The Law of Health and Safety at Work

Norman Selwyn

LLM, Dip Econ (Oxon),
Barrister

CRONER @ CCH

Croner.CCH Group Limited
145 London Road
Kingston upon Thames
Surrey KT2 6SR
Tel: 020 8547 3333

Published by
Croner.CCH Group Limited
145 London Road
Kingston upon Thames
Surrey KT2 6SR
Tel: 020 8547 3333

First published January 1982
First Edition 1982
Second Edition 1993
Third Edition 1994
Fourth Edition 1995
Fifth Edition 1996
Sixth Edition 1997
Seventh Edition 1998
Eighth Edition 1999
Ninth Edition 2000
Tenth Edition 2001

© N M Selwyn

British Library cataloguing in Publication Data. A CIP Catalogue Record for this book
is available from the British Library

ISBN 1 85524 601 5

Printed by Thomson Litho, Glasgow

PREFACE

Although the subject of health and safety at work is of vital importance to every employer, employee and self-employed person, there is an apparent dearth of books which explain the complex legal requirements in a manner which can be readily understood and appreciated by those who are most affected. The aim of this book is to fill that gap. It should be of interest to employers, company secretaries, managers, trade unionists, safety officers, safety representatives, enforcement officers and lawyers, as well as to students who are seeking to be in employment in the future.

The book is intended to be a guide, not a bible. The aim is to promote knowledge, yet at the same time to give understanding. In other words, I have tried not only to state the law, but also to explain it. If the consequence has been a certain amount of over simplification, I believe that this is a price well worth paying. However, the reader will appreciate that when legal problems arise in practice, it may be necessary to consult the actual statutory provisions, or, where necessary, seek expert legal advice.

Health and safety is an ubiquitous subject and it is not easy to draw boundaries. There is no obvious delineation between health and safety at work and health and safety generally. Road traffic, environmental issues, consumer protection, etc all overlap with health and safety at work. Thus I have included some material on "peripheral"; matters, but if the line has been drawn somewhat arbitrarily, it is perhaps better to do so than not to draw one at all.

The *raison d'être* of the law on health and safety at work is not always easy to discover, for there are differing social objectives to be achieved. The law is intended to be partly preventative, partly punitive, and partly compensatory. The rules are an amalgam of contract, tort and criminal law. Statutory provisions are interwoven with judicial decisions, and, in recent years, Approved Codes of Practice have assumed a greater importance in giving practical guidance. Each industry has its own peculiar problems. Each firm has its own difficulties. Each incident has its own unique features. These variations make the task of preventing accidents difficult for those involved. But however complex these matters may be, ignorance of the legal requirements is the least excuse.

The law on health and safety at work is constantly changing, particularly with the introduction of new regulations and Codes of Practice. Judicial interpretation of the legislation is becoming more significant, even going so far as to extend the impact of health and safety regulations into the fields of sex, race and disability discrimination. It is essential for all concerned with this subject, be they employers, employees, lawyers, students, trade union officials, etc to keep up to date with all the latest developments, and, where appropriate, implement those aspects of the law which are relevant to their own circumstances.

There have been few legislative changes since the last edition of this book. Mention is made of the Genetically Modified Organisms (Contained Use) Regulations 2000, the Construction (Design and Management) (Amendment) Regulations 2000, and the Ionising Radiations (Medical Exposure) Regulations 2000. The potential impact of the Human Rights Act 1998 has been noted, and there has been some re-arrangement of the material, as well as the inclusion of a number of significant legal decisions. The coming year is likely to see an increase in legislative activity, with a number of significant changes, including a new law on corporate killing, changes to the regulations concerning safety representatives, a requirement for some employers to report on their health and safety activities, an increase in penalties for offences and so on. There will also be new Codes of Practice, including one on health and safety responsibilities of directors. A busy year lies ahead!

I have tried to state the law according to the sources available to me as at 1 June 2001.

Norman Selwyn
Solihull, West Midlands

June 2001

CONTENTS

Table of Statutes

Table of Regulations and Orders

Table of Cases

CHAPTER 1

Law and legal institutions

The background to health and safety law

1.1　　Legislative intervention in pursuance of the cause of health and safety dates from the Health and Morals of Apprentices Act 1802. This Act was designed to protect young children working in cotton and woollen mills and other factories where more than twenty persons were employed. At that time it was the custom to put four children in a bed during the day and four more in the same bed at night while the daytime occupants were working. It was this type of abuse at which the Act was aimed. Other pieces of minor legislation were passed in the ensuing years, but the real breakthrough came in 1833 when the Factory Act was passed. It provided that four factory inspectors were to be appointed with powers of investigation and prosecution. From that time on the factory movement gathered momentum, although the motives of some of the protagonists were not always of high altruism. Sometimes the legislation was designed to restrict the hours of work of women and young children (indirectly benefiting adult male labour), while other enactments were concerned with establishing safe working conditions. Perhaps the worst feature was the multiplicity of legislation — in 1876 a Factory Commission reported that the law was in a complete state of chaos, with no less than nineteen different enactments to be considered. It was not until the Factory and Workshop Act of 1901 that a comprehensive piece of factory legislation was enacted, when all the previous law was consolidated into one statute. One of the more interesting innovations was to give the power to the Secretary of State to make regulations for particular industries, a power which was used extensively to control a large number of different industrial processes. In 1916, this power was extended to permit Welfare Orders to be made dealing with washing facilities, first aid provisions, and so on. A further major breakthrough came in 1937 when the Factories Act was passed. It swept away the old distinctions between the different types of premises (textile factories, workshops, etc) and made detailed provisions for health, safety and welfare. Minor amendments were made in 1948 and

1959, and the various statutes were consolidated once more by the Factories Act 1961, the bulk of which has now been repealed and replaced by new health and safety regulations and Approved Codes of Practice.

1.2   The mining industry was an obvious subject for protective legislation, and in 1842 a Mines and Collieries Act was passed, which was mainly concerned with regulating hours and working conditions of women and children. Work in quarries was brought within the scope of the law by the Metalliferous Mines Regulations Act 1872, and a further major reform took place in 1911 with the passing of the Coal Mines Act. These provisions were strengthened and brought up to date in the Mines and Quarries Act 1954 which, together with regulations made, lays down a comprehensive protective code of legislation for these industries.

1.3   Health and safety legislation for the non-industrial worker came somewhat later. In 1886, the Shop Hours Regulation Act restricted the hours of work of young persons, and the Seats for Shop Assistants Act 1899 may be regarded as an important welfare statute. After many attempts had been made to give legislative cover to office workers, an Offices Act was passed in 1960, but this (and other legislation) was superseded by the Offices, Shops and Railway Premises Act 1963 (now almost totally repealed). Other statutes which regulated hours of work include the Employment of Women, Young Persons and Children Act 1920, Hours of Employment (Conventions) Act 1936 and Young Persons (Employment) Act 1938.

1.4   The original intention of the framers of the legislation was that health and safety laws would be enforced through the use of criminal sanctions, but for two reasons this emphasis changed over the years. The first was the gradual realisation that a rigorous policy of enforcement by the factory inspectorate would probably lead to the shutdown of large sections of British industry, already fighting hard to maintain its position against competition from foreign countries which were not necessarily inhibited by such constraints. The policy would also clutter up the courts and require a massive expansion of the machinery for bringing prosecutions. The second and possibly more significant reason for the change in emphasis was the ability of injured workers to bring civil actions in respect of injuries suffered as a result of their employers' failure to observe the statutory duties. This action for breach of statutory duty was first successful in the case of *Groves v Lord Wimborne* in 1898 and, because of the absolute nature of many of the statutory duties, became a fruitful source of financial solace. But the result was to divert the objects of the law away from prosecution and prevention towards a system of civil compensation. As Goddard LJ stated in *Hutchinson v London and North Eastern Rly Co* in 1942, "The real incentive for the observance by employers of their statutory duties is not their liability to substantial fines, but the possibility of heavy claims for damages." Even this, however, was not entirely correct, for most employers realised the value of taking out insurance policies against such claims (a requirement which was made compulsory in 1969) with the result that both the civil and criminal law ceased to be major deterrents.

1.5   At the same time as these developments were taking place, the common law of the country was also becoming active. In a leading case decided in 1837 (*Priestley v Fowler*) a claim based on an allegation of negligence by an employer towards his employee failed, but a few years later, in 1840, a young girl successfully sued when she was seriously injured in a mill accident and was awarded damages (*Cottrell v Stocks*). From then on, common law claims were bogged down with problems arising from the doctrine of "common employment (abolished in 1948 by the Law Reform (Personal Injuries) Act), the inability to sue at common law if the injured worker had also claimed under the Workman's Compensation Act (amended by the National Insurance (Industrial Injuries) Act 1946), and the inability to claim if the employee had been contributorily negligent (amended by the Law Reform (Contributory Negligence) Act 1945). By 1970, the law on health and safety was largely concerned with issues of compensation.

1.6   In 1970, a committee on health and safety at work was appointed under the chairmanship of Lord Robens, which reported two years later. In their report, the Robens Committee reached some fundamental conclusions. First, although it was generally recognised that we had in this country the finest regulatory system of legal controls anywhere in the world, this did not prevent the annual carnage which took place, evidenced by the numbers who were killed or injured. Second, much of our law was obscure and unintelligible to those whose actions it was intended to influence. There was a haphazard mass of legislation, intricate in detail, difficult to amend and frequently out-of-date. Third, the various enforcement authorities had overlapping jurisdictions which caused some confusion.

1.7   But the main conclusion of the Robens Committee was that there was one single cause, above all else, for accidents and ill health at work. This was apathy. Apathy at the top, apathy at the bottom, apathy at all levels in between. True, there were a few dedicated people who worked hard at trying to influence people's attitudes, but these rarely had sufficient power or authority to override considerations of production, and in the main, health and safety had a low priority in almost all workplaces. In an attempt to overcome this attitude, the Robens Committee made a number of far-reaching proposals. The first was to devise a system whereby all employers and all employees became aware that health and safety was the concern of everyone, and not just a matter for the dedicated few. As the report stated, "Our present system encourages too much reliance on State regulation, and rather too little on personal responsibility and voluntary, self-generating effort." Next, it was suggested that there was a need for a single comprehensive framework of legislation which would cover all work activity, supported and supplemented by a series of controls to deal with specific problems, and assisted by voluntary standards and more flexible codes of practice. Finally, a more unified enforcement authority was needed, having overall responsibility for initiating legal proposals and giving assistance and advice, possessing stronger enforcement powers, and with the ability to delegate its enforcement functions when necessary.

1.8   The result was the passing of the Health and Safety at Work, etc Act 1974 (HSWA), an important piece of legislation which adopts a fundamentally different approach to the whole subject. In the first place, the Act applies to all employed persons, wherever they work (except domestic servants in private households). This brought into the protective umbrella an estimated eight million "new entrants" who were not hitherto covered by previous legislation. Next, as well as laying down duties for employers and employees, the Act imposes certain legal requirements on those who manufacture, import, design or supply articles and substances which are to be used at work. Some of the provisions (eg safety policies, safety representatives) are designed to bring about a greater personal involvement of all concerned. New institutions were created, new enforcement powers were enacted, and new concepts, such as the use of Approved Codes of Practice, were introduced. The "old" law, eg the Factories Act, the Offices, Shops and Railway Premises Act, etc was intended to remain in force for the time being, although the ultimate objective was to gradually repeal and replace it by new regulations which will be supplemented by Approved Codes of Practice and guidance literature.

1.9   It must not be assumed that HSWA is the answer to all our problems, or that it is a perfect piece of legislation. On the contrary, despite the criticism levelled by the Robens Committee against the legalistic and unintelligible nature of the then existing law, the Act is turgid, soporific and in parts about as meaningful as medieval metaphysics. Further, it is basically a criminal statute, with appropriate penalties for breaches, and does not confer on anyone the right to make a claim for compensation. This means that most of the cases will start and finish in the magistrates' courts, with the result that there is very little opportunity for authoritative interpretations of the complex legal language. In the twenty years since the Act was passed, there have been relatively few legal decisions from higher courts, and thus problems and queries remain.

1.10   On the positive side, the Act has acted as a catalyst for considerable management activity and as a greater awareness of responsibility has brought about increased concern for the health and safety of employees. It is, perhaps, too early to judge the psychological impact of the Act, or to evaluate its success, for although it is possible to note some downward trends in the numbers of accidents, there are many other factors which need to be taken into account, and we can never know how many accidents did not happen as a result of a more safety-conscious approach. Whether the encouraging reduction in accident rates over the past decade has been due to a greater awareness of the legal requirements, to pro-active safety policies, to changes in manufacturing processes, or to a reduction in the numbers employed in those industries which were traditionally a major source of accidents and ill health, is always going to be a matter for debate. Meanwhile, if the propaganda which surrounds the Act brings about a greater awareness that health and safety is everyone's concern, and not merely a matter for those who have a specialised interest in the problem, nothing but good will be the result.

1.11   Since 1974, the Act has been amended by the Consumer Protection Act 1987 (in particular strengthening s.6), the Criminal Justice Act 1991 and the Offshore Safety Act 1992, which have increased the penalties which may be imposed for various breaches. The progressive repeal of the Factories Act and other primary legislation has continued and, more recently, there has been a spate of new health and safety regulations (supplemented by Approved Codes of Practice and Guidance Notes) consequent on our membership of the European Union. Although various amendments to the Act are being actively considered at the present time, its basic principles will remain.

1.12   In 1989, the Council of Ministers of the European Union adopted the health and safety "Framework Directive" (89/391/EEC) which deals with the general principles to be applied throughout the Union on health and safety in all work activities (except domestic service). The primary duty for ensuring health and safety at work was placed upon employers, although self-employed persons and employees were also embraced. Five additional "daughter" Directives were subsequently adopted dealing with more specific proposals, ie Workplace Directive (89/654/EEC), Use of Work Equipment Directive (89/655/EEC), Personal Protective Equipment Directive (89/656/EEC), Manual Handling of Loads Directive (90/269/EEC) and Display Screen Equipment Directive (90/270/EEC). Further Directives have been adopted on Carcinogens, Biological Agents, Temporary Workers, Asbestos Workers Protection, Construction Sites, Safety Signs, Pregnant Workers and Young Persons. A number of other Directives with health and safety implications have either been adopted or are currently being discussed with a view to adoption (see Chapter 10).

1.13   Following the adoption of the Framework and first five daughter Directives, the Health and Safety Commission (HSC) issued six Consultative Documents, with proposals for new regulations to implement the Directives, together with Approved Codes of Practice or Guidance Notes. After extensive consultation, six new regulations were approved by Parliament, and except for specified transitional periods, came into force as from 1 January 1993.

1.14   The HSC took the view that whilst in general the Health and Safety at Work Act 1974 was adequate as a means of achieving the appropriate standards, the Directives were more prescriptive and detailed, and thus it was necessary to extend the law in order to meet the new standards required by the Directives. It was hoped to achieve the desired results by avoiding any disruption with the basic framework laid down in HSWA, and at the same time to continue with the process of modernising the law and repealing out-of-date legislation. Thus the new regulations, together with the Approved Codes of Practice and Guidance Notes should meet the EU standards, and UK law has been adapted accordingly within the existing framework.

1.15   As a general principle, health and safety regulations may give rise to civil as well as criminal liability. Thus where certain familiar statutory provisions, which have hitherto been a prolific source of civil litigation, have been repealed, civil proceedings may in general be brought under the new regulations in due course. But attention must be paid to the individual regulations in order to determine whether civil claims may be brought. All the regulations impose criminal liabilities.

1.16   However, there is as much danger from having too much law as having too little law. Equally, it is necessary that legal provisions do not overlap, are not out-of-date, and do not create administrative burdens which outweigh their usefulness. In December 1992, the Government invited the Health and Safety Commission to review all workplace legislation as part of a deregulation initiative, although it was emphasised that there was no intention of undermining any necessary and existing health and safety standards. Following the receipt of the review by the HSC (and proposals from seven Business Deregulation Task Forces) the Deregulation and Contracting Out Act 1994 was passed. Section 37 of the Act empowers the Secretary of State, by Order, to repeal or revoke any pre-1974 legislation on health and safety issues, although before doing so he must consult with the HSC and other appropriate persons (although post-1974 health and safety legislation can be repealed under the 1974 Act, it was doubtful if he had the power to do so in respect of pre-1974 legislation without making provision for replacement legislation). About 100 regulations and Orders were identified as possible candidates for revocation without any loss of health and safety standards, as well as seven pieces of primary legislation, including the remaining parts of the Factories Act 1961 and the Offices, Shops and Railway Premises Act 1963. Many of these provisions have now been revoked or repealed, and the Deregulation Task Force has now been replaced by the Better Regulation Unit, now based in the Cabinet Office. It has published a policy document entitled *Principles of good regulation* which recommends that regulations and enforcement should be measured against the five principles of transparency, accountability, targeting, consistency and proportionality. The legal requirements relating to risk assessments, provision of information to employees and others, and the provision of instruction and training are all currently being looked at to see if some form of rationalisation, clarity and simplicity could be achieved. Approved Codes of Practice are being looked at to ensure that they do indeed contain practical guidance. Thus there is likely to be a thorough overhaul of legislation on health and safety matters within the next few years, which will hopefully lead to a more streamlined and simplified system of legal requirements, with no loss of effectiveness so far as controls are concerned.

1.17   The present situation, therefore, is that the law on health and safety at work is an amalgam of criminal law, civil law, and preventative measures. Breaches of the various statutory provisions (and regulations made thereunder) are capable of being criminal offences, in respect of which the wrongdoer may be fined or (in rare circumstances) imprisoned. Civil claims for compensation may arise in respect of injuries received as a result of a failure by the employer to observe the statutory requirements (other than HSWA and other legislation as specified), or a failure to carry out those duties imposed by the common law of the land. The preventative measures can be found in the new enforcement notices which may be issued, the greater involvement of the workforce by the appointment of safety representatives and the creation of safety committees, as well as in the more detailed requirements of the new health and safety regulations, in particular with regard to the requirements for employers to carry out risk assessments, undertake health surveillance, appoint safety advisers and so on. Health and safety is also being used to give remedies to workers and employees in employment tribunals, when the employer fails to carry out his legal responsibilities.

1.18   This mixture of legal objectives is reflected in the decided cases which explain and expand on the nature of the legal duties. For practical reasons, the majority of these cases stem from civil claims, although in recent years there has been an increasing number of decisions in the employment tribunals which add to our understanding of the legal rules. Care must always be taken not to elevate all such decisions to absolute principles, for the statute is always paramount, and individual cases can only be decided on their own special facts. Legal interpretation is more of an art than a science.

Sources of law

Legislation

1.19   The prime source of law in the UK consists of Acts of Parliament. With the important exception noted below relating to the Treaty of Rome, an Act of Parliament is the supreme law of the land. Parliament, it is said, can make or unmake any law whatsoever. In strict theory, this could lead to severe problems, but in reality there are clearly political and practical limits on what Parliament in fact will do.

1.20   Statute law commences with the introduction of a Bill into either House of Parliament. This will receive a formal First Reading when it is published. The House will then hold a full debate on the general principles behind the proposed legislation, and a vote may be held on a proposal to give the Bill a Second Reading. If successful, the Bill will then be sent to a committee, where it is considered in detail, and amendments may be made. Next, the Bill is presented to a report stage of the full House, when the amendments are considered, and finally, the Bill will receive its Third Reading. It will then go to the other House, where a similar procedure is adopted. When both Houses have passed the Bill, it is presented to the Queen for the Royal Assent, which, by convention, is never refused.

1.21   However, although the Bill is now an Act, its implementation may be delayed in whole or in part. Modern legislation frequently contains powers which enable the appropriate Minister to bring the Act into force in various stages, often with transitional provisions. In those cases the law will not come into force until the date specified in a Commencement Order.

Regulations

1.22   An Act may confer upon a Minister the power to make new or additional law by means of regulations. Such subordinate legislative power has many advantages, for it enables technical proposals to be passed, it is speedier than the procedure adopted for an Act, and enables the law to be amended by a simpler procedure. Regulations must be laid before Parliament, and are considered by the Joint Committee on Statutory Instruments, which has members from both Houses. They are not concerned with the policy or merits of the regulations, only the technical competence of the Minister to make them. For example, the committee will ascertain whether the regulations are within the powers which are conferred by the parent Act, and whether they contain any unusual or unexpected use of that power. Some regulations will only become law after an affirmative vote by both Houses of Parliament, but the majority will become law when they are made. However, they can subsequently be vetoed by a negative vote within 40 days of laying. Regulations which are made under HSWA are of this type (see s.82(3)).

1.23   Regulations have the full force of law until they are revoked or amended in some way. It is possible for them to supersede specific provisions of the parent Act. In *Miller v William Boothman & Sons Ltd* , the plaintiff was injured while working on a circular saw, the fencing of which complied with the Woodworking Machinery Regulations 1922. It was argued on his behalf that the employers were still liable for his injury, as they were in breach of the requirements of s.14 of the Factories Act to fence every dangerous part of any machinery. The argument was rejected. The Minister had exercised the power vested in him to exclude the provisions of the Act by regulation, and the latter prevailed.

1.24   As has already been indicated, one of the main objects of HSWA is to replace the existing statutory provisions over a period of time with a more streamlined system in which regulations will play a major part. These will fall generally into different categories. First, there will be those regulations which will apply to most or all employment situations (eg the Reporting of Injuries, Diseases and Dangerous Occurrences Regulations 1995). Second, there will be those regulations which are designed to control a particular hazard (eg Lifting Operations and Lifting Equipment Regulations 1998). Third, there are those which will refer to a particular hazard or risk which may be found in a number of industries or processes (eg the Control of Lead at Work Regulations 1998). Fourth, regulations may be introduced in order to further the streamlining process or because the old provisions were out-of-date (eg the Health and Safety (First Aid) Regulations 1981). Others may be introduced consequent upon the discovery of a loophole in the law which may have come to light because of some litigation (the Abrasive Wheels Regulations 1970 (now themselves revoked) were made in order to nullify the decision of *Summers (John) & Sons Ltd v Frost*). As a general rule, regulations are designed to supplement and strengthen the provisions of the various Acts of Parliament, spelling out the requirements in greater detail.

1.25   Health and safety regulations made under HSWA, s.15 may be for any of the following purposes:

(a) repeal or modify any existing statutory provision

(b) exclude or modify in relation to any specific class of case any of the provisions of ss.2–9 (Chapter 3) or any existing statutory provision

(c) make a specific authority responsible for the enforcement of any relevant statutory provision

(d) impose requirements by reference to the approval of the Commission or other specified body or person

(e) provide that any reference in a regulation to a specific document shall include a reference to a revised version of that document

(f) provide for exemptions from any requirement or prohibition

(g) enable exemptions to be granted by a specified person or authority

(h) specify the persons or class of persons who may be guilty of an offence

(i) provide for specified defences either generally or in specified circumstances

(j) exclude proceedings on indictment in relation to certain offences

(k) restrict the punishment which may be imposed in respect of certain offences.

1.26   In addition to the above, Schedule 3 to HSWA contains detailed provisions about the contents of such regulations, sufficient, it is thought, to completely replace the old law, and wide enough to enable the Secretary of State and the Commission to do almost anything in order to promote "the general purposes" of the Act. In particular, however, we may note two further important provisions. The first is the power to prohibit the carrying on of any specified activity or the doing of any specified thing without a licence granted for that purpose, which may be subject to conditions. The second is contained in s.79 of the Act, which amends s.16 of the Companies Act 1967 (see now Companies Act 1985, s.235 and Schedule 10, Part IV) so as to enable the Secretary of State to prescribe cases whereby directors' reports will contain such information about the arrangements in force for that year for securing the health, safety and welfare at work of the employees of that company (and any subsidiary company), and for protecting other persons against risks to health resulting from the activities at work of the employees. To date, no action has been taken to implement this provision.

1.27 A breach of a duty imposed by regulations is, of course, punishable as a criminal offence. Additionally, a breach may give rise to civil liability, except insofar as the regulations provide otherwise.

The making of regulations

1.28 Health and safety regulations are made by the Secretary of State as a result of proposals made to him by the Health and Safety Commission (HSC). He may also make them on his own initiative, but before doing so he must consult with the HSC·and with any other appropriate bodies. If the HSC makes the proposals, it too must consult with appropriate government departments and other interested bodies (HSWA, s.50). The normal practice is for the HSC to initiate proposals in the form of a Consultative Document, which is given a wide circulation to interested bodies, such as employers' associations, trade unions, trade associations, and so on. Comments received are considered, and the proposals may be modified in the light of these. Draft regulations are then publicised, amended if necessary, and the regulations, in their final form, are presented to the Secretary for State, to be laid before Parliament.

1.29 Responsibility for health and safety matters now rests with the Department of the Environment, Transport and the Regions, although it would not be unusual for certain health and safety regulations to emanate from another government department (eg Defence, Transport, Health, etc).

Orders

1.30 Historically, Orders were promulgated by the Queen in her Privy Council, exercising the royal prerogative. This procedure was a convenient way of avoiding Parliamentary scrutiny, but since the Statutory Instruments Act 1946 this is no longer so, and Orders are now subject to annulment on a resolution of either House of Parliament (see HSWA, s.84(4)). Modern practice is to confer on the appropriate Minister the power to make Orders, which again can only be exercised within the powers conferred. For example, s.84 of HSWA empowers the Queen by Order in Council to extend the provisions of the Act outside Great Britain (see Health and Safety at Work Act 1974 (Application outside Great Britain) Order 2001), whereas s.85 enables the Secretary of State to make Commencement Orders.

1.31 As a rough guide, the distinction between a regulation and an Order is that the former is a means whereby the power to make substantive law is exercised, whereas the latter gives the force of law to an executive act.

Bye-laws

1.32 Local authorities have power to pass bye-laws for the administration of their own area. These must be within the powers conferred by the parent Act of Parliament, and must also be reasonable. It is possible to challenge the validity of a bye-law in the courts. Model bye-laws, drawn up by the Department of the Environment, Transport and the Regions are frequently adopted by local authorities.

Judicial precedent

1.33 The bulk of British law is contained in the decisions made by the judges in cases which come before them in the courts. When a judge decides a case, he will state his reasons for that decision. Frequently, the case will be reported in one of the many series of law reports (official or commercial) which exist. From the report, it may be possible to cull the narrow reason for the decision, ie the *ratio decidendi*. Anything else uttered in the course of the decision is regarded as *obiter dicta*, ie things said by the way. Distilling the *ratio* of a case, and distinguishing it from *obiter dicta*, is a legal art.

1.34 Strictly speaking, it is only the decisions of the higher courts which become binding precedents. Other decisions are said to be "persuasive". Thus a decision of the House of Lords will bind all lower courts, and can only be changed by a further decision of the House of Lords itself (a rare occurrence) or by an Act of Parliament. A decision of the Court of Appeal will also bind lower courts but not, of course, the House of Lords. All other lower courts only create persuasive precedents.

1.35 However, lawyers will attempt to avoid inconvenient precedents (when necessary) by using their legal ingenuity. Thus it may be possible to distinguish a previous decision on the ground that the facts are not identical, or that there are material differences sufficient to warrant not following an earlier decision. Since the *ratio* of a case is uncertain, inconvenient remarks may be brushed aside as being *obiter dicta*, on the ground that they were not essential for the actual decision.

A court may be asked to refuse to follow a precedent because it was decided *per incuriam*, ie without a full and proper argument on the point in issue. Frequently, there will be an abundance of precedents, and each side will quote those which support its argument. Occasionally, the point may never have arisen for decision before, and the court must reach its conclusions on first principles, thus creating a precedent. It is because of these points that the vagaries, as well as the richness, of British law emerges, but it will also be seen why litigation is so uncertain.

Approved Codes of Practice

1.36   For the purpose of providing practical guidance, in recent years Parliament has authorised a number of organisations to issue Codes of Practice, which, though not having the force of law, may be taken into consideration by the courts and tribunals in appropriate circumstances. So far as this book is concerned, s.16 of HSWA conferred on the Health and Safety Commission (HSC) power to approve and issue Codes of Practice for the purpose of providing practical guidance with respect to any of the general duties laid down in ss.2–7 of the Act, or any health and safety regulations or existing statutory provision. The HSC may also approve other codes which are drawn up by other persons or organisations (eg British Standards). The HSC cannot approve a code without first obtaining the consent of the Secretary of State, and prior to obtaining this, it must consult with government departments and other appropriate bodies. Codes may be revised from time to time and the HSC may, if necessary, withdraw its approval from a particular code.

1.37   A failure on the part of any person to observe the provisions contained in an Approved Code of Practice does not, of itself, render that person liable to any criminal or civil proceedings, but in any criminal proceedings, if a person is alleged to have committed an offence concerning a matter in respect of which an Approved Code of Practice is in force, the provisions of that Code are admissible in evidence, and a failure to observe it constitutes proof of the breach of duty, or contravention of the regulation or statutory provision in question, unless the accused satisfies the court that he complied with the requirement of the law in some other equally efficacious manner. Codes, therefore, are guides to good safety practice. If a person follows the requirements of the Codes it is unlikely that he will be successfully prosecuted for an offence. If he fails to follow the Code, he may be guilty of an offence unless he can show that he observed the specific legal requirements in some other way (HSWA s.17).

1.38   The purpose of making increased use of Codes of Practice is to avoid built-in obsolescence in legal requirements, and to give practical guidance for the benefit of those upon whom duties are placed by virtue of a statute or regulation. HSWA contains no guidance on the status of Codes of Practice in civil proceedings, but it is likely that a failure to observe their provisions could constitute *prima facie* evidence of negligence, which would have to be rebutted by evidence to the contrary.

Guidance Notes

1.39   The HSC and Health and Safety Executive (HSE) frequently issue Guidance Notes, sometimes alongside Codes and sometimes independently. Guidance Notes contain practical advice and sound suggestions, and are frequently more informative than the Codes (see for example, the Guidance Notes attached to the Safety Representative and Safety Committee Regulations, which are far more helpful than the actual Code). Although the Guidance Notes have no legal standing, it is possible to use them as evidence of the state of knowledge at the time of issue. For example, in *Glyn Owen v Sutcliffe* an Environmental Health Officer (EHO) issued an improvement notice requiring a self-employed shoe repairer to install ventilation in his shop, following complaints about the strong smell of solvent fumes. At an appeal before an employment tribunal, the EHO referred to an HSE Guidance Note, and also to one issued by the British Adhesive Manufacturers Association, both of which warned of the dangers of inhaling solvent vapour, and suggested suitable ventilation and vapour extraction. The employment tribunal affirmed the improvement notice, for the shoe repairer was in breach of his duty under the Act to himself as well as to others (s.3(2)). In *Burgess v Thorn Consumer Electronics (Newhaven) Ltd* it was held that if employers do not warn employees of the dangers referred to in the Guidance Notes, they may be liable to employees for negligence, as the Guidance Notes indirectly give rise to a duty of care.

The European Union

1.40   As from 1 January 1973, the UK became a member of the European Union (EU) and by the European Communities Act 1972 (s.2), all obligations arising out of the various treaties which set up the EU are to be given legal effect in this country without further enactment. European law is of particular importance to the study of domestic law on health and safety at work. First, since the object of the EU is economic harmonisation, it would distort market forces if one country could economise on health and safety matters to the disadvantage of others. Second, a number of changes have been brought about in our domestic law in order to conform to European standards. Third, the EU has recently introduced the "social dimension" whereby positive steps are to be taken to increase protections offered to workers from the risks of accidents and ill health at work, and generally raise standards of employment protection throughout the EU. Thus the impact of European law on domestic law is gathering momentum and cannot be ignored. In order to understand European law, we must examine the treaties, the institutions and the nature of European law.

The Treaty of Rome

1.41 This Treaty was signed in 1957 by the six founding States (France, West Germany, Italy, Belgium, The Netherlands and Luxembourg). The UK, Ireland and Denmark acceded to the Treaty in 1973, Greece in 1981, Spain and Portugal became full members in 1992 and Austria, Finland and Sweden joined in 1995. The original Treaty required unanimity between all the Member States before laws could be passed. So far as is relevant, Article 137 of the Treaty stated that one of the objects of the Community was to harmonise laws relating to "employment, labour law and working conditions, basic and advanced training, social security, protection against occupational accidents and diseases, occupational hygiene, law of trade unions, and collective bargaining between workers and employers".

1.42 In 1986, the Single European Act was signed in The Hague and Luxembourg, making certain amendments to the Treaty of Rome. These amendments were given effect in this country by the European Communities (Amendment) Act 1986. One significant change made was the introduction of a system of "qualified majority voting"; on certain issues. Each State has been allocated a certain number of votes (Germany, Italy, France and the UK have 10 votes each, Spain has eight, Belgium, The Netherlands, Portugal and Greece have five, Austria and Sweden have four, Denmark, Finland and Ireland have three and Luxembourg has two). A qualified majority decision requires 62 out of the 87 votes available to pass a particular proposal. The significance is that qualified majority voting can be used to pass proposals relating to health and safety matters in the working environment under Article 138 of the Treaty (see Chapter 10).

1.43   The numbering of the Articles was altered by the Treaty of Amsterdam in 1999, so that Article 48 (free movement of workers) is now Article 39, Article 118 (promotion of employment and working conditions) is now Article 137, Article 119 (equal pay for equal work) is now Article 141, and so on.

The Maastricht Treaty

1.44   In 1992, the Treaty on European Union (the Maastricht Treaty) was signed, expanding the scope of the Community's existing responsibilities, and introducing new policy areas. The ultimate aim is to create European citizenship, a single currency as part of economic and monetary union, a common foreign policy and a common defence policy. The concept of "subsidiarity" was also introduced so that matters which could more usefully be dealt with at local or national level would not be the subject of Community action unless there was no other way the objectives could be achieved. The UK Government had opted out (by Protocol) of certain provisions of the Treaty, including the final stage of monetary union.

EU institutions

Council of Ministers

1.45   This is the supreme policy making body of the EU. Each meeting of the Council is attended by a minister from each Member State. Usually, this will be the respective foreign secretaries, but sometimes, when specific detailed proposals are being discussed, the respective "portfolio" ministers will attend. One member of the Council will hold the presidency for six months and then the position rotates. The Council is assisted by a Secretariat (comprising a staff of some 2000) and preparatory work for the meetings is undertaken by frequent meetings of senior civil servants from the respective countries, known as the Committee of Permanent Representatives (COREPER).

The European Commission

1.46   This is sometimes described as being the "bureaucracy" of the EU, but perhaps a more accurate description would be the "engine room". There are 20 commissioners (Germany, France, Italy and the UK each appoint two commissioners, the other Member States each appoint one). However, although appointed by their respective countries, commissioners are totally independent of them. Each commissioner has certain departmental responsibilities and is assisted by a cabinet and directorate general. Decisions are taken on a collegiate basis.

1.47   The European Commission has the responsibility of initiating and drafting proposals for approval by the Council. It acts as a mediator between States, and as a "watch dog" to ensure that EU rules are being observed. Indeed, if the Commission considers that a Member State is failing to comply with an EU law, it can take enforcement action by referring the alleged breach to the European Court of Justice (ECJ) for a ruling (see below).

European Parliament

1.48   This body sits in Strasbourg and consists of 626 Members of the European Parliament (MEPs) elected directly from each Member State. It can express an opinion to the Council of Ministers on proposals which emanate from the Commission, can submit questions to both institutions, and can, as a final sanction, dismiss the Commission on a vote of censure passed by a two-thirds majority. The Single European Act introduced a co-operation procedure, whereby the views of the Parliament must be established prior to the Council of Ministers reaching a common position on any particular proposal (see Chapter 10).

European Court of Justice

1.49   This court sits in Luxembourg, and comprises 15 judges and nine advocate generals. Appointments are made for six years. The court gives rulings on the interpretation of European law, either on a reference from the Commission, at the request of the courts of a Member State or on a claim brought by an individual person or corporation in a Member State. Once it has given its ruling the matter is then referred back to the courts of the Member State for compliance.

European Agency for Safety and Health at Work

1.50   A new EU-wide European Health and Safety Agency has been established, with headquarters in Bilbao, Spain. Its objectives are to promote improvements in health and safety at work by raising awareness and improving the availability of health and safety information. It will also provide technical, scientific and economic information to Member States, EU institutions and others involved with health and safety at work, and will set up a network to provide and disseminate relevant information within the EU. An Administrative Board, consisting of representatives of each Member State, three members of the Commission, six representatives from employers' organisations and six representatives from trade union organisations, will meet twice each year, and the Agency will be headed by a Director with appropriate staff.

1.51   The Agency will also organise training courses for safety experts, ensure the compatibility of national data on health and safety, and identify data in need of harmonisation. An annual report will be sent to all Member States, the Council of Ministers, the European Commission, and the European Parliament.

1.52   A great part of its work involves the dissemination of information, particularly via its website *(www.eu.osha.es)*. In this way, expertise in all EU countries can be made available to anyone needing advice and information. The Agency seeks to assist people to find practical solutions to health and safety problems which arise in the workplace, investigate methods of communicating health and safety solutions to smaller organisations, and, in particular, address the information needs of fragmented workforces.

1.53   There are a number of other European institutions concerned with health and safety at work, including the Advisory Committee on Safety, Hygiene and Health Protection, which consist of representatives of employers' organisations, trade unions and Member States. This committee is consulted by the European Commission on draft Directives at an early stage, prior to consultation with the European Parliament.

European law

The Treaty of Rome

1.54   The Treaty of Rome is the supreme law of all Member States. If an Article of the Treaty is clear, precise, requires no further implementation and does not give discretion to Member States, then it is directly applicable, and does not require the Member States to pass domestic legislation to give it effect. The main significance of this rule relates to the way Article 141 of the Treaty which requires that there should be equal pay for equal work has been invoked by courts when national law has failed to ensure compliance, (eg *Secretary of State for Scotland v Wright*). Also significant is Article 39, which requires the free movement of workers within the EU without discrimination (*Van Duyn v Home Office (No. 2)*).

Regulations

1.55   Once a regulation has been passed by the Council of Ministers, it becomes part of the laws of Member States, and overrides any contrary domestic provision. No implementing legislation is needed. A number of regulations have been passed dealing with the transportation of goods, vehicle movements generally, etc. For example, EU Regulation 3820/85 controls the hours of work of drivers of goods and passenger vehicles throughout the Union (see *Prime v Hosking*). More recently, the Council of Ministers adopted the Existing Substances Regulations (EEC/793/93) establishing a framework for the notification and assessment of existing chemical substances.

Directives

1.56   A Directive passed by the Council of Ministers is binding on Member States as to the results to be achieved, but generally leaves a choice as to form and method. There are a number of problems relating to the precise legal effect of a Directive, but it is generally accepted that in the field of health and safety they are not directly applicable in Member States, and do not, by themselves, give rise to any enforceable EU right. Health and safety generally is a topic for considerable activity by the EU and a number of Directives have been passed which are either in force or due to come into force within the near future (see Chapter 10). Indeed, the HSC must keep a very close eye on European Directives:

(a) to ensure that our existing laws comply

(b) to ensure that future changes do not conflict, and

(c) to consider ways in which European standards can be implemented.

Decisions

1.57   A decision may be given by the European Commission on any particular case referred to it, either by a Member State, an individual or a corporate body. The decision is only applicable to that case and has no value as a binding precedent.

Recommendations

1.58   The Council of Ministers may make recommendations, which have no binding effect. However, they may be considered by national courts when dealing with a problem arising out of the interpretation of domestic law. In *Grimaldi v Fonds des Maladies Professionelles*, the ECJ held that national courts should take recommendations into account when determining disputes before them, particularly when they purport to clarify the interpretation of laws passed to implement them, or when they are designed to supplement binding EU measures.

European Charter for Fundamental Social Rights

1.59   Following the amendment to the Treaty by the Single European Act, the Commission produced a Charter for Fundamental Social Rights. Some of these proposals were regarded as being controversial and it was not entirely clear whether they could be passed by the qualified majority voting system or require a unanimous vote. For example, the Working Time Directive (93/104/EEC) (see paragraph 10.25) was challenged by the UK Government, which sought to have it annulled in whole or in part, on the ground that there was no direct and objective link between it and health and safety, and therefore it should have been considered under Article 94, which requires unanimous approval. However, the ECJ upheld the validity of the Directive (apart from the "Sunday rest day" provisions), holding that a broad interpretation should be given to the powers contained in Article 139 (see *United Kingdom v Council of the European Union*). Other proposals are generally accepted. Currently, Directives are being introduced concerning a number of matters raised by the Charter. Less controversial are the health and safety Directives, which are discussed in Chapter 10. However, it is clear that the European Union is now the major driving force behind health and safety legislation generally, as well as the impetus behind environmental protection and protection from major hazards.

The judicial system in England and Wales

Criminal courts

Magistrates' courts

1.60   These courts are presided over by Justices of the Peace, who are generally non-lawyers, appointed by the Lord Chancellor on the recommendation of a local advisory committee. The aim is to select magistrates from a wide cross-section of the local community, so that the bench is a balanced one. Magistrates are advised on points of law by a (usually) legally qualified clerk, but it is the responsibility of the bench to determine the facts and to make a decision. In certain large cities, full-time district judges (formerly known as stipendiary magistrates) may be found. These are qualified lawyers and are paid a stipend. A district judge will usually sit alone, whereas lay magistrates will normally sit in benches of three.

1.61   A magistrates' court has some civil jurisdiction (mainly concerned with matrimonial disputes) but the bulk of the work is criminal, and indeed, over 94% of all criminal cases start and finish in the magistrates' courts. True, the overwhelming majority of these are motoring offences, but a fair amount of petty crime is also dealt with. The powers of punishment are normally limited to imposing a maximum fine of £5000 (£20,000 in certain circumstances), or to send someone to prison for up to six months, although the relevant statute will usually contain the maximum penalties. Sometimes, in respect of continuing offences, a fine may be imposed for each day in which the offence is continued.

1.62   Procedurally there are three types of offences. First, there is a summary offence, which can only be dealt with before a court of summary jurisdiction, ie the magistrates' court. Second, there is an indictable offence which results in a formal document, known as an indictment, being drawn up. An accused will be brought before the magistrates for them to determine whether or not there is sufficient evidence (or *a prima facie* case) to commit the accused to the Crown Court for trial (hence these are known as committal proceedings) where the case will be heard before a judge and jury. Third, there are those cases which are triable either way (ie summarily or on indictment) depending on the option exercised by the accused and the gravity of the case, which may cause the magistrates to decide to send the matter for trial or to hear it themselves.

1.63 So far as health and safety legislation is concerned, some offences under the Health and Safety at Work, etc Act 1974 (HSWA) are summary, others are triable either before the magistrates or at the Crown Court, depending on the seriousness of the offence.

1.64 The overlap between certain statutory provisions may cause some problems. For example, an obligation imposed by a health and safety regulation may be an absolute one (ie the thing must or must not be done, as the case may be, see paragraph 1.105), whereas under HSWA, an offence may be committed only if the accused failed to take steps which were reasonably practicable. In the former case, a failure to do the thing required is an offence, and the fact that it was difficult, or even impossible, to carry out the obligation is no defence, whereas in the latter case, the accused may be able to show that it was not reasonably practicable to do more than he in fact did.

1.65 If a person wishes to appeal from the decision of the magistrates' court on a point of law, this is done by way of a "case stated" to the Queen's Bench Divisional Court. Either the prosecution or the defence may so appeal. Appeals against conviction and/or sentence may be made by the accused to the Crown Court, and will take the form of a rehearing before a judge (without a jury).

Crown Court

1.66 This court will hear indictable offences and those cases (usually of a more serious nature) which the prosecution or defence have elected to have tried before the Crown Court. Such cases are heard before a judge and jury. It is the function of the judge to ensure that the trial is conducted fairly, and to sum up for the jury on points of law. The jury returns a verdict depending on the facts. Under HSWA, offences are punishable by an unlimited fine, and eight particular offences (see paragraph 3.178) may be additionally punished by a term of imprisonment of up to two years. In recent years, there are signs that the courts are prepared to impose stiff penalties for breaches of health and safety law. There are several instances where custodial or suspended prison sentences have been imposed, for example for failure to comply with a prohibition notice. Recently, a sentence of 12 months' imprisonment (as well as a fine) was imposed on a company director who failed to ensure that protective clothing was supplied to a worker who came into contact with a deadly chemical, and who, in consequence, was killed. Substantial fines have also been imposed, the highest recorded being of £1.7 million (see paragraph 3.179). An appeal against conviction and/or sentence will lie to the Court of Appeal.

Divisional Court

1.67 The Queen's Bench Divisional Court is presided over by (usually) the Lord Chief Justice, who will normally sit with two other judges. This court will hear appeals by way of "case stated" from the decisions of the magistrates' courts. The Divisional Court also hears appeals from decisions of employment tribunals relating to prohibition and improvement notices. The reason appeals against enforcement notices go to this court (instead, as one might expect, to the Employment Appeal Tribunal) is because a failure to comply with one of these enforcement notices is a criminal offence and the Divisional Court is basically a criminal appeal court, hearing appeals from inferior courts and tribunals.

Civil courts

County Court

1.68 This is a civil court, which formerly had limited jurisdiction. However, as a result of recent changes, the County Court now has concurrent jurisdiction with the High Court in all matters other than specified exceptions. In particular, personal injury claims which are likely to involve less than £50,000 must be started in the County Court. Cases will be heard by a county court judge or a circuit judge. "Small claims" of less than £5000 may be heard by a district judge in a special informal procedure.

High Court of Judicature

1.69 For all practical purposes, this is the major civil court, and is presided over by a High Court Judge, sitting in the Queen's Bench Division (there are other specialised courts at this level which deal with commercial matters, admiralty claims, divorce, probate, etc). Juries have long been abolished in all but the most exceptional civil cases and thus the judge will be the sole arbiter of law and fact. This court is based in the Strand in London, but will also hear cases in various parts of the country. So far as this book is concerned, civil claims for industrial accidents, etc are usually heard in this court.

Other courts, etc

Court of Appeal

1.70   This court acts as the appeal court from the decisions of the Queen's Bench in civil matters, the Queen's Bench Divisional Court in criminal matters, from the Crown Court and County Court and the Employment Appeal Tribunal (EAT). It is presided over by the Master of the Rolls who sits with two other Lord Justices of Appeal. Appeals may only be made on a point of law, and thus cases will consist entirely of legal argument.

House of Lords

1.71   In its legal capacity, the House of Lords is the highest court in the land. It consists of "Law Lords", ie judges who have been "promoted" from the lower courts. The Lord Chancellor (a political appointee) is entitled to sit, as is any ex-Lord Chancellor. Normally, the House will sit with five members present, but as in theory the House of Lords is part of the legislature, the judgments consist of "speeches". By convention, only the Law Lords and Lord Chancellors (past and present) will attend when the House is sitting in its legal capacity. Once a decision of the House of Lords is given on a point of law, it will bind all lower courts until the House gives a different ruling, or until the decision is changed by an Act of Parliament. But precedence must always be given to European law, as interpreted by the European Court or the House of Lords itself.

1.72   For example, in *Equal Opportunities Commission v Secretary of State for Employment*, the House of Lords held that provisions in the Employment Protection (Consolidation) Act 1978 which restricted the rights of part-time workers to obtain redundancy payments and unfair dismissal rights were incompatible with Article 141 of the Treaty of Rome and the Equal Treatment Directive (75/117/EEC), a ruling which forced Parliament to amend the relevant provisions of the Employment Protection (Consolidation) Act 1978.

Employment tribunals

1.73   Formerly known as industrial tribunals (renamed employment tribunals by the Employment Rights (Dispute Resolution) Act 1998), these were created in 1964, and now have a wide jurisdiction relating to problems arising out of modern employment legislation. For the purpose of this book, employment tribunals have three important functions, namely to hear appeals against the decision of an inspector to impose a prohibition or improvement notice, to hear claims for unfair dismissal, sex, race and disability discrimination, and to hear other claims arising out of the Employment Rights Act 1996 (ie refusal to give time off work to safety representatives, a failure to pay for such time off work, protection in health and safety cases, and a refusal to pay medical or maternity suspension pay). An employment tribunal consists of a legally qualified chairman, with two "wingmen". Decisions of employment tribunals, though not regarded as precedents, are valued for their reasoning and guidance. Any person may represent a party before an employment tribunal, costs are not normally awarded to the winner (but see paragraph 3.166), and proceedings are generally more informal than in other courts. An appeal against a decision of an employment tribunal on a point of law relating to cases concerning improvement and prohibition notices will go to the Queen's Bench Divisional Court, but appeals on all other matters will go to the Employment Appeal Tribunal.

Employment Appeal Tribunal

1.74   This is a specialised court whose main function is to hear appeals on points of law from the decisions of employment tribunals. It will consist of a High Court judge and two wingmen chosen from each side of industry. Again, procedure is relatively more informal than in other courts, legal representation is not insisted upon, costs are not normally awarded to the winner, and the procedure is designed to hear cases with a maximum amount of simplicity and a minimum amount of delay. A further appeal may be made to the Court of Appeal.

The judicial system in Scotland

1.75   For historical reasons, Scotland has its own distinctive legal system, with its own procedure and, to some extent, legal rules. Acts of

Parliament which apply to Scotland must be specifically stated to be so, and frequently Parliament will enact legislation which is parallel to English law.

District Court

1.76   Minor criminal offences are heard summarily by the District Court, which is presided over by Justices of the Peace or a stipendiary magistrate.

Sheriff Court

1.77   More serious criminal offences are heard in the sheriffs' court. Under the summary procedure, the sheriff can impose a fine of up to £5000 and/or a prison sentence of up to three months (for offences under the Health and Safety at Work Act, the maximum punishment can be £20,000 and/or six months' imprisonment). Under the solemn procedure (where the sheriff sits with a jury of 15) trial is by way of indictment, and an unlimited fine and/or up to two years' imprisonment may be imposed. Certain civil cases can also be heard.

High Court of Justiciary

1.78   This court only hears trials on indictment and has unlimited powers of punishment.

Court of Criminal Appeal

1.79   Appeals from the district court, sheriff's court and the High Court of Justiciary are heard by the Court of Criminal Appeal which consists of three judges.

Court of Session

1.80   This is the major civil court in Scotland. The Outer House has originating jurisdiction and the Inner House acts as a court of appeal. A further appeal lies to the House of Lords.

1.81   So far as the subject of health and safety at work is concerned, there are no differences in the legal rules applied in England and Wales and Scotland. Insofar as cases from Scotland are cited in this book, certain terminology has been transposed into the English equivalent for the sake of consistency and simplicity. In England and Wales, prosecutions may be instituted in the magistrates' court by a Health and Safety Executive (HSE) or local authority inspector, whereas in Scotland the inspector will send a report to the procurator fiscal, who will decide whether or not to prosecute.

Woolf reforms of civil procedure

1.82   Following a report of a committee set up by Lord Woolf, new civil procedure rules have been introduced. The aim is to replace the old system, which was slow, cumbersome and costly, with a new simplified system which will be fairer, speedier and cheaper. Judges will be able to take a more active role by setting strict timetables, documents will have to be disclosed at an early stage, new terminology has been adopted (see Appendix 4), Latin tags will be abolished, and early settlements will be encouraged. A failure to comply with the new rules may result in costs being awarded against a party to the proceedings. The overriding objective is to ensure that personal injury litigation is dealt with justly and speedily. In particular, alternative dispute resolution, and mediation or arbitration, will be encouraged.

1.83   Pre-action protocols have been issued for different types of claims, requiring the disclosure of documents and exchange of information within specified time limits. The aim is to ensure that each side to the dispute is aware of the other side's case as early as possible, so that the precise issues can be identified. A failure to comply with the protocols could lead to essential evidence being excluded, or an award of costs being made against the party in default.

1.84   A claimant must send the first letter of claim containing all the essential information, and the defendant (or the insurers) must respond within 21 days, and either admit or deny liability within three months. If there is a denial, it must be accompanied by all the relevant documentation. If expert evidence is required (eg a medical or other report), the parties will be encouraged to agree on a single expert, who will prepare a non-partisan independent report. A defendant corporation must appoint an appropriate person to make a "reasonable search" for documents which will be relevant to the case (see paragraph 7.217) and he must certify that he has understood the duty of disclosure and discharged it to the best of his knowledge. Documents must be disclosed timeously.

1.85   Claims will generally fall into three categories, ie:

(a) small claims, with a financial value of up to £5000 (or personal injury claims up to £1000)

(b) fast track claims, which have a value of between £5001 and £15,000. The court will set a strict timetable for the conduct of such cases, and generally they should not last for more than one day in court, and

(c) multi-track claims, where the value of the claim exceeds £15,000. Here, the court will take an active role, and arrange case management conferences so that the progress of the claim can be discussed, and strict timetables laid down.

1.86 Pre-action protocols have already been created for personal injury cases of less than £15,000 in value, and further protocols will be issued in the near future. These set out the time table within which the various procedural steps should be taken, the lists of documents which should be considered for submission, agreement on an expert's report and so on. The statement of case (ie the claim form and defence) must be in plain English, and, in particular, the defendant must state which facts are accepted, which are denied, state the defendant's version of the events, and identify those facts of which the defendant has no knowledge and requires the claimant to prove.

1.87 The new system will not only require full documentation of incidents by health and safety managers, but, as will be seen (paragraph 7.219), should act as an impetus towards ensuring that assessments, testing, maintenance work, training, etc are all carried out, and results recorded, so that proper disclosure statements can be made.

The divisions of substantive law

1.88 All the laws of Great Britain may be found in the thousands of volumes of statutes and judicial decisions which line the shelves of law libraries. For convenience, we tend to subdivide subjects under different headings, each with their own special rules and application. Thus, if a person dies, interested parties will want to know something about the law of wills, or probate, or succession, as the case may be. If someone buys a house, he will get involved with land law, or conveyancing, and so on. In the field of occupational health, safety and welfare, we are mainly concerned with employment law, which is an amalgam of the law relating to contract, tort and crime. Each of these requires a brief examination.

Contract law

1.89   Most people enter into contracts almost every day of their lives. When they buy a newspaper, go on a train journey, eat a meal in a restaurant, etc they are entering into a contract. The law on this subject is made up largely of judicial decisions, supplemented by certain statutory provisions and can be found in any recognised textbook on the subject. Occupational health and safety is fundamentally based on the existence of a contract of employment, and certain aspects of this will be dealt with in Chapter 9. There is some force in the view that the duties which employers owe to employees to ensure their safety and health at work are based on contract as well as tort (*Matthews v Kuwait Bechtel Corporation*, see paragraph 8.3).

Law of tort

1.90   A tort is a civil wrong, ie a wrongful act by one person which gives a right to the injured party to sue for a legal remedy, which is usually, but not exclusively, an action for damages. Torts are subclassified under a number of well-known headings; thus defamation, trespass, nuisance, negligence, etc are all torts each with their own special rules and legal requirements. We will be concerned to a large extent with the tort of negligence, which is the breach of a legal duty to take care not to cause damage or injury to another. Thus an employer owes a duty to take care in order to ensure the health and safety of the employees (see Chapter 8), as well as to others who may be adversely affected by the work activities.

Crime

1.91   A crime is an act which is punishable by the state in the criminal courts. Parliament has taken the view that employers and others who fail to comply with certain minimum health and safety standards shall be punished, in order to deter others from breaking the law. It cannot be pretended that the actual amount of the fines imposed acts as a great deterrent, for these seldom reflect the hazard created, nor the ability of the employer to pay. Nonetheless, the adverse publicity and the tarnishing of reputation is regarded as being undesirable. Modern management will take the view that health and safety is an objective to be pursued for its own sake, not through fear of punishment.

1.92   It is clear that the object of criminal law must be prevention, not retribution, rectification of hazards, not punishment for indifference. The criminal law should always be a weapon of last resort, rather than an instant reaction when offences are discovered. Certainly, this is the philosophy behind the Health and Safety Executive (HSE) inspectorate, for the number of prosecutions undertaken will represent only a small fraction of the number of breaches which may be discovered.

Criminal offences

1.93   As has been noted, a breach of health and safety legislation is generally a criminal offence. However, this does not imply that the only criminal offences are those which are in breach of the relevant statutory provisions, for the general criminal law is also capable of being invoked. In particular, in recent years the crime of manslaughter has been raised in cases where death has occurred due to recklessness or dangerous conduct which is itself an unlawful act. The first successful prosecution for manslaughter was brought in 1990, when a company director pleaded guilty following the death of an employee at his factory.

1.94   More difficult, and perhaps more controversial, have been recent instances of bringing charges of corporate manslaughter against companies. The problem is that in general, the crime of manslaughter requires the accused to have *mens rea*, ie a "guilty mind", which is an essential ingredient in the crime. Can a company have "a mind" of its own (irrespective of the minds of its employees and/or directors) so as to possess the necessary *mens rea*? Several attempts have been made in recent years to establish the offence of corporate manslaughter, generally without success. In *R v Great Western Trains Co*, charges of corporate manslaughter arising out of the Southall train disaster were dismissed, the judge holding that "it was still necessary to look for a directing mind and identity whose gross negligence it is that fixes the company with criminal responsibility". The Attorney General sought the opinion of the Court of Appeal on a question of law, and it was held that for a non-human defendant to be convicted of the crime of manslaughter by gross negligence, there must be evidence establishing the guilt of an identified human individual for the same crime (*Attorney-General's Reference (No. 2 of 1999)*). Thus prosecutions for corporate manslaughter will only succeed where smaller companies are concerned, for it will then be easier to show that there is an identifiable person who could be fastened with guilt. In a case arising out of the

Lyme Bay disaster, when four teenagers died whilst out canoeing at an activity centre, charges of corporate manslaughter succeeded. The centre was convicted of four counts of manslaughter and its managing director was also convicted, and sentenced to three years imprisonment. The difficulties in securing a conviction for corporate manslaughter has meant that few prosecutions are contemplated, although, in recent years, two successful prosecutions have been brought. Both involved small companies, where a senior person could be identified as having day-to-day control of the companies' activities. The Law Commission has put forward proposals for three new offences which might be used to meet an obvious gap in the law, namely "reckless killing", "killing by gross carelessness" and "corporate killing". The present Government is consulting on these proposals, and, if legislation follows in the near future, health and safety will be moved firmly to boardroom level.

1.95   In respect of work-related deaths, a protocol for liaison has been agreed between the HSE, the Director of Public Prosecutions, and the Association of Chief Police Officers, recognising their respective functions and ensuring co-operation and co-ordination of activities. Thus, the HSE is responsible for enforcing health and safety legislation, the police authorities will investigate to ascertain if a serious criminal offence has been committed, and the Crown Prosecution Service has to decide whether there is sufficient evidence to warrant prosecution for manslaughter.

1.96   For the purpose of this book, the overwhelming number of criminal offences which may be committed are those specified in the various statutory provisions. It is quite possible for a single occurrence to give rise to more than one offence. For example, the HSE may decide to prosecute for a breach of the Health and Safety at Work, etc Act 1974 (HSWA) at the same time as for a breach of other legislation.

Defence of due diligence

1.97   A statutory provision may provide that it is a defence for an accused to show that he or she used due diligence to secure compliance with the law. This is a question of fact, and the standard of proof is that of the balance of probabilities (*R v Carr-Briant*). If the accused is an incorporated association (eg a limited company) the prosecution would need to show that the failure to comply was due to the act or omission of a person who can be identified with the controlling mind and will of the company. The default by a subordinate will not necessarily be that of the company. In *Tesco Supermarkets Ltd v Natrass*, a supermarket advertised a washing powder at a discount rate. A customer sought to purchase the item, but was told the special rate stock had been exhausted. The supermarket was prosecuted under the Trade Description Act. In its defence it was argued that the store manager had been responsible for the breach because his system of daily checks had broken down, and further argued that the company had done all it could to ensure that the offence would not be committed. It was held that the company was entitled to plead the defence of due diligence. The store manager did not act *as* the company, but *for* the company. The *mens rea* of the company could only be derived from the actions of those officers who represented the company's controlling mind. It is this "controlling mind" theory which make prosecutions for those offences which require *mens rea* (eg manslaughter) difficult to sustain.

The overlap of the law

1.98   Since there are no clear boundaries between legal concepts, an act may frequently have two or more legal implications. Thus an accident at work may result in a prosecution for a criminal offence; the same incident may result in a civil claim being brought for compensation. Indeed, in civil proceedings, the fact that there has been a criminal conviction in respect of the relevant incident is admissible in evidence (Civil Evidence Act 1968, s.11) for the purpose of proving that the defendant committed the offence, although it is not conclusive, and rebutting evidence may be given. The majority of legal decisions on health and safety which explain and interpret the various statutory provisions arise out of civil proceedings, a fact which indicates how the law on occupational health and safety tends to work in practice.

Statutory interpretation

1.99   It is the task of the courts to interpret the words used by Parliament, not to legislate, although there can be little doubt in practice that by doing the former they achieve the latter. In recent years, the courts have taken a broader view in respect of reforming legislation and sought to interpret the words by seeking the intentions of Parliament. Indeed, the House of Lords have recently held that when construing a statute, reference may be made to Parliamentary material (eg *Hansard*) where the legislation is ambiguous or obscure, or leads to an absurdity (see *Pepper v Hart*). An exploration of this aspect of judicial innovation is beyond the scope of this book.

1.100   All modern Acts of Parliament contain a section which deals with interpretation, and they will also define special terms where necessary. The Health and Safety at Work, etc Act 1974 (HSWA) contains four sections (ss.52, 53, 76, 82) which are concerned with the meaning of words and phrases used in the Act, and this practice is to be found in other relevant statutes and regulations. It is to these that reference should be made in the first instance. Words used in health and safety regulations are generally construed in accordance with the parent Act.

1.101   The Interpretation Act 1978 can be looked to for assistance in some circumstances. By that Act, unless the contrary is intended, a reference to a male includes a reference to a female, and vice versa, and a reference to the singular includes the plural. A "person" includes a body of persons (whether corporate or unincorporate), "month" means calendar month, and so on.

1.102   There are a number of rules for statutory interpretation which are well known and used in legal circles, sometimes with Latin tags. There is the "literal rule", whereby the courts will look at the ordinary and grammatical sense of the words used. If this leads to absurdity or inconsistency, the "golden rule" may be applied, whereby a construction is given which leads to a sensible interpretation, taking into account the whole statute. The tag *ejusdem generis* (of the same species) may be used on occasions. For example, if a statute referred to "any car, van, bus or other vehicle" it is doubtful if the latter phrase would include a bicycle, as the species is clearly motorised transport.

1.103   Sometimes, the courts may look to the interpretation already given to a particular word or phrase when used in another enactment, particularly when the two statutes are dealing with the same or similar subject matter. Thus words used in the Offices, Shops and Railway Premises Act used to be construed on the same lines as identical words used (and judicially explained) in the Factories Act. This is known as construing *in pari materia* (in similar circumstances). (As has been noted (see paragraph 1.82), Latin tags are no longer to be used, but they are still to be found in older cases.)

1.104   The following are some of the words and phrases which are to be commonly found in the law on health and safety generally.

"Shall"; "Shall Not"

1.105   These words impose an absolute obligation to do (or not to do) the act or thing in question, and it is not permissible to argue that it is impracticable, difficult or even impossible to do it (or not to do it). Thus, when the Factories Act, s.14 stated that "Every dangerous part of any machinery shall be securely fenced", it imposed an absolute obligation to securely fence, and a failure to do so may have resulted in criminal proceedings or, if someone is injured because of a failure to securely fence, a civil action for compensation. If it was impossible to use the machine when securely fenced, then the Act implicitly prohibited its use (*Summers (John) & Sons Ltd v Frost*) or the occupier of the factory used it at his peril.

1.106   An absolute obligation may be laid down in regulations made under an Act. In *Stark v Post Office* a postman was injured when a part of the front brake of his delivery bicycle broke. It was held the Post Office were in breach of regulation 6(1) of the Provision and Use of Work Equipment Regulations 1992 (see paragraph 6.53) which provides that "Every employer shall ensure that work equipment is maintained in an efficient state, in efficient working order and in good repair". The regulations imposed an absolute obligation on the employer, who was liable for damage for the tort of breach of statutory duty.

"So far as is practicable"; "best practicable means"

1.107   This is a high standard, but not an absolute one because if it is impossible to do something, then clearly it is not practicable to do it (*Jayne v National Coal Board*). If something is practicable, it must be done; if the best practical means are required, then it is up to the person on whom the obligation is placed to find the best practicable means, and to constantly bring his knowledge up to date. However, it is not practicable to take precautions against a danger which is not known to exist, although once the danger is known, it becomes practicable to do something about it (*Cartwright v GKN Sankey Ltd*). The test is one of foresight, not hindsight (*Edwards v National Coal Board*). The standard of practicability is that of current knowledge and invention (*Adsett v K and L Steelfounders and Engineers Ltd*). Once something is found to be practicable, it is feasible, and it must be done, no matter how inconvenient or expensive it may be to do it. The burden of proof to show that it was not practicable to do something, or to do more than was in fact done, is on the person upon whom the obligation is placed (in civil proceedings) and upon the defendant or accused in criminal proceedings (HSWA, s.40).

"Reasonably practicable"

1.108   This phrase causes more concern to practitioners than any other, although there is no magic or mystery about it. It should be looked at in the following way.

1.109   First, we start off with the presumption that if something is practicable, the courts will not lightly hold that it is not reasonably practicable (*Marshall v Gotham & Co*).

1.110   Second, it is a somewhat lesser standard than "practicable". It is permissible to take into account on the one hand the danger or hazard or injury which may occur, and balance it, on the other hand, with the cost, inconvenience, time and trouble which would have to be taken to counter it. As Asquith LJ stated in *Edwards v National Coal Board*, "Reasonably practicable" is a narrower term than "physically possible" and seems to me to imply that a computation must be made by the owner in which the quantum or risk is placed in one scale and the sacrifice involved in the measures necessary for averting the risk (whether in money, time or trouble) is placed in the other, and that, if it be shown that there is a gross disproportion between them the risk being insignificant in relation to the sacrifice the defendants discharge the onus on them. Moreover, this computation falls to be made by the owner at a point in time anterior to the accident." By way of example, we may cite *Marshall v Gotham & Co.* where, although the roof of a mine had been tested in the usual way, it collapsed because of the existence of a rare geological fault. It was held that the employers were not liable for the injuries to the plaintiff which ensued. The court held that, "The danger was a very rare one. The trouble and expense involved in the use of precautions, while not prohibitive, would have been considerable. The precautions would not have afforded anything like complete protection against the danger". In the circumstances, the employers had done all that was reasonable.

1.111 Third, in criminal proceedings, it shall be for the accused to prove that it was not reasonably practicable to do more than was in fact done to satisfy the duty or requirement (HSWA, s.40). However, this can be established by the defendant by the ordinary burden of proof, ie on the balance of probabilities.

1.112 Fourth, in the last analysis, it will be for the court to decide, as a question of fact, based on the evidence which can be adduced, whether or not something was reasonably practicable. In the Crown Court, this will be decided by the jury (*R v Nelson Group Services (Maintenance) Ltd* (see paragraph 3.80)). In the last resort, therefore, the issue can only be determined after the event when it has been tested in court.

1.113 For example, in *Martin v Boulton & Paul Ltd*, an employee of the defendants was injured while erecting a steel beam, and the defendants were prosecuted for failing to provide, so far as was reasonably practicable, a safe system of work. The magistrate found that the method adopted by the defendants was a universal practice adopted in the steel erection industry and dismissed the charge. On appeal by way of "case stated", the Divisional Court held that the existence of a universal practice did not, by itself, lead to the conclusion that there was no other reasonably practicable way of doing something. There may be evidence to suggest that despite the universal practice, there were other ways of doing the work which were safer and therefore reasonably practicable. Thus evidence of a universal practice does not discharge the burden of proof which lies on the defendant, though it is a factual matter which can be taken into account, along with all the other evidence.

1.114 Indeed, it would not be impossible for different courts and tribunals to come to contrary conclusions on identical facts if perceptions differ. The passage of time, greater knowledge and experience, accident statistics, as well as the "inarticulate major premise" of those hearing cases, may account for a different end result. For example, an employment tribunal in *International Stores Ltd v Johns* quashed a prohibition notice imposed on an unguarded meat-slicing band saw, whereas in *Gateway Foodmarkets Ltd v Eastwood*, a similar notice on an identical machine was upheld.

"Relevant statutory provisions"

1.115   This means the provisions of Part 1 of HSWA (including health and safety regulations made under the Act), plus the following provisions, which are contained in Schedule 1 of HSWA.

	Provisions which are relevant statutory provisions
The Explosives Act 1875	The whole Act except ss.30 to 32, 80 and 116 to 121
The Boiler Explosions Act 1882	The whole Act
The Boiler Explosions Act 1890	The whole Act
The Alkali, etc Works Regulation Act 1906	The whole Act
The Revenue Act 1909	Section 11
The Anthrax Prevention Act 1919	The whole Act
The Employment of Women, Young Persons and Children Act 1920	The whole Act
The Celluloid and Cinematograph Film Act 1922	The whole Act
The Explosives Act 1923	The whole Act
The Public Health (Smoke Abatement) Act 1926	The whole Act
The Petroleum (Consolidation) Act 1928	The whole Act
The Hours of Employment (Conventions) Act 1936	The whole Act except section 5
The Petroleum (Transfer of Licences) Act 1936	The whole Act
The Hydrogen Cyanide (Fumigation) Act 1937	The whole Act
The Ministry of Fuel and Power Act 1945	Section 1(1) so far as it relates to maintaining and improving safety, health and well-being of persons employed in and about mines and quarries in Great Britain
The Coal Industry Nationalisation Act 1946	Section 42(1) and (2)
The Radioactive Substances Act 1948	Section 5(1)(a)

The Alkali, etc Works Regulation (Scotland) Act 1951	The whole Act
The Fireworks Act 1951	Sections 4 and 7
The Agriculture (Poisionous Substances) Act 1952	The whole Act
The Emergency Laws (Miscellaneous Provisions) Act 1953	Section 3
The Mines and Quarries Act 1954	The whole Act except section 151
The Factories Act 1961	The whole Act except section 135
The Public Health Act 1961	Section 73
The Pipelines Act 1962	Sections 20 to 34, 37 and 42, Schedule 5
The Offices, Shops and Railways Premises Act 1963	The whole Act
The Nuclear Installations Act 1965	Sections 1, 3 to 6, 22 and 24A
The Mines and Quarries (Tips) Act 1969	Sections 1 to 10
The Mines Management Act 1971	The whole Act
The Employment Medical Advisory Service Act 1972	The whole Act except ss.1 and 6 and Schedule 1
The Mineral Workings (Offshore Installations) Act 1971	The whole Act
The Petroleum and Submarine Pipelines Act 1975	Sections 26, 27 and 32
The Petroleum Act 1978	Sections 11(2(2a)), 21 to 24
The Gas Act 1986	Sections 16, 47(3)–(4)

1.116   Since the passing of HSWA, many of the above provisions have been repealed in whole or in part or superseded in some way. A number of other Acts were added to this list by the Railways Act 1993, relating to the operation of railways.

"Prescribed"

1.117   If something is to be prescribed, it has to be specifically referred to at some future time. Thus, if a statute states that something shall be done "in prescribed cases" then the power exists for someone (eg the Secretary of State) to prescribe the cases where that thing shall be done, and until the power is exercised, nothing has happened. For example, s.2(7) of HSWA states that in prescribed cases an employer shall establish a safety committee, and the Safety Representatives and Safety

Committees Regulations 1977 specify that this shall be done when at least two safety representatives request the employer, in writing, to establish such a committee. If something has to be prescribed under the Act, it will be done by regulations (s.53(1)).

"At work"

1.118 An employee is at work throughout the time when he is in the course of his employment, but not otherwise (s.52(1)(b)). The phrase "course of his employment" is not capable of precise definition and legal authorities based on civil cases have, as a matter of policy, given it a somewhat liberal construction. These authorities do not necessarily bind in criminal law. In *Coult v Szuba*, the defendant was employed to work at the Scunthorpe site of the British Steel Corporation. The site had 39 miles of roads. The defendant, who was due to start work at 6am, clocked in at 5.41am and then drove along a road to the place where he was due to work. On the way, he was involved in an accident with another car due to the defendant's fault. He was prosecuted for an offence under s.7(a) of HSWA for failing to take reasonable care of the safety of himself and others while at work. The magistrates dismissed the charge, and their decision was upheld by the Divisional Court on appeal. On the facts of the case, it was not possible to say that the defendant was in the course of his employment at the time of the accident (this case may be contrasted with *Bolton Metropolitan Borough Council v Malrod Insulations Ltd*, paragraph 3.29).

1.119 It will be noted that trainees and others on work experience are "at work" for the purpose of s.52(1)(b) even though they are not employees in the legal sense (see paragraph 3.13).

Burden of proof

1.120 In criminal cases, the general rule is that it is for the prosecution to prove its case, in the hallowed phrase "beyond reasonable doubt". However, in some circumstances, the burden of proof is on the defendant. For example, s.17 of HSWA requires the accused to show that he observed the specific statutory provision otherwise than by observing the Approved Code of Practice; s.40 of HSWA requires the accused to show that it was not practicable or not reasonably practicable to do more than in fact was done, etc. However, this burden can be discharged by proof on the balance of probabilities (*R v Carr-Briant*).

1.121 In civil cases, the rule is that the burden is upon the plaintiff to prove his case on the balance of probabilities. In this, he may be assisted by some principles of evidence.

(a) Res ipsa loquitor

1.122 If something is under the control of the defendant, and an accident occurs in circumstances such that it would not have happened unless there had been a want of care by the defendant, then a presumption is raised that the defendant has been negligent. The burden is then put on the defendant to explain the accident, and to show that there was no want of care on his part. In other words, "the facts speak for themselves". However, the defendant may be able to show a convincing reason why he was not negligent (eg the accident was caused by the fault of a third party) in which case the burden of proof is thrown back to the plaintiff to prove his case in the usual manner.

(b) Shifting presumptions

1.123 Sometimes, the mere statement of facts will give rise to an inferential presumption which may cause the burden of proof to shift from one party to the other, requiring it to be rebutted by evidence. For example, in *Gardiner v Motherwell Machinery and Scrap Co Ltd*, the plaintiff sued in respect of dermatitis which he alleged was contracted at work. Lord Reid said, "When a man who has not previously suffered from a disease contracts that disease after being subjected to conditions likely to cause it, and when he shows that it starts in a way typical of the disease caused by such conditions, he establishes a *prima facie* presumption that his disease was caused by those conditions." Thus if a person contracts bronchitis after working in dusty conditions, or suffers deafness after being exposed to excessively noisy conditions, an evidential presumption arises that those conditions caused the disease or injury in question.

The scope of the law

1.124 For historical reasons, the UK is made up of four countries, namely England, Wales, Scotland and Northern Ireland. Although there is a general common law operating throughout the UK, there are some procedural differences. A reference to Great Britain excludes Northern Ireland.

1.125 England and Wales may be regarded as one country for legal purposes as no difference exists in the law or procedure (certain problems may arise over the use of the Welsh language, but this is irrelevant for our purposes). Scotland, on the other hand, retains its own legal system, which has certain distinctive terminology, procedure and sometimes different legal rules. As a general principle, the law on health and safety in Scotland is the same as in England and Wales and will be so treated throughout this book. Acts of Parliament will usually state whether or not they apply to Scotland, and if they do not, it is frequently necessary to enact further legislation in order to bring the countries into harmony. Some Acts apply to England, Wales and Scotland, and merely note the different terminology by reference to the appropriate Scottish words. Although there is now a Scottish Parliament, this body will not make any changes to employment, industrial relations, and health and safety law (Scotland Act 1998, Schedule 5), as these powers are reserved for the Westminster Parliament. Equally, the Welsh Assembly has no such law-making powers (Government of Wales Act 1998, ss.21–23). Northern Ireland, however, has its own legal system, though at the present time it is governed direct from the UK Parliament and will usually follow the pattern already laid down for Great Britain. The Health and Safety at Work (Northern Ireland) Order 1978 created the Health and Safety Agency, with functions and responsibilities similar to those of the Health and Safety Commission (HSC). The Health and Safety Agency has been renamed as the Health and Safety Executive by the Health and Safety at Work (Amendment) (Northern Ireland) Order 1998.

1.126 The Isle of Man and the Channel Islands are not part of the UK (Royal and Parliamentary Titles Act 1927).

1.127 By the Health and Safety at Work Act (Application Outside Great Britain) Order 2001, as amended, the provisions of HSWA are extended to cover offshore oil and gas installations, pipeline work, offshore construction work, certain loading and unloading operations, and shipbuilding, repair work, floating accommodation vessels and diving operations which take place outside British territorial waters. This is additional to the provisions of the Mineral Workings (Offshore Installations) Act 1971, the Petroleum and Submarine Pipelines Act 1975 and regulations made thereunder. At the present time, approximately 40 sets of regulations apply to the offshore installation industry.

1.128 It may be noted at this stage that the Offshore Safety Act 1992 transferred responsibility for health and safety on offshore installations from the Department of Energy to the Health and Safety Executive (HSE), following recommendations made in the Cullen Report, which enquired into the Piper Alpha disaster.

The Human Rights Act 1998

1.129 In order to prevent a recurrence of the horrors and atrocities which took place before and during the Second World War, the European Convention for the Protection of Human Rights and Fundamental Freedoms was signed in 1950. The Human Rights Act 1998 is designed to give effect to those rights and freedoms by effectively incorporating the Convention into UK law. Basically, there are four principles which apply, as follows.

1. When determining a question which arises in connection with a Convention right, a court or tribunal must take account of any judgment, decision, declaration or advisory opinion of the European Court of Human Rights.
2. So far as it is possible to do so, primary and subordinate legislation must be read and given effect to, in a way which is compatible with Convention rights.
3. If a court (not a tribunal) is satisfied that a provision of primary legislation is incompatible with the convention, it may make a declaration of incompatibility.
4. It is unlawful for public authority to act in a way which is incompatible with a Convention right.

1.130 So far as the law of health and safety at work is concerned, the Human Rights Act 1998 is likely to have very limited application. Article 6 of the Convention guarantees a person (which term includes an artificial legal body, such as a limited company) the right to a fair trial in civil and criminal proceedings. This means that each party to a case must have a reasonable opportunity of presenting his case; there must be a public hearing and judgment, with a reasoned decision; the hearing must take place within a reasonable time, and must be before an independent and impartial tribunal. There is no reason to suspect that the UK legal system is wanting in this respect. Article 8 of the Convention guarantees respect for private life, family life, home and correspondence, and although there have been cases before the European Court which have taken the view that state bodies could be in breach of Article 8 if they fail to take appropriate steps to prevent environmental harm, the likelihood of public authorities in the UK falling foul of this provision is somewhat remote.

1.131   In theory, if the Health and Safety Executive (HSE) refused to investigate a major injury, or failed to prosecute in respect of a serious offence, or failed to take some action which would have prevented a major injury, or failed to enforce a legal provision designed to prevent a major injury, then such actions may give rise to a complaint under the Human Rights Act 1998. There may well be cases where the powers of HSE inspectors will be challenged, and where a defendant complains that the right to a fair trial has been violated, but existing laws should be adequate to resolve such issues, and it will be rare that resort to the Human Rights Act 1998 will be needed.

CHAPTER 2

The institutions of health and safety

The role of Government

2.1   The prime responsibility for overseeing health and safety legislation is a political function of the relevant government department. Following a recent reshuffle all matters relating to health and safety at work have been transferred from the Department of the Environment, Transport and Regions (DETR) to the Department of Transport, Local Government and the Regions (DTLR). The head of the department is a Secretary of State (with a seat in the Cabinet) assisted by various junior ministers, one of whom will have been designated as having a special responsibility for occupational health and safety matters. Other problems of health and safety, which are partly concerned with the occupation and partly of general concern to the whole community are dealt with by other departments. Powers relating to the control of industrial pollution are now exercisable by the new Environment Agency created by the Environment Act 1995. The former responsibility of the Department of Energy for occupational health and safety on offshore installations has now been assigned to the Health and Safety Executive (HSE). Similarly, the Railway Inspectorate has been transferred from the Department of Transport to the HSE.

2.2   The Secretary of State appoints the Chairman of the Health and Safety Commission (HSC) and not less than six nor more than nine other members. As to three of these appointees, he must first consult with such organisations representing employers as he considers appropriate, as to a further three, he must consult with trade union organisations, and as to the remainder, he must consult with organisations representing local authorities and other bodies concerned with matters of health, safety and welfare. He must also approve the appointment by the HSC of the Director General of the HSE and of the two other members. He exercises a general control over the Commission by approving (with or without modifications) proposals submitted to him, and may give directions to the Commission with respect to its functions. He will make regulations and give his consent to the issue of Codes of Practice by the HSC.

Health and Safety Commission

2.3   The Health and Safety Commission (HSC) was created by the Health and Safety at Work, etc Act 1974 (HSWA), s.10, and has the prime responsibility for administering the law and practice on occupational health and safety. As already noted, it consists of a chairman and up to nine members. Details of the terms of appointment and constitution of HSC can be found in Schedule 2 to HSWA.

General duties (s.1(1))

2.4   The general duty of HSC is to do such things and make such arrangements as it considers appropriate for the general purposes laid down in s.1(1) of HSWA, (as amended), which are:
  (a) securing the health, safety and welfare of persons at work
  (b) protecting persons other than persons at work against risks to health or safety arising out of or in connection with the activities of persons at work
  (c) controlling the keeping and use of explosives or highly flammable or otherwise dangerous or environmentally hazardous substances, and generally preventing the unlawful acquisition, possession and use of any such substance
  (d) protection of the public from personal injury, fire, explosions and other dangers arising from the transmission or distribution of gas through pipes, or from the use of gas supplied through pipes (Gas Act 1986, s.18(1))
  (e) securing the safety, health and welfare of persons on offshore installations or engaged on pipeline work, the safety of such installations, preventing accidents on or near them, and securing the proper construction, safe operation, and safe dismantling of offshore installations and pipelines (Offshore Safety Act 1992, s.(1))
  (f) securing the proper construction and safe operation of railways, including protection of the public from personal injury and other risks arising from the construction and operations of railways (Railways Act 1993, s.117(2)).

2.5   It will be noted that the HSC is no longer responsible for controlling emissions into the atmosphere of noxious or offensive substances (s.1(1)(d), which related to the emission of noxious substances into the atmosphere from premises, was repealed as from 16

December 1996, see Environmental Protection Act 1990 (Commencement No. 18) Order 1996), and control over industrial pollution is now the responsibility of the Environment Agency or local authorities, depending on the type and size of process involved.

Particular duties of HSC (s.11(2))

2.6   Additionally, the HSC has the following duties:
 (a) assist and encourage persons concerned with matters relevant to any of the above general purposes to further them
 (b) make such arrangements as it considers appropriate for the carrying out of research, the publication of results, the provision of training and information connected therewith, and to encourage research and the provision of training and information by others
 (c) make arrangements for ensuring that government departments, employers, employees, employers' organisations, trade unions and others concerned are provided with an information and advisory service and are kept informed and adequately advised
 (d) submit proposals for the making of regulations by the appropriate authority (ie via the minister responsible).

2.7   The HSC shall also submit to the Secretary of State from time to time particulars of what it proposes to do for the purpose of performing its functions. It must ensure that its activities are in accordance with proposals approved by the Secretary of State, and give effect to any directions given by him.

Powers (s.13)

2.8   The HSC may do anything (except borrow money) which is calculated to facilitate, or is conducive or incidental to, the performance of its functions, and in particular may:
 (a) enter into agreements with any government department or other person for that department or person to perform any function on behalf of HSC or the HSE (eg the HSC has made an "agency agreement" with the National Radiological Protection Board for the latter to perform certain functions relating to ionising and other radiations)
 (b) make agreements whereby the HSC performs functions on behalf of any other minister, government department or other public

authority, being functions which, in the opinion of the Secretary of State, can appropriately be performed by the HSC (but not the power to make regulations or other legislative instruments)

(c) provide services or facilities which may be required by any Government department or public authority

(d) appoint persons or committees to provide the HSC with advice (see paragraph 2.18)

(e) pay travelling and/or subsistence allowances and compensation for loss of remunerative time in connection with any of the functions of the HSC

(f) pay for any research connected with the functions of the HSC and to disseminate (or pay for the dissemination of) information derived from such research

(g) make arrangements for the making of payments to the HSC by other parties who are using facilities and services provided by the HSC.

Investigations and inquiries (s.14)

2.9   If there is an accident, occurrence, situation or other matter which the HSC thinks necessary or expedient to investigate in order to fulfil any of the general purposes of the Act (above) or with a view to the making of regulations for those purposes, it may direct the HSE or any other person to carry out that investigation and make a report (s.14(2)(a)).

2.10   As an alternative, and with the consent of the Secretary of State, the HSC may direct that an inquiry shall be held into the matter (s.14(2)(b)). The result of the investigation or inquiry may be made public, in whole or in part, as the HSC thinks fit.

2.11   The distinction between an investigation and an inquiry is that an inquiry is a formal, public affair into a matter in which there is general public interest as to its outcome, whereas an investigation is more informal and may be carried out in a manner determined by the investigator, though he must still observe the rules of natural justice, and receive evidence from any person who may be able to contribute worthwhile information.

2.12   The Health and Safety Inquiries (Procedure) Regulations 1975 as amended, lay down the procedure for the conduct of inquiries under s.14(2)(b). The date, time and place shall be fixed (and may be varied) by the HSC, who shall also give 28 days' notice to every person entitled to appear whose name and address is known. It must also publish a notice of the intention to hold the inquiry in one or more newspapers (where appropriate, circulating in the district in which the subject matter of the inquiry arose) giving the name of the person who has been appointed to hold the inquiry and of any assessors appointed to assist.

2.13   The following persons shall be entitled to appear at the inquiry as of right:
(a) the Commission
(b) any enforcing authority concerned
(c) in Scotland, the Procurator Fiscal
(d) any employers' association or any trade union representing employers or employees concerned
(e) any person who was injured or who has suffered damage as a result of the incident, or his personal representatives
(f) the owner or occupier of any premises in which the incident occurred
(g) any person carrying on the activity which gave rise to the incident.

2.14   Other persons may appear at the inquiry, but only at the discretion of the person appointed to hold it. Anyone wishing to appear at an inquiry may do so in person, or may be represented by a lawyer or by any other person.

2.15   The person appointed to conduct the inquiry may, either on his own volition or on the application of any person entitled or permitted to appear, require the attendance of any other person in order to give evidence or to produce any document, and it is an offence, punishable by a fine of up to £5000 to fail to comply with such requirement.

2.16   The conduct of the inquiry will be the responsibility of the appointed person, and it will be held in public unless a Minister of the Crown directs that part or all of the inquiry shall be held in private because it would be against the interests of national security to allow certain evidence to be given in public. Also, a private session may be held if information is likely to be disclosed which relates to a trade secret, on an application made by a party affected. Otherwise, the procedure to be followed will be at the discretion of the appointed person, which he will state at the commencement of the proceedings, subject to any submissions made by any person appearing (or their representatives). He will also inform them as to any proposals he may have regarding an inspection of any site, will determine the order of the witnesses, permit opening statements, examination and cross-examination, hear evidence on oath, permit documents to be introduced as evidence and allow them to be inspected and copied. He may receive any written submissions, and if necessary, adjourn the proceedings from time to time.

2.17   After the inquiry has been concluded, a report, containing the findings of fact and any recommendations, will be made to the HSC.

Advisory committees

2.18   A number of advisory committees have been created in order to provide the HSC with specialised advice and information. These will usually consist of representatives from each side of industry, academic and industrial experts, and officials from the HSE. They will report to the HSC, and may make recommendations. Examples of existing Standing Advisory Committees dealing with specific subjects are as follows.

Advisory Committee on Toxic Substances

2.19   This committee was set up to advise the HSC on methods of controlling health hazards to persons at work (especially in connection with the COSHH regulations, see paragraph 6.316) and also to the general public consequent on or arising from the use of toxic substances. The committee has representatives from industry, local authorities and other expert advisors.

Advisory Committee on Dangerous Substances

2.20   This committee considers methods of securing the safety of persons at work and related risks to the general public arising from the manufacture, import, storage, conveyance and use of materials which are flammable or explosive, and the transportation of a wide range of dangerous substances. Its membership includes representatives from industry, local authorities and other experts.

Advisory Committee on the Safety of Nuclear Installations

2.21   This committee advises on all aspects of nuclear safety. It is chaired by an independent member and has scientific and industrial advisors.

Advisory Committee on Dangerous Pathogens

2.22   This committee will advise the HSC and the Departments of Health and Agriculture on matters relating to all classes of pathogens which are dangerous to human beings. As well as representatives from both sides of industry it has a number of medical and scientific experts It will advise the HSC on the general standards of safe working to be observed in laboratories, point out any improvements necessary, consider new hazards, and make recommendations concerning proposed regulations, Approved Codes of Practice and guidance generally.

Advisory Committee on Genetic Modification

2.23   This committee gives guidance on the planned release of genetically manipulated organisms for agricultural and environment purposes, including risk assessment and notification of proposals to carry out such work. It also deals with guidelines for the health surveillance of persons involved in genetic manipulation in laboratories, etc and the setting up of safety committees.

Occupational Health Advisory Committee

2.24   As its name implies, this committee is concerned with all aspects of occupational health, and has professional as well as industry membership.

Advisory Committee on Ionising Radiations

2.25   This committee advises on the health hazards from ionising radiations, and makes recommendations to ensure adequate protection for employees and others who are exposed to such. The committee also ensures that UK legislation meets standards laid down in EC Directives.

Industrial Advisory Committees (IACs)

2.26 A number of industry-based advisory committees and joint standing committees have been set up with a view to stimulating action to promote the health and safety of workers within particular industries and to protect the general public from related hazards arising from such activities. As a general rule, the HSE provides the secretariat and chairmen, with the rest of the membership drawn from the main organisations in the industry. Each Industrial Advisory Committee (IAC) will draw up its own plan of work (short term and long term) reviewing specific problems which need to be tackled, which is submitted to the HSC for approval. Proposals for action to be taken may also be placed before the HSC for consideration.

2.27 Currently there are some 15 IACs, dealing with the following industries: adventure activity, agriculture, ceramics, chemicals, construction, deep mined coal, education, foundries, health services, oil, paper and board, printing, railways, rubber and textiles.

Ad hoc committees

2.28 The HSC will sometimes set up a committee to deal with a particular problem. For example, the Advisory Committee on Asbestos was created to consider and investigate the special hazards to health arising from the use of asbestos in industry. It issued several reports which, together with its final report contained a number of specific recommendations, and a new Approved Code of Practice (together with Guidance Notes) was published giving practical advice on the precautions to be observed when working with asbestos insulation and asbestos coatings.

2.29 The HSC is constantly updating its strategic planning, in an effort to prioritise its activities, as well as paying attention to its continuing aims. In a recent consultation paper, *Revitalising health and safety*, it announced its targets for the next decade, to include a reduction in working days lost through work-related injury and ill-health by 30%, a reduction in the incidence of people suffering from work-related ill-health by 20%, and a reduction in the rate of fatal and major injury accidents by 10%. To achieve these targets, a ten-point strategy supported by a 44–point action plan was introduced, to provide incentives and practical support for employers, as well as new measures to be taken against those employers who do not meet their health and safety responsibilities.

Health and Safety Executive

2.30   The Health and Safety Executive (HSE) was established by s.10 of HSWA. It is headed by a director general appointed by the HSC with the approval of the Secretary of State, and two other members appointed by the HSC with like approval after consultation with the director general. The HSE, which has its headquarters in London, controls the various branches of the Inspectorate.

2.31   The HSE has undergone considerable organisational changes, with a view to increasing its efficiency and effectiveness. It is now responsible for the Railway Inspectorate, and, since 1992, offshore oil and gas safety. The basic work of inspections and field services is done by the Field Operations Directorate (incorporating the former Factories, Agricultural and Quarries inspectorates and the Employment Medical Advisory Service (EMAS)), which constitutes nearly 50% of all the HSE staff. The Field Operations Directorate has been recently reorganised into seven regional offices (see Appendix 1). Other divisions (health policy, special hazards, safety and general policy, etc) provide essential backup services and combine policy with operational responses.

2.32   In addition, the HSE controls the activities of the EMAS (see paragraph 2.64). Thus, although industry has to deal with one unified body, in practice specialists from the different branches may be encountered, as well as other enforcement bodies (eg fire authority, local authorities, see below). Each inspectorate will obviously deal with those matters in respect of which it has been assigned.

National Interest Groups

2.33   The internal organisation of the HSE is designed to permit a greater degree of industrial specialisation. This is done by means of National Interest Groups (NIGs), which exist for the following sectors: metals and minerals; services; construction; agriculture and wood; fibres and polymers; safety issues; engineering; utilities; customer services; and occupational health (see Appendix 1). Any inspector may approach a specialist of one of the NIGs for assistance and information. In addition, a number of area offices have National Responsibility Groups (NRGs) for certain processes in respect of which NIGs do not exist.

Duties of the HSE

2.34   It is the duty of the HSE to exercise on behalf of the HSC such of the latter's functions as it may care to direct that the HSE shall exercise, and to give effect to any directions given to it by the HSC. However, except for the purpose of giving effect to directions given to the HSC by the Secretary of State, the HSC cannot give the HSE any directions as to the enforcement of the relevant statutory provisions in any particular case (s.11(4)). In other words, the HSE alone will decide when and how to enforce the law in individual cases.

2.35   The HSE may also provide a Minister of the Crown with information in connection with any matter with which he is concerned and provide him with advice. The HSE can do anything (except borrow money) which is calculated to facilitate, or is conducive or incidental to, the performance of any function within its statutory obligations. The duty of HSE to enforce the relevant statutory provisions is limited by the extent that some other authority is responsible for their enforcement (see para 3.171 below).

Enforcement (ss.20–26)

2.36   The HSE has a number of actual and potential powers whereby it may seek to ensure compliance with the relevant statutory provisions. Primarily, however, it will seek to give advice and assistance to any employer or other person who is seeking ways of meeting the necessary standards. Persuasion, rather than compulsion, has always been the style adopted by the inspectorate, for the object has always been to establish high standards of health and safety rather than to punish offenders. Thus an inspector may give verbal or written advice as to the steps which need to be taken to ensure compliance with the statutory duties. If remedial steps are not taken, or where the dangers are so obvious or imminent that immediate action is necessary, the powers of issuing improvement or prohibition notices may be exercised. As a last resort, criminal proceedings may be brought by an inspector (see *Campbell v Wallsend Slipway & Engineering Co Ltd*) which are usually instituted when there has been an incident, or after prior warnings have been given, or where the employer in question has a bad record of compliance. In other words, the inspectors will usually start off with advice, persuasion and encouragement. If these fail, resort may be had to compulsion or sanctions. For the principles of enforcement action see paragraph 3.171.

2.37   Every enforcement authority has the power to appoint as inspectors (under whatever title they may think fit) such persons having suitable qualifications as it thinks necessary for enforcing the relevant statutory provisions within its field of responsibility, and may also terminate the appointment (HSWA, s.19). However, it is submitted that this does not take inspectors outside the protection of the relevant provisions of the Employment Rights Act 1996, particularly in respect of rights not to be unfairly dismissed.

Powers of inspectors (s.20)

2.38   When an inspector is appointed, he will be given a document specifying which of the powers conferred on him by the relevant statutory provisions are to be exercisable by him, and he may only exercise those powers within the area of the responsibility of the enforcing authority which appointed him (see *Laws v Keane*). When seeking to exercise those powers, he must produce, on request, his instrument of appointment. The powers of inspectors are as follows.
   1. At any reasonable time, or, if there is a dangerous situation, at any time, to enter premises which he has reason to believe it is necessary to enter for the purpose of carrying into effect any relevant statutory provision.
   2. To take with him a constable if he has reasonable cause to apprehend any serious obstruction in the execution of his duty.
   3. To take with him any person duly authorised by the inspector's authority, and any equipment or materials required for any purpose for which the power of entry is being exercised.
   4. To make such examination and investigation as may be necessary.
   5. To direct that any premises or anything therein shall be left undisturbed so long as it is reasonably necessary for the purpose of examination or investigation.
   6. To take such measurements and photographs and make such recordings as he considers necessary for the purpose of examination or investigation.

7. To take samples of any article or substance found in any premises and in the atmosphere in or in the vicinity of any such premises; the Secretary of State may make regulations concerning the procedure to be adopted in such cases.

8. In the case of any article or substance likely to cause danger to health or safety, to cause it to be dismantled or subjected to any process or test, but he may not destroy or damage it unless it is for the purpose of exercising his powers. If the person who has responsibilities in relation to those premises so requests, the inspector will exercise this power in that person's presence, unless he considers that it would be prejudicial to the safety of the State to do so. In any case, before exercising these powers, he must consult with appropriate persons for the purpose of ascertaining what dangers, if any, there may be in doing what he proposes to do.

9. In the case of any article or substance likely to cause danger to health or safety, to take possession of it, and detain it for so long as is necessary in order to examine it, to ensure that it is not tampered with before he has completed his examination, or to ensure that it will be available for use as evidence in any proceedings for an offence, or in respect of matters arising out of the issuing of an improvement or prohibition notice. He must leave a notice giving particulars of the article or substance, stating that he has taken possession of it, and, if it is practicable to do so, leave a sample with a responsible person.

10. If he is conducting an examination or investigation under (4) above, to require any person whom he has reasonable cause to believe to be able to give any information to answer such questions as the inspector thinks fit, and to sign a declaration of the truth of his answers. However, no answer given in response to an inspector's questions shall be admissible in evidence against that person or his husband or wife in any proceedings.

11. To require the production of, inspect, and take copies of any entry in any books or documents which are required to be kept, and of any book or document which it is necessary for him to see for the purpose of any examination or investigation under (4) above, but not if the production is refused on the ground of legal professional privilege.

12. To require any person to afford him such facilities and assistance within that person's control or responsibilities, as are necessary for him to exercise his powers.

13. Any other power which is necessary for the purpose of exercising any of the above powers.

Obtaining information (s.27)

2.39   In order to discharge their functions, the HSC, the HSE or any other enforcing authority may need further information. To obtain this, s.27 gives power to the HSC, with the consent of the Secretary of State, to serve on any person a notice requiring him to furnish the HSC, the HSE or any other enforcing authority with such information about such matters as may be specified in the notice, and to do this in such form and manner, and within such time, as may be specified.

2.40   No information obtained under this power shall be disclosed without the consent of the person by whom it was furnished, but this does not prevent the disclosure:
  (a) to the HSC, or the HSE, a government department or any other enforcing authority
  (b) by the recipient of the information to any person for the purpose of any function conferred on the recipient by any relevant statutory provision
  (c) to an officer of a local authority, water authority, or river purification board, or to a constable, in each case to a person who is authorised to receive it
  (d) by the recipient, as long as it is in a form which is calculated to prevent it from being identified as relating to a particular person or as a particular case
  (e) of any information for the purpose of any legal proceedings or any investigation or inquiry held by virtue of s.14(2) (above) or any report made as a result thereof.

Disclosure of information by inspectors (s.28)

2.41   A person exercising powers of entry or inspection under s.14(4)(a), or general powers of inspection, etc under s.20 may not disclose any information obtained by him (including, in particular, any information with respect to any trade secret obtained by him in any premises into which he has entered by virtue of such powers) except:
  (a) for the purpose of his functions, or
  (b) for the purpose of any legal proceedings, or any investigation or inquiry held by virtue of s.14(2), or a report thereof, or

(c) with the consent of the person who furnished the information in pursuance of a requirement imposed under s.20, and with the consent of the person having responsibilities in relation to the premises where the information was obtained in any other case (s.28(7)).

2.42   However, an inspector is expressly authorised by s.28(8) to disclose information to employed persons or their representatives if it is necessary for him to do so for the purpose of assisting in keeping them adequately informed about matters affecting their health, safety or welfare. Normally, this information will be communicated to safety representatives, but in the absence of these, it can be to a shop steward, or to representatives of employee safety, or to individuals or even their legal representatives, should this be necessary. The information which can be disclosed is:

(a) factual information obtained by him as a result of the exercise of any of his powers under s.20 (above) or as a result of a person who is holding an inquiry under s.14 (above) exercising his right to enter and inspect premises (see s.14(4)(a)), as long as the information relates to the premises where the employees are employed, or to anything which was or is in there, or was or is being done there, and

(b) information with respect to any action which he has taken or proposes to take in or in connection with those premises.

2.43   If the inspector does give such information to employees or their representatives, he must also give the same information to the employer.

Disclosure for civil proceedings (s.28(9))

2.44   Section 116 of the Employment Protection Act 1975 added a new subsection (s.28(9) to HSWA), which permits the disclosure by an inspector of information to a person who is likely to be a party to any civil proceedings arising out of an accident, occurrence or other situation. He will do this by providing a written statement of the relevant facts observed by him in the course of exercising any of his powers.

2.45   Thus, in a civil action for damages (see Chapter 8) either the plaintiff or the defendant may request the information from an inspector.

Additional powers

2.46 As we shall see, an inspector may serve a prohibition notice, an improvement notice, and in England and Wales may prosecute offenders. He may seize and render harmless any article or substance likely to be a cause of danger, and is responsible for the enforcement of the employer's duty to display the certificate of insurance under the provisions of the Employers' Liability (Compulsory Insurance) Act 1969.

Power of an enforcing authority to indemnify inspectors (s.26)

2.47 A person who is aggrieved by any action of an inspector who has exceeded his powers may always bring a civil action against him. If the circumstances are such that the inspector cannot legally claim the right of indemnity from the appointing authority, the latter may nonetheless indemnify him in whole or in part against any damages, costs, or expenses ordered to pay or incurred if the authority is satisfied that the inspector honestly believed that he was acting within his powers and that his duty as an inspector required or entitled him to do the act in question.

2.48 An aggrieved person may also pursue a complaint against an inspector, the HSE or the HSC through the machinery laid down in the Parliamentary Commissioner Act 1967 (which created the investigatory role of the Ombudsman).

2.49 When an inspector is carrying out his functions as such, he owes no duty of care when giving advice about safety improvements, even though the fortunes of a business enterprise might be adversely affected. In *Harris v Evans and the HSE*, the plaintiff wished to use a mobile telescopic crane for bungee jumping, and was informed by the HSE to comply with the Code of Practice issued by the Standard Association of British Bungee. He did this, but subsequently another inspector advised the local authority that the crane should not be used unless it had been certified by the manufacturer or by a competent person appointed by the National Certification System for Insurance Inspection Bodies. Such certification proved to be impossible, but the local authority served a prohibition notice until he obtained certification. An appeal against the prohibition notice was dismissed by an employment tribunal. However, the Secretary of State for Employment indicated that there was no technical evidence to show that there was an unacceptable level of risk in using mobile cranes for bungee jumping, and that the advice given by the inspector to obtain certification was wrong. The local authority then withdrew the prohibition notice. The plaintiff sued for the financial loss he had suffered as a result of the (alleged) negligent advice given by the HSE inspector to the local authority. It was held that his claim must fail. The advice given was in pursuance of a statutory function, and did not give rise to a duty of care on the part of the inspector. The plaintiff had protection by way of an appeal to an employment tribunal, and it would not be right to permit an aggrieved person to recover via a negligence action the damage cause to his business by a notice which had been upheld by an employment tribunal.

2.50 The HSC has published a leaflet *What to expect when a health and safety inspector calls*, as a guide for businesses, employees and their representatives.

Local authorities

2.51 One of the problems disclosed by the Robens Committee was the overlapping jurisdiction of the different enforcement authorities. Thus, a shoe repair shop since it was both a factory and a shop could be visited by the factory inspector and a local authority inspector, each concerned with his own responsibilities. To prevent this happening, s.18 of HSWA enables the Secretary of State, by regulation, to make local authorities responsible for certain prescribed activities, to facilitate the transfer of responsibilities between HSE and local authorities, and to deal with uncertain areas.

2.52 For the purpose of enforcement of the relevant statutory provisions, a local authority is (in England and Wales) a district council, a London Borough Council, the sub-treasurer of the Inner Temple, the under-treasurer of the Middle Temple, or the Council of the Isles of Scilly. In Scotland, the enforcing local authority is an islands or district council.

2.53 The enforcement functions are carried out by officials who have a number of different titles, although they are increasingly being known as Environmental Health Officers (EHOs). EHOs are usually members of the Chartered Institution of Environmental Health (CIEH), the qualification for which is either passing the Institution's Diploma in Environmental Health, or obtaining a degree or post-graduate diploma in environmental health from a recognised institution of higher education. The Institution has over 7000 members, most of whom are employed by local authorities throughout the country. EHOs have all the powers of an HSE inspector (see above).

2.54   The Health and Safety (Enforcing Authority) Regulations 1998 drew a clear line between the responsibilities of the HSE and local authorities. The regulations basically apply three principles, namely allocation of premises shall be based on the concept of the main activity carried on, dual inspection is to be avoided, and there shall be no self-inspection by enforcing authorities. Local authorities will be allocated responsibility for premises as specified in Schedule 1 of the regulations.

Enforcement

Local authority enforcement

2.55   The following are the main activities which determine whether local authorities will be enforcing authorities.
1. The sale or storage of goods for retail or wholesale distribution except:
    (a) at container depots where the main activity is the storage of goods in the course of transit to or from dock premises, an airport or a railway
    (b) where the main activity is the sale or storage for wholesale distribution of any substance or preparation dangerous for supply
    (c) where the main activity is the sale or storage of water or sewage or their by-products or natural or town gas
    and for the purposes of this paragraph where the main activity carried out in premises is the sale and fitting of motor car tyres, exhausts, windscreens or sunroofs the main activity shall be deemed to be the sale of goods.
2. The display or demonstration of goods at an exhibition for the purposes of offer or advertisement for sale.
3. Office activities.
4. Catering services.
5. The provision of permanent or temporary residential accommodation including the provision of a site for caravans or campers.
6. Consumer services provided in a shop except dry cleaning or radio and television repairs, and in this paragraph "consumer services"

means services of a type ordinarily supplied to persons who receive them otherwise than in the course of a trade, business or other undertaking carried on by them (whether for profit or not).

7. Cleaning (wet or dry) in coin-operated units in launderettes and similar premises.
8. The use of a bath, sauna or solarium, massaging, hair transplanting, skin piercing, manicuring or other cosmetic services and therapeutic treatments, except where they are carried out under the supervision or control of a registered medical practitioner, a dentist registered under the Dentists Act 1984, a physiotherapist, an osteopath or a chiropractor.
9. The practice or presentation of the arts, sports, games, entertainment or other cultural or recreational activities except where the main activity is the exhibition of a cave to the public.
10. The hiring out of pleasure craft for use on inland waters.
11. The care, treatment, accommodation or exhibition of animals, birds or other creatures, except where the main activity is horse breeding or horse training at a stable, or is an agricultural activity or veterinary surgery.
12. The activities of an undertaker, except where the main activity is embalming or the making of coffins.
13. Church worship or religious meetings.
14. The provision of car parking facilities within the perimeter of an airport.
15. The provision of childcare, or playgroup or nursery facilities.

Activities for which the HSE is the enforcing authority

2.56   Where the main activity carried on in non-domestic premises is not covered by Schedule 1, HSE is the enforcing authority. This would cover factories, etc. In addition, the HSE is the enforcing authority for local authorities premises, police and fire authorities, international organisations, the Crown, s.6 of the HSWA (manufacturers, etc see paragraph 3.91) and the following activities, set out in Schedule 2.

1. Any activity in a mine or quarry in respect of which notice of abandonment has been given under s.139(2) of the Mines and Quarries Act 1954.
2. Any activity in a fairground.
3. Any activity in premises occupied by a radio, television or film undertaking in which the activity of broadcasting, recording or

filming is carried on, and the activity of broadcasting, recording or filming wherever carried on, and for this purpose "film" includes videos.

4. The following activities carried on at any premises by persons who do not normally work in the premises:
   (a) construction work if:
      (i) regulation 7(1) of the Construction (Design and Management) Regulations 1994 (which requires projects that include or are intended to include construction work to be notified to the Executive) applies to the project which includes the work; or
      (ii) the whole or part of the work contracted to be undertaken by the contractor at the premises is to be external fabric or other external part of a building or structure, or
      (iii) it is carried out in a physically segregated area of the premises, the activities normally carried out in that area has been suspended for the purpose of enabling the construction work to be carried out, the contractor has authority to exclude from that area persons who are not attending in connection with the carrying out of the work and the work is not the maintenance of insulation on pipes, boilers or other parts of heating or water systems or its removal from them
   (b) the installation, maintenance or repair of any gas system, or any work in relation to a gas fitting
   (c) the installation, maintenance or repair of electricity systems
   (d) work with ionising radiations except work in one or more of the categories set out in Schedule 3 to the Ionising Radiations Regulations 1999.

5. The use of ionising radiations for medical exposure (within the meaning of regulation 2(1) of the Ionising Radiations Regulations 1999).

6. Any activity in premises occupied by a radiography undertaking in which there is carried on any work with ionising radiations.

7. Agricultural activities, and any activity at an agricultural show which involves the handling of livestock or working of agricultural equipment.

8. Any activity on board a seagoing ship.

9. Any activity in relation to a ski slope, ski-lift, ski-tow or cable-car.

10. Fish, maggot and game breeding, except in a zoo.

11. Any activity in relation to a pipeline within the meaning of regulation 3 of the Pipelines Safety Regulations 1996.

12. The operation of a railway.

2.57   Where premises are multi-occupied, each part separately occupied is regarded as separate premises for the purpose of enforcement allocation.

2.58   In order to establish a certain amount of consistency of approach, the HSE has established a Local Authority Unit (LAU), which prepares guidance for Environmental Health Officers (EHOs). The LAU provides the secretariat for the HSE local authority Enforcement Liaison Committee (HELA) which acts as a forum for the exchange of information and informal discussions and also attempts to arrive at practical co-operation between the HSE and local authorities. Additionally, each HSE area office has a liaison officer, whose task it is to maintain links with local authorities and provide advice and assistance, with particular reference to the provisions of training and the dissemination of information. The HSC has published a policy statement on the approach to be taken to enforcement of health and safety legislation by the HSE and local authority environmental health departments (MISC 30: *HSE enforcement policy statement*, available from HSE Books).

Self inspection

2.59   On the principle that there shall be no self inspection, the HSE will inspect the premises of the local authorities, and the local authorities will inspect those belonging to the HSE (even though it is a Crown body). Although it might be expected that local authorities should be regarded as good employers and aware of their responsibilities, there have been several cases where they have been prosecuted by the HSE and convicted of offences under HSWA. Hopefully, this is an indication of human weakness within the organisation, rather than a wilful or neglectful disregard of the standards on health and safety.

Transfer of authority

2.60   Regulation 5 of the 1998 regulations enables the responsibility for enforcement to be transferred in a particular case from the HSE to a local authority, or from a local authority to the HSE. This may be done by HSC or by agreement between the enforcing authority which has current responsibility and the authority to which it is proposed to transfer. The new enforcing authority will then give notice of the transfer to persons affected by it. If the transfer has been made by the HSC, notice will be given to both enforcing authorities.

2.61   In cases of uncertainty, in respect of any premises, part of premises or any activity, responsibility may be assigned to the local authority or HSE as appropriate by the other enforcement authority. Alternatively either authority may apply to HSC, and if it thinks that uncertainty exists it will take into account the views expressed, inform each party of the views expressed by the other (*R v Health & Safety Commission, ex parte Spelthorne Borough Council*) and assign accordingly, giving notice to the authorities and persons affected by it. Any proposal to transfer the responsibility for premises occupied or controlled by the Crown can only be done with the combined agreement of the HSE, the local authority, and the government department concerned.

2.62   However, if there is a change in the main activity being carried on at the premises, there is an automatic transfer of responsibility from one enforcing authority to the other. It is not necessary to go through the formal procedure for effecting a transfer, because this would result in there being a period of time when there would be no one charged with the task of enforcement (*Hadley v Hancox*).

2.63   It will be recalled that responsibility for enforcing legislation relating to air pollution (including s.5 of HSWA) has been transferred to the Environment Agency, or local authorities, as appropriate (see paragraph 2.5).

Employment Medical Advisory Service (EMAS)

2.64   There has been a medical branch of the Factory Inspectorate since 1898, but the new streamlined medical service was created by the Employment Medical Advisory Service Act 1972, and it commenced operations in 1973. Its existence was continued by virtue of Part II of HSWA, and EMAS is now an integral part of the HSE.

2.65   The functions of EMAS are laid down in s.55 of HSWA, and are as follows:
  (a) securing that the Secretary of State, the HSC, employers' organisations, trade unions, and occupational health practitioners can be kept informed and adequately advised on matters of which they ought to take notice, concerning the safeguarding and

improvement of the health of persons who are employed or who are seeking employment or training for employment

(b) giving to employed persons and persons seeking employment or training for employment, information and advice on health in relation to such employment or training

(c) other purposes of the functions of the Secretary of State relating to employment.

2.66 EMAS is headed by a Director of Medical Services, with Senior Employment Medical Advisors to be found throughout the various regions of the country. There is also a Chief Employment Nursing Advisor, and specialist advisors in toxicology, respiratory diseases, pathology research, and the medical aspects of rehabilitation. From its head office, EMAS controls a force of Employment Medical Advisors (EMAs) who are qualified registered medical practitioners and Employment Nursing Advisors (ENAs) who are also qualified in occupational health.

2.67 In order to exercise its statutory functions, EMAS has responsibility for:

(a) advising the inspectorate on the occupational health aspects of regulations and Approved Codes of Practice

(b) regular examinations of persons employed on known hazardous operations

(c) other medical examinations, investigations and surveys

(d) giving advice to the HSE, employers, trade unions and others about the occupational health aspects of poisonous substances, immunological disorders, physical hazards (noise, vibrations, etc) dust, and mental stress, including the laying down of standards of exposure to processes or substances which may harm health

(e) research into occupational health

(f) advice on the provision of occupational medical, nursing and first aid services

(g) advice on the medical aspects of rehabilitation and training for and replacement in employment.

Powers of EMAS

2.68 An employment medical advisor has the same power of entry and investigation as inspectors have under s.20 (above) by virtue of an appointment as such. He can examine workers in those employments which regulations require that they shall be examined at regular intervals, (eg Control of Lead at Work Regulations 1998), but he cannot force a person to be examined against his will. Nor will he prescribe any treatment, but will refer workers to their own family general practitioner.

2.69 Advice is also given on the medical aspects of employing young persons (ie below the age of 18).

2.70 ENAs are an integral part of the service and will visit premises on request or as a result of a visit by an inspector, and give advice and assistance to employers, trade unions, safety officers, safety representative, etc. They will also give advice to the Disablement Resettlement Officers and others about the advisability of employing someone who has a health problem, enforce the Health and Safety (First Aid) Regulations 1981 and undertake biological monitoring.

2.71 Thus information about suspected health hazards will reach EMAS from a number of sources, enabling an investigation to take place, and advice given on how hazards can be reduced or eliminated. EMAS is frequently used as an advisory service and is constantly engaged in research into health problems, in collaboration with HSE.

Other institutions

Royal Society for the Prevention of Accidents

2.72 Royal Society for the Prevention of Accidents (RoSPA) is the largest independent safety organisation in Europe. A major part of its activities is concerned with occupational health and safety and it publishes three journals on the subject: (1) *Occupational Safety and Health*, (2) *RoSPA Bulletin*, (3) *Safety Express*. RoSPA also organises conferences and training courses, and gives advice and assistance to members. Its address is Cannon House, The Priory, Queensway, Birmingham B4 6BS. Tel: 0121 248 2000.

British Safety Council

2.73 A non-profit-making independent body, financed entirely by subscriptions from its members, the BSC provides information and training on all aspects of health and safety, will undertake loss control surveys, issues posters and booklets, runs a National Safety Award scheme, and issues a Diploma in Safety Management. BSC also publishes a magazine *Safety Management* and a newsletter *Health and Safety at Work Act.* The address is 62–64 Chancellor's Road, Hammersmith, London W6 9RS. Tel: 020 8741 1231.

British Standards Institution

2.74 The British Standards Institution (BSI) was incorporated by Royal Charter in 1929, and has as its objectives:
  (a) to co-ordinate the efforts of producers and users for the improvement, standardisation and simplification of engineering and industrial materials so as to simplify production and distribution and eliminate national waste of time and material in the production of unnecessary varieties of patterns and sizes of articles used for one and the same purpose
  (b) to set up standards of quality and dimensions, prepare and promote the adoption of BSI specifications and schedules, revise, alter and amend these from time to time as experience and circumstances may require
  (c) to register, in the name of the Institution, marks of all descriptions, and to approve, affix, and license the affixing of such marks
  (d) to take any other action as may be necessary or desirable to promote the objectives of the Institute.

2.75 The Institution is governed by an executive board consisting of 35 members, who appoint a director general. Over 1000 technical committees perform the day-to-day work of developing appropriate standards. When these are agreed, the final standard can be adopted. The Institute is financed from government funds, sales revenue and individual subscriptions.

2.76 Manufacturers who adopt the approved standards are entitled to use the BSI Kite Mark, but must agree to supervision and sample testing.

2.77 The Institution increasingly works closely with the International Organisation for Standardisation and other European organisations which have objects similar to its own. BSI is a member of the European Committee for Standardisation (CEN) and the Committee for Electrotechnical Standardisation (CENELEC) (see paragraph 10.37).

Safety Equipment Association

2.78   The Safety Equipment Association (SEA) replaced the Industrial Safety Protective Equipment Manufacturers' Association, and provides a forum for the discussion and promotion of the collective voice representing manufacturers, distributors and end-users of safety equipment. It will also assist with the improvements to international standards relating to the correct selection, training, education and use of personal safety equipment to end-users throughout the world. It will concentrate on technical and training duties, and will compile a database to inform members about methods of dealing with the European market.

2.79   An associated organisation is the Safety Equipment Distributors Association (SEDA) which comprises distributors of products of SEA members. SEDA feeds back information from the user, thus helping in the improvement in the design, comfort, and wearability of the product. It is anticipated that SEDA will wind up when its members are absorbed into SEA.

2.80   A new body, called the British Safety Industry Federation has recently been formed. It will represent the views of the industry to the Government and to various European Institutions.

Institution of Occupational Safety and Health

2.81   This is the professional institute for safety professionals, and currently has over 20,000 members. The Institution's examining body is the National Examination Board in Occupational Safety and Health (NEBOSH) (see paragraph 5.186).

CHAPTER 3

Health and Safety at Work, etc Act 1974

The scope of the Act

3.1   The Health and Safety at Work, etc Act 1974 (HSWA) is based on principles and details which are fundamentally different from other health and safety legislation. These differences are designed to bring about a greater awarenesss of the problems which surround health and safety matters, a greater involvement of those who are, or who should be, concerned with improvements in occupational health and safety and a positive movement away from the apathy and indifference which tended to surround the whole subject.

3.2   In the first place, the Act applies to people, not to premises. It covers all employees in all employment situations with minor exceptions, eg domestic servants. We will not be concerned with problems of interpretation as to whether or not certain premises are, or are not, a factory, a shop, an office, etc. The nature or location of the work is irrelevant. At one stroke, the Act brought within the ambit of protective legislation some 7–8 million people (the "new entrants") who were hitherto not covered by the various statutes then in force, eg Factories Act 1961. Subject only to the exception in respect of domestic employees (see paragraph 3.17) every employer needs to know and to carry out duties required under the Act. Further, the Act requires all employers to take account of the fact that persons who are not in their employment may be affected by work activities, and there are additional duties in this regard. Obligations are placed on those who manufacture, design, import or supply articles or substances for use at work to ensure that these can be used in safety and are without risks to health.

3.3   Next, the Act is basically a criminal statute, and does not give rise to any civil liability (but see paragraph 3.18). No tort action in respect of a breach of statutory duty can be brought; prevention and punishment (rather than compensation) is the keynote. However, to assist the courts when interpreting the Act, regard may be had to legal precedents which have arisen from civil as well as criminal proceedings, provided, of course, that it is appropriate to do so in the context. Additionally the inspectorates are given powers of enforcement in order to eliminate or minimise hazards before an incident occurs, rather than take action afterwards.

3.4 It should be noted that subject to the defence of reasonable practicability, the Act imposes absolute criminal liability. It is not possible, for example, for a corporate employer to avoid liability for an offence on the ground that the "directing mind" or senior management were not involved, or that they had delegated control or supervision of safety matters to competent persons. Under the Act, there is no defence of due diligence (see paragraph 1.97). Thus employers (whether incorporated or not) cannot escape liability on the grounds that they were not personally to blame for a breach of the Act (*R v British Steel plc*).

3.5 Finally, there are some provisions which are designed to bring about a greater personal involvement and individual responsibility so as to actively encourage and promote health and safety, being part of the greater self-regulatory system which the Robens Committee thought to be desirable. Safety policies, risk assessments, safety representatives and safety committees should increase the awareness that the main responsibility for the elimination of accidents and ill-health in employment lies with those who create the dangers.

3.6 The new requirement that employers should carry out assessments (see paragraph 7.180) will focus minds on key problem areas, health surveillance and monitoring should assist in dealing with certain illnesses at an early stage, and also act as a warning sign of possible deficiencies in health and safety practices. Employers are required to give information, training, etc not only to their own employees, but sometimes to non-employees. In other words, health and safety is now high on the agenda.

3.7 How successful the Act has been, or will be in the future, is something we may never know. It is impossible to state how many accidents did not happen as a result of this legislation. Statistics may illustrate trends, and perhaps even lead to some satisfaction, but these are notoriously inconclusive. New machinery, new processes, new designs, new substances, etc may decrease hazards irrespective of legislative arrangements. If nothing else, the Act should play a positive role in ensuring that technological change does not increase the exposure to risks at work. On the other hand, the increasing consciousness of the problems, the growing acceptance that health and safety is the concern of all from the most senior person in the organisation to the most junior, the vast increase in training opportunities and the general streamlining of legal rules should all have a considerable effect in reducing the annual accident figures progressively each year. There must be a limit, however, to the power of the law to influence human conduct, for a majority of accidents occur in situations where there is no actual breach of a legislative provision, but are regarded as common occurrences or human failings (slipping, tripping, falling, etc) which legal control can only prevent if it can induce a state of mind. A knowledge of the legal framework may make a positive contribution to this.

3.8   The Act is sometimes referred to as an "enabling Act". This is merely descriptive of the role envisaged by the Robens Committee, ie that all the old law should be progressively swept away, and replaced by a single statute, supplemented by regulations and Codes of Practice. Since 1974, this pattern has been adopted, so that by the turn of the century the major legislative provisions which were pre-1974 had considerably reduced significance or relevance.

3.9   The Act is divided into four parts. Part I will be the subject of this chapter; Part II provides for the continuation of the Employment Medical Advisory Service (see Chapter 2); Part III (now repealed) made amendments to the Building Regulations (and was the main reason for the curious addition of the word "etc" in the title of the Act) and Part IV contains some miscellaneous provisions. There are also 10 Schedules to the Act.

Application of the Act

3.10   The Act applies to all employment in Great Britain (ie England, Wales and Scotland) but not in Northern Ireland. However, by the Health and Safety at Work (Northern Ireland) Order 1978 the provisions of the Act have been repeated so far as Northern Ireland is concerned, with some modifications. The Act does not apply to the Isle of Man or to the Channel Islands, but does apply to the Isles of Scilly.

3.11   By the Health and Safety at Work (Application outside Great Britain) Order 2001 the provisions of the Act have been extended to cover persons working on offshore installations and pipeline work within British territorial waters or the UK sector of the continental shelf, as well as to certain diving and construction work carried on within territorial waters. These provisions are in addition to the Mineral . Workings (Offshore Installations) Act 1971 and the regulations made thereunder, the Petroleum and Submarine Pipelines Act 1975, and the Offshore Safety Act 1992.

Application to the Crown

3.12   The provisions of Part I apply to the Crown with the exception of ss.21–25 and 33–42. This means that it is not possible to issue improvement or prohibition notices against the Crown or in respect of Crown premises. However, Health and Safety Executive (HSE) has taken to issuing Crown Notices (see paragraph 3.116) which have a moral effect. Also, it is not possible to prosecute the Crown for any offence committed (based on the theory that the Queen cannot be prosecuted in her own courts), but s.48(2) provides that ss.33–42 (ie the criminal sanctions sections) shall apply to persons in the service of the Crown as they apply to other persons. This means that an individual Crown employee who commits an offence (eg under ss.7, 8, 37, etc) can be prosecuted if necessary. By the National Health Service and Community Care Act 1990, s.60, the National Health Service is not to be regarded as part of the Crown for the purpose of health and safety legislation. Thus prosecutions may be carried out and enforcement notices issued against the NHS.

Trainees

3.13   By the Health and Safety (Training for Employment) Regulations 1990 a person is to be treated as being at work for the purpose of HSWA if he is being provided with relevant training, which is defined as being work experience provided pursuant to a training course or programme, or training for employment, except training provided on a course run by an educational establishment, or training given under a contract of employment. In other words, for the purposes of HSWA, persons on all training for employment schemes (as opposed to training in employment) are to be regarded as employees at work, even though technically they are not employees. The employer, for the purpose of the regulations, is the person whose undertaking is providing the training.

Police

3.14   The Police (Health and Safety) Act 1997 applies the provisions of HSWA to holders of the office of constable (ie police, including police cadets), even though they are not employed under a contract of employment, the deemed employer being the chief officer of police, or Director General of the National Criminal Intelligence Service, or the National Crime Squad. The various provisions of the Employment Rights Act 1996 (ie ss.44, 48, 49 and 100, see paragraph 5.170) giving protection to employees when exercising health and safety rights also apply. The Police Federation is to be treated as a recognised trade union for the purpose of appointing safety representatives under s.2(4) of HSWA (see paragraph 5.99).

3.15   The Police (Health and Safety) Regulations 1999 provide that a person who holds the office of constable or appointment as a police cadet shall be treated as being an employee of the relevant officer for the purpose of all regulations made under HSWA, the only proviso being that a police officer shall be treated as being at work only when he is on duty. Various police staff associations are to be treated as recognised trade unions for the purposes of the Safety Representative and Safety Committees Regulations 1977. Regulation 4(1) of the Personal Protective Equipment at Work Regulations 1992 is amended so that where the characteristics of any policing activity are such that compliance with the duty to provide suitable protective equipment would inevitably conflict with the exercise of police powers or the performance of police duties, the requirement shall be complied with so far as is reasonably practicable. A minor amendment has also been made to regulation 4(4) of the Provision and Use of Work Equipment Regulations 1998, so that the requirements of suitability relating to work equipment used by the police for arrest, restraint, self-defence or as deterrent equipment will only apply to the health and safety of police officers and cadets.

3.16   The ACOP accompanying the Management of Health and Safety at Work Regulations 1999 has amended the earlier code so as to reflect the sometimes inherently dangerous work undertaken by the police, fire-fighters and other emergency service workers.

Domestic employees

3.17   Section 51 provides that none of the statutory provisions shall apply in relation to a person by reason only that he employs another, or is himself employed, as a domestic servant in a private household.

Civil liability (s.47)

3.18   As we have already noted, HSWA is essentially a criminal statute enforced by criminal sanctions. Section 47 specifically provided that nothing in Part I (which contains the relevant provisions so far as this book is concerned) shall be construed as conferring any right of action in any civil proceedings in respect of a failure to comply with any duty imposed by ss.2–7 or a contravention of s.8. Thus no civil action under HSWA can be brought for a breach of statutory duty as a result of an accident. However, if a prosecution is brought under the Act and is successful, it would appear, under the provisions of s.11 of the Civil Evidence Act 1968, that the fact of that prosecution may be raised and pleaded in an action for damages caused by negligence, leaving the defendant with the burden of proving that he was not negligent. Additionally, s.47(2) provides that any breach of duty imposed by health and safety regulations shall be actionable in a civil claim except in so far as the regulations provide otherwise. HSWA does not alter the present rights at common law (see Chapter 8), but does not add to them except as stated.

The general purposes (s.1)

3.19   The provisions of the Act shall have effect with a view to:
  (a) securing the health, safety and welfare of persons at work
  (b) protecting persons other than persons at work against risks to health or safety arising out of or in connection with the activities of persons at work
  (c) controlling the keeping and use of explosives or highly flammable or otherwise dangerous or environmentally hazardous substances, and generally preventing the unlawful acquisition, possession and use of such substances.

3.20   It will be noted that by the Health and Safety at Work (Application to Environmentally Hazardous Substances) Regulations 1996 (as amended) the reference in s.1(1)(c) of HSWA to dangerous substances shall include a reference to environmentally hazardous substances, for the purpose only of making regulations under s.15 in order to implement various EC Directives, which are concerned with the transportation by road or rail of dangerous goods, and emissions from the storage and distribution of petrol.

3.21   The general purposes of the Health and Safety at Work Act have been extended to include the following:
   (a) securing the safety, health and welfare at work of persons on offshore installations or engaged on pipeline works
   (b) securing the safety of such installations and preventing accidents on or near them
   (c) securing the proper construction and safe operation of pipelines and preventing damage to them
   (d) securing the safe dismantling, removal and disposal of offshore installations and pipelines (see Offshore Safety Act 1992, s.1, which has the effect of transferring responsibility for all aspects of offshore safety from the Department of Energy to HSE).

3.22   The general purposes of the Act shall also include safety matters relating to on-shore pipelines, in particular:
   (a) securing the proper construction and safe operation of pipelines and preventing damage to them
   (b) ensuring that, in the event of an accidental escape or ignition of anything in a pipeline, immediate notice of the event will be given to persons who will or may have to discharge duties or take steps in consequence of the happening of the event
   (c) protecting the public from personal injury, fire, explosions and other dangers arising from the transmission, distribution, supply or use of gas (including liquid gas) (see Offshore Safety Act 1992, s.2(1), repealing, *inter alia*, s.18(1) of the Gas Act 1986).

3.23   Finally, the general purposes of the Act also include:
   (a) securing the proper construction and safe operation of railway systems, including locomotives, rolling stock and other vehicles used on such systems
   (b) protecting the public (whether passengers or not) from personal injury and other risks arising from the construction and operation of railway tramways or trolley vehicle systems (Railways Act 1993, s.117(2)).

3.24   The general scheme of things is to progressively replace all the enactments specified in Schedule 1 of the Act (and regulations, etc made thereunder) by a system of regulations and Approved Codes of Practice which are designed to maintain and improve standards of health, safety and welfare. Since 1974, this policy has been steadily followed. Virtually all of the Factories Act 1961 and the Offices, Shops and Railway Premises Act 1963 have been repealed in addition to other enactments. New regulations have been introduced, and Codes of Practice have been approved. It is therefore essential for all concerned to keep up to date with the latest developments with a field of law which is constantly changing.

The general duties (s.2(1))

3.25   *It shall be the duty of every employer to ensure, so far as is reasonably practicable, the health, safety and welfare at work of all his employees*

3.26   This is the prime duty under the Act, in respect of which all the other subsequent duties imposed by s.2 are more detailed. As we have seen (see Chapter 1), what is reasonably practicable is a question of fact and evidence in each case.

3.27   It must be borne in mind that the duty, placed fairly and squarely on the employer, is a strict one, subject to the defence of reasonably practicable. If the employer is an individual (or an identifiable group of individuals), it would not be difficult to place liability for a failure to comply with s.2(1). However, most employers are corporate bodies, and the question arises: is liability placed on the employer only for the acts or omissions of directors or senior management, or can the corporate body also be liable for the wrongful acts of more junior personnel? In *R v Gateway Foodmarkets* there was a lift operating in a supermarket, and the company's head office had made arrangements with a reputable firm for regular maintenance and a call-out service. However, there was a faulty electrical contact, which caused the lift to frequently jam. The defect could be cured manually, and the contractors told the store personnel how to do it so as to avoid them having to be called out each time the lift jammed. This practice was unauthorised and no-one at the company's head office knew about it. Following a routine maintenance, contractors left open a trap door in the control room floor. The following day an employee went into the control room in order to free the contact. Unfortunately, he did not see that the trap door was open, and he fell to his death. The company was prosecuted for a breach of s.2(1).

3.28   For the company, it was argued that s.2(1) does not render them liable for the acts or omissions of an employee who could not be regarded as the embodiment of the company (in this case, the store manager who had carried out this practice). It was submitted that the section was limited to the acts or omissions of "the directing mind" of the company, ie senior management and/or head office personnel. However, the Court of Appeal decided to follow the general approach laid down in *R v Associated Octel Co Ltd* (see paragraph 3.73). The onus is on the employer to show that all reasonable precautions were taken by it and by its employees and agents on its behalf. There is no clear legal basis for distinguishing between "management" and other more junior employees. If all reasonable precautions have been taken, then it is not material that the acts of an individual are those of a senior or junior employee. Thus, although the company may have taken reasonable precautions at a senior level, there was a failure at store management level, for which the company was liable under s.2(1), and a conviction was upheld. However, the Court of Appeal left open the question whether an employer would be liable in circumstances where the only negligence or failure to take reasonable precautions had taken place at some more junior level.

3.29   The duty is owed to employees while they are in the course of their employment, but is not confined to the times when the employee is actually working. The duty is broken if the employer makes available unsafe plant or an unsafe system of work, etc even though these have not yet been put into operation or use. In *Bolton Metropolitan Borough Council v Malrod Insulations Ltd*, contractors were engaged to strip asbestos insulation, for which task a special decontamination unit was to be used. Before the work had commenced, an Environmental Health Officer (EHO) inspected the decontamination unit, and discovered several defects, which could have given rise to electric shocks. The contractors were prosecuted for a breach of ss.2(1) and 2(2) of the Act. In their defence, it was argued that no offence could be committed until the employees were "at work" using the decontamination unit. The argument was upheld in the Crown Court, but the decision was reversed by the Divisional Court. The employer's duty under s.2(2) was "to provide" safe plant and safe systems of work, and thus the duty arose in respect of employees who *will be* at work, as well as those who *are* at work. To hold otherwise would mean that an inspector who came on to the premises at the end of a working day and discovered breaches of the law would be powerless to take any action because the employees were not actually at work at the time of the inspection, a conclusion which is not consistent with the statutory health and safety provisions. Further, the duty under s.2(1) of the Act applies to the employer's duty to all his employees, not just to those employees who are engaged on a specific process. An employee can be exposed to a risk of injury from unsafe plant even though he is not engaged on the process or work being carried on.

3.30 It must be borne in mind that the Act does not prevent dangerous work; it is designed to ensure that work — even dangerous work — can be done in a way that is safe. Thus in *Langridge v Howletts Zoo & Port Lympne Estates Ltd*, a local authority issued a prohibition notice designed to prevent keepers entering an enclosure in a wild animal park where there were tigers roaming around freely. This followed an incident when a keeper had been mauled to death by a tiger. The notice would have prohibited keepers from entering the enclosure unless the tigers were anaesthetised, immobilised or otherwise made safe. The owners of the animal park argued that it was necessary for keepers to enter the enclosure in order to achieve "bonding", so that the tigers could be successfully released into the wild. An employment tribunal modified the notice to allow the previous practice to continue, albeit with a new system of work designed to reduce the risks to the keepers. On an appeal, the judge held that if the council's submissions were upheld, then certain types of dangerous work would be proscribed. The Act is not concerned with what work is being done, but with the manner of performing it. On the facts of the case, the council's appeal was dismissed.

3.31 The phrase "health, safety and welfare" is not defined. Clearly, health includes mental as well as physical health and safety refers to the absence of any foreseeable injury. Welfare, on the other hand, is a somewhat elusive concept. Schedule 3 of HSWA provides that regulations may be made for "Securing the provision of specified welfare facilities for persons at work, including, in particular, such things as adequate water supply, sanitary conveniences, washing and bathing facilities, ambulance and first aid arrangements, cloakroom accommodation, sitting facilities and refreshment facilities." It is clear that this list is not an exhaustive definition of welfare, and indeed, some of them may well be regarded as health matters. Social clubs may be generally regarded as being part of a firm's welfare facilities, but since employees do not use them in the course of their employment, they are not within the scope of the Act. There is no obligation on an employer to concern himself with health, safety or welfare matters which arise outside the employment, although this is being done increasingly as part of advanced personnel policies.

3.32   The duty of an employer under ss.2–9 is owed to each employee individually, as well as collectively. Thus special care must be taken where employees with special needs are employed, eg persons with disabilities, young or inexperienced workers, pregnant women, etc (see Chapter 7).

Particular duties (s.2(2))

3.33   The above general duty is particularised by five specific duties placed on the employer, which spell out the general duty in detail. These duties, which as we have noted are essentially criminal in nature, are very similar to the duties of care which an employer owes to his employees at common law and which are frequently raised in civil actions (see Chapter 8). They must all be fulfilled "as far as is reasonably practicable". Thus meanings which have been given to certain words and phrases in civil actions may be used as an aid in interpreting the words used in the Act, for although the issues in criminal and civil proceedings are different, the canons of statutory interpretations (see paragraph 1.99) generally apply to both types of proceedings.

3.34   It must further be borne in mind that the particular duties which follow are spelt out in even greater detail by the new regulations outlined in subsequent chapters, ie Management of Health and Safety at Work, Provision and Use of Work Equipment, Workplace (Health, Safety and Welfare), Personal Protective Equipment at Work, Manual Handling Operations and Health and Safety (Display Screen Equipment). Thus, s.2 of HSWA must be read in conjunction with these and other regulations.

3.35   *To provide and maintain plant and systems of work that are so far as is reasonably practicable, safe and without risks to health* (s.2(2)(a))

3.36   An employer "provides" when the plant, etc is in a place where it can be easily come by, or when he gives clear directions as to where it can be obtained (*Norris v Syndic Manufacturing Co Ltd*). Thus, in *Woods v Durable Suites* the employee was working with a synthetic glue, which could cause dermatitis unless certain precautions were taken. The employers instructed the employee in the proper procedure to be followed and provided washing facilities and a barrier cream, but the employee did not take the necessary precautions and contracted dermatitis. It was held that the employers had fulfilled their common law duty of care, for they had provided the necessary precautions. They were under no duty to compel the employee to use the barrier cream or to stand over him to ensure that he used the washing facilities.

3.37   The duty to provide may be observed even though the employee does not use that which is provided. In certain cases, however, it has been held that the employers' common law duty may be something more than the passive one of providing and includes the more active duty of encouraging, persuading and even insisting on the use of the precautions (see Chapter 8). On other occasions the law may well go further and place an obligation on the employee *to use* the precautions supplied, eg under the Personal Protective Equipment at Work Regulations 1992 (see Chapter 6). But if the employer fails to provide the necessary equipment, or provides defective equipment, he will be in breach of his duty. In *Lovett v Blundells and Crompton & Co* the employee erected a makeshift staging in order to do his work. This collapsed and he was injured. It was held that the employer had not provided adequate equipment for the work to be done in safety.

3.38   Once having provided the necessary plant, etc the employer must ensure that it is maintained and in a condition which makes it fit for use. Plant and systems of work are "maintained" safe when they are kept in efficient working order at all times. Thus if there is a single failure of a component, this will normally be sufficient evidence that the equipment has not been properly maintained. Under the absolute provisions of the Factories Act 1961 it was never a defence for an employer to argue that he could not have discovered the defect before an accident occurred (*Galashields Gas Co v O'Donnell*), but under s.2(2)(a) the burden on the employer is to fulfil his obligation so far as is reasonably practicable. Maintenance is a matter of forethought and foresight. There must be a proper system of regular inspection with the reporting of defects to a responsible person. In *Barkway v South Wales Transport Co* a coach crashed owing to a burst tyre and the plaintiff's husband was killed. Although the defendants could show a system of testing and inspecting tyres, they did not require their drivers to report incidents which could produce impact fractures and were thus held liable for negligence.

3.39   Maintenance also requires the rectification of known defects, either by repairs or replacement, as necessary. In *Taylor v Rover Car Co Ltd* the employee was injured when a splinter of steel flew from the top of a chisel he was using. The chisel had previously been used by a leading hand on the production line, who had himself been injured when a splinter had flown off, but this incident was not reported. It was held that the employers were liable, for they should have had a system whereby defective tools were reported and withdrawn from circulation and replaced by ones which were not defective.

3.40   Routine maintenance, as well as revealing defects, can prolong the life of the plant or machinery, etc thus creating a cost benefit for the employer as well as making it safe for the user. It is further suggested that manufacturers of articles for use at work should include maintenance schedules along with the articles they sell, as being part of "the conditions necessary to ensure that when put to use it will be safe and without risks to health" (see paragraph 3.91).

3.41   Section 53(1) states that the term "plant" includes any machinery, equipment or appliance. In accordance with the *ejusdem generis* rule of interpretation, it is unlikely that the word includes "buildings" of any kind (contrary to the popular use of the word) as these would be covered by s.4 of the Act (see paragraph 3.82). But the definition is not exhaustive, and there is no indication of what else may be included. At common law, a van was held to be "plant" (see *Bradford v Robinson Rentals Ltd*, see paragraph 8.31).

3.42   Systems of work was defined by Lord Greene in *Speed v Thomas Swift & Co Ltd*, who said, "It may be the physical layout of the job — the setting of the stage, so to speak — the sequence in which the work is to be carried out, the provision in proper cases of warnings and notices, and the issue of special instructions." To this we may add the provision of safety equipment and the taking of adequate safety precautions. Whatever system of work is adopted, the employer must ensure, so far as is reasonably practicable, that it is a safe one.

3.43   *To ensure, so far as is reasonably practicable, safety and the absence of risks to health in connection with the use, handling, storage and transport of articles and substances* (s.2(2)(b))

3.44   In appropriate cases, protective clothing, proper equipment and tools, etc must be provided in relation to use. The handling must be organised in a safe manner, eg excessive weights should be considered, contamination should be guarded against, dangerous parts should be covered, etc. Storage facilities must be adequate and safe, eg proper racks provided, fork-lift truck drivers must be instructed in proper stacking techniques. The transportation must be done in a safe manner: loads must be properly tied down, with an even distribution of weight, goods must be packed properly so as to be safe when being transported.

3.45   *To provide such information, instruction, training and supervision as is necessary to ensure, so far as is reasonably practicable, the health and safety at work of all employees* (s.2(2)(c))

3.46   Thus, information must be given to employees about the hazards involved in the work, and the precautions to be taken to avoid them. Since the employer will, in most cases, be in a better position to know of those hazards, he must provide the information, not wait for the employees to request it. In addition to the general requirement of s.2(2), there are a number of specific statutory provisions which require an employer to provide detailed information to employees in particular circumstances (see Chapter 5).

3.47   The information which is provided must be accurate and meaningful. In *Vacwell Engineering Ltd v BDH Chemicals Ltd* the plaintiff purchased a quantity of boron tribromide from the defendant. The chemical was delivered in ampoules which were labelled "Harmful vapour". The chemical was poured on to some water, and an explosion resulted, causing damage to the plaintiff's premises. It was held that the defendants were liable for negligently labelling a dangerous substance. The information given was misleading and did not accurately describe the hazard.

3.48   Proper and clear instructions must be given as to what is to be done, and what must not be done, for workers performing routine tasks are frequently heedless of their own safety. Greater care must be taken when dealing with employees whose command of English is weak so that they understand clearly the nature of the dangers and the precautions to be taken. Young and inexperienced workers must be given clear instructions.

3.49 The employer's duty to provide information and instruction to ensure the health and safety of his own employees includes a duty to provide such information and instruction to the employees of a subcontractor where this is necessary to ensure the health and safety of the employees. In *R v Swan Hunter Shipbuilders Ltd*, the employers distributed a booklet to their employees giving practical rules for the safety of users of oxygen equipment, in particular warning of the dangers of oxygen enrichment in confined spaces. The booklet was not distributed to employees of a subcontractor except on request. A fire broke out on a ship which the appellants were building and because an employee of a subcontractor left an oxygen hose in the deck, the fire became intense because that part of the ship, which was badly ventilated, became oxygen enriched. As a result, eight workmen were killed. The appellants were prosecuted on indictment for a breach of s.2(2)(a) (failure to provide a safe system of work), s.2(2)(c) (failure to provide information and instruction) and s.3(1) (duty to non-employees). The appellants were convicted in the Crown Court, and an appeal was dismissed by the Court of Appeal. If the provision of a safe system of work for the benefit of an employer's own employees involved the provision of information and instruction as to potential dangers to persons other than his own employees, then the employer was under a duty to provide such information and instruction. In the circumstances, it was reasonably practicable to do so.

3.50 Training in safe working practices should be undertaken on a regular basis; where special courses are available, employees should be required, not merely encouraged, to go on them (eg for fork-lift truck drivers, or when handling heavy weights). Where appropriate, "in-house" training can be given. The employee is under a legal duty to co-operate with the employer (s.7(2), see paragraph 3.107), and hence a refusal to go on an appropriate training course, as well as being a possible offence under the Act, may well be grounds for fair dismissal (see Chapter 9). Sometimes regulations will specify the actual training to be given, including the syllabus, but otherwise the training may be carried out by the employer or an independent body. As long as it is adequate, the requirements of HSWA will be met.

3.51   A failure to provide training for employees could lead to an improvement notice being issued. In *Sunner v Radford*, a local authority inspector while inspecting a supermarket noticed that a fork-lift truck was not being operated correctly. He also discovered that the two employees who drove the truck had never received any formal training. He served an improvement notice requiring the employer to send the men on a course of training for fork-lift truck drivers, and, on appeal, an employment tribunal upheld the notice. The employer had failed to provide such training as was reasonably practicable to ensure the safety of employees at work.

3.52   A suitable and satisfactory system of supervision must be provided with properly trained and competent supervisors who have authority to ensure that safety precautions are implemented, safety equipment used, and safe systems followed. Young and inexperienced employees in particular must be properly supervised.

3.53   *So far as is reasonably practicable, to ensure the maintenance of any place of work under the employer's control in a condition that is safe and without risks to health, and the provision and maintenance of means of access and exit that are safe and without such risks* (s.2(2)(d))

3.54   Thus premises must be safe and maintained safe. Obstacles must be removed, dangerous wiring replaced, defective floors and stairs repaired, roads, pavements, pathways, doors, etc must all be safe.

3.55   *The provision and maintenance of a working environment that is, so far as is reasonably practicable, safe, without risks to health, and adequate as regards facilities and arrangements for the welfare of employees at work* (s.2(2)(e))

3.56   Thus the employer must pay proper regard for systems of noise control, eliminate noxious fumes and dust, lighting must not be excessive or inadequate. Welfare arrangements and facilities must be adequate, eg toilet accommodation, washing facilities, cloakroom arrangements, etc. Ergonomic factors, such as seating, posture, reaching, etc may also need to be considered.

3.57   It will be recognised that the above statutory duties bear a strong resemblance to those duties owed by an employer to an employee at common law (see Chapter 8) spelt out in greater detail. Under s.2 of HSWA these duties may only be enforced by criminal sanctions or by the use of an enforcement notice (see paragraph 3.116).

3.58   The general nature of the employer's obligations under s.2(2) are spelt out in even greater detail by regulations, in particular the "six pack" regulations originally passed in 1992 in order to comply with EU Directives (see Chapters 5 and 6).

Safety policies (s.2(3))

3.59   Every employer shall prepare (and as often as may be appropriate revise) a written statement of his general policy with respect to:

(a) the health and safety at work of his employees, and

(b) the organisation and arrangements in force for the time being for carrying out that policy

and bring the statement and any revision of it to the notice of all his employees.

3.60   However, this duty does not apply to any employer who carries on an undertaking in which for the time being he employs less than five employees (Employers' Health and Safety Policy Statements (Exception) Regulations 1975).

3.61   In *Osborne v Bill Taylor of Huyton Ltd* the employer owned and controlled 31 betting shops. Each shop employed three people, but two of them were entitled to have a day off work each week during which time relief staff were employed. An improvement notice was served on the employer requiring him to prepare a written safety policy and when he failed to do so he was prosecuted for contravening the notice. The Divisional Court held that the words "for the time being" meant "at any one time" and thus the relief staff were to be excluded when determining the number of employees employed for the purpose of the Exception Regulations. However, the further question to be asked was whether the employer was carrying on 31 separate businesses or one business in 31 different places. In the latter case the employer would not be excluded from the duty to prepare a written safety policy. It was held that there was one business with more than five employees employed at any one time, and therefore the prosecution could succeed. To determine whether there is a single business run through a number of outlets, or whether a person has set up a series of separate businesses (albeit that each of those businesses are of the same nature) it is necessary to look at the manner in which the activities are run. If there is a series of separate legal bodies running each enterprise, almost certainly each will be a separate undertaking. Control from the centre is an indication that there is a single undertaking.

3.62   The drawing up of the safety policy is the beginning of the commitment of the employer to safety and health at work. There is no standard policy, no precedent which can be adopted. Each employer must work it out for himself, bearing in mind the nature of the hazards involved and the precautions and protections needed. General advice on the drawing up of safety policies may be sought from a number of sources (employers' associations, safety organisations, etc) but the responsibility is placed fairly and squarely on the shoulders of each employer. Studies have revealed that whilst some policy statements lay down a general commitment, they lack details of "the organisation and arrangements in force" for the carrying out of the policy. Moreover, there is a need to constantly revise the policy statement when appropriate.

3.63   The Act requires the statement to be brought to the notice of all employees. This is not done merely by affixing a policy statement to a notice board. Some employers issue the statement as a paper communication which conforms with the law but is not necessarily good practice, for sheets of paper are frequently lost or destroyed. Perhaps the best method is by introducing the policy statement on an induction course and publishing it together with the works rules or information handbook which is given to employees. Particular attention should be paid to those employees whose command of English is limited and steps must be taken to draw attention to the policy in a language they understand.

3.64   A safety policy can be drawn up in the following manner.

General statement

3.65   This will specify the commitment of the employer to a standard at least as high as that required by law. It should make clear that management considers it to be a binding commitment and that safety will rank as a prominent and permanent feature of all activities. The objectives should be spelt out, eg to reduce and eliminate accidents, to achieve a safe and healthy working environment, and so forth.

Organisation

3.66 The distribution of responsibility should be detailed, starting with the management board, through the different levels of management, supervision, safety officer and safety representatives, medical personnel and ending with the responsibilities of employees. Where there are a number of sites or departments, responsibilities should be fixed as appropriate. It is probably good practice to identify the person responsible in each case, either by name or by position. The lines of communication for dealing with grievances, complaints or suggestions about health and safety matters should be stated.

Arrangements in force

3.67 The existence of the arrangements must be stated in relation to the objectives to be achieved in each case. For example, on health, state details of the first aid facilities, fire precautions, medical arrangements, etc. On safety, specify training, supervision, safety equipment, safety precautions, safety rules, maintenance practices, etc. On welfare, specify washing facilities provided, requirements relating to ventilation, heating, lighting, etc. Stress the need for all employees to be involved in good housekeeping, to co-operate with management and to report any defects or potential hazards.

Review

3.68 Safety policies should be reviewed (and revised if necessary) when there are changes in the law, new processes introduced, new hazards revealed, or when health and safety problems are revealed.

3.69 Safety policies cannot be adequately reviewed unless there is periodic monitoring. This may well be one of the functions of the safety committee but the prime responsibility must always rest with senior management. The statement should be dated and signed by the senior person in the organisation so that employees will recognise that it is an authoritative document and will note the ongoing commitment.

3.70 Safety policies should be seen to work. They should not be a mere formality to satisfy the curiosity of visiting inspectors.

General duties owed to others (s.3)

3.71   Every employer is under a duty to conduct his undertaking in such a way as to ensure, so far as is reasonably practicable, that persons not in his employment who may be affected thereby are not exposed to risks to their health and safety. A similar duty is imposed on self-employed persons, in respect of themselves and other persons not being their employees (s.3(2)). The Genetically Modified Organisms (Contained Use) Regulations 2000 provide that in relation to an activity involving genetic modification the reference to a self-employed person shall include a reference to any person who is not an employer or employee in relation to any activity involving genetic manipulation. This would include, for example, a research student.

3.72   Section 3 is designed to give protection to the general public or other non-employees to ensure that they are not at risk from workplace hazards, etc. Thus, it would be an offence under the Act (irrespective of any other heading of legal liability) if a construction firm were to permit an explosion to take place which causes windows to break in nearby houses, or for a firm to permit the seepage of a poisonous chemical into a private water supply. Visitors who come on to the employer's premises, subcontractors who come to work there, students who are on a university campus, etc are all within the class of persons who may be affected by the way the undertaking is being carried on. Whether such people have a right of civil action is irrelevant to the criminal liability of the employer in respect of a breach of the duty.

3.73   To establish criminal liability under s.3(1), it is not necessary to show that the employer had any control over the operation in question as part of his undertaking. It is sufficient to show that the operation in question came within the employer's conduct of his undertaking. The question of control, however, may be relevant to the defence of "reasonably practicable". Thus in *R v Associated Octel Co Ltd* the company had closed down production processes for pre-planned annual maintenance. The task of repairing the lining of a tank within the chlorine plant was entrusted to a specialist contractor. As the plant was designated a major hazard site under what is now the Control of Major Accident Hazards Regulations 1999 (see paragraph 6.235) the company was obliged to submit a safety case to HSE. The case required contractors to conform to a permit-to-work system. However, this was not properly implemented, with the result that an employee of the contractor was seriously burned. The company was convicted of an offence under s.3(1). On appeal, it was argued that it was not liable for the actions of independent contractors, and that it was the contractor who was conducting the undertaking. The latter should have been responsible for deciding how the work was to be done and the precautions to be taken. However, the Court of Appeal dismissed the appeal, and this decision was confirmed by the House of Lords. The term "undertaking" meant "enterprise" or "business". The cleaning, maintenance or repair of plant, machinery or buildings necessary for carrying on the business was part of the undertaking, whether carried out by the employer's employees or by independent contractors. Thus there was *prima facie* liability under s.3(1). The House of Lords also disapproved of an earlier decision in *RMC Roadstone Products Ltd v Jester*, which appears to suggest that the liability of an employer under s.3(1) for acts of sub-contractors depended on there being actual or shared control over the conduct of the undertaking.

3.74   It is a question of fact in each case whether the activity can be described as being part of the employer's undertaking. Thus if an independent contractor comes on to an employer's premises to do some repair work to the employer's machinery, the work will fall within s.3. If, on the other hand, the independent contractor takes the machinery away for repair, and does it on his own premises, the employer will have no control over the way the work is done, and thus s.3 will not apply.

3.75   The House of Lords further pointed out that if an employer engages an independent contractor to do work which forms part of the employer's undertaking, he must stipulate for whatever conditions are needed to avoid those risks and are reasonably practicable. The employer cannot, having omitted to do so, say that he was not in a position to exercise control. Thus once the "undertaking" test has been satisfied, in the sense that the work is for the business or ancillary to it, the only defence for an employer is that he took such steps as were reasonably practicable. The form of control, if any, he has over the independent contractor is basically irrelevant. Thus if the employer has no control whatsoever over the way an independent contractor did the work, it might not be reasonably practicable for him to do other than rely on the contractor to take the necessary precautions, but it is possible to stipulate that such precautions must be taken, and to take whatever supervisory steps as are possible to ensure that those precautions are implemented. Further, if the employer is aware of special hazards, or the work involves the co-ordination of activities between several contractors, or between the contractor and the employer's employees, then again the employer must take reasonably practicable steps. A large organisation, with a high level of expertise, would have more control over the activities of a contractor than a small employer would. Some employers would have a higher level of competence or expertise than others. On the facts of the instant case, *Associated Octel* had assumed sufficient measure of control over the safety precautions as to bring them within s.3(1).

3.76 Further, "the risks" to which non-employees should not be exposed to include the possibility of danger or injury, and s.3(l) is not confined to actual accidents or instances of ill health. In *R v Board of Trustees of the Science Museum*, it was alleged that an air-conditioning system at the Science Museum exposed members of the public to risks to their health from *Legionella pneumophilia* (LP), because there was a failure to institute a system of regular cleaning and disinfection, etc. For the Museum it was argued that the prosecution had to show that members of the public actually inhaled the bacterium, but this argument was rejected by the Court of Appeal. The term "risk" conveys the notion of possible danger, not actual danger. This is in accordance with the purposive construction which the courts give to the Act so as to promote the preventative aims.

3.77 The duty imposed by s.3(1) is wide enough to include the duty to provide information and instruction to persons who are not in the employer's employment (*R v Swan Hunter Shipbuilders Ltd* (see paragraph 3.49)).

3.78 The words "conduct his undertaking" do not appear to apply to the effects which a deleterious product may have on an ultimate consumer, where the ordinary law of negligence (as in *Donoghue v Stevenson*) or the provisions of the Consumer Protection Act 1987 will apply.

3.79 A person may be "conducting his undertaking" even though his "business" is closed. In *R v Mara*, the accused was a director of a small cleaning company which had a contract to clean the premises of a supermarket each weekday morning. It was also agreed that the cleaning machines used by the company would be left on the supermarket's premises to be used by the latter's employees. The accused knew that an electric cable on a cleaning machine was defective.

An employee of the supermarket used the cleaning machine and because of the defect was electrocuted. The accused was charged with consenting to and conniving with (see s.37, *post*) a breach of the Health and Safety at Work Act, s.3(1), in that the company had failed to conduct its undertaking in such a way as to ensure that persons not in its employment were not exposed to risks to their health and safety. For the accused it was argued that at the time of the accident the company was not carrying on its undertaking because it was closed and the only undertaking being carried on was that of the supermarket. This contention was rejected by the Court of Appeal. It was the business of the company to provide cleaning services. To do this it cleaned the premises on weekday mornings and left the cleaning machines for the use of employees of the supermarket. Those employees were clearly persons who may be affected by the way the company carried on its undertaking and the conviction was upheld.

3.80 The fact that the offence was committed by an employee, or an appointed safety adviser, will no longer amount to a defence for any contravention of any statutory provision. Thus in *R v Nelson Group Services (Maintenance) Ltd* the company was involved in the installation, servicing and maintenance of gas appliances. A fitter, who had been properly trained to perform his work competently, left a gas fitting in a condition which exposed the occupier of the house to health and safety risks. It was held that the employer had done everything reasonably practicable to ensure that the employee had a safe system of work laid down, had the appropriate skills and instruction, was subject to adequate supervision, and had been provided with safe plant and equipment for the proper performance of the work. An isolated act of neglect by the employee performing the work did not render the employer criminally liable. However, regulation 21 of the Management of Health and Safety at Work Regulations 1999, appears to have closed this line of defence. It provides that nothing in any relevant statutory provision shall operate so as to afford a defence in any criminal proceedings for a contravention of those provisions by reason of any act or default of an employee or a person appointed to provide health and safety assistance (see paragraph 5.72). But the ACOP accompanying the regulations states that in practice, enforcement inspectors will doubtless take into account the circumstances of the case before deciding on the appropriateness of enforcement action, including the fact that the employer has taken reasonable steps to satisfy himself of the competency of the employee or safety assistant concerned.

3.81   In such cases as may be prescribed, and in the circumstances and prescribed manner, it shall be the duty of every employer and every self-employed person to give to persons who are not his employees, but who may be affected by the way he conducts his undertaking, the prescribed information about such aspects of the way he conducts his undertaking as might affect their health or safety (s.3(3)). This subsection is clearly designed to ensure that persons living near to some hazardous operation have some form of advance notification of what they may expect if something goes wrong and the necessary action they should take. To date, no regulations requiring the disclosure of any such information have been made. However, under the Control of Major Accident Hazards Regulations 1999, operators who control installations carrying out certain dangerous activities must prepare a site emergency plan for dealing with any major accident and may be required to provide information to the public (see paragraph 6.235).

General duties of controllers of premises (s.4)

3.82   This section imposes duties on people who have the control over non-domestic premises, or of the means of access thereto or exit therefrom, or of any plant or substances therein, which are used by persons (who are not employees) as a place of work or as a place where they may use plant or substances provided there for their use. The duty is to take such measures as it is reasonable for a person in his position to take to ensure, so far as is reasonably practicable, that the premises, the means of access and exit, and any plant or substance in or provided for use there, is or are safe and without risks to health.

3.83   Residential premises are clearly domestic premises, but the common parts of those premises, ie those parts which are not exclusively used for domestic purposes, are non-domestic. In *Westminster City Council v Select Managements Ltd*, the defendants owned and managed a block of flats. An improvement notice was served on them relating to the lifts and electrical installations which serviced the common parts of the flats. They appealed against the notice, arguing that the lifts, etc were "domestic premises" within the meaning of s.4 of the Act. The validity of the notice was upheld by the Court of Appeal. The common parts of the block of flats (eg the hallway, lift, stairs, landing, etc) were non-domestic premises. These common parts were available to persons who were not in the employment of the flat owners as a place of work or as a place where they may use plant (eg the lifts). Thus an improvement notice could properly be served.

3.84   It would appear from this decision that premises will be regarded as being non-domestic if they are not in the exclusive occupation of the occupants of a private dwelling.

3.85   Section 4 is the criminal counterpart of the civil liability contained in the Occupiers' Liability Act 1957 (and the Occupiers' Liability (Scotland) Act 1960) (see paragraph 8.87) and would apply in those cases where an employee is using premises which are not controlled by the employer, eg a visiting window cleaner. However, the effect of the section is somewhat wider than that. Thus a coin-operated launderette would be covered, even though no one was employed there, for a customer would be using plant or substances provided for use. Universities would have a duty under this section to ensure that their premises (libraries, etc) are safe; schools have duties towards their pupils using laboratories, etc. In *Moualam v Carlisle City Council* the defendant operated a children's play-centre, and was convicted following his failure to comply with a number of improvement notices. His appeal was dismissed. The premises were non-domestic, the children were using plant (ie equipment) there, and he had control over the premises. Section 4 is not limited to persons who are at work.

3.86   Further, a person who, by virtue of any contract or tenancy, has an obligation to maintain or repair any premises used by others as a place of work or as a place where they may use plant or substances, or to maintain the means of access or exit, or to ensure the safety or absence of risks to health arising from the use of such plant or substances, will be the person upon whom the above duty will lie, s.4(3). For example, a maintenance contractor who is responsible for the maintenance of plant, or a specialist advisor who has to deal with the control of a dangerous substance, will have those duties imposed by this section to persons other than his employees.

3.87   When a person makes available premises for the use of another person, the reasonableness of the measures taken to ensure the safety of those premises must be determined in the light of the controller's knowledge of the anticipated use of those premises and of his knowledge of the actual use. In *Austin Rover Group Ltd v Inspector of*

Factories, an employee of a firm of subcontractors was killed while working on the premises of Austin Rover. On the facts of the case, Austin Rover had given clear instructions, and the accident was caused by employees of the subcontractor acting contrary to those instructions. The prosecution of Austin Rover was dismissed. If premises are not a reasonably foreseeable cause of injury to anyone acting in a way in which a human being may reasonably be expected to act in circumstances which may reasonably be expected to occur, then it would not be reasonable to take further measures to prevent the occurrence of unknown and unexpected events.

3.88   For the purpose of s.4, the premises in question must be used by the person in control by way of a trade, business or other undertaking (whether for profit or not). The question may well arise as to whether the word "undertaking" is to be construed *ejusdem generis* with "trade or business", as implying some form of commercial activity.

Duty to prevent pollution (s.5, now repealed)

3.89   Section 5 of HSWA dealt with the duty of controllers of prescribed premises to prevent the emission into the atmosphere of noxious or offensive substances. The enforcement of pollution control has now been transferred to the Environment Agency, exercising powers conferred in the Environment Act 1995. Consequently, s.5 was repealed as from 16 December 1996 (Environmental Protection Act 1990 (Commencement No.18) Order 1996). In its place, a two-tiered system of environmental control has been instituted; processes and substances covered by the Environmental Protection Act are listed in the Environmental Protection (Prescribed Processes and Substances) Regulations 1991 (as amended). Those classified as "Part A" processes are subject to a regime of integrated pollution control supervised by the Environment Agency, whereas "Part B" processes remain the responsibility of local authorities, which are only concerned with air pollution. The Act provides that for all prescribed processes, the Best Available Technique Not Entailing Excessive Cost (BATNEEC) must be used to control pollution.

3.90   Superimposed on to this legislation is the Pollution Prevention and Control Act 1999, which is designed to implement EC Directive 91/61/EC on integrated pollution prevention and control (IPPC). There were certain differences between the existing UK provisions and the requirements of the Directive, which would have created problems, and so the Act was passed to enable a coherent regime, compatible with existing systems, to be created by Regulations. The Regulations will implement the Directive's provisions concerning integrated pollution prevention and control, regulate activities which are capable of causing environmental pollution, and prevent or control emissions capable of causing any such pollution. These Regulations may be made by the Secretary of State, the National Assembly for Wales, and the Scottish Executive.

General duties of designers, manufacturers, importers and suppliers (s.6)

3.91   Section 6 lays down duties on any person who designs, manufactures, imports or supplies any article for use at work, and on any person who manufactures, imports or supplies any substance for use at work. The basic objective is to introduce safety measures at source, rather than leave this to the ultimate user. Before we consider the nature of these duties, we must first ascertain the scope of the above words.

3.92   "An article for use at work" is defined as being "any plant designed for use or operation (whether exclusively or not) by persons at work and any article designed for use as a component in any such plant". The word "plant" includes "any machinery, equipment or appliance". A "substance" is "any natural or artificial substance (including micro-organisms) whether in solid or liquid form, or in the form of gas or vapour" (s.53). "Work" in this connection means at work as an employee or as a self-employed person. Thus a sale to a "do-it-yourself" enthusiast is not within s.6, for although he may be working, he is not at work. Consumer sales are not included within the Act, but since s.53 states that the article need not be exclusively designed for use at work, an item which is capable of being used at work is within the scope of the section even though it is also capable of being a consumer item. It may be that a test will emerge which asks if it was reasonably foreseeable that an employer would purchase the item for use at work.

3.93   The article or substance must be "for use". Thus if it is part of the stock-in-trade, or is purchased for resale purposes, the section does not apply. Nor does it apply to goods which are manufactured, etc for export, for the Act does not apply extraterritorial.

3.94   "Supply" in this connection means the supply of an article or substances by way of sale, lease, hire or hire purchase, whether as a principal or as an agent for another However, s.6(9) recognises the commercial nature of hire-purchase agreements, conditional sales agreements, and credit-sales agreements, and draws a distinction between the ostensible supplier and the effective supplier. The ostensible supplier is in reality merely financing the transaction even though in the course of the transaction he may become the legal owner of the goods in question. The liability under s.6 is on the effective supplier, ie the manufacturer, etc who sells to the finance company, who then sells to the customer. A similar provision is to be found in the Health and Safety (Leasing Arrangements) Regulations 1992, whereby if the ostensible supplier is merely acting as a financier for a leasing arrangement made between the effective supplier and the customer, then, subject to certain conditions, the effective supplier and not the ostensible supplier will have the duties of s.6 imposed on him.

3.95   It will be noted that in respect of articles the designer has certain duties, as well as manufacturers, importers and suppliers. It is not clear whether this means the person who actually designs the product or the employer of the designer. It is likely that HSE policy will be to leave the employee to be prosecuted under s.7, and take action against the employer of the designer under s.6. This is because subsection (7) of s.6 reminds us that the duties only apply "to things done in the course of a trade, business or undertaking carried on by him" and presumably it is the employer of the designer who is carrying on the trade, business or undertaking. If the employer had no reason to suspect that the designer was incompetent, or had made a faulty design, presumably he could rely on the defence that he took all steps which were reasonably practicable.

3.96   Section 6 of HSWA was amended by the Consumer Protection Act 1987 (Schedule 3). It is clear that there is a close connection between occupational safety and consumer safety generally, and indeed it will frequently occur that goods are manufactured, etc for consumers as well as for persons at work. It was recognised that it is strongly desirable to introduce enforcement at the earlier point of supply and the ultimate use for which the goods are intended should not be particularly relevant. In other words, safety has to be built into the design and manufacture of the product, rather than at the user end. Thus more extensive obligations were placed on those who put goods into circulation. A new subsection (6(1)A) was added relating to articles of fairground equipment, although this is more for the protection of the general public than for persons at work. Again, however, the obligations relating to safety were placed at the earlier point in time, ie with the manufacturer, etc.

3.97   Section 6 lays down six duties in respect of articles, and five duties in respect of substances.

Articles

3.98   The six duties in respect of articles are as follows.
1. It shall be the duty of any person who designs, manufactures, imports or supplies any article for use at work to ensure, so far as is reasonably practicable, that the article is so designed and constructed that it will be safe and without risks to health at all times when it is being set, used, cleaned or maintained by a person at work. However, s.6(10) goes on to state that the absence of safety, or, a risk to health shall be disregarded in so far as it is shown to be an occurrence which could not reasonably be foreseen. Further, in determining whether the duty has been performed, regard shall be paid to any relevant information or advice which has been provided by the designer, manufacturer, importer or supplier.
2. Designers, manufacturers, importers and suppliers must carry out (or arrange for the carrying out) of such testing and examination as may be necessary for the performance of the above duty, but there is no need to repeat any testing or examination which has previously been carried out, in so far as it is reasonable for him to rely on the results thereof.
3. Designers, manufacturers, importers and suppliers must take such steps as are necessary to ensure that the person supplied by him with the article is provided with adequate information about the use for which it has been designed or tested, and about any condition necessary to ensure that it will be safe and without risks to health when it is being set, used, cleaned or maintained.
4. Designers, manufacturers, importers and suppliers must take such steps as are necessary to secure, so far as is reasonably practicable, that persons who have been provided with information are also provided with any revisions of the information as are necessary by reason of it becoming known that there is a serious risk to health or safety.

5. It is the duty of designers and manufacturers (but not importers or suppliers) to carry out (or arrange for the carrying out of) any necessary research with a view to the discovery and elimination or minimisation of any risks to health or safety to which the design or article may give rise. Again there is no need to repeat any research which has already been done insofar as it is reasonable to rely on the results thereof.

6. It shall be the duty of any person who erects or installs any article for use at work in any premises where the article is to be used by persons at work, to ensure, so far as is reasonably practicable, that nothing about the way the article is erected or installed makes it unsafe or a risk to health when it is being set, used, cleaned or maintained by a person at work. New duties are placed on installers by the Provision and Use of Work Equipment Regulations 1998.

Substances

3.99   The five duties in respect of substances are as follows.

1. It shall be the duty of any person who manufactures, imports or supplies any substance to ensure, so far as is reasonably practicable, that the substance will be safe and without risks to health at all times when it is being used, handled, processed, stored or transported by a person at work or in premises to which s.4 of the Act (see paragraph 3.82) applies. Again, the absence of risks to health or safety may be disregarded insofar as the occurrence was one which could not be reasonably foreseen, and regard shall also be had to any relevant information or advice provided by the person by whom the substance was manufactured, imported or supplied.

2. To carry out or arrange for the carrying out of such testing and examination as may be necessary to perform the above mentioned duty. However, it is not necessary to repeat any testing or examination which may have been previously carried out insofar as it is reasonable for him to rely on the results thereof.

3. To take such steps as are necessary to secure that persons supplied by him with the substance are provided with adequate information about any risks to health or safety to which the inherent properties of the substance may give rise, about the results of any relevant tests carried out and about any conditions necessary to ensure that the substance will be safe and without risks to health at all times when it is being used, handled, processed, stored, transported and disposed of.

4. To take such steps as are necessary to secure, so far as is reasonably practicable, that persons supplied with the information are provided with all revisions of the information as are necessary by reason of it becoming known that there is a serious risk to health or safety.

5. A manufacturer of a substance is under a duty to carry out (or arrange to carry out) any necessary research with a view to discovering and, so far as is reasonably practicable, the elimination or minimisation of any risks to health or safety to which the substance may give rise at all times when it is being used, handled, processed, stored or transported. Again, there is no need to repeat any research which has been carried out previously insofar as it is reasonable to rely on the results thereof.

3.100   The above duties only extend to a person in respect of things done in the course of a trade, business or other undertaking carried on by him (whether for profit or not) and to matters within his control, s.6(7). This appears to exclude employees from the scope of s.6 (though not, of course, from s.7). Whether the matters are within the control of a person is a question of fact. If he has the right of control, but fails or refuses to exercise it, the matters are still within his control.

Indemnity clauses (s.6(8))

3.101   Where a person designs, manufactures, imports or supplies an article to or for another person on the basis of a written undertaking by that other person to take specific steps sufficient to ensure, so far as is reasonably practicable, that the article will be safe and without risks to health when it is being set, used, cleaned or maintained, the undertaking will have the effect of relieving the first-mentioned person from the duty of ensuring that it is designed and constructed so as to be safe, to such an extent as is reasonable having regard to the terms of the undertaking. Thus if a person supplies second-hand machinery to another on the basis of that other's assurance that he will ensure that it is properly serviced and examined before being put to use, or where a manufacturer supplies machinery made specifically to certain specifications or to a certain design, the supplier or manufacturer may be relieved from legal responsibility under s.6(l)(a). However, there must be a written assurance, which implies a specific commitment in the instant case, not a general standard commitment. Further, the exclusion is only from the liability under s.6(1)(a), not from the liability imposed by ss.6(1)(b) or 6(1)(c) or 6(2). In other words, the obligations to test, provide information and carry out research, remain. Further, the terms of the undertaking may be looked at to discover the extent to which the designer, etc is to be absolved. The HSE appear to take the view that this may lead to a partial relief, depending on the terms of the undertaking, but this may be misleading. A breach of s.6 is a criminal offence; either an offence has been committed or it has not. There is no such thing as "partially guilty". Mitigating circumstances can only arise if an offence has been committed, and the extent of the mitigation will be for the court to determine.

Further liability of importers

3.102   Nothing in ss.6(7) or (8) shall relieve an importer of any article or substance from any of his duties under the Act as regards anything done or not done which was within the control of a foreign designer or foreign manufacturer of an article or substance. Thus importers of unsafe products may be liable for the acts or omissions of foreign designers or manufacturers even though they have no control over their activities (s.6(8A)).

The effect of s.6

3.103   The exact scope and meaning of s.6 has still to receive authoritative judicial interpretation, for although there have been some prosecutions, there appears to be a marked reluctance on either side to challenge these findings in the High Court. The purpose is to try to ensure that acceptable levels of health and safety are built into articles and substances at the design and manufacturing stage, whether by way of compliance with recognised standards (eg BSI) or HSE Guidance Notes or other acceptable tests. But the fact that the manufacturer, etc may be in breach of his duty under s.6 is irrelevant to the employer's liability under the general law to take reasonable care to ensure the health and safety of his employees, or the duty to fence or guard dangerous machinery (see regulation 11 of the Provision and Use of Work Equipment Regulations 1998). A modern practice is for purchasers of products for use at work to make the contract conditional upon compliance by the supplier with s.6 of HSWA, thus leaving it open for the purchaser to reject the product. It will be recalled that nothing in HSWA gives rise to any civil liability, but it would be an interesting argument if the purchaser rejected a product on the grounds that a failure to comply with the requirements of s.6 rendered the product not of satisfactory quality as required by the Sale and Supply of Goods Act 1994.

General duties of employees (s.7)

3.104   Two main duties are placed on an employee.

3.105   Section 7(1) *To take reasonable care for the health and safety of himself and of others who may be affected by his acts or omissions at work*

3.106   Thus an employee who refuses to wear safety equipment or use safety precautions is liable to be prosecuted under this section. Further, if through his carelessness or negligence someone else is injured, he could again be prosecuted. Thus an employee who is prone to horseplay or skylarking, with the result that he or another is injured, commits an offence. A supervisor who encourages an employee to take an unsafe short cut or to remove effective guards may equally be guilty under this section.

3.107   Section 7(2) *As regards any duty or requirement imposed on his employer or other person by or under any of the relevant statutory provisions, to cooperate with him insofar as is necessary to enable that duty or requirement to be performed or complied with*

3.108   This duty to co-operate is potentially very wide. An employee who announces that he intends to refuse to wear a safety belt or refuses to use a safety precaution provided by his employer in pursuance of the latter's duty under s.2 is failing to co-operate with the employer and thus a prosecution may again succeed.

3.109   In addition, the Management of Health and Safety at Work Regulations 1999 impose further duties on employees to report dangerous situations and shortcomings in the employer's protection arrangements (see paragraph 5.54).

Interference or misuse (s.8)

3.110   *No person shall intentionally or recklessly interfere with or misuse anything provided in the interests of health, safety or welfare in pursuance of any of the relevant statutory provisions*

3.111   This obligation is again wider than the corresponding provision in the Factories Act which referred to wilful conduct in the sense of being deliberate or perverse. Intentional or reckless conduct does not need to be perverse.

3.112   It should be noted that s.8 is not restricted to employees and could, for example, apply to visitors, burglars, etc.

Duty not to charge (s.9)

3.113   *No employer shall levy or permit to be levied on any employee of his any charge in respect of anything done or provided in pursuance of any specific requirement of the relevant statutory provisions*

3.114   This provision originally applied only to the specific requirements of relevant statutory provisions, but most of these have now been repealed by virtue of the Personal Protective Equipment at Work Regulations 1992 (see paragraph 6.111). Section 9 now applies to all personal protective equipment deemed necessary by those regulations.

Enforcement of the Act

3.115   A breach of the Act or of health and safety regulations can be dealt with in two ways. First, there are the powers given to the inspectors to issue enforcement notices or to seize and destroy. Second, a prosecution may take place in respect of the commission of a criminal offence.

Enforcement notices (ss.21–24)

3.116   There are two types of enforcement notices which may be issued. These are (1) improvement notice and (2) prohibition notice (which may be immediate or deferred). In addition, the inspectorate have taken to issuing Crown Notices in respect of premises belonging to the Crown, but although there is no legal basis for such notices (it will be recalled that ss.21–24 do not bind the Crown) they have a moral and persuasive effect. A failure to comply with a Crown Notice would lead to an approach by the HSE to the Government department concerned, and the Government has announced that in such circumstances the necessary action would be taken to ensure compliance. Moreover, a copy of the Crown Notice will be given to the representatives of the employees, thus drawing attention to the hazard.

3.117 The HSE can also issue a Crown Censure, which is a formal recording of a decision that, but for Crown immunity, there was sufficient evidence to warrant the bringing of a prosecution against the Crown body concerned, for a breach of health and safety law.

3.118 Enforcement notices may be issued by HSE inspectors and Environmental Health Officers (EHOs) of a local authority, all of whom must act within the powers contained in the instrument of their appointment. However, it must be shown that the premises concerned are within the scope of the relevant legislation. In *Dicker & Sons v Hilton* a notice was served requiring the appellant to comply with s.36 of the Factories Act which laid down that air receivers shall be cleaned and examined by a competent person every 26 months. The notice was cancelled on appeal when the employment tribunal learned that the appellant ran a one-man business. Since his premises were not a factory (which is defined as being premises where persons are employed) the relevant statutory provision did not apply.

Improvement notice (s.21)

3.119 If an inspector is of the opinion that a person:
 (a) is contravening a relevant statutory provision, or
 (b) has contravened one or more provisions in circumstances that make it likely that the contravention will continue or be repeated,

then he may serve an improvement notice, which must state:

 (a) that he is of that opinion
 (b) the provisions in question
 (c) particulars of the reasons for his opinion.

3.120 The improvement notice will also require that person to remedy the contravention or matters occasioning the contravention within such period as the notice may specify, but not earlier than 21 days after the notice has been served (which is the period in which the person affected may lodge an appeal against the notice).

3.121 In other words, if there is a statutory requirement that a certain thing shall be done (or not done) an inspector may serve a notice requiring the thing be done (or not done) any time after 21 days.

3.122   But the fact that a period of grace is permitted does not absolve the person concerned from any criminal or civil liability in respect of anything which may happen prior to the notice taking effect.

3.123   An inspector may (but is not bound to) attach a schedule of the remedial steps to be taken (s.23). If he does, and it is unclear or vague, this will not affect the validity of the notice (*Chrysler (UK) Ltd v McCarthy*) but the tribunal may clarify or alter the schedule.

3.124   If the requirement of the statutory provision is absolute, then there can be no defence in the case of a breach (*Ranson v John Baird*). If the statutory requirement is to do that which is reasonably practicable, the employment tribunal may exercise its own judgment in accordance with the circumstances of the case when hearing an appeal. Thus in *Roadline (UK) Ltd v Mainwaring*, an improvement notice required an employer to provide heating in a transit shed. The employment tribunal thought that the cost of doing so was excessive in relation to the marginal improvement which would result.

3.125   Section 3(2) of the Act requires every self-employed person to conduct his undertaking so as to ensure, so far as is reasonably practicable, that he and other persons who may be affected thereby are not exposed to risks to their health and safety. In *Jones v Fishwick* an environmental health officer served an improvement notice on a butcher requiring him to use a chain mail apron whilst boning meat. Applying the "cost/risk" analysis the employment tribunal noted that there had been a number of serious accidents in that industry during boning out procedures, and the cost of acquiring a chain mail apron was £32.40. Thus it was reasonably practicable to take the necessary precautions and the improvement notice was confirmed.

3.126   Before issuing an improvement notice, the inspector will discuss with the duty holder the breaches of law concerned, and the action needed to be taken by the duty holder to ensure compliance. The duty holder will be given the opportunity to discuss issues with the inspector before formal action is taken, and, if possible, resolve points of difference. If the inspector decides to issue the improvement notice, the inspector will tell the duty holder what needs to be done, why and by when.

Prohibition notice (s.22)

3.127　If an inspector is of the opinion that activities are being carried on or are likely to be carried on in relation to which any of the relevant statutory provisions apply, and which involve or will involve a risk of serious personal injury, he may serve a prohibition notice. This will:

(a) state that the inspector is of such an opinion

(b) specify the matter which in his opinion is giving or will give rise to the risk of serious personal injury

(c) if the matter also involves a contravention of a relevant statutory provision, he will state the statutory provision, and give particulars of the reason as to why he is of that opinion and

(d) direct that the activities to which the notice relates shall not be carried on by or under the control of the person on whom the notice has been served unless the matters specified in the notice (and any associated contraventions of statutory provisions) have been remedied.

3.128　The prohibition notice will take effect immediately (immediate prohibition notice) if it so declares or at the end of the period specified in the notice (deferred prohibition notice). Again, the inspector may but is not bound to, attach a schedule of the remedial steps to be taken. It will be noted that to issue a prohibition notice, the inspector need only be satisfied that the activities complained of give rise to a risk of serious personal injury and there is no need for there to be a breach of a relevant statutory provision (*Roberts v Day*). However, if he has little information on which to form such an opinion, the notice may be cancelled by the employment tribunal (*Bressingham Steam Preservation Co Ltd v Sincock*).

3.129　There must be substrata of fact on which an inspector can form his "opinion" that there has been a breach of the general duties under the Act, and ideally this should be demonstrable by a risk assessment carried out which is at least as thorough as that required by an employer under the Management of Health and Safety at Work Regulations 1999 (see Chapter 5) and other legislation. This would include a consideration of the risk, the nature of the hazard, the preventative measures already taken and the cost of further measures, and so on. Equally, the employer's own risk assessment is capable of being used to counter the inspector's opinion, by showing additional factors, such as the training given, the supervision employed, the use in actual practise, the low number of previous incidents, the search for suitable alternatives, and expert evidence (if available) as to the reasonably safe equipment or systems of work as appropriate. The employment tribunal will then be in a position to make an informed evaluation, and decide if the inspector's "opinion" is sustainable.

Supplementary provisions (s.23)

3.130   As already noted, an improvement and prohibition notice may (but need not) include directions as to the measures to be taken to remedy any contravention, for the inclusion of details of the precise nature of the breach, and the remedial matters which will have to be taken to remedy it, is an option, not an obligation (*MB Gas Ltd v Veitch*). The measures to be taken may be framed by reference to any Approved Code of Practice or may give a choice as to different ways of taking remedial action. However, if the improvement notice refers to a building, or a matter connected with a building, the notice may not direct that measures shall be taken which are more onerous than the requirements of any building regulations which are applied in respect of new buildings. If the notice refers to the taking of measures affecting the means of escape in the case of fire, the inspector must first consult the fire authority.

3.131   In the case of an improvement notice or a deferred prohibition notice, these may be withdrawn at any time by the inspector before the date on which they are to take effect, and also the period for compliance may be extended by him provided an appeal is not pending.

3.132   Once the matter which has been the subject of an improvement or prohibition notice has been attended to, or the person to whom it is addressed has complied with any requirement contained therein, the activity may be carried on without any further need to contact the inspector, although prudence may well advise such a course in order to ensure that he is satisfied with the rectification. This is particularly important in view of the fact that a failure to comply with the requirements of an enforcement notice exposes the offender to potentially severe punishment. However, the prohibition notice does not lapse on compliance. It continues in force so long as the activities in question are being carried on, for there is no procedure to remove it, although appeals can be made.

Appeals against enforcement notices (s.24)

3.133 A person on whom a prohibition or improvement notice has been served may appeal to an employment tribunal within 21 days of its receipt, and the tribunal may confirm or cancel the notice. If it is confirmed, this may be done in its original form, or with such modifications as the employment tribunal thinks fit. An appeal may be made on a point of law or of fact.

Procedure for appeals

3.134 The Employment Tribunals (Constitution and Rules of Procedure) Regulations 2001, Schedule 4, lay down the procedure to be followed for the making of an appeal against the decision of an inspector to issue a notice. The appellant shall send a Notice of Appeal to the Regional Office of Employment Tribunals, stating:
  (a) his name and address for service of documents
  (b) the date of the notice appealed against
  (c) the address of the premises concerned
  (d) the name and address of the respondent (ie the inspector)
  (e) particulars of the requirements or directions appealed against, and
  (f) the grounds for the appeal.

3.135 The appeal must be lodged within 21 days from the date of the service of the notice on the appellant, although the employment tribunal may extend the time limit on application if it is satisfied that it was not reasonably practicable to bring the appeal earlier. The 21 day time limit runs from the date of the receipt of the notice (*DH Tools Co v Myers*).

3.136 If the appeal is against the imposition of an improvement notice the lodging of the appeal will automatically suspend the operation of the notice until the appeal is disposed of. If the appeal is against the imposition of a prohibition notice the appellant may apply for it to be lifted pending the hearing of the appeal, although the notice will continue to take effect despite the fact that an appeal is pending. Since a prohibition notice which takes immediate effect can have serious repercussions on the employer's business, appeals against them are often heard as a matter of urgency, if necessary the very next day (*Hoover Ltd v Mallon*).

3.137   Employment tribunals have wide powers to deal with preliminary matters prior to the appeal. They can require further and better particulars of the application, grant disclosure of documents, issue attendance orders compelling witnesses to attend and so on. As a rule, at least 14 days' notice of the date of the hearing is given, unless a speedier hearing can be arranged by agreement between the parties. The hearing will normally be in public, unless a party applies for it to be heard in private on grounds of national security or if there may be evidence the disclosure of which would be seriously prejudicial to the interests of the appellants undertaking other than its effect on collective bargaining. Either side may be represented by a solicitor, barrister or any other person whom he desires to represent him, including a trade union official or the representative of an employers' association. If written submissions are made, these must be sent to the employment tribunal seven days prior to the hearing and a copy must be sent at the same time to the other party.

3.138   Each side is entitled to make an opening statement, give evidence on oath, call witnesses, cross-examine witnesses from the other side, introduce documentary or other evidence and make a closing submission. The tribunals do not appear (to date) to have found it necessary to appoint assessors to assist them, but they can, and do, visit the premises in order to make their own informed judgment (eg *Wilkinson v Fronks*).

3.139   The tribunal will then make its decision, which may be a unanimous one or by a majority. If the tribunal consists only of two members, the chairman has a casting vote. The decision may be given orally or in writing after consideration, but it will always be promulgated in writing and a copy sent to each side.

Grounds for appeal

3.140   An appeal may be lodged on the ground that the inspector lacked the legal power to impose an enforcement notice. This may be because the premises are not covered by the relevant statutory provisions (*Dicker & Sons v Hilton*, above) or because the inspector has misinterpreted the statutory provision in question. But the fact that the employer has complied with the requirements previously laid down by some official authority is not by itself sufficient objection to a subsequent requirement made on grounds of health or safety. In *Hixon v Whitehead*, the appellant had received permission from the district environmental health officer to store 4000kg of liquified petroleum gas on the premises. As a result of complaints from local residents, another inspector issued a notice limiting the holding to 500kg. The notice was affirmed by the employment tribunal. There was no question of estoppel arising against the local authority, for the tribunal had to consider the avoidance of serious injuries to employees and to other persons who may be affected. Similarly, in *Williamson Cliff Ltd v Tarlington* the company installed a tank containing 29,000 gallons of butane. Planning permission had been given for this after a fire hydrant had been installed. Subsequently another inspector insisted that a spray system be installed. Although the employment tribunal expressed sympathy with the company which had installed the correct system initially, only to find that they were now required to add another one even though there was no new knowledge in relation to safety, the improvement notice was confirmed. The overriding consideration was the safety of employees and other persons who were likely to be affected should an explosion occur.

Appeals against improvement notices

3.141   An improvement notice may be issued if there is a breach of a relevant statutory provision. This may be HSWA or any other appropriate legislation or regulations. The provision in question may be an absolute one, or prefaced by the requirement that something shall be done "so far as is reasonably practicable". In either case, the issues will be determined largely by the evidence which can be adduced.

3.142   Thus in *Murray v Gadbury* a farmer and his labourer used a rotary grass cutter for 26 years without incident. An inspector issued an improvement notice requiring the farmer to have the cutter guarded in accordance with the Agriculture (Field Machinery) Regulations 1962. It was argued that since the machine had been used for such a long time without accident, the notice was unnecessary. The employment tribunal rejected the appeal and confirmed the notice. The farmer appealed to the Divisional Court, claiming that the law only required him to do that which was reasonably practicable. Again, the appeal was dismissed. The provisions of the regulations were quite clear and were mandatory. On the other hand, in *Associated Dairies v Hartley*, the appellants, who used roller trucks, provided safety footwear for employees at cost price. One day the wheel of a truck ran over the foot of an employee who was not wearing protective footwear, causing a fracture. An inspector issued an improvement notice requiring the employers to provide suitable safety footwear free of charge. An appeal against this notice was allowed. There was no statutory requirement that such footwear should be provided and the obligation under s.2 of HSWA to make arrangements for securing safety at work is subject to the limitation "so far as is reasonably practicable". In determining whether or not a requirement was reasonably practicable, it was proper to take into account the time, trouble and expense of the requirement and to see if it was disproportionate to the risks involved. In this case, it would cost £20,000 in the first year to provide the boots, and £10,000 each year thereafter. On the other hand, the likelihood of such an accident occurring was fairly remote and there was no evidence that employees would use the boots if they were provided free. The tribunal concluded that the present arrangement whereby the employers made safety footwear available was satisfactory.

3.143   The fact that employees are content with existing arrangements is also irrelevant. In *File Tile Distributors v Mitchell* the firm had a cold water supply, with a gas ring and kettle on which they could heat water. Employees used this method without complaint, but an improvement notice requiring the firm to provide running hot water was upheld. The statutory requirements are designed to improve facilities for employees and their acquiescence in lower standards must be discounted.

3.144   Nor is it relevant that there has not been a previous accident or dangerous occurrence. In *Sutton & Co Ltd v Davies* the inspector issued an improvement notice requiring a machine to be fenced. The company produced evidence that there had not been an accident arising from this particular machine in 27 years. Nonetheless, the notice was affirmed. The requirements of the statute were absolute. One need not wait for an accident to happen before condemning a system as being dangerous or unsafe.

3.145   The fact that it is financially and physically possible to comply with an improvement notice does not mean that it is reasonably practicable to do so. In *West Bromwich Building Society v Townsend* an inspector served an improvement notice on a branch of a building society requiring them to erect anti-bandit screens for the protection of employees. The society appealed to an employment tribunal and the inspector sought to treat the appeal as a test case for all building societies in the area. The employment tribunal held that the risks were more than minimal, and that the measures required were financially and physically possible. Thus the notice was confirmed. On a further appeal, the Divisional Court reversed the decision. The employment tribunal had concentrated on the general desirability of having anti-bandit screens, whereas they should have decided whether screens were needed for this particular office. Further, they had decided that it was physically and financially possible to erect the screens, instead of whether it was reasonably practicable to do so.

3.146 The statutory requirements are not met by providing substitutes, unless some other equally efficacious method is permitted by the legislation. In *Belhaven Brewery Co v McLean* the inspector issued an improvement notice requiring the company to securely fence transmission machinery by the use of an interlocking device attached to the doors or gates. This would switch off the power when the doors were opened. The company argued that this would be very expensive and they wanted to deal with the problem by erecting safety screens. They would also put up a notice warning employees of the danger. Since the employees were of sufficient intelligence to see that the gates were in position while the plant was working, and since there was a high level of supervision, they wanted the notice cancelled or modified. The notice was confirmed without modification. The requirements of s.13 of the Factories Act could not be met by erecting a screen. Moreover, under s.2(1) of HSWA it was reasonably practicable to fit the interlocking device. The sacrifice in terms of cost was not disproportionate to the risk and dangers.

3.147 Employment tribunals are more willing to allow appeals to the extent that the appellant requires more time to comply with the requirements of the notice. In *Campion v Hughes* an improvement notice was issued requiring the employer to make changes to the means of escape in the event of fire. It was held that the appeal would be allowed only for the purpose of extending the time for compliance. One of the requirements was that the fire escape be made on land which belonged to the local authority, and consent for doing the work had not been given. An extension of time for a further three months was given in order to enable the employer to obtain the appropriate consent.

3.148 Similarly, in *Porthole Ltd v Brown* a firm enlarged its kitchen on the ground floor and this took away the stairway which led to the first floor lavatory used by employees. An outside stairway was erected to provide the necessary access to the lavatory, and an inspector issued an improvement notice requiring this to be covered. The operation of the notice was suspended to permit the firm to obtain the consent of the landlord and planning permission from the local authority.

3.149   An unusual extension of time arose in the case of *Cheston Woodware Ltd v Coppell*, where an improvement notice was issued requiring the appellant to fit an exhaust appliance to a planing machine used for thicknessing. The firm pointed out that if the machine was being used for thicknessing and surfacing, no such exhaust appliance would be required by the Woodworking Machines Regulations 1974. The tribunal agreed that this was somewhat odd, and postponed the operation of the notice to enable the appellant to apply for an exemption certificate.

3.150   As a general rule, an appeal cannot succeed merely because the employer is unable financially to comply with the requirements. In *Harrison (Newcastle-under-Lyme) Ltd v Ramsey* an improvement notice was issued requiring the company to clean and paint its walls in accordance with s.1(3) of the Factories Act. The company appealed on the ground that it could not afford to spend the money on the work, in view of its grave financial position. The notice was confirmed by the tribunal. To hold otherwise would enable an employer to ignore the statutory requirements because of expense and undercut his competitors who were so complying.

3.151   However, the employment tribunals are not totally unsympathetic with the financial plight of firms, and will take into account the record of compliance in the past. In particular, they are more likely to postpone (as opposed to cancel) the operation of an improvement notice where the matter concerns a "health" rather than a "safety" aspect (*R A Dyson & Co. Ltd v Bentley*).

3.152   An improvement notice may be successfully challenged on the ground that the employer is in fact complying with the statutory requirements. In *Davis & Sons v Leeds City Council* the tenancy of a flat above a small bakery shop was subject to a condition that employees at the shop could use the toilet facilities at all times. An improvement notice was issued requiring the shop occupiers to provide readily accessible sanitary facilities instead of this arrangement, in order to comply with s.9(1) of the Offices, Shops and Railway Premises Act 1963 (OSRPA). The employment tribunal allowed an appeal against the notice. Section 9(5) of the Act recognised that facilities might have to be shared with others, and in a circular addressed to local authorities the (then) Ministry of Labour had stated that the effect of s.9(5) would be that "workers in a lock-up shop might have to use the conveniences and facilities in adjacent premises". The tribunal, having visited the premises, concluded that the toilet facilities in the flat were conveniently accessible, and cancelled the notice.

3.153   A similar result was reached in *Alfred Preedy & Sons Ltd v Owens*, where an improvement notice was served alleging that a stone stairway leading to a storage room was in a dangerous condition. The tribunal cancelled the notice after hearing evidence from a witness with a long experience in property management and maintenance that the defects were minimal and of no practical significance.

3.154   A notice may be successfully challenged on the ground that the inspector has misunderstood the application of the statutory provision. In *NAAFI v Portsmouth City Council* an improvement notice was served requiring the appellants to maintain a constant temperature of 55 F, so as to conform with s.6(1) of OSRPA. The appellants argued that as the premises were used for the storage of fresh food, a temperature of between 41 and 50 F was adequate. The tribunal noted that s.6(3)(b) of the Act provides for an exception where it is a room in which the maintenance of a reasonable temperature would cause the deterioration of goods, provided employees had conveniently accessible means of keeping themselves warm. Since a warm room was provided, together with suitable clothing, the notice was cancelled.

3.155   Nor may an inspector impose a non-statutory requirement. In *Chethams v Westminster Council* a notice was issued because the appellants were allegedly in breach of regulation 7(1) of the OSRPA (Hoists and Lifts) Regulations. The notice required that the latest British Standards for lifts be adopted. This requirement was struck out, because British Standards are merely a guide for new work and are not a statutory provision.

3.156   The fact that the breach in question is a trivial one is irrelevant. In *South Surbiton Co-operative Society v Wilcox* an improvement notice required the employers to replace a wash basin which was cracked. On appeal, the notice was confirmed. The surface of the basin was not "impervious" as required by the Washing Facilities Regulations 1964, and consequently it was not "properly maintained" in accordance with s.10(2) of OSRPA. That the infringement was trivial was irrelevant to the validity of the notice.

3.157   Nor does the validity of the notice depend on the instructions for remedying the defect being precise. In *Chrysler (UK) Ltd v McCarthy* two improvement notices were issued following a fire at the company's premises. Appeals were lodged on the ground that one of the notices was imprecise. On a preliminary point of law, the tribunal dismissed the appeal, and this was confirmed by the Queen's Bench Divisional Court. It was pointed out that employment tribunals have wide powers under s.24 of HSWA to modify the requirements of the notice as they think fit in the circumstances. However, when the matter was returned to the tribunal, it felt that they lacked sufficient information on which to make such a modification, and the notice was suspended to permit the parties to agree between themselves what requirements should be laid down.

3.158   When modifying the notice, an employment tribunal may add to the inspector's requirements as well as vary them (*Tesco Stores Ltd v Edwards*). If the requirements of the inspector are vague or imprecise, the employment tribunal may exercise its power to amend them (*Chrysler (UK) Ltd v McCarthy*), but there is no power which enables the employment tribunal to amend a notice so as to include further allegations that an employer is in breach of other provisions of the Act (*British Airways Board v Henderson*).

Appeals against prohibition notices

3.159   A prohibition notice may be issued if the inspector considers that there is a risk of serious personal injury, irrespective of whether or not there is a breach of any relevant statutory provision. Consequently, a certain amount of subjectivity is involved in the formation of such opinion and accordingly this assessment can be challenged. In *Nico Manufacturing Co Ltd v Hendry* a power press operated by the company was examined and tested by a competent person who found certain defects. In accordance with the Power Presses Regulations 1965 he made a report to the company and to the inspector of factories. A few weeks later a director of the company operated the press, and when this came to the attention of the inspector, he issued a prohibition notice. An appeal was lodged on the grounds that the worn state of the press did not constitute a likely source of danger to the employees and that the deprivation of the use of the machine would cause a serious loss of production and endanger the jobs of other employees. It was held that the notice would be confirmed. The employment tribunal preferred the evidence of the expert witness called on behalf of the inspector in so far as his evidence as to the danger was in conflict with that of the company's technical director. Although there was a small likelihood that the press would break up, there was a danger that parts would fracture which would constitute a serious danger to operatives.

3.160   Thus if a defect could lead to a catastrophic failure, or there was a substantial risk of a serious injury, the employment tribunal is unlikely to be impressed by arguments of financial hardship or loss of profits. In *Grovehurst Energy Ltd v Strawson*, a prohibition notice was served on the company preventing it from using a receiver, which had been declared unsuitable for further use by a qualified engineer who had carried out a statutory inspection on the firm's boilers and receivers. The company was finding some difficulty in obtaining a replacement receiver and so it applied for the prohibition notice to be suspended. The managing director of the company (who was a qualified engineer) was confident that a replacement receiver would be available in a few weeks, and offered to take extra precautions until it arrived. If he were unable to use the existing receiver, he would suffer a considerable loss of profit. Nonetheless, the employment tribunal affirmed the notice. The consequences of a catastrophic failure would have been very serious, and the receiver was a substantial risk of injury to anyone who happened to be passing at the time of a failure and to others who worked nearby.

3.161   However, if a machine or process has been in use for a long time without any history of accident or injury, it may be easier to challenge the inspector's view that the activities will involve a risk of serious personal injury. In *Brewer & Sons v Dunston* an inspector issued a prohibition notice on a hand-operated guillotine. The company had used the machine for eighteen years without incident, and also had nine other similar machines. The tribunal, having visited the premises and seen the machine in operation, were satisfied that there was no risk of serious personal injury and cancelled the notice.

3.162   The employment tribunals take a similar attitude to appeals based on expense or a request for an extension of time as they do with improvement notices. Thus in *Otterburn Mill Ltd v Bulman* the company operated four machines with no guards. After making a number of visits to the premises, the factory inspector insisted that the appropriate guards be fitted, and when this was not done, he issued deferred prohibition notices requiring the guards to be fitted within three months. The company appealed against the time limit imposed, and requested that they should be allowed to fence one machine every six months, as they did not have the necessary finance to make the improvements. This argument was rejected by the tribunal. It would not be right to insist that a prosperous company should do the work in a short time, while a struggling company should be given a much longer period. However, since it was a deferred notice, in that the risk was not imminent, the time taken to put the matter right was always a factor to be taken into account. As the last (and only) accident recorded at the factory was about nine years ago, the tribunal was prepared to grant an extension of time in respect of one machine, in order to avoid serious embarrassment to the company.

3.163   The number of enforcement notices issued will, of course, vary from year to year, but there is little doubt that they are, and will continue to be, used increasingly by the enforcement authorities. Currently, the HSE issues about 9000–11,000 enforcement notices each year. Local authority inspectors issue twice that number. Additionally, HSE issues about 50 Crown Notices each year.

Application for review

3.164   An application may be made within 14 days after the promulgation of the decision to an employment tribunal to review its decision, on the grounds that:
- (a) the decision was wrongly made as a result of an error on the part of the tribunal staff
- (b) a party did not receive notice of the proceedings
- (c) the decision was made in the absence of a party
- (d) new evidence has come to light since the making of the decision, the existence of which was not previously known or foreseen
- (e) the interests of justice require a review.

3.165   It must be remembered that an application for review is not an appeal against the decision of the employment tribunal, and thus it must fall strictly within one of the above five grounds. The application may be refused by a chairman of tribunals sitting on his own if he thinks that it stands no reasonable prospect of success. In making the application, the appellant should state the facts or evidence upon which he seeks to base his case. If the tribunal decides to hear the application, it may vary or revoke the original decision and order a rehearing, or dismiss the application.

Costs

3.166   Unlike other proceedings before employment tribunals, costs are normally awarded against the loser to the party who wins the case. The amount awarded may be a specific sum, or, in default of agreement between the parties, the amount may be taxed in accordance with the County Court scales, as directed. However, the award of costs is always a matter for the discretion of the tribunal. Thus in *South Surbiton Co-operative Society v Wilcox* (see paragraph 3.156) an improvement notice was confirmed on appeal, but because the breach in question was a trivial one, the employment tribunal refused to make an order for costs.

Further appeals

3.167   An appeal from a decision of an employment tribunal which relates to an enforcement notice can only be made to the Queen's Bench Divisional Court on a point of law.

Failure to comply

3.168   A failure to comply with the requirements of a prohibition notice or an improvement notice is a criminal offence under s.33(1)(g) of the Act. The offence is an absolute one, and it is no defence to argue that the accused had done that which was reasonably practicable in the circumstances. The question of reasonably practicable and allied matters must be raised on appeal to an employment tribunal, not as a defence in the magistrates' or Crown Court (*Deary (HM Inspectors of Factories) v Mansion Upholstery Hide Ltd*).

Power to deal with imminent danger (s.25)

3.169   Where an inspector finds any article or substance in any premises which he has power to enter, and has reasonable cause to believe that, in the circumstances in which he finds it, the article or substance is a cause of imminent danger of serious personal injury, he may seize it and cause it to be rendered harmless (whether by destruction or otherwise). Before doing so, if it is reasonably practicable to do so, he must take a sample and give it to a responsible person at the premises where it was found, marked in a manner sufficient to identify it. After the article or substance has been seized and rendered harmless, the inspector will prepare and sign a written report giving particulars of the circumstances in which the article or substance was seized and dealt with by him, and shall:

(a) give a signed copy to a responsible person at the premises where it was found, and
(b) unless that person is the owner, give a copy to the owner. If the inspector cannot ascertain the name or address of the owner, the copy will be given to the responsible person in question.

3.170 Additionally, for the purpose of facilitating the exercise of any power by an enforcing authority, a customs official may seize any imported article or substance, and detain it for not more than two working days (s.25A).

Prosecutions for criminal offences (ss.33–42)

3.171 Historically, the various branches of the inspectorate have always sought to ensure compliance with health and safety legislation by giving advice and using persuasion, rather than compulsion. Prosecutions for offences are generally used as the weapon of last resort. The HSC has produced a revised *Enforcement policy statement*, setting out the general principles and approach which the Commission expects health and safety enforcing authorities (HSE and local authorities) to follow, based on principles of proportionality in applying the law and ensuring compliance, consistency of approach, targeting of enforcement action, transparency about how the regulator operates, and accountability for the regulator's actions. Enforcing authorities must use their discretion in deciding whether to initiate a prosecution. There must be a realistic prospect of a conviction, and the prosecution must be in the public interest. Factors which will be taken into account include:

(a) whether a death occurred as a result of a breach of legislation
(b) the gravity of the alleged offence, the seriousness of actual or potential harm, and the general record of the offender
(c) whether there has been a reckless disregard of health and safety requirements

(d) repeated or persistent poor compliance

(e) work carried out without, or in serious breach of, a licence

(f) any failure to comply with a written warning or improvement or prohibition notice

(g) any evidence of inspectors having been intentionally obstructed in the lawful course of their duties.

3.172   In addition, prosecution will be expected when:

(a) false information has been wilfully supplied, or there has been an intent to deceive

(b) there have been serious failures in the management of health and safety

(c) it is appropriate to draw general attention to the need for compliance with the law, and a conviction may deter others from similar failures.

3.173   The HSE has also developed an *Enforcement management model* which establishes a framework within which inspectors may make informed enforcement decisions, proportionate to the risks or seriousness of any breach, and assist in ensuring consistency of enforcement action.

3.174   In England and Wales, the decision to bring a prosecution rests with the enforcing authority, by an inspector, or by or with the consent of the Director of Public Prosecutions (s.38 of the HSWA). An inspector, if authorised by the enforcing authority, may conduct the prosecution before a magistrates' court even though he is not a solicitor or a barrister (s.39). However, the inspector has no power to delegate the institution of those proceedings to someone else (eg a local authonty's solicitor, see *R v Croydon Justices, ex parte WH Smith Ltd*). In Scotland, the decsion is taken by the Procurator Fiscal, either on the recommendation of an enforcing authority or on the Procurator Fiscal's own initiative.

3.175   The HSC has now decided to publish in its Annual Report the names of all the companies and individuals who have been convicted in the previous 12 months of breaking health and safety legislation, following prosecutions by HSE. Their names will also appear on a website (to be found at www.hse-databases.co.uk.prosecutions).

3.176   Under a new protocol agreed between the HSE, the Association of Chief Police Officers and the Crown Prosecution Services, a CID officer will have to attend the scene of any sudden death in the workplace to assess whether a charge of manslaughter may be brought.

3.177   Sentencing powers were last altered by the Criminal Justice Act 1991 and the Offshore Safety Act 1992.

3.178   Prosecutions under HSWA may be brought in respect of the following offences.

Offence	Summary conviction	On indictment
1. Failure to discharge a duty under ss.2–6	£20,000	Unlimited fine
2. Contravening ss.7–9	£5,000	Unlimited fine
3. Contravening health and safety regulations	£5,000	Unlimited fine
4. Contravening any requirement made by regulations relating to investigations or enquiries made by the Commission, etc under s.14, or obstructing anyone exercising his powers	£5,000	—
5. Contravening any requirement under s.20 (powers of inspectors)	£5,000	—
6. Contravening any requirement under s.25 (power of the inspector to seize and render harmless articles or substances likely to cause inminent danger)	£5,000	Unlimited fine
7. Preventing a person from appearing before an inspector or from answering questions under s.20(2)(j) (examinations and investigations)	£5,000	—
8. Contravening a requirement or prohibition imposed by an improvement notice	£20,000 and/or 6 months' imprisonment	Unlimited fine and/or 2 years' imprisonment

9. Contravening a requirement or prohibition imposed by a prohibition notice	£20,000 and/or 6 months' imprisonment	Unlimited fine and/or 2 years' imprisonment
10. Intentionally obstructing an inspector	£5,000	—
11. Contravening a notice served by the Commission under s.27(1) requiring information	£5,000	Unlimited fine
12. Using or disclosing information in contravention of s.27(4) (disclosure by the Crown or certain Government agencies of information to the Commission or Executive)	£5,000	Unlimited fine and/or 2 years' imprisonment
13. Making a false or reckless statement in purported compliance with a statutory provision, or for the purpose of obtaining the issuance of a document under any statutory provision	£5,000	Unlimited fine
14. Intentionally making a false entry in any register, book, or other document required to be kept, or to making use of such entry, knowing it to be false	£5,000	Unlimited fine
15. With intent to deceive, using a document issued under a relevant statutory provision	£5,000	Unlimited fine
16. Pretending to be an inspector	£5,000	—
17. Failing to comply with an order of the court under s.42 (order to remedy)	£20,000 and/or 6 months' imprisonment	Unlimited fine and/or 2 years' imprisonment
18. Acting without a licence which is necessary under a relevant statutory provision	£5,000	Unlimited fine and/or 2 years' imprisonment

19. Contravening the terms of such a licence	£5,000	Unlimited fine and/or 2 years' imprisonment
20. Acquiring, using or possessing explosives contrary to the relevant statutory provisions	£5,000	Unlimited fine and/or 2 years' imprisonment
21. Breach of regulations made for the purpose of s.1(1) of the Off-shore Safety Act 1992	£5,000	Unlimited fine and/or 2 years' imprisonment

3.179   The HSE prosecutes between 1000 and 2000 cases each year, and local authorities just under 1000. The conviction rate is about 90%. Average fines appear to be on the increase, and are currently around the £4000 mark. In recent years there are signs that the courts are prepared to impose stiff penalties for breaches of health and safety law. There are several instances where custodial and suspended prison sentences have been imposed, for example for failure to comply with a prohibition notice. Recently, a sentence of 12 months' imprisonment (as well as a fine) was imposed on a company director who failed to ensure that protective clothing was supplied to a worker who came into contact with a deadly chemical, and who, in consequence, was killed. Substantial fines have also been imposed. For example, in 1997 four companies were fined a total of £1.7 million following the collapse of a ferry walkway at Ramsgate Docks, which led to the death of six people, and a similar fine was imposed on a civil engineering firm following the collapse of railway tunnelling.

3.180   For many years critics have suggested that the level of fines imposed by the courts for breaches of health and safety legislation has been too low, but in a recent decision the Court of Appeal gave guidance on the criteria to be adopted by magistrates and judges, which will undoubtedly result in significantly higher fines being imposed. In *R v Howe & Sons (Engineers) Ltd*, it was stated that a fine needs to be large enough to bring the message home to managers and shareholders that the purpose of enforcing health and safety legislation is to achieve a safe environment for those who work in a workplace and for other members of the public who may be affected. The court suggested a three-stage approach should be adopted, ie criteria, aggravating factors and mitigating factors.

3.181   The criteria to be adopted when assessing the gravity of the breach is for the court initially to see how far the defendant fell short of the appropriate standard of reasonably practicable. Sometimes, it will be a matter of chance whether death or serious injury results from a serious breach, but if death does result, the penalty should reflect the public disquiet at the unnecessary loss of life. A deliberate breach is to be regarded seriously. The size of a company and its financial strength or weakness cannot affect the degree of care that is required, because those firms lacking in-house expertise can obtain assistance from the HSE or other sources. The degree of risk, the extent of the danger, the extent of the breach (ie whether an isolated incident or one which continued over a period) and the defendant's resources and the effect of a fine on the business should all be taken into account. If a company wishes to make any submissions about its ability to pay a fine, it should produce the annual accounts prior to the hearing, which should be examined carefully. If these are not produced, the court will draw any necessary conclusion about the company's ability to pay a fine.

3.182 The aggravating factors to be taken into account will include a failure to heed warnings, and where the defendant either specifically ran a risk to save money or deliberately profited financially from the failure to take necessary health and safety steps. A deliberate breach of health and safety legislation with a view to profit will always seriously aggravate the offence.

3.183 Mitigating factors which a court can take into account include a prompt admission of responsibility and a timely admission of guilt. It will also count in a defendant's favour if steps were taken immediately to remedy any deficiencies after these were drawn to his attention. A previous good safety record will also help by way of mitigation.

3.184 Subsequently, the Court of Appeal in *R v Friskies Petcare (UK) Ltd* gave further guidance on the approach to sentencing policies. It was suggested that HSE should list, in writing, for the assistance of the court, the aggravating features alleged to exist, and the defendant should then be invited to outline the mitigating features which it says the court should take into account. In this way, both sides will know and understand the basis on which the court can make its appropriate decision. It was further suggested that large fines, in excess of £500,000, tend to be reserved for those cases where a major public disaster occurs, or where breaches of legislation put large numbers of the public at risk of serious injury. A high fine is appropriate where safety has been deliberately sacrificed for profit.

Burden of proof (s.40)

3.185   As a general rule, it is for the prosecution to prove its case beyond reasonable doubt. However, s.40 provides that if the offence consists of a failure to comply with a duty or requirement to do something "so far as is practicable" or "so far as is reasonably practicable" or to "use the best practicable means", it shall be for the accused to prove that it was not practicable or not reasonably practicable to do more than was in fact done or that there was no better practicable means than was in fact used to satisfy the duty or requirement. However, when this burden is placed on the accused, he need only satisfy the court on the balance of probabilities that what he has to prove has been done (*R v Carr-Briant*).

Offences due to the fault of another person (s.36)

3.186   Where the commission of an offence by any person is due to the act or default of some other person, that other person shall be guilty of an offence and may be charged and convicted whether or not proceedings are taken against the first-mentioned person (s.36(1)). If an offence is committed by the Crown, but the Crown cannot be prosecuted (see paragraph 3.12) and the offence is due to the act or default of a person other than the Crown, that person shall be guilty of the offence and may be charged and convicted accordingly (s.36(2)). Thus employees of the Crown may be convicted, even though the Crown itself is immune.

Offences by directors, managers, secretaries, etc (s.37)

3.187   Where an offence committed by a body corporate is proved to have been committed with the consent or connivance of, or attributable to any neglect on the part of, any director, manager, secretary or other similar officer of the body corporate, or a person who was purporting to act in such capacity, then he, as well as the body corporate shall be guilty of that offence and shall be liable to be proceeded against (s.37(1)). A director consents to the commission of an offence when he is well aware of what is going on and agrees to it. He will be deemed to connive to an offence when he is equally well aware of what is going on but his agreement is tacit, not actively encouraging what happens, but letting it continue and saying nothing about it (*Huckerby v Elliot*). He will be committing an act of neglect if he is under a duty to do something and fails to do it, or if he does it in a negligent manner. This section was considered in *Armour v Skeen*, where the Strathclyde Regional Council and its Director of Roads were both prosecuted for a breach of safety regulations, lack of a safe system of work and failing to notify an inspector that certain work was being undertaken. As a result of these failures, an employee of the council was killed. The alleged neglect on the part of the Director of Roads was a failure to have a sound safety policy for his department, failing to provide information to his subordinates and a failure to provide training and instructions in safe working practices. He was convicted of the offences and the conviction was upheld on appeal. The fact that s.2 of HSWA imposes a duty on the employers to provide a safe system of work did not mean that there was no duty on his part to carry out that duty. Section 37(1) refers to "any neglect", not to the neglect of a duty imposed. The offences were committed by the body corporate, but were due to his neglect. Further, although his title as "Director of Roads" did not mean he was a "director" within the meaning of s.37(1), he was within the ambit of the words "manager or similar officer".

3.188   Persons who purport to act as directors, managers, secretaries or similar officers are equally liable. Thus if a person acts as a director even though he has been disqualified from doing so under the Companies Act, he is purporting to act as such. Nor do the words "purporting to act" imply that there is a fraudulent or false intention in so acting. Anyone who acts in a managerial capacity may be held liable under s.37(1) whatever title he may have. If the affairs of the body corporate are being managed by its members (eg a workers' co-operative), then the acts of a member which are in connection with his managerial functions are within the meaning of this section (s.37(2)).

3.189   A director does not escape responsibility for health and safety matters by appointing a third party to carry out the necessary duties. The director must make sure that an independent third party is competent and properly supervised, but the director has to accept greater responsibility for the safety of employees and others than those who are engaged on a part-time basis to assist (*R v Ceri Davies*).

3.190   For a person to be convicted under this section, it must be shown that he has some responsibility for the making of management decisions, and be in a position of responsibility. In *R v Boal*, the accused was the assistant general manager of Foyle's bookshop. He had been given no management training, and in particular, none in health and safety matters, or fire precautions. He was, however, in charge of the shop while the general manager was away on a week's holiday. During this period, the premises were visited by officers from the local fire authority, who discovered that there were serious breaches of the fire certificate which had been issued. Foyle's and the accused were charged with a number of offences under the Fire Precautions Act 1971 — Foyle's as the "body corporate" and the accused because the 1971 Act provides that "...where an offence committed by a body corporate is proved...to be attributable to any neglect on the part of any director, manager, secretary or other similar officer of the body corporate he as well as the body corporate shall be guilty of that offence...".

3.191   Foyle's were convicted on 11 counts, and were fined. The accused pleaded guilty to 3 counts, and was found guilty of seven others. He was sentenced to 3 months' imprisonment, suspended for 12 months. He then appealed against the conviction on the ground that he was not a "...manager or other similar officer..." within the meaning of the Act.

3.192   The Court of Appeal (Criminal Division) allowed his appeal. A person was "a manager" if he had power of "...the management of the whole of the affairs of the company..." or was, "...entrusted with power to transact the whole of the affairs of the company..." or was "managing in a governing role the affairs of the company itself". The Court further thought that the intended scope of s.23 of the Fire Precautions Act was "...to fix with criminal liability only those who are in a position of real authority, the decision makers within the company who have both the power and responsibility to decide corporate policy and strategy. It is to catch those responsible for putting proper procedures in place; it is not meant to strike at underlings."

3.193   The HSC is currently considering a draft Code on health and safety responsibilities of directors, which would apply to incorporated bodies and senior management boards in the public sector. The Code would require that:

(a) a formal acknowledgement is made of the collective role in providing health and safety leadership

(b) all board members would accept their individual responsibility for providing that leadership

(c) all board decisions would reflect the commitment to health and safety, as laid down in the policy statement

(d) the board would ensure the active participation of all staff in improving health and safety

(e) a member of the board would be appointed with specific responsibility for health and safety matters.

3.194   It appears that the Code will not have the status of an Approved Code of Practice but will provide guidance for directors so that they will be aware of the need to promote health and safety matters when making decisions affecting the operation of the business.

Additional powers of the court (s.42)

3.195   If a person is convicted of an offence under any of the relevant statutory provisions in respect of any matter which appears to the court to be something which is in his power to remedy, the court may (in addition to, or instead of, any other punishment) order him, within such time as may be fixed, to take specified steps to remedy the matter. An application may be made to the court for an extension of time within which to comply with the order.

3.196   If a person is convicted of an offence under s.34(4)(c) (acquiring, possessing or using an explosive article or substance in contravention of a relevant statutory provision), the court may order the article or substance to be forfeited or destroyed or dealt with in such other manner as the court may order. Before making a forfeiture order the court must give an opportunity to the owner (or any other person with an interest in the article or substance) an opportunity to show cause why the order should not be made.

3.197   A failure to comply with an order under s.42 (eg if a person fails to take the necessary remedial action) is punishable by a fine of up to £20,000, and/or six months' imprisonment on summary conviction, and an unlimited fine and/or two years' imprisonment if convicted in the Crown Court.

Disqualification of directors

3.198   Under the Company Directors Disqualification Act 1982, s.2, the court may disqualify a person from being a director of a company if he is convicted on an indictable offence, whether on indictment or summarily, if the offence was in connection with the management of the company. A magistrates' court may impose a disqualification for up to 5 years, whilst the higher court may disqualify for up to 15 years. To date, eight directors have been disqualified as a result of serious health and safety offences (eg, a failure to comply with a prohibition notice). The disqualification can be in addition to any other penalty imposed.

Time limits for prosecutions

3.199   By virtue of s.127 of the Magistrates' Courts Act 1980 a prosecution for a summary offence must be commenced by the laying of an information (ie issuing a summons) within six months from the date of the commission of the offence. However, s.34 of HSWA specifies that in certain cases an extension of the time limit may be possible. These are:
  (a) where there has been a special report made by a person holding an investigation under s.14(2)(a) (see paragraph 2.9)
  (b) where a report is made by a person holding an inquiry under s.14(2)(b) (see paragraph 2.10)
  (c) a coroner's inquest is held touching the death of a person which may have been caused by an accident happening at work, or a disease contracted at work
  (d) a public enquiry is held into a death so caused under Scottish legislation

and it appears from the report, inquest or inquiry that a relevant statutory provision was contravened, then summary proceedings may be commenced at any time within three months from the making of the report, or the conclusion of the inquest or inquiry (s.34(1)).

3.200   If an offence is committed by a designer, manufacturer, importer or supplier (ie s.6 offences) then summary proceedings may be commenced at any time within six months from the date when the enforcing authority had sufficient evidence, in its opinion, to justify a prosecution (or, in Scotland, to justify the making of a report to the Lord Advocate). A certificate of an enforcing authority stating that such evidence came to its knowledge on a specified date shall be conclusive evidence of that fact (ss.34(3), (4), (5)). However, this provision appears to be otiose since the passing of the Criminal Law Act 1977 (see *Kemp v Leibherr (GB) Ltd*) because s.6 offences are hybrid offences (ie triable either summarily or on indictment).

3.201   When an offence is committed by reason of a failure to do something within a fixed time, the offence shall be deemed to continue until that thing be done and time will not run until then (s.34(2)).

Indictable offences

3.202   Because of the maxim "Time does not run against the Crown" a prosecution in respect of an indictable offence is never barred by time limits. Since most of the offences under HSWA are triable either way (ie potentially indictable), the six months' time limit has limited effect and applies to those offences which are summary only. Hybrid offences are deemed to be indictable offences so far as time limits for prosecution are concerned (*Kemp v Leibherr (GB) Ltd*).

3.203   However, it will be recalled that Article 6 of the European Convention on Human Rights (see para 1.129) provides that in the determination of civil and criminal rights and obligations, everyone is entitled to a fair and public hearing within a reasonable time. It is therefore likely that a prosecution brought long after the enforcing authority was aware of the essential facts would be dismissed under the Human Rights Act 1998.

CHAPTER 4

Other statutory provisions

Employers' liability insurance

4.1 Under the Employers' Liability (Compulsory Insurance) Regulations 1998 (made under the Employers' Liability (Compulsory Insurance) Act 1969, every employer (subject to certain exceptions, see below) must take out and maintain an insurance policy with an authorised insurer against bodily injury or disease sustained by employees arising out of and in the course of employment. The policy must now provide cover of at least £5 million arising out of any one occurrence, although a "cap" of £10 million is usually imposed by the Association of British Insurers. Where the employer is a holding company, the insurance cover will be in respect of that company together with any subsidiaries as if they were a single employer. The actual policy may not contain certain exemption clauses (eg excluding liability if the employer does not take reasonable care to protect his employees against injury, or if he fails to perform a statutory duty, etc) but can require the employer to contribute a sum to the insurer in respect of the satisfaction of any claim made.

4.2 A contract of insurance is one of *uberrimae fidei*, ie of the utmost good faith, and the proposer must disclose all the information which would affect the mind of a prudent insurer. If, therefore, the employer fails to make such disclosure, the policy may be void, and as well as being without the necessary cover to meet a claim the employer will be liable for a criminal offence. It must be stressed that the Act applies to every employer carrying on a trade or business, including sports and social clubs, as long as a person is an employee within the legal definition. It is not necessary to take out an insurance policy if the employer engages persons as independent contractors, domestic servants (who are not employed for the purposes of a business), close relatives and persons who are not normally resident in Great Britain and who are working here for fewer than 14 consecutive days.

4.3 The certificate of insurance must be in a form prescribed, and kept by employers for 40 years, so that claims relating to insidious injuries (which might not be immediately apparent) can be dealt with. The certificate (or copies) must be displayed at each place of business at which the employer employs any relevant employee of the class or description to which the certificate relates, and must be of such size and legibility that it may be easily seen and read. It must also be reasonably protected from being defaced or damaged.

4.4 An inspector can request to see the certificate of insurance, and also the policy itself (on reasonable notice being given). The inspector may also request sight of policies issued in previous years, so as to investigate possible past infringement.

4.5 There are a number of employers who are exempt from the requirements of the regulations, generally speaking, because they are big enough to carry out their own insurance (eg mutual insurance association for shipowners), or where claims can be settled out of public funds (eg magistrates' courts' committees) or are already under a statutory duty to insure (eg licensees under the Nuclear Installations Act 1965). A full list of exempt employers can be found in Schedule 2 of the regulations. There are also special provisions for offshore installations (see Offshore Installations and Pipeline Works (Management and Administration) Regulations 1995).

4.6 Any employer who is not insured in accordance with the Act shall be guilty of an offence punishable by a fine of £1000 for each day when he is in default and if the offence is committed with the consent, connivance, or facilitated by the neglect of any director, manager, secretary or other officer, then he, as well as the employer (if a body corporate) shall be guilty of an offence and punishable accordingly.

4.7 It is also an offence, punishable by a fine of £1000, to:
    (a) fail to display the certificate or a copy of the insurance certificate
    (b) fail to send the certificate or a copy to the inspector when so required
    (c) fail to produce the certificate or a copy on demand by an inspector
    (d) refuse to allow the inspector to inspect the actual policy document.

4.8 The fact that the employer has a valid policy in force does not confer any automatic right to compensation for an injured employee, as this must be determined by reference to the legal rights of the parties (see Chapter 8). However, it does mean that if an employee succeeds in his claim, there will be funds available with which to satisfy the judgment.

4.9   A failure by an employer to take out the necessary insurance, although a criminal offence, does not give rise to civil liability. In *Richardson v Pitt-Stanley* the plaintiff was injured during the course of his employment. His employer, a limited company, had not taken out employers' liability insurance. The plaintiff obtained judgment against the company, but it went into liquidation, with no assets to satisfy the judgment. The plaintiff then brought an action against the company's director and company secretary, claiming that as they had consented to or connived with a breach of the Act, they were personally liable for the loss sustained by him. The Court of Appeal dismissed his claim. Whether a breach of statutory duty (see paragraph 8.9) which involved criminal liability also gave rise to a civil cause of action was a question of construction. There was no express provision in the Employers' Liability (Compulsory Insurance) Act 1969 creating civil liability on the part of the directors or secretary of a corporate body for failing to insure under the Act, and it was not possible to imply such liability. The Act only created a criminal offence.

Fire certificates and fire precautions

4.10   The law relating to fire certificates and general fire safety is contained in the Fire Precautions Act 1971, as amended by HSWA, the Fire Safety and Safety of Places of Sport Act 1987, the Fire Precautions (Factories, Offices, Shops and Railway Premises) Order 1989 and the Fire Precautions (Workplace) Regulations 1997, as amended.

4.11   The following places of work must have a fire certificate, ie offices, shops, railway premises and factories where:
  (a) more than 20 persons are employed at any one time
  (b) more than 10 persons are employed to work at any one time elsewhere than on the ground floor, or
  (c) the premises is part of a larger building which meets the conditions in (a) or (b) above, or
  (d) explosive or highly flammable materials are stored or used.

4.12   Also, certain other premises, such as hotels and boarding houses with six or more units of sleeping accommodation, must have a fire certificate.

4.13 In respect of certain special premises, in terms of the Fire Certificates (Special Premises) Regulations 1976, as amended, the HSE will issue the fire certificate. Otherwise it will be issued by the local fire authority who can, however, grant an exemption on the ground that the fire risk to occupants is not sufficiently serious as to warrant the issue of a certificate. If exemption is not granted, the authority will inspect the premises and must be satisfied that the means of escape, the method of escape, the means of fighting fire and the fire warning systems are adequate. If they are, a fire certificate will be issued. If not, the fire authority will issue a notice stating the necessary steps which must be taken before a certificate can be issued.

4.14 The Fire Precautions (Factories, Offices, Shops and Railway Premises) Order 1989 provides that certain premises may be exempt from the need to have a fire certificate. The exemption applies to offices, shops, factories and railway premises in which:

    (a) not more than 20 persons work at any one time, and

    (b) not more than 10 people work at any one time elsewhere than on the ground floor.

4.15 This exemption will not arise if the premises form part of a larger building where the total number working there exceeds 20 (or exceeds 10 working elsewhere than on the ground floor) or the premises is a factory where explosive or highly flammable materials are stored or used in sufficient quantities as to constitute a fire risk.

4.16 However, even though the premises may be exempt, the employer must still provide adequate means of escape and adequate means of fighting fire under the Fire Precautions (Workplace) Regulations 1997, as amended.

Fire Precautions (Workplace) Regulations 1997/99

4.17 The Fire Precautions (Workplace) Regulations came into force on 1 December 1997 and are designed to implement parts of the EC Framework and Workplace Directives. However, the European Commission was concerned that the regulations did not entirely meet the requirements of the Directives, particularly with regard to certain "excepted workplaces". The result was that the 1997 Regulations were amended in 1999.

Applications of the regulations

4.18 Every employer shall ensure that he complies with the requirements of the regulations in respect of every workplace (other than an excepted workplace) which is to any extent under his control, so far as those requirements relate to matters within in his control. Further, any person who has control of a workplace (other than an excepted workplace) shall ensure that the workplace complies with any applicable requirement of the regulations, so far as it relates to matters within his control. A person who has, by virtue of any contract or tenancy, an obligation to maintain or repair any workplace, or has an obligation in relation to the safety of any workplace, shall be treated as being the person who has control of the workplace to the extent of his obligation.

Fire-fighting equipment (regulation 4(1))

4.19 Where necessary (eg whether due to the features of a workplace, the activities carried on there, any hazard present, or any other relevant circumstances), in order to safeguard employees in case of fire, a workplace shall be equipped with appropriate fire-fighting equipment, and with fire detectors and alarms. This obligation is to be complied with to the extent that the provision of such equipment and detectors is appropriate, taking into account the dimension and use of the buildings at the workplace, the equipment they contain, the physical and chemical properties of the substances likely to be present, and the maximum number of people that may be present at any one time. Any non-automatic fire-fighting equipment so provided shall be accessible, simple to use, and indicated by signs.

Fire-fighting measures (regulation 4(2))

4.20 Where necessary in order to safeguard the safety of his employees in case of fire, an employer shall take measures for fire fighting in the workplace (taking into account the nature of the activities carried on, the size of the undertaking and the workplace, and persons other than employees who may be present) and, in particular, nominate employees to implement those measures. The number of such nominated employees, their training, and the equipment available to them must be adequate, taking into account the workplace concerned, and the specific hazards involved there. The employer must also arrange any necessary contacts with external emergency services, particularly those involved in rescue work and fire fighting.

Emergency routes and exits (regulation 5)

4.21   Where necessary, in order to safeguard the safety of employees in case of fire, routes to emergency exits from a workplace, and the exits themselves, shall be kept clear at all times. Emergency routes and exits shall lead as directly as possible to a place of safety, and the number, distribution and dimensions of emergency routes and exits shall be adequate having regard to the use, equipment and dimensions of the workplace, and the maximum number of persons that may be present at any one time. In the event of danger, it must be possible for employees to evacuate the workplace quickly and as safely as possible. Emergency doors shall open in the direction of the escape route, sliding or revolving doors shall not be used for exits specifically intended as emergency exits, and emergency doors shall not be so locked or fastened that they cannot be easily and immediately opened by a person in an emergency. Emergency routes and exits must be indicated by signs, and routes and exits requiring illumination shall also be provided with emergency lighting of adequate intensity in case of failure of normal lighting.

Maintenance (regulation 6)

4.22   Where necessary, in order to safeguard the safety of employees in case of fire, the workplace and any equipment and devices provided under regulations 4–5 (above) shall be subject to a suitable system of maintenance, and be maintained in an efficient working order and in good repair.

Excepted workplaces

4.23   The 1997 Regulations did not apply to certain "excepted workplaces", which were:
(a) premises for which a fire certificate was in force (or for which an application for one is pending under the 1971 Act)
(b) premises which had a safety certificate under the Safety of Sports Grounds Act 1975 or the Fire Safety and Safety Places of Sports Act 1987

(c) surface railway stations, and premises to which the Fire Certificate (Special Premises) Regulations 1976 apply.

4.24   However, these particular provisions were removed from the regulations by the Fire Precautions (Workplace) (Amendment) Regulations 1999. The only excepted workplaces now are:
(a) construction sites (see Construction (Health, Safety and Welfare) Regulations 1966)
(b) workplaces in or on a ship (within the meaning of the Merchant Shipping Act 1995)
(c) workplaces in or on offshore installations (see Offshore Installations and Pipelines Works (Management and Administration) Regulations 1995)
(d) workplaces in or on a vehicle for which a licence (or exemption) is in force under the Vehicle Excise and Registration Act 1994
(e) a workplace in a field, wood, or other land forming part of an agricultural undertaking, which is not part of a building and is situated away from the undertaking's main building
(f) workplaces which are used by self-employed persons or are private dwellings.

Amendments to the Management Regulations

4.25   The Fire Precautions (Workplace) Regulations 1997 are not part of the "relevant statutory provisions" for the purposes of issuing approved codes of practices, or enforcement and offences under HSWA (see paragraph 3.1), but they are added to certain provisions found in the Management of Health and Safety at Work Regulations 1999 (see paragraph 5.4). Thus the provisions in the Management Regulations relating to risk assessment (regulation 3), health and safety assistance (regulation 7), co-operation and co-ordination (regulation 11), and host employers' undertakings (regulation 12), now include references to the Fire Precautions (Workplace) Regulations 1997, in addition to the relevant statutory provisions. The requirement for employers to provide information for employees (regulation 10) is extended to include giving employees information relating to the measures taken for fighting fire, and the identity of persons nominated to implement those measures. Where two or more employers share a workplace (regulation 11), they must now also co-ordinate measures in order to comply with the relevant statutory provisions and the Fire Precautions (Workplace) Regulations 1997.

Enforcement and offences

4.26   The Fire Precautions (Workplace) Regulations 1997 are enforced by the fire authorities, acting through inspectors appointed under the Fire Precautions Act 1971.

4.27   A person will be guilty of an offence if being required to do so, he fails to comply with any provision of the workplace fire precautions legislation, and that failure places one or more employees at risk of death or serious injury in case of fire. However, it will be a defence for the person charged to prove that he took all reasonable precautions and exercised due diligence to avoid the commission of an offence.

4.28   Where a fire authority is of the opinion that a person has failed to comply with any provision of workplace fire precautions legislation, the authority may serve an enforcement notice, stating why they are of that opinion, specifying the steps they consider necessary to remedy that failure, requiring those steps to be taken within 21 days, and explaining how, where, within what period and on what grounds an appeal may be made against the notice. The appeal must be made within 21 days of the serving of the notice to the magistrates' court (or sheriffs court in Scotland), and the bringing of the appeal suspends the notice until the appeal has been disposed of or withdrawn. The court may cancel the notice, or affirm it, either in its original form or with such modifications as the court thinks fit. It is an offence to contravene any requirement imposed by an enforcement notice.

Employee consultation

4.29   The Safety Representatives and Safety Committee Regulations 1977, and the Health and Safety (Consultation with Employees) Regulations 1996 are amended so as to require consultation with employees over the arrangements for appointing or nominating employees for the purpose of implementing the measures for fire safety (see regulation 4(2) above).

Proposed legislation

4.30   The Government has recently published a consultation document seeking views on a radical overhaul of all fire safety legislation, which is currently considered to be somewhat of a patchwork quilt. The proposals, if adopted, would lead to the repeal of the 1971 Act and the 1997 and 1999 regulations, as well as a number of other legislative provisions, and take fire safety out of the ambit of HSWA, with a new regime to be enforced by the fire authorities. However, there appears to be a delay in finalising the proposals.

Protection of the environment

4.31   Basically, health and safety legislation is concerned with the protection of workers and those affected by work activity. There is an obvious link between these objectives and the need for general environmental protection, and in many cases there is an overlap. As governments became more aware of the need to prevent pollution of the environment, both on a national and international level, new strategies have been developed, and complex legislative provisions enacted.

4.32   The Environmental Protection Act 1990 (EPA), together with other relevant legislation (Water Resources Act 1991, the unrepealed parts of the Control of Pollution Act 1974, etc) provide the basic framework of pollution control legislation. The 1990 Act established two systems of control: Integrated Pollution Control, administered by the Environment Agency (formerly HM Inspectorate of Pollution (HMIP)) in England and Wales, and the Scottish Environment Protection Agency (formerly HM Industrial Pollution Inspectorate) in Scotland; and control of air pollution for all other specified processes is the responsibility of local authorities. These authorities are responsible for all aspects of pollution control carried on by polluting industrial processes. Certain prescribed processes require prior authorisation before they may be operated and such permission will not be granted unless various conditions are met, including ensuring that the Best Available Techniques Not Entailing Excessive Cost (BATNEEC) are used for preventing the release of substances prescribed into any environmental medium and for rendering harmless any other substance which might cause harm if so released. The Department of the Environment has issued a guidance document giving its interpretation of BATNEEC. "Best" means the best technology available anywhere in the world; patented processes are "available" if they are available under licence; "techniques" include operational factors (numbers and qualifications of staff, training, supervision, etc) as well as the design, construction, lay out and maintenance of buildings; to determine whether the technique entails "excessive cost" one considers whether the additional costs are justified by the corresponding reduction in emissions. To enable the enforcing authorities to apply consistent standards when applying BATNEEC, process Guidance Notes have been prepared, to which they may have regard.

4.33   It is a criminal offence to break a condition to which an authorised process is subject. Additionally, in criminal proceedings, it shall be for the operator to show that there was no better technique available not entailing excessive cost than the one used. Enforcing authorities have power to issue prohibition notices, they may vary authorisations already granted and revoke them. There is a right of appeal to the Secretary of State.

4.34   Integrated pollution control inspectors have very wide powers under the Act. They may enter, inspect and examine premises, take measurements, photographs, samples, etc require persons to give information and produce documents, and so forth, very much on the lines of HSE inspectors (see paragraph 2.38). Public registers will be kept of applications for authorisations and other information, with certain safeguards for the necessity for withholding information on the grounds of national security or commercial confidentiality.

4.35   EC Directive 91/61/EC (Integrated Pollution Prevention and Control) was largely inspired by UK legislation, but there were certain differences which would have made full implementation difficult. Consequently, the Pollution Prevention and Control Act 1999 was passed to enable a coherent integrated regime to be implemented by regulation, which will be, in effect, superimposed on the 1990 Act (see paragraph 3.90).

4.36   The Genetically Modified Organisms (Contained Use) Regulations 2000 implement EC Directives 90/219/EEC, 94/51/EC, and 98/81/EC, and replace the 1992 Regulations. Any activity involving genetic modification of micro-organisms is prohibited unless the person undertaking the activity has ensured that a risk assessment has been carried out. The person carrying out the assessment is required to establish a safety committee to advise. Before the first use of any premises involving such activity, the HSE must be notified, and certain specified information provided. The consent of the HSE must be obtained before the work commences, which may be varied or revoked. A person who carries out an activity which involved the genetic modification of micro-organisms, or organisms other than micro-organisms, must apply the appropriate containment measures. All waste containing genetically modified micro-organisms must be made inactive, and there is a requirement for enhanced public access to information via an expanded public register of notifications.

4.37 The Biological Agents Directive (90/679/EEC) has been implemented in the UK by incorporation into the COSHH regulations 1999 (see paragraph 6.316).

Food safety

4.38 The provisions of the Food Safety Act 1990 are peripheral to health and safety at work legislation, but are mentioned here in brief for the sake of completeness. Generally speaking, local authorities are to be the "food authorities" and they will appoint "authorised officers" (usually Environmental Health Officers (EHOs)) to act in matters arising under the legislation. It is an offence to render food so as to be injurious to health (eg by adding or abstracting anything), or to sell food not complying with food safety requirements. An authorised officer may inspect and seize suspected food and may also serve improvement and/or prohibition notices. In many ways the Act is an enabling Act, and the precise measures to be taken in order to deal with its provisions will be found in regulations. The Food Safety (General Food Hygiene) Regulations 1995 require food proprietors to ensure that food preparagraphtion, processing, manufacturing, packaging, storing, transportation, distribution and sale are carried out in a hygienic manner. The Regulations also contain provisions relating to training, personal hygiene of food handlers, reporting of diseases capable of being transmitted through food, and require proprietors to carry out food safety risk assessments. The temperature of food is controlled by the Food Safety (Temperature Control) Regulations 1995, which define certain temperatures which must be achieved during various food-related processes.

Product safety

4.39 The General Product Safety Regulations 1994 are designed to implement Directive (92/59/EEC), and impose requirements concerning the safety of products intended for consumers, placed on the market by producers or supplied by distributors. There is a general obligation that a product shall not be placed on the market unless it is safe, the producer must provide information to the consumer informing of any risks the product might present, and the measures to be taken to counter those risks. Distributors must act with due care to ensure the product is safe and the relevant information is provided. The regulations do not apply to second-hand products which are antiques, or products supplied for repair or reconditioning before use, or where there are EU rules governing the safety of the particular product.

Health, safety and welfare in factories

4.40   As has been noted, one of the main objects of HSWA was the repeal of much of pre-1974 legislation, to be replaced by new regulations and codes of practice. A prime candidate for repeal was the Factories Act 1961, which, although a major source of civil and criminal litigation, only gave statutory protection to those working in factories (as defined). Much of the Act has already been repealed, and replaced by regulations applicable to all employment situations (eg first aid, fire precautions, removal of dust and fumes, use of lead compounds, etc). Following the introduction of the "six pack" regulations in 1992 (see Chapters 5 and 6), further parts of the Act were repealed, and are only of relevance insofar as they concern litigation arising out of incidents which occurred when they were in force.

4.41   The Factories Act 1961 only applies to factories as defined under the Act (s.175, and see *J & F Stone Lighting and Radio Ltd v Haygarth*). Its provisions were designed to protect all persons who worked in a factory, whether or not they were employed by the owner, occupier or employer, including self-employed persons, visitors, etc.

4.42   The following provisions of the Factories Act will remain in force for the time being.

Medical examinations (s.10A)

4.43   If an Employment Medical Advisor (EMA) (see Chapter 2) is of the opinion that a person's health has been or is being injured (or that it is possible that he is or will be injured) by reason of the work he is doing, the EMA may serve a notice on the factory occupier requiring the occupier to permit a medical examination of that person to take place. The notice will state the time, date and place of the examination, which must be at reasonable times during working hours. Every person to whom it relates shall be informed of its contents and of the fact that he is free to attend for that purpose. If the examination is to take place in the factory, suitable accommodation shall be provided.

Teagle openings (s.24)

4.44   Every teagle opening or similar doorway used for hoisting or lowering goods or materials shall be securely fenced and shall be provided with a handrail on each side. The fencing shall be properly maintained and, except when the hoisting or lowering of goods or materials is being carried on, shall be kept in position.

Explosive or inflammable substances (s.31)

4.45   Where, in connection with any grinding, sieving or other process giving rise to dust which may cause an explosion on ignition, all practicable steps shall be taken to prevent such explosion by enclosure of the plant, by removal or prevention of accumulation of dust, and by the exclusion or effective enclosure of possible sources of ignition. This section is designed to deal with the dangers inherent in the grinding of coal or other carbonaceous material and other dust likely to explode if ignited. Unless the plant is so constructed as to withstand the pressure likely to be produced from any such explosion, all practicable steps shall be taken to restrict the spread and effects by the provision of chokes, baffles, vents or other equally effective appliances. Special provisions must be taken in connection with the grinding of magnesium (Magnesium (Grinding of Castings and Other Articles) Special Regulations 1946).

4.46   Before any part of a plant which contains explosive or flammable gas or vapour under pressure is opened, the flow shall be effectively stopped by a stop valve or otherwise, and before the fastening is removed, the gas or pressure must be reduced to atmospheric pressure.

4.47   Any tank plant or vessel which has contained any explosive or flammable substance shall not be subjected to any welding, brazing or soldering operation, or any cutting operation, which involves the application of heat for the purpose of taking it apart unless all practicable steps have been taken to remove the substance, or to render it non-explosive or non-flammable. Once such operation has been carried out, no explosive or inflammable substance shall be allowed to get into the relevant container until the metal has cooled sufficiently to prevent the risk of ignition taking place. The HSE has the power to make certain exemptions from these latter provisions.

Water sealed gas holders (s.39)

4.48 Every gasholder which has a storage capacity of at least 140m³/5000 cubic feet shall be of sound construction and properly maintained. They must be examined externally by a competent person at least every two years, and a record containing the prescribed particulars entered into or attached to the general register (see the Gasholders (Record of Examinations) Order 1938).

Certificate of fitness (s.119)

4.49 If an inspector is of the opinion that the employment of a young person in a factory or a particular process is prejudicial to his health or to the health of other persons, he may serve a written notice to this effect on the occupier. The latter will not be able to continue to employ that young person in that place or on that process until the employment medical adviser has examined him and certified that he is fit to work in the factory or on the process.

Special applications (ss.121–127)

4.50 These sections make special provisions for applying the requirements of the Act (with appropriate modifications) to parts of buildings let off as a separate factory, electrical stations, charitable or reformatory institutions, docks, wharves, warehouses, ships, building operations and works of engineering construction.

Notices and returns (s.137)

4.51 Every person who occupies premises as a factory must, one month prior to going into occupation, send to the inspector a notice stating the name or title of the occupier, the postal address of the factory, the nature of the work, stating whether or not mechanical power is being used, the name of the local authority and other prescribed particulars.

General Register (s.140)

4.52 Every factory shall have a General Register (Form F31 is available for this purpose, obtainable from HSE Books). The following information is still currently required to be recorded in the Register (see Factories Act General Register Order 1973):

Part 1   Name and address of occupier, nature of work carried on Certificate as to means of escape in case of fire
Part 2   Particulars of young persons employed
Part 5   Particulars of washing, painting, whitewashing, etc.

4.53 There are separate registers for docks wharves, quays and warehouses, and building operations and works of engineering construction.

4.54 Attached to the General Register shall be kept all other matters which are required to so be, and other matters specified in the appropriate regulations.

4.55 The General Register shall be kept for inspection by an inspector or employment medical advisers for at least two years after the date of the last entry.

Enforcement of the Act (s.155)

4.56 The main liability for criminal penalties is placed on the occupier of the factory, or, in certain cases, the owner. If a person contravenes the provisions of a regulation or order made under the Act which expressly imposes a duty on him, then that person shall be guilty of an offence, and the owner or occupier shall not be guilty of an offence unless it is proved that he failed to take all reasonable steps to prevent the contravention (s.155(2)). The onus is on the prosecution to prove that the occupier or owner failed to take all reasonable steps to prevent the contravention (*Wright v Ford Motor Co Ltd*).

Penalties

4.57 The Factories Act 1961 is one of the existing statutory provisions for the purpose of s.33(3) of HSWA (see Schedule 1), and therefore offences are punishable by a fine of up to £5000 on summary conviction and an unlimited fine in respect of a conviction on indictment (Criminal Justice Act 1992, ss.35–62).

Application to the Crown

4.58   The Act applies to factories belonging to or in the occupation of the Crown and to building operations or works of engineering construction undertaken by or on behalf of the Crown (s.173).

Health, safety and welfare in offices, shops and railway premises

4.59   Following the passing of the "six pack" regulations (see Chapter 6) most of the provisions of the Offices, Shops and Railway Premises Act 1963 have been repealed (except in relation to registrars of births, marriages and deaths and members of a police force, when the Act will still apply).

4.60   The Act applies to offices, shops and railway premises, defined in s.1 as being premises wherein persons are employed under a contract of employment (or apprenticeship) for a total of 21 or more hours a week. Thus if only voluntary labour is used, the Act does not apply (however, other replacement legislation will, eg Workplace Regulations or PUWER). Nor does the Act apply if the only persons employed are close family members. Also excluded are premises of home workers, premises which form part of a factory, premises to which an exemption order applies, or premises used for a temporary or transitional purpose of not more than six weeks in the case of a fixed structure or six months in the case of a moveable structure.

4.61   The following provisions remain in force for the time being.

Multi-occupancy buildings (s.42)

4.62   A building which is under the ownership of one person but parts of which are leased or licensed to another must have clean common parts, and all furniture, furnishings and fittings in such common parts shall be kept in a clean state. Effective provision shall be made for securing and maintaining in common parts suitable and sufficient lighting (whether natural or artificial), and all glazed windows and skylights shall, so far as is reasonably practicable, be kept clean on both sides and free from obstruction (except when whitewashed or shaded for the purpose of reducing heat or glare). Floors, stairs, steps, passages and gangways shall be of sound construction and properly maintained, and shall, so far as is reasonably practicable, be kept free from any substance likely to cause any person to slip. Staircases shall be provided with a substantial handrail or handhold, and any open stairway shall be guarded by the provision and maintenance of efficient means of preventing any person from accidentally falling through the space.

4.63   In the event of a contravention of this section, the owner of the building will be guilty of an offence.

Notification of employment (s.49)

4.64   Before a person begins to employ persons in any office, shop or railway premises, he shall serve on the appropriate authority (ie the enforcement authority) two copies of a notice containing the necessary information. The Schedule to the Notifications of Employment of Persons Order 1964 contains the notice in a prescribed form for use for the purpose of this section. A failure to comply may lead to a fine on summary conviction.

Offences (s.63)

4.65   Since most of the obligations imposed by the Act are placed on the occupier of the premises, it is he who will be primarily liable. If the Act provides that some other person shall be held responsible as well as the occupier, then both shall be liable. The owner is liable in certain multi-occupancy situations (see above).

Defences (s.67)

4.66   It shall be a defence for a person charged with an offence under the Act or a regulation to prove that he used all due diligence to secure compliance with that provision (see paragraph 1.97). This defence is, of course, applicable to criminal proceedings, not to civil liability, although in the latter case a plea of "no negligence" may equally succeed. "Due diligence" and "reasonable care" are similar concepts. In *J H Dewhurst Ltd v Coventry Corporation* the defence of due diligence failed, for although the defendants had given the boy instructions, put up notices, and had received regular visits from the inspectors without adverse comment, the court considered that in view of the statutory prohibition, there was a special obligation to provide the necessary supervision. However, the defence succeeded in *Tesco Supermarkets Ltd v Natrass* (see paragraph 1.97).

Power to modify agreements (s.73)

4.67   If a person is prevented from doing any structural or other alteration to the premises necessary to comply with a provision of the Act because of the terms of a lease or agreement, he may apply to the local county court, which may make an order modifying or setting aside the terms of that lease or agreement as the court thinks just and equitable. If such alterations do become necessary, the court may also apportion the expense of doing so between the parties having an interest in the premises.

Application of the Act (s.83)

4.68   Insofar as the Act imposes duties which may give rise to civil liability (based on an action in tort) the Act is binding on the Crown (except in respect of the Armed Forces). So far as enforcement is concerned, although the HSE can inspect Crown premises it is not possible to prosecute the Crown in the criminal courts.

Offshore Safety Act 1992

4.69   This Act makes existing offshore safety legislation "relevant statutory provisions" for the purpose of HSWA. The effect is to transfer responsibility for offshore safety from the Department of Energy to the HSC/HSE, thus making the HSE responsible for the enforcement of all safety legislation relating to offshore activities. Further, the reform of existing offshore legislation can now be achieved by means of health and safety regulations made under s.15 of HSWA.

4.70   The Offshore Installations (Safety Case) Regulations 1992 came into force in 1993 (except for certain requirements relating to well operations which came into force in 1995). These regulations require operators and owners of offshore installations to submit a "safety case" to the HSE. The objective of the safety case is to describe management systems and demonstrate that safety standards are adequate to avoid major accidents.

Working in agriculture

4.71   Every year a number of people are killed working in agriculture and related industries. There are thousands of non-fatal accidents, but it is suspected that there is considerable under-reporting in the industry.

4.72   Agricultural workers frequently work alone in remote places where immediate attention is not readily available. Supervision is minimal. The industry is highly mechanised, yet the general working environment is far from ideal and many dangerous substances are used. These facts illustrate the need for strong protective legislative measures and a greater need for educating workers in safe practices and procedures. The annual reports from the HSE's Agricultural Inspectorate discuss many of the hazards which arise whilst working on farms and considers some of the special problems. The Agricultural Industry Advisory Committee is engaged in a wide programme of work in looking at improvements which can be made to increase safety in the industry generally. A permanent office and a Health and Safety Information Centre has been established at Stoneleigh in Warwickshire, which aims to provide up-to-the-minute advice and information on a wide range of health and safety problems.

4.73   Following the introduction of the "six pack" regulations (see Chapters 5 and 6), most of the relevant provisions of the Agriculture (Safety, Health and Welfare Provisions) Act 1956 have been repealed. Still in force is s.7 of the Act which provides that it is an offence to cause or permit a child to ride on or to drive a vehicle or machine or agricultural implement in contravention of the Prevention of Accidents to Children in Agriculture Regulations 1998. These provide that no child (ie a person below the age of 13) shall ride on certain agricultural vehicles while they are being used in the course of agricultural operations. The vehicles in question are tractors, self-propelled agricultural machines, trailers, trailers into which a conveyor mechanism is built, machines mounted on or towed by tractors, binders or mowers drawn by animals. A child may ride on the floor of a trailer or on any load carried by a trailer, provided it has four sides each of which is higher than the load. A child shall not drive a tractor or self-propelled vehicle or machine while it is being used in the course of agricultural operations, or ride on agricultural implements.

4.74   HSE has issued a Code of Practice and Guidance Notes (ACOP L116: *Preventing accidents to children in agriculture*) on preventing accidents to children in agriculture.

4.75   The Health and Safety (Repeals and Revocations) Regulations 1996 have repealed (under the Deregulation and Contracting Out Act 1994) a number of legislative provisions relating to agriculture; these were outdated and have been superseded by the "six pack" regulations. Thus, regulations that specifically dealt with threshers and balers, ladders, field machinery, workplaces, poisonous substances, etc are no longer in force.

CHAPTER 5

Health and safety management

5.1 In this Chapter, we shall consider some of the legal requirements which are the minimum requirements of a health and safety management programme.

5.2 Successful health and safety management begins with a commitment by all concerned within an organisation, but in particular, by the decision-makers, whose actions (or inaction) will have a powerful influence on the attitudes of the rest of the workforce. But the commitment should not be just lip-service. A structured and planned approach must be adopted and implemented, and appropriate resources made available. Health and safety must always be regarded as a prime responsibility of all levels of management, and not solely of those who have been given specific assignments. An attitude of indifference or a lack of knowledge displayed by those who are in senior positions will quickly percolate throughout the organisation.

5.3 The success of a health and safety management programme will be proportionate to the effort put into a structured approach to the problem. It is generally accepted that there are five steps to be adopted, and the input required at each stage will usually depend on the particular problems encountered and solutions adopted. HSE has published a booklet HSG65: *Successful health and safety management*, to which reference may be made. Also the British Standards publication, BS 8800: 1996 *Guide to occupational health and safety management* may be of use.

1. *Policy:* The policy on health and safety should not just be confined to the written statement which needs to be given to all employees under s.2(3) of HSWA (see paragraph 3.59), but a policy which demands that health and safety considerations be given top priority by all levels of management, and a commitment to find the resources to meet that policy. Appropriate health and safety rules and procedures should be adopted not only with regard to systems of work, but for purchasing tools, equipment, materials, services, etc. All the activities of the organisation can be considered with a view to the implementation of the policy.

2. *Organisation:* The overall responsibility for overseeing the implementation of the policy should be a function of senior

management, but particular responsibilities can be assigned in specific areas. Effective communication will be needed, competence established, and participation encouraged at all levels.

3. *Planning:* The actual implementation of the policy through the established health and safety organisation will be the subject of detailed planning. Risk assessments should be undertaken, training needs identified, shortcomings noted and rectified, control methods introduced, and so on. Each organisation will adopt the methods most suited to deal with its own particular problems, and find its own solutions.

4. *Measuring performance:* Once predetermined standards and objectives have been laid down, it will then be possible to measure performance, so as to identify those areas where further action needs be taken and further improvements made. It should also identify underlying causes or weaknesses, and generally tighten up on existing health and safety practices.

5. *Reviewing performance:* Health and safety audits, operated systematically and on a regular basis, will then reveal the success or otherwise of the health and safety management programme. Statistics can be analysed, incidents examined, lessons learned, and recommendations for further action made. New or developing knowledge can be noted and considered, and the experiences of other organisations taken into account. Successful health and safety management frequently depends on the ability to foresee problems before they arise, rather than dealing with them once they have arisen.

Management of Health and Safety at Work Regulations 1999

5.4   The original Management Regulations were passed in 1992 in order to implement the provisions of the Framework Directive (89/391/EEC) and the Temporary Workers Directive (91/383/EEC). The regulations were amended in 1994 in order to implement the Pregnant Workers Directive (92/85/EEC) and again in 1997 in order to implement the Protection of Young Persons at Work Directive (94/33/EEC). Further amendments were made in the Fire Precautions (Workplace) Regulations 1997.

5.5 All these provisions have now been consolidated in the Management of Health and Safety at Work Regulations 1999, which came into force at the end of that year, with additional provisions relating to the general principles of prevention set out in Directive (89/391/EEC), and some further minor amendments to the Health and Safety (First Aid) Regulations 1981, Mines Miscellaneous Health and Safety Provisions Regulations 1995, Construction (Health Safety and Welfare) Regulations 1996, and Fire Precautions (Workplace) Regulations 1997.

5.6 The regulations apply to all work activities to which HSWA applies, including offshore activities and trainees, but not to merchant shipping. The Secretary of Defence may, in the interests of national security, exempt the armed forces from certain obligations, (other than regulations 16–18), and members of the armed forces from certain requirements (other than regulation 14). Generally speaking, the breach of a duty imposed by the regulations does not confer a right of action in any civil proceedings, other than regulations 16(1) (risk assessment for new or expectant mothers) and regulation 19 (protection for young workers). The reason is that the regulations are to be regarded as an extension of the duties set out in ss.2–8 of HSWA, which is essentially a criminal statute, but the exceptions are required in order to comply with the provisions of Directive (891/391/EEC) regarding adequate remedies.

5.7 The 1999 Regulations were accompanied by a new Approved Code of Practice (ACOP L21).

Risk assessment (regulation 3)

5.8 Every employer shall make a suitable and sufficient assessment of:
  (a) the risks to the health and safety of his employees to which they are exposed whilst they are at work, and
  (b) the risks to the health and safety of persons not in his employment arising out of or in connection with the conduct by him of his undertaking,

for the purpose of identifying the measures he needs to take to comply with the requirements and prohibitions imposed on him by or under the relevant statutory provisions and Part II of the Fire Precautions

(Workplace) Regulations 1997. A similar duty is placed on self-employed persons, with regard to the risks to his own health and safety, and the safety of others not in his employment.

5.9 The assessment shall be reviewed by the employer or self-employed person if there is reason to suspect it is no longer valid, or there has been a significant change in the matters to which it relates. If on review, changes to the assessment are required, these are to be made.

5.10 An employer shall not employ a young person (ie under the age of 18) unless he has made or reviewed an assessment, taking particular account of:
  (a) the inexperience, lack of awareness of risks and the immaturity of young persons
  (b) the fitting out and layout of the workplace and the workstation
  (c) the nature, degree and duration of exposure to physical, biological and chemical agents
  (d) the form, range and use of work equipment and the way it is handled
  (e) the organisation of processes and activities
  (f) the extent of health and safety training provided or to be provided to young persons, and
  (g) the risks from agents, processes and work listed in the Annex to Council Directive (94/133/EC) on the protection of young people at work (Annex A deals with ionising radiation, work in high pressure atmosphere, biological and certain chemical agents, and certain types of work connected with explosives, high voltage electrical hazards, dangerous animals, dangerous gases, and work where there is a risk of a structural collapse, etc).

5.11 The requirement to make an assessment for young persons does not apply to occasional work or short-term working involving domestic service in a private household, or work regulated as not being harmful, damaging or dangerous to young people in a family undertaking.

5.12 If the employer employs five or more employees, he shall record the significant findings of the assessment, and any group of his employees identified by it as being specially at risk. Normally this would be done in writing, but it could be recorded by some other means (eg electronically) as long as it is retrievable for use or examination.

5.13   Although Regulation 3 does not give rise to civil liability, a failure to carry out a risk assessment, which would have identified a potential source of injury (eg the need to vary working practices so as to avoid work related upper limb disorder) could be evidence of negligence in a civil claim for damages (*Godfrey v Bernard Matthews plc*). In a criminal case, if it is alleged that an employer failed to carry out an adequate and sufficient risk assessment so as to properly assess the risks involved, the prosecution must specify in what respects the risk assessment was alleged to be inadequate. It is not enough merely to rely on the fact that an accident happened (*Heermac VOF v Munro*).

5.14   The ACOP suggests that a risk assessment involves an identification of the hazards, and an estimation of the risks, taking into account the existing precautions available and used, and a consideration of what else needs to be done. The employer (or self-employed person) should be able to decide what measures need to be taken in order to comply with his duties under the relevant statutory provisions.

5.15   A risk assessment will be "suitable and sufficient" if it enables the employer (or self-employed person) to identify the risks arising from work. To do this, employers should look at appropriate sources of information, eg relevant legislation, suppliers' manuals, manufacturers' instructions, the trade press, or seek advice from a competent source. The risk assessment should be appropriate to the nature of the work, and identify the period of time for which it is likely to remain valid. It should identify what the hazards are, who might be exposed to harm (and how) as well as evaluate the risks. This will enable the employer to prioritise the measures which need to be taken to comply with the relevant statutory provisions.

5.16   Risk assessments should be reviewed at regular intervals, but in particular when the nature of the work changes or there has been a further appreciation of hazards or risks. The monitoring of health and safety arrangements required by regulation 5 may reveal further hazards which can be the subject of a revised assessment.

5.17   There are no fixed rules about how a risk assessment should be carried out, for this will depend on the nature of the undertaking and the type of hazards and risks present. For small undertakings it can be a simple process based on judgement, and will require no specialist skills or complicated techniques. At the other extreme, it may be the basis for a complete safety case. In intermediate cases, specialist advice may be necessary in respect of unfamiliar risks. Separate assessment exercises may be necessary in particular operations or groups of hazards. The views of employees, safety representatives, advisers, etc, should be taken into account. A structured approach should always be adopted.

5.18　　In particular, the ACOP suggests that a risk assessment should:
(a) ensure that the significant risks and hazards are addressed
(b) ensure that all aspects of the work activitiy are reviewed, including routine and non-routine activities, and those which are not under the immediate supervision of the employer, eg relating to contractors, loaned employees, the self-employed, homeworkers, mobile workers, etc
(c) take account of non-routine operations, including maintenance, cleaning operations, loading and unloading of vehicles, emergency response arrangements, etc
(d) take account of the management of incidents such as interruptions to the work activity, including the procedures which should be followed
(e) be systematic in identifying the risks and hazards — activities should be looked at in groups, eg machinery, transport, substances, electrical, etc, and sometimes an operational approach is appropriate, eg production, despatch, office work, etc
(f) take account of the way the work is organised, and the effect this can have on health
(g) take account of the risks to the public
(h) take account of the need to consider fire risks — if necessary, a separate assessment should be carried out.

5.19　　Where an assessment is required to be made under some other regulation (eg COSHH, etc see paragraph 6.316) which will cover in part the obligation to make an assessment under the Management Regulations, it need not be repeated as long as it remains valid. On the other hand, an assessment under the Management Regulations may reveal that a further assessment should be made under the other regulation.

Principles of prevention to be applied (regulation 4)

5.20　　Where the employer implements any preventative and protective measures, he shall do so on the basis of the principles set out in Schedule 1 to the regulations. This involves:

(a) avoiding risks
(b) evaluating risks which cannot be avoided
(c) combating the risks at source
(d) adapting the work to the individual, especially as regards the design of the workplace, the choice of work equipment, and the choice of working and production methods, with a view, in particular, to alleviating monotonous work and work at a pre-determined work-rate and to reduce their effect on health
(e) adapting to technical progress
(f) replacing the dangerous by the non-dangerous or less dangerous
(g) developing a coherent overall prevention policy which covers technology, organisation of work, working conditions, social relationships and the influence of factors relating to the working environment
(h) giving collective protective measures priority over individual protective measures, and
(i) giving appropriate instructions to employees.

Health and safety arrangements (regulation 5)

5.21   Every employer shall make and give effect to such arrangements as are appropriate, having regard to the nature of his activities and the size of his undertaking, for the effective planning, organisation, control monitoring and review of the preventative and protective measures. Where the employer employs five or more employees, he shall record these arrangements.

5.22   The ACOP suggests that a health and safety management system should consist of five elements:
  (a) *Planning*. Once a systematic approach to the completion of a risk assessment has been adopted, priorities and objectives can be set for eliminating hazards and reducing risks. A programme should be adopted, deadlines set, risk control methods selected, and performance standards developed.
  (b) *Organisation*. This includes involving employees and their representatives in carrying out risk assessments, deciding on preventative protective measures, and implementing those requirements. Effective means of communication should be established, health and safety information communicated to employees, and competence secured by the provision of adequate information, instruction and training.

(c) *Control*. Health and safety responsibilities should be well co-ordinated, those with responsibilities given time and resources to discharge them effectively, standards set, and adequate and appropriate supervision provided.

(d) *Monitoring*. Adequate routine inspections and checks should ensure that preventative and protective measures are in place and are effective. The underlying causes of incidents and accidents should be adequately investigated, remedial action taken, and lessons learnt.

(e) *Review*. Priorities established for any necessary remedial action discovered necessary as a result of the monitoring, to ensure that suitable action is taken in good time and is completed. The whole management system needs to be reviewed to ensure that it remains effective.

Health surveillance (regulation 6)

5.23   Every employer shall ensure that his employees are provided with such health surveillance as is appropriate having regard to the risks to their health and safety which are identified by the assessment.

5.24   The ACOP suggests that once the risk assessment has been done, it should be possible to identify the circumstances when health surveillance is required by specific health and safety regulations (eg under COSHH, etc). Health surveillance should also be introduced when:

(a) there is an identifiable work related disease or adverse health condition

(b) valid detection techniques are available

(c) there is a reasonable likelihood that the disease or condition may occur under the particular working conditions, and

(d) surveillance is likely to further the protection of the employees to be covered.

5.25   The object of surveillance is to detect adverse effects of ill-health at an early stage, thus preventing further harm. Additionally, the effectiveness of control measures can be checked, as well as the accuracy of the risk assessment. If health surveillance is appropriate, individual health records should be kept. Health surveillance procedures will depend, for their suitability, on the circumstances.

Health and safety assistance (regulation 7)

5.26   Every employer shall employ one or more competent persons to assist him in undertaking the measures he needs to take to comply with the requirements of the relevant statutory provisions and the Fire Precautions (Workplace) Regulations. This does not apply to a self employed person (who is not in partnership with another person), where he has sufficient training and experience or knowledge to undertake those measures himself. Nor does regulation 7 apply to a partnership which employs persons where at least one of the partners has sufficient training and experience or knowledge and other qualities to carry out the measures needed to ensure compliance with the statutory requirements and prohibitions, and can properly assist the partnership in carrying out those measures.

5.27   If the employer appoints more than one person, he shall make arrangements to ensure adequate co-operation between them. The number of persons appointed and the time and means made available to them to fulfil their functions shall be adequate having regard to the size of the undertaking, the risks to which employees are exposed, and the distribution of those risks throughout the undertaking.

5.28   The person designated to provide health and safety assistance need not be an employee of the employer. However, if an outside consultant is appointed, the employer must inform him of all the factors known to the employer which may affect the health and safety of any person who may be affected by the conduct of the undertaking. The employer must also give the outside consultant access to the information referred to in regulation 10 (below), as well as details of persons working under a fixed term contract or employed in an employment business. But if there is a competent person in the employer's employment, he shall be appointed as a safety assistant under regulation 7 in preference to an outside consultant.

5.29   A person shall be regarded as being competent if he has sufficient training and experience or knowledge and other qualities to enable him properly to assist in carrying out the measures which the employer needs to take in order to comply with the statutory provisions.

5.30   The ACOP states that it is the employer's responsibility to ensure that those who are appointed to assist with health and safety measures are competent to carry out the tasks assigned to them (taking into account the complexities of the work situation and the skills required), and to ensure that they are given adequate information and support. The appointment of a competent person should be included among the health and safety arrangements under regulation 5 (above), and safety representatives should be consulted on the arrangements for the appointment for competent assistance.

Procedures for serious and imminent danger and for danger areas (regulation 8)

5.31 Every employer shall establish, and give effect to, appropriate procedures to be followed in the event of serious and imminent dangers to persons at work in his undertaking. Competent persons shall be nominated to implement evacuation procedures. The procedures shall, so far as is practicable, require any persons at work who are exposed to serious and imminent danger to be informed of the nature of the hazard, and of the steps to be taken to protect them from it. They should be able to stop work and immediately proceed to a place of safety and, save in exceptional circumstances specified in the procedures (eg emergency services) require the persons concerned to be prevented from resuming work while there is a danger.

5.32 The employer shall ensure that none of his employees has access to any area occupied by him which it is necessary to restrict access on grounds of health and safety unless the employee concerned has received adequate health and safety instruction.

Contacts with external services (regulation 9)

5.33 Every employer shall ensure that any necessary contacts with external services are arranged, particularly as regards first aid, emergency medical care, and rescue work.

5.34 The ACOP states that, procedures should be established for any worker to follow if situations presenting serious and imminent danger were to arise. This should set out the nature of the risk and how to respond to it, additional procedures to cover risks beyond those caused by fire and bombs (eg a release of toxic gases), the additional responsibilities of particular employees who may have specific tasks to perform (eg shutting down plant), the role, responsibilities and authority of the competent people nominated to implement detailed action, and details of how and when the procedures are to be activated so that employees can proceed in good time to a place of safety.

5.35   Emergency procedures should be written down, under regulation 5 (above) and made known to the safety assistants under regulation 7 (above), to employees under regulation 10 (below) and to non-employees under regulation 12 (below). They should form part of any induction course (regulation 13, below). Test exercises should be carried out.

5.36   Work should not be resumed after an emergency if a serious danger remains. After the emergency has passed, consideration should be given to a review of the risk assessment.

Information for employees (regulation 10)

5.37   Every employer shall provide his employees with comprehensible and relevant information on:
  (a) the risks to their health and safety identified by the assessment
  (b) the preventative and protective measures
  (c) procedures dealing with serious and imminent dangers, danger areas, and fire fighting measures
  (d) the identity of persons nominated to implement evacuation procedures and fire fighting measures; and
  (e) the risks which have been notified to him by another employer with whom the workplace is shared.

5.38   Before employing a child (ie a person who is not above compulsory school leaving age) the employer shall provide the child's parents with comprehensible and relevant information on:
  (a) the risks to health identified by the assessment
  (b) the preventative and protective measures
  (c) any information provided to him by another employer with whom the workplace is shared concerning the risks to the employees' health and safety arising from the conduct by that other employer of his undertaking (regulation 11(1)(c)).

5.39   However, this requirement does not apply to occasional work or short-term work involving domestic service in a private household, or work regulated as not being harmful, damaging or dangerous to young people in a family undertaking.

5.40   The Guidance Note states that the information should be capable of being understood by the employees concerned and will thus take into account their level of training, knowledge and experience. Special attention should be given to persons with language difficulties or physical disabilities which may affect their receipt of information (eg blind persons, persons whose mother tongue is not English, etc).

5.41   Persons who are on fixed term contracts are required to have additional information (see regulation 15, below).

Co-operation and co-ordination (regulation 11)

5.42   Where two or more employers share a workplace (whether on a temporary or permanent basis), each employer shall:
  (a) co-operate with other employers concerned so far as is necessary to enable them to comply with their statutory duties
  (b) take all reasonable steps to co-ordinate health and safety measures with those which the other employers are taking to comply with statutory provisions, and
  (c) take all reasonable steps to inform the other employers concerned of the risks to their employees' health and safety arising out of the conduct by him of his undertaking.

5.43   This regulation also applies to employers who are sharing the workplace with self-employed persons, and to self-employed persons who are sharing with other self-employed persons.

5.44   The ACOP points out that where a worksite is under the control of a main employer, other employers (or self-employed persons) on the site should assist in assessing shared risks and co-ordinating any necessary measures. Equally, the controlling employer will have to establish site-wide arrangements and this information should be passed on, as appropriate. If there is no employer in control, joint arrangements should be agreed and consideration given to the appointment of a health and safety co-ordinator.

Visiting workers (regulation 12)

5.45   Every employer, and every self-employed person, shall ensure that the employer of any visiting employees is provided with comprehensible information on:

(a) the risks to the visiting employees' health and safety arising out of the conduct of the undertaking, and

(b) the measures taken to ensure compliance with the statutory requirements in so far as they relate to those visiting employees.

5.46   The employer shall then ensure that every visiting worker is provided with appropriate instructions and comprehensible information regarding any risks to that person's health and safety which arise out of the conduct of the employer's undertaking. Employers must also ensure that the employer of any visiting employee, as well as the visiting employee, is provided with sufficient information to identify the person responsible for evacuation procedures.

5.47   In other words, an employer owes a duty to the employer of any visiting employee who comes on to his premises, and to the visiting employee as well.

5.48   The ACOP points out that the risk assessment should have identified risks to people who come on to the employer's premises. Thus, comprehensible information on those risks, and the measures to be taken to control them, should be given to visiting workers. If necessary, the information can be provided through a written permit-to-work system. Information provided to employees under regulation 10 should be provided to visiting workers either directly or through their own employer.

Capabilities and training (regulation 13)

5.49   When entrusting tasks to his employees, every employer shall take account of their capabilities as regards health and safety. The employer shall also ensure that his employees are provided with adequate health and safety training:

(a) when they are recruited, and

(b) on being exposed to new or increased risks because of being transferred, or given new responsibilities, or when new equipment, new technology, or new systems of work are introduced.

5.50   The training should be repeated periodically where appropriate, and adapted to take account of new or changed risks. Training should take place in working hours.

5.51   The employer should ensure that the demands of the job do not exceed the employees' ability to carry out the work without risk to themselves or others. Account should be taken of the employees' capabilities, and the level of their training, knowledge and experience. Managers should be aware of relevant legislation, and be competent to manage health and safety effectively. Health and safety training should take place during normal working hours, but if it is necessary to arrange training outside working hours, this should be treated as an extension of time at work, and compensated accordingly.

5.52   The Guidance Notes state that training needs are likely to be greatest on recruitment. Basic training should include the arrangements for first aid, fire and evacuation procedures, as well as general health and safety matters. Refresher training may be needed if particular skills are used infrequently.

Employees' duties (regulation 14)

5.53   Every employee shall use any machinery, equipment, dangerous substances, transport equipment, means of production or safety device provided to him, in accordance with any training received by him and any instructions provided to him by his employer in compliance with the statutory provisions.

5.54   Every employee shall inform his employer (or the person responsible for health and safety matters):
  (a) of any work situation which a person with his training and instruction would reasonable consider to represent a serious and immediate danger to health and safety, and
  (b) of any matter which a person with his training and instruction would reasonably consider represented a shortcoming in the employer's protection arrangements for health and safety.

5.55   This duty arises in so far as the situation affects the employee's own health and safety, or arises out of his own activities at work. Also, the matter must be one which has not previously been reported to the employer or his safety advisor.

5.56   The ACOP points out that employees have certain duties under s.7 of HSWA, but this regulation clearly goes much further. The employee must report to his employer any work situation which might give rise to a serious or imminent danger to himself or to others if it flows from the work activity. Further, he should report shortcomings in the employer's arrangements even when no danger exists, so that the employer can take remedial action. However, this does not reduce the responsibility of the employer to comply with his statutory duties.

Temporary workers (regulation 15)

5.57 If an employer engages a worker on a fixed term contract, or engages a person employed by an employment business, the employer must provide that person with comprehensible information on:

(a) any special occupational qualification or skills required to be held by that employee if he is to carry out his work safely, and

(b) any health surveillance required to be provided to that employee.

5.58 This information is to be provided before the employee concerned commences his duties.

5.59 Where an employer is seeking to have work done by persons who will be provided by an employment agency, he must provide the person carrying on that business with comprehensible information on:

(a) any special occupational qualifications or skills required to be held by the employees if they are to carry out their work safely, and

(b) the specific features of the jobs to be filled by those employees in so far as those features are likely to affect their health and safety.

5.60 The person carrying on the employment agency shall pass on the information to the employees concerned.

5.61 The Guidance Notes point out that both the user employer and the person carrying on the employment business have duties to provide information to the employees concerned.

Risk assessment for new or expectant mothers (regulation 16)

5.62 Where persons working in an undertaking include women of child-bearing age, and the work is of a kind which could involve risk to the health and safety of a new or expectant mother, or to that of her baby, from any processes or working conditions, or from physical, biological or chemical agents, including those specified in Annexes I and II of Directive 92/185/EEC on measures to encourage improvements in the health and safety at work of pregnant workers and workers who have recently given birth or who are breast-feeding, the assessment required by regulation 3(1) (above) shall include an assessment of such risks.

5.63   Annex I of the Directive provides a non-exhaustive list of agents, processes and working conditions in respect of which an employer must make an assessment and decide what measures need to be taken. These include physical agents likely to cause foetal lesions and/or likely to disrupt placental attachment, particularly shocks, vibrations, handling of loads entailing risks, noise, ionising radiation, extremes of cold and heat, movements and posture, travel and mental and physical fatigue. Also specified are certain biological agents and certain chemical agents, in so far as it is known that they endanger the health of a woman or her foetus. Certain industrial processes and underground mine workings are also specified. Annex II to the Directive provides for a non-exhaustive list of agents and working conditions to which a pregnant woman must not be exposed, and a further list of agents to which a woman who is breast feeding must not be exposed.

5.64   It should be noted that a breach of regulation 16 may give rise to civil as well as criminal liability. This is to comply with a requirement to that effect contained in Directive 92/185/EEC.

5.65   The requirement to carry out such a risk assessment is not limited to when a woman is pregnant. The regulations require a risk assessment to be carried out when an employer employs a woman of child-bearing age even before she is pregnant. The assessment is designed to ascertain whether the work could be a risk to her health, or the health of her child, should she become pregnant (*Day v T Pickles Farms Ltd*). What is not clear is at what age does a woman cease to be of child-bearing age. There does not appear to be a requirement to undertake an assessment under regulation 16 of a woman who has had a hysterectomy, because there would not be a risk to her as a new or expectant mother. However, a regulation 3 assessment would need to be carried out in the usual way.

5.66   Regulation 16(2)–(4), and regulation 17, make further provisions for the steps to be taken by an employer to alter a woman's working conditions or working hours, or to suspend her, or suspend her from night work, in certain circumstances (see paragraph 7.6). Regulation 18 makes it clear that the employer will not be required to take this action unless the employee has notified the employer in writing that she is pregnant, has given birth within the previous six months, or is breastfeeding.

5.67   HSE has issued a Guidance Note (HSG122; *New and expectant mothers at work; a guide for employers*) which includes a table of hazards to which employers should pay attention when carrying out risk assessments, and advice on subsequent action to be taken.

Protection of young persons (regulation 19)

5.68   Every employer shall ensure that young persons employed by him are protected at work from any risks to their health and safety which are a consequence of their lack of experience, or absence of awareness of existing or potential risks, or the fact that the young person has not yet fully matured.

5.69   No employer shall employ a young person for work:
   (a) which is beyond his physical or psychological capacity
   (b) involving harmful exposure to agents which are toxic or carcinogenic, cause heritable genetic damage or harm to the unborn child or which in any way chronically affects human health
   (c) involving harmful exposure to radiation
   (d) involving the risks of accidents which it may reasonably be assumed cannot be recognised or avoided by young person owing to their insufficient attention to safety or lack of experience or training
   (e) in which there is a risk to health from:
      (i) extreme cold or heat
      (ii) noise, or
      (iii) vibration.

5.70   However, the above restrictions do not prevent the employment of a young person (who is not a child) for work:
   (a) where it is necessary for his training
   (b) where the young person will be supervised by a competent person, and
   (c) where any risk will be reduced to the lowest level that is reasonably practicable.

5.71   Nor does regulation 19 apply to occasional work or short-term working involving domestic service in a private household, or work regulated as not being harmful, damaging or dangerous to young people in a family undertaking (regulation 2(2)).

Provisions as to liability (regulation 21)

5.72 In criminal proceedings for the contravention of any relevant statutory provision, it will not be a defence for an employer to argue that the contravention was due to the act or default of an employee of his, or of a person appointed as a health and safety assistant under regulation 7 (this regulation has effectively closed the escape route revealed in *R v Nelson Group Services*, see paragraph 3.80). The Guidance Notes state that in practice, the enforcing authorities will take account of the circumstances of each case before deciding on the appropriateness of any enforcement action. Thus if an employer has taken reasonable steps to satisfy himself of the competence of the person concerned, this will be taken into account. In the event of a prosecution, such factors may go to mitigation, but cannot affect liability.

Exclusion of civil liability (regulation 22)

5.73 The general principle in the Management Regulations is that a breach does not give rise to civil liability. However, civil and criminal proceedings may be brought in respect of a breach of regulation 16(1) (risk assessment for women of child-bearing age) and regulation 19 (protection of young persons).

Hours of work

Working Time Regulations 1998/99

5.74 New regulations came into force in October 1998, (amended in 1999) designed to implement the provisions of the Working Time Directive (93/104/EC), and the Young Workers Directive (94/33/EC). Technically, these Directives should have been implemented by 23 November 1996, and thus in theory those employers who are emanations of the State (see *Foster v British Gas*) and private employers were exposed to *"Francovitch"*type claims. In *Gibson v East Riding of Yorkshire* it was held that Article 7 of the Directive, which provided for workers to have four weeks holiday pay was directly enforceable against the State, because it was clear and precise, and gave rise to no ambiguity or conditionality. Nor was it subject to any derogations. Further, the applicant was entitled to four weeks holiday entitlement, because the UK Government had not, at that time, exercised the option (which it subsequently did) to limit the right to three weeks until November 1999.

5.75 Generally, the regulations give a series of new rights to "workers", a term which is wider than, "employees", and applies additionally to a person working under a contract "to do or perform personally any work or services for another party to the contract whose status is not by virtue of the contract that of a client or customer of any profession or business undertaking carried on by the individual" (regulation 2(1)). This clearly covers casual, freelance and some self-employed workers, other than self-employed persons who are pursuing a professional or business activity on their own account. However, advantage has been taken of a number of derogations and exceptions permitted by the Directive, and potentially by means of workplace or collective agreements.

5.76 The main provisions of the Working Time Regulations 1998/99 are as follows:

(a) *Regulation 4 (maximum weekly working time).* Unless his employer has first obtained the worker's agreement in writing to perform such work, a worker's working time, including overtime, shall not exceed an average of 48 hours for each seven day period in any applicable reference period. The reference period is 17 weeks, although in certain circumstances (regulation 21, special cases) the reference period can be 26 weeks, or 52 weeks if permitted by a collective agreement or a workforce agreement (regulation 23(b)). The opting out agreement may be for a specific period, or apply indefinitely. If there is no provision in the agreement to terminate it by notice, then the worker may terminate it by giving seven days' notice. If the agreement can be terminated by notice, the notice period shall not exceed three months.

To calculate the average hours in any reference period, the formula to be applied is: $(A + B) \div C$.

This requires some explanation. In any reference period, there will be days when the employee will not work, eg because of annual holidays, sick leave, maternity leave, etc. Clearly, to exclude those days from the calculation would distort the average hours worked. Therefore, those "excluded days" must be added back in to the calculation. "A" is the total number of hours worked during the reference period; "B" is the total number of hours worked immediately after the reference period during the number of days equivalent to the number of excluded days. "C" will be the number of weeks in the reference period. Thus the formula $((A + B) \div C)$ will give the average number of hours in the reference period, which will, in effect, be extended by the equivalent number of "excluded" days.

If a relevant agreement provided for successive 17 week reference periods, then each reference period will be self-contained, for the purpose of calculating average working hours. In the absence of any such agreement, the reference period will be a "rolling" 17-week period, ie each week will be the start of a new 17 week reference period.

(b) *Regulation 6 (length of night work).* The normal hours of work for a night worker (defined in regulation 2) shall not exceed eight in any 24 hour period, again, the average being assessed over a 17 week period (which can be fixed successive 17 week periods, as set out in a relevant agreement, or, failing such agreement, a "rolling" 17 week period). In *R v Attorney General for Northern Ireland, ex parte Burns* the applicant worked a cycle of 15 shifts of 8 hours duration. During five of these, at least three hours of her working time fell between 11pm, and 6am. It was held that she was a night worker within the meaning of regulation 6. It was noted that the Directive defined a night worker as a person who works at night "as a normal course", and this phrase was to be construed as meaning "as a regular feature".

An employer shall ensure that no night worker whose work involves special hazards or heavy physical or mental strain, works for more than 8 hours in any 24 hour period. The work shall be regarded as involving special hazards or physical or mental strain if it is identified as such in a collective agreement or a workforce agreement, or in a risk assessment carried out under the Management of Health and Safety at Work Regulations 1999. Further, a night worker will be entitled to a free health assessment before he takes up the assignment, with further such assessments at regular intervals. A young worker (ie between the ages of 15–17 inclusive) must not work between the hours of 10pm and 6am unless he has had a free health assessment before commencing the assignment, and thereafter at such regular intervals as may be appropriate in his case (regulation 7). If a registered medical practitioner advises the employer that a worker employed by him is suffering from health problems connected with night work, then, if possible, the employer should transfer the worker to other work for which he is suited, and undertaken at times so that he ceases to be a night worker.

To calculate the average working hours of a night worker, the normal working hours during the reference period must be divided by the number of working days in that period. The formula is: $A \div (B - C)$. Again, an explanation is required.

From the number of 24 hour periods during the reference period ("B") must be deducted the number of hours (divided by 24 to equate days) which comprise or are included in the weekly rest periods, as provided for in regulation 11 ("C"). The amount of the normal working hours during the reference period ("A") can thus be ascertained by dividing the normal working hours during the reference period by the number of working days in that period.

If a worker has worked for less than 17 weeks, the average will be calculated by reference to the period since the worker started to work for the employer.

(c) *Regulation 8 (pattern of work).* Where the pattern according to which the employer organises work is such as to put the health and safety of a worker employed by him at risk, in particular because the work is monotonous or the work-rate is pre-determined, the employer shall ensure that the worker is given adequate rest breaks.

(d) *Regulation 9 (records).* The employer shall keep up-to-date records of all workers who have opted out of the maximum weekly working time (see regulation 4(2)), and records of the maximum weekly working time, length of night working, and health assessments, etc of night workers, in respect of each worker in relation to whom they apply, and keep such records for two years.

(e) *Regulation 10 (daily rest).* An adult worker is entitled to a rest period of not less than eleven consecutive hours in each 24 hour period during which he works for an employer, although a young worker is entitled to a rest period of twelve consecutive hours.

(f) *Regulation 11 (weekly rest periods).* An adult worker is entitled to an uninterrupted rest period of not less than 24 hours in each seven day period during which he works for his employer, although this can be changed to two uninterrupted periods of 24 hours in each 14 day period, or one uninterrupted period of 48 hours in each 14 day period. A young worker is entitled to a rest period of not less than 48 hours in any seven day period, although this can be altered in certain circumstances .

(g) *Regulation 12 (rest breaks).* Where an adult worker's daily working time is more than six hours, he is entitled to a rest break, which shall be for an uninterrupted period of 20 minutes (unless a collective agreement or workforce agreement specifies otherwise), to be spent away from the workstation. A young worker who works for more than four and a half hours shall be entitled to a rest break of at least 30 minutes, spent away from the workstation.

(h) *Regulation 13 (annual leave entitlement).* A worker is entitled to four weeks annual holidays each year and to receive his normal weekly pay during his holidays, calculated in accordance with ss.221–224 of the Employment Rights Act 1996 (ERA) (regulation 16). Where a worker is paid for a public bank holiday, this will count towards entitlement to annual leave. If the employment is terminated during the leave year, the worker will be entitled to a proportionate pay in lieu. To qualify for the right, the worker must have been employed for 13 weeks, thereafter entitlement is proportionate to the length of employment in the relevant leave year. Leave entitlement is only in respect of the holiday year in which it is due, and may not be replaced by a payment in lieu except on termination of the worker's employment.

5.77 To ascertain how much leave is owed on termination, the formula to use is $(A \times B) - C$ where "A" is the period of leave the worker is entitled to under the Regulations, "B" is the portion of the leave year which has expired prior to the effective date of termination, and "C" is the period of leave already taken by the worker. If a relevant agreement so permits, a worker who has already taken holiday entitlement in excess, of his statutory entitlement can be required to compensate the employer, either by way of a payment, or by doing additional work.

5.78 It goes without saying that clauses sometimes found in existing employment contracts which specify that an employee dismissed for reason of gross misconduct shall not be entitled to accrued holiday pay are no longer valid.

5.79   The worker may give notice to the employer of the dates when he wishes to take his holidays, subject to the employer requiring the worker to take his holidays on particular dates. The worker must give twice the number of days' notice as days leave he wishes to take. The employer can prevent the employee taking leave on a particular day by giving notice equivalent to the same number of days as the employer wishes to prevent the leave occurring on. However, the notice provisions are capable of being overridden by a relevant agreement, which may provide for longer (or shorter) periods of notice.

5.80   The commencement of the leave year should be specified in a relevant agreement, or, if there is no such agreement, it will run from the date the worker commenced employment, or when the Regulations came into effect.

Exclusions

5.81   There are a number of excluded sectors of employment and specified activities to which specific regulations do not apply, as follows.

5.82   *Regulation 18*:
   (a) Employment in the following sectors of activity:
       (i) air, rail, road, inland waterway and lake transport
       (ii) sea fishing
       (iii) other work at sea, or
   (b) the activities of doctors in training, or
   (c) where characteristics peculiar to certain specified services, such as the armed forces or the police, or to certain specific activities in the civil protection services, inevitably conflict with the Regulations.

5.83   The above workers are excluded from regulation 4 (maximum weekly working time), regulation 6 (length of night work), regulation 7 (health assessment for night workers), regulation 8 (safe pattern of work), regulation 10 (daily rest periods), regulation 11 (weekly rest periods), regulation 12 (rest breaks) regulation 13 (annual leave) and regulation 16 (annual leave pay).

5.84   *Regulation 19*: Domestic servants in a private household are excluded from regulation 4 (maximum weekly working time), regulation 6 (length of night work), regulation 7 (health assessment for night workers), regulation 8 (safe pattern of work).

5.85   *Regulation 20*: Workers who, on account of the specific characteristics of the activities engaged in, or where the duration of the working time cannot be measured or predetermined, or which can be determined by the worker himself. In particular:

(a) managing executives or other persons with autonomous decisions making powers, or

(b) family workers, or

(c) workers officiating at religious ceremonies in churches and religious communities.

5.86   The above workers are excluded from regulation 4 (maximum weekly working time), regulation 6 (length of night work), regulation 10 (daily rest), regulation 11 (weekly rest period) and regulation 12 (rest breaks).

5.87   Where such workers' working time is partly measured, pre-determined, or determined by the worker, and partly not, the weekly working time and night work provisions will apply only in relation to that part of the worker's work which is measured, pre-determined or determined by the worker himself.

5.88   *Regulation 21*: There is a limited exclusion for the following group of workers:

(a) workers whose activities are such that his place of work and place of residence are distant from one another, or whose different places of work are distant from one another

(b) where a worker is engaged in security and surveillance activities requiring a permanent presence in order to protect property and persons, particularly security guards and caretakers or security firms

(c) workers whose activities involve the need for continuity or service or production, particularly:

(i) services relating to the reception, treatment or care provided by hospitals or similar establishments, residential institutions and prisons

(ii) work at docks or airports

(iii) press, radio, television, cinematographic production, postal and telecommunications services and civil protection services

(iv) gas, water and electricity production, transmission and distribution, household refuse collection and incineration

(v) industries in which work cannot be interrupted on technical grounds

(vi) research and development activities

(vii) agriculture.

(d) where there is a foreseeable surge of activity, particularly in:

(i) agriculture

(ii) tourism, and

(iii) postal services

(e) where the worker's activities are affected by:

(i) an occurrence due to unusual and unforeseeable circumstances, beyond the control of the worker's employer

(ii) exceptional events, the consequences of which could not have been avoided despite the exercise of all due care, or

(iii) an accident or the imminent risk of an accident.

5.89 In respect of the above group of workers, the following regulations do not apply, namely, regulation 6 (length of night work), regulation 10 (daily rest periods), regulation 11 (weekly rest periods) and regulation 12 (rest breaks). However, if a worker is required to work during what would normally be a rest period, the employer shall allow him to have a compensatory period of rest, or, if this is not possible, afford him appropriate protection (regulation 24).

5.90 Regulation 23 provides that a collective agreement or a workforce agreement may modify or exclude the following regulations in relation to particular workers, namely regulation 6 (length of night work), regulation 10 (daily rest), regulation 11 (weekly rest period) and regulation 12 (rest breaks). So far as regulation 4 (maximum weekly working time) is concerned, such agreement can substitute a different period over which the average can be worked out, not exceeding 52 weeks (in place of 17 weeks).

5.91 There are also a number of other limited exclusions in respect of workers in the armed forces, young workers employed on ships, and young workers affected by force majeure (regulations 25–27). There are also special rules for agricultural workers (Schedule 2)

Enforcement

5.92 The regulations can be enforced in three ways. First, inspectors from the Health and Safety Executive (or, in appropriate circumstances, the enforcement officers of local authorities) are responsible for the enforcement of the following provisions (see regulation 28):

(a) the duty of the employer to take reasonable steps to ensure that the provisions relating to the 48 hour week have been complied with. The inspectors will also have the right to inspect the employer's records in relation to workers who are subject to an opting out agreement

(b) the duty of the employer to take reasonable steps to ensure compliance with the limit on average hours for night workers, and the absolute limit on length of night work for night workers whose work involves special hazards or heavy physical or mental strain

(c) the provision of free health assessments for adult workers who work at night, and also health and capacities assessments for young workers

(d) the duty of the employer to transfer night workers to day work if, in the opinion of a registered medical practitioner, night workers suffer from health problems as a result of working at night

(e) the duty of the employer to provide adequate rest breaks where the pattern of work is such as to put the health and safety of the worker at risk, particularly if the work is monotonous or repetitive

(f) the duty of the employer to keep records showing that the 48 hour week, the limits on night work, and the provisions relating to free health assessments or health and capability assessments is complied with

(g) the duty of the employer to provide equivalent compensatory rest, or to provide appropriate protection, when the hourly night work limits are modified or excluded by a collective or workforce agreement.

5.93   In respect of the above matters, an employer may be prosecuted in the magistrates courts, where a fine of up to £5000 may be imposed, or an unlimited fine imposed in the Crown Court. Enforcement officers may also issue an Improvement Notice, requiring the employer to rectify matters specified therein, in order to ensure compliance with the statutory requirements, and a failure to comply with such Notice can lead to a fine of up to £20,000, and/or six months imprisonment in the magistrates court, or an unlimited fine and/or up to two years imprisonment in the Crown court.

5.94   The second way in which the Regulations can be enforced is by way of a complaint by a worker to an employment tribunal, alleging that the employer has failed to comply with any of the following provisions:

(a) the daily rest periods for adult or young workers (regulation 10)

(b) the weekly rest periods for adult or young workers (regulation 11)

(c) rest break periods for adult or young workers (regulation 12)

(d) entitlement to annual leave (regulation 13)

(e) entitlement to equivalent compensatory rest, where the provisions of regulations 10, 11 and 12 have been excluded or modified

(f) entitlement to compensatory rest where the provisions of regulations 10 and 11 have been excluded in respect of young workers serving in the armed forces, or where the force majeure exemption applies

(g) the duty of the employer to pay a worker statutory annual leave pay, or pay for leave outstanding on the termination of employment (regulations 14, 16).

5.95 A complaint to an employment tribunal must be brought within three months from the date on which it is alleged that the exercise of the right should have been permitted, or, in the case of holiday pay, from the date when the payment should have been made, although the employment tribunal may extend the period if it was not reasonably practicable to bring the complaint earlier. If the complaint is well founded, the employment tribunal may make a declaration, and may award compensation of such amount as the tribunal consider to be just and equitable, having regard to the employer's default in refusing to permit the worker to exercise the right in question, and any loss sustained by the worker attributable to that default. In the case of holiday pay, the amount due will be awarded.

5.96 A worker will also have the right (s.45A Employment Rights Act (ERA)) not to be subjected to any detriment because:

(a) he refused to comply with a requirement that the employer imposed which would be in contravention of the regulations

(b) he refused to forgo a right conferred by the regulations

(c) he failed to sign a workforce agreement or an individual agreement opting out of the regulations

(d) he performed any functions or activities as a workforce representative, or as a candidate in an election for workforce representatives

(e) he brought proceedings against the employer to enforce a right conferred by the regulations

(f) he alleged that the employer had infringed a right conferred by the regulations.

5.97   An employee (not a worker) also has the right not to be unfairly dismissed for any of the above reasons (s.101A, ERA), and also the right not to be unfairly selected for redundancy (s.105(4A), ERA). Again, the complaint must be brought within three months from the date of the act complained of, with the usual extension of time if it was not reasonably practicable to bring the complaint earlier. If the complaint is upheld, the employment tribunal will make a declaration, and may make an award of compensation, on just and equitable principles. If the employee was unfairly dismissed, no qualifying period of employment is required, interim relief is available, and the minimum basic award, as well as an additional award (of between 26 and 52 weeks pay) may be made as appropriate.

5.98   The third way of enforcing the regulations is to seek an appropriate remedy for breach of contract of employment. In *Barber v RJB Mining (UK) Ltd*, pit deputies, although contractually obliged to work for 42 hours a week, regularly worked a considerable amount of overtime, in excess of 48 hours. They were asked to sign an agreement opting out of their rights under the regulations, but refused, and they sought from the court a declaration to the effect that they need not work at all until such time as their average working hours fell below the limit specified in regulation 4(1). The High Court granted the declaration. It was held that it was clearly the intention of Parliament that their contract of employment should be read so as to provide that an employee should work no more than 48 hours a week during the relevant reference period. Thus the regulation 4(1) created a free-standing right which took effect as a contractual term in the contracts of employment of the pit deputies.

Safety representatives

5.99   One of the more important innovations to be found in HSWA is contained in s.2(4), which enabled the Secretary of State by regulations to provide for the appointment by recognised independent trade unions of safety representatives from among the employees, who will represent them in consultation with the employers and have other prescribed functions. It will then be the duty of every employer to consult with such representatives with a view to the making and maintenance of arrangements which will enable him and his employees to cooperate effectively in promoting and developing measures to ensure the health and safety at work of the employees, and in checking the effectiveness of such measures (s.2(6)).

5.100 The relevant regulations have been made (Safety Representatives and Safety Committees Regulations 1977, as amended by the Management of Health and Safety at Work Regulations 1992) together with an ACOP and non-statutory Guidance Notes. In addition, there is an ACOP on time off for the training of safety representatives. These are all published in one document, L87: *Safety representatives and safety committees*.

Appointment of safety representatives (s.2(4))

5.101 A safety representative may be appointed by an independent trade union which is recognised by the employer for the purpose of collective bargaining. To be a trade union, it must be on the list of trade unions maintained by the Certification Officer under s.2 of the Trade Union and Labour Relations (Consolidation) Act 1992. It will be an independent trade union if it has applied for and received a Certificate of Independence from the Certification Officer (issued if it can show that it is not under the domination or control of the employer, whether by way of the provision of financial benefits or otherwise) under s.6 of the same Act. It will be a recognised trade union if the employer recognises it for the purpose of negotiations relating to or connected with one or more of the matters specified in s.244 of the 1992 Act. There is no need to have a formal agreement concerning recognition; it is a question of fact, to be determined by the circumstances of each case as to whether or not the employer does recognise the trade union concerned (*National Union of Tailors and Garment Workers v Charles Ingram & Co Ltd*).

5.102 Only an independent trade union which is recognised for the purposes of collective bargaining is legally entitled to appoint safety representatives. In *Cleveland County Council v Springett*, union representatives, who were members of the Association of Polytechnic Teachers, claimed that they had been denied time off work with pay in accordance with the regulations. The union was not formally recognised by the local authority which ran the polytechnic, although it was represented on the national Burnham Committee, a body which made recommendations on teachers' pay. It was held that this did not constitute recognition by the employer. Further, the fact that the union had had previous dealings with the employer when representing an individual employee of the polytechnic did not constitute recognition for the purpose of collective bargaining.

5.103 If an employer refuses to consult with the appointed safety representatives on the ground that he does not recognise the trade union concerned, it is likely that the HSE will invoke the aid of the Advisory Conciliation and Arbitration Service (ACAS) to provide advice. The Employment Relations Act 1999 has introduced a statutory scheme whereby a trade union will have to be recognised when the majority of the relevant workforce so desire.

5.104 The system whereby the legal right to appoint safety representatives is confined to trade unions has been the subject of some criticism. It is argued that it tends to perpetuate the divisions in industry between "us" and "them". Safety, after all, should be the concern of all, be they employers, managers, employees, union officials, and so on, and it is wrong that safety representatives are to be seen against the backcloth of the battleground of industrial relations. Against this, it is argued that the disputes which may arise over the functions and rights of a safety representative can more readily be resolved within the existing framework of collective bargaining machinery, and that to place the safety representative outside that machinery is to leave no avenue available for the resolution of disputes.

5.105 Although a safety representative is appointed by the recognised trade union, he need not be a member of the trade union. The only requirements are that he shall, so far as is reasonably practicable, have been employed by his employer throughout the preceding two years or have had at least two years' experience in similar employment (Safety Representatives, etc Regulations, regulation 2). Again, this raises some argument in practice. Some trade unions will appoint shop stewards to be the safety representatives, on the ground that they are better trained, will not be overawed by management, and can handle the appropriate dispute procedures. On the other hand, this can cause some problems, for, as a shop steward, he may be subject to the processes of re-election, or there may be a conflict arising out of his functions as a shop steward and those he exercises as a safety representative. For example, if there are disciplinary proceedings being taken against an employee (see Chapter 9) who has acted in breach of safety rules, the shop steward who has to represent his member will have to reconcile his actions with his belief that the safety rules must be upheld. To avoid such conflict, some trade unions will refuse to appoint shop stewards and look to other members to carry out this important work. This has the added advantage of spreading the workload and training opportunities, and involving more members in the activities of the union. Clearly, no single pattern will meet all the circumstances, and the matter must be regarded from a pragmatic viewpoint.

5.106 Neither the regulations nor the ACOP specify how many safety representatives should be appointed by the trade union concerned, and certain difficulties may well exist in multi-union situations. The Guidance Notes attached to the regulations suggest that the appropriate criteria should be based on:
  (a) the total number of employees in the workplace
  (b) the variety of different occupations
  (c) the size of the workplace and the variety of workplace locations
  (d) the operation of shift systems
  (e) the type of work activity and the degree and character of inherent dangers.

5.107 A person who has been appointed safety representative shall cease to be such when:
  (a) the trade union which appointed him notifies the employer in writing that the appointment has been terminated
  (b) he ceases to be employed at the workplace; however, if he was appointed to represent employees at more than one workplace, he shall not cease to be a safety representative so long as he continues to be employed at any one of them
  (c) he resigns.

Consultations with safety representatives

5.108 Once an employer has been notified in writing by or on behalf of a trade union that a person has been appointed as a safety representative, and of the group of employees he is to represent, the safety representative shall have the right to be consulted by the employer with a view to the making and maintaining of arrangements which will enable the employer and his employees to co-operate effectively in promoting and developing measures to ensure the health and safety at work of the employees, and to check the effectiveness of those measures (HSWA, s.2(6)). The Management of Health and Safety at Work Regulations 1992 introduced new consultation provisions to the Safety Representative, etc Regulations which require the employer to consult with the safety representatives in good time with regard to:

(a) the introduction at the workplace of any measure which may substantially affect the health and safety of the employees who are represented by the safety representative

(b) his arrangements for appointing or nominating his safety assistant/advisor and person responsible for evacuation procedures

(c) any health and safety information required to be provided by the employer to employees the safety representative concerned represents

(d) the planning and organisation of any health and safety training required to be provided by the employer to the employees the safety representative represents, and

(e) the health and safety consequences of the introduction of new technologies into the workplace.

5.109   The employer shall also provide such facilities and assistance as safety representatives may reasonably require for the purpose of carrying out their statutory functions.

Functions of safety representatives

5.110   Regulation 4 of the Safety Representatives and Safety Committees Regulations lays down a number of functions which a safety representative shall be entitled to perform. These are:

(a) to investigate potential hazards and dangerous occurrences at the workplace (whether or not they are drawn to his attention by the employees he represents) and to examine the causes of accidents at the workplace; this right is not confined to having time off work (with pay) to make the investigation inside the workplace, for there may be circumstances when it is necessary to go outside in order to investigate (eg to interview an injured employee at home, see *Dowsett v Ford Motor Co*, see paragraph 5.129)

(b) to investigate complaints by any employee he represents relating to that employee's health, safety or welfare at work

(c) to make representations to the employer on the above matters

(d) to make representations to the employer on general matters affecting the health, safety or welfare at work of the employees at the workplace

(e) to carry out inspections (see below)

(f) to represent employees in consultations at the workplace with inspectors of HSE or any other enforcing authority

(g) to receive information from inspectors (see paragraph 2.42)

(h) to attend meetings of the safety committee where he attends in his capacity as safety representative in connection with any of the above functions.

5.111 As an employee, the safety representative is subject to the general requirements imposed by ss.7–8 of HSWA (see Chapter 3) but no function conferred on him as noted above shall impose any duty on him. This means that he cannot be prosecuted for a failure to perform his duty as a safety representative, or for performing his duties badly. Nor can he be sued civilly for a failure to perform his statutory duty, although he is subject to the ordinary law of negligence in the usual way (see Chapter 8).

5.112 A safety representative is expected to act responsibly, and, in particular, he should not ignore established internal procedures. In *O'Connell v Tetrosyl Ltd*, a safety representative was dismissed because he made direct calls to the Factory Inspectorate concerning alleged breaches of safety regulations. The employers considered his actions to be misconduct, because he should have drawn management's attention to the matters before going to an outside body. By a majority, an employment tribunal had found his dismissal to be fair and an appeal against that decision was rejected by the Employment Appeal Tribunal. The employers had reasonable grounds for believing that he had bypassed internal procedures by going to the outside body, and this conduct did constitute a fair reason for dismissal.

5.113 Following the enactment of the Trade Union Reform and Employment Rights Act 1993, safety assistants, safety representatives, members of safety committees, and employees generally, have protection against being subjected to a detriment or being dismissed, when taking certain actions connected with their functions as such, or health and safety generally (see Employment Rights Act 1996, see paragraph 5.165).

Inspection of the workplace

5.114   Safety representatives are entitled to inspect the workplace or any part of it on three occasions.

5.115   First, if they have not inspected it within the previous three months. They must give reasonable notice to the employer in writing of their intention to do so. More frequent inspections may be carried out with the agreement of the employer.

5.116   Second, where there has been a substantial change in the conditions of work (whether by way of the introduction of new machinery or otherwise), or where new information has been published by the HSC or HSE relevant to the hazard since the last inspection. Then, after consulting with the employer, a further inspection may be carried out notwithstanding that less than three months have elapsed since the last inspection.

5.117   Third, where there has been a notifiable accident or dangerous occurrence (see Chapter 6) or a notifiable illness has been contracted there, and:
  (a) it is safe for an inspection to be carried out, and
  (b) the interests of the group of employees represented by the safety representatives might be involved.

5.118   In these circumstances, the safety representatives may carry out an inspection of the part of the workplace concerned (and so far as is necessary to determine the cause, they may inspect any other parts of the workplace). Where it is reasonably practicable for them to do so, they shall notify the employer of their intention to carry out the inspection.

5.119   The duties of a health and safety representative are not confined to examination of accidents and records on the employer's premises. In *Healey v Excel Logistics Ltd* the applicant was a safety representative. One of his colleagues had a serious accident while making a delivery to a supermarket, and he decided to visit the site in question, and also made an approach to the manager of the supermarket. The employer felt that this action was tantamount to gross misconduct, and so he was dismissed. An employment tribunal held that his dismissal was fair, because he was not carrying out an inspection of the workplace under the Safety Representative and Safety Committee Regulations 1977, but had gone to the supermarket to pry into health and safety matters without permission. On appeal, the Employment Appeal Tribunal reversed the decision, and held the dismissal to be unfair. One of the duties of a safety representative was to investigate potential hazards and dangerous occurrences at the workplace. He had been dismissed because he wanted to look at the accident report book at the supermarket in order to examine the cause of an accident at the workplace, an activity which was within his function as a safety representative.

5.120 The employer shall provide such facilities and assistance as the safety representatives may reasonably require, including facilities for independent investigation by them and private discussions with employees, but the employer or his representative is entitled to be present in the workplace during the inspection.

Inspection of documents

5.121 For the performance of their duties, safety representatives are entitled, on giving reasonable notice to the employer, to inspect and take copies of any document relevant to the workplace or to employees they represent which the employer is required to keep by virtue of any relevant statutory provision. Thus, they can inspect and take copies out of the general register, reports of the examination of hoists, lifts, cranes, etc. However, they are not entitled to see a copy of the fire certificate issued under the Fire Precautions Act 1971 as this is not one of the relevant statutory provisions. Nor are they entitled to inspect or take copies of any document consisting of or relating to any health record of an identifiable individual.

Disclosure of information to safety representatives

5.122 Safety representatives will be entitled to receive information from two main sources. First, regulation 7(2) requires the employer to make available information within his knowledge which is necessary to enable the safety representatives to perform their functions. However, the employer need not disclose:

(a) information the disclosure of which would be against the interests of national security

(b) any information which he could not disclose without contravening a prohibition imposed by or under an enactment

(c) any information relating specifically to an individual, unless that individual has consented to it being disclosed

(d) any information, the disclosure of which would, for reasons other than its effect on health, safety or welfare at work, cause substantial injury to the employer's undertaking or, where the information was supplied to the employer by some other person, to the undertaking of that other person

(e) any information obtained by the employer for the purpose of bringing, prosecuting or defending any legal proceedings.

5.123 Nor do the regulations require the employer to disclose any document or to allow the inspection of it if it does not relate to health, safety or welfare at work.

5.124 The restriction concerning the discovery of documents used for the purpose of legal proceedings was an issue before the House of Lords in *Waugh v British Railways Board* (see Chapter 8) where it was held that for a document to be privileged, the dominant purpose in preparing it must have been for its use in possible litigation. Thus, if an accident report is prepared as a matter of routine practice in order to establish the cause, and is subsequently required for the purpose of litigation, the safety representative will be entitled to see it, for the dominant purpose in preparing it was not for the purpose of litigation.

5.125 The Approved Code of Practice makes a number of recommendations concerning the nature of the information which should be disclosed to safety representatives. These include:

(a) information about the plans and performance of the undertaking and any changes proposed in so far as they affect the health and safety at work of employees

(b) information of a technical nature about the hazards of health and the precautions deemed necessary to eliminate or minimise them, in respect of plant, machinery, equipment, processes, systems of work, and substances in use at work, including any relevant information provided by consultants and designers, or the manufacturer, importer or supplier of any article or substance used at work

(c) information which the employer keeps relating to the occurrence of any accident, dangerous occurrence or notifiable disease, and any statistical records relating to those matters
(d) any other information specifically relating to matters affecting health and safety at work, including the results of any measurements taken by the employer (or person acting on his behalf) in the course of checking the effectiveness of his health and safety arrangements
(e) information on articles or substances which an employer issues to his home workers.

5.126 The second source of information for safety representatives may come from the inspector, who, by virtue of s.28(8) of the HSWA may give information to employees or their representatives to ensure that they are adequately informed about matters affecting their health, safety or welfare (see above and paragraph 2.42). This may be factual information relating to the premises or anything therein, or information regarding any action taken or proposed to be taken by the inspector (eg the issuing of a prohibition or improvement notice). The inspector must give the like information to the employer.

Time off work for safety representatives

5.127 A safety representative is entitled to have time off work, with pay, during his working hours, for the purpose:
(a) of performing his functions as a safety representative
(b) to undergo training in aspects of those functions as may be reasonable having regard to the ACOP issued by the HSC.

5.128 If his pay does not vary with the amount of work done, then he shall be paid as if he had worked throughout the whole of the time. If his pay varies with the amount of work done, then he shall be entitled to be paid his average hourly earnings for his work or, if no fair estimate of his earnings can be made, the average hourly earnings for work of that description of persons in comparable employment or, if there are no such persons, then the average hourly earnings which are reasonable in the circumstances. A part-time employee, who goes on a full time training course in health and safety matters, is entitled to be paid on the same basis as a full-time employee attending such courses (*Neath v Port Talbot County Borough Council*).

5.129   The right to investigate hazards and dangerous occurrences is not confined to having time off (with pay) to make an investigation inside the workplace. In *Dowsett v Ford Motor Co* an employee was injured in an accident. The applicant, who was the safety representative, investigated the incident, and concluded that no further action was necessary. Five weeks later, he attended a meeting of the works safety committee where the safety engineer gave a report on the incident. The applicant wanted to have time off work with pay to visit the employee at home in order to make further enquiries, but this was refused, so he made an application to the employment tribunal. It was held that the regulations were sufficiently wide to enable the safety representative to go outside the workplace if it was necessary to perform his functions. However, this was a question of fact and degree. In this case, he had not done anything for five weeks, and would not have acted had he not heard the report at the safety committee. Consequently, it was not necessary to make any further enquiries. In principle, however, the employment tribunal made it quite clear that there could be circumstances where it would be necessary to interview the injured person (or others) and to perform this function satisfactorily it may be necessary to go outside the workplace.

Training of safety representatives

5.130   The ACOP on *Time off work for the training of safety representatives* states that as soon as possible after they have been appointed they should be permitted to have time off work to attend basic training facilities approved by the TUC or their own trade union. Further training, similarly approved, should be undertaken when they have special responsibilities, or when this is necessary because of changed circumstances or new legislation. The trade union should inform management of the course it has approved and supply a copy of the syllabus if the employer asks for it. The trade union should give a few weeks' notice, and the number of safety representatives attending at one time from the same employer should be that which is reasonable in the circumstances, bearing in mind the availability of the relevant courses and the operational requirements of the employer. Unions and management should endeavour to reach agreement on the appropriate numbers and arrangements, and refer any problems to agreed procedures. Health and safety training for safety representatives is not limited to training that is necessary to enable the representative to perform his functions. The issue is whether the training is reasonable for aspects of his functions (*Rama v South West Trains*).

5.131   It will be recalled that the status of the Code of Practice is not of a rule of law; it is guidance to good practice. Thus there is no absolute rule that training should be only on a union approved course. In *White v Pressed Steel Fisher Ltd* the applicant was appointed safety representative by the T&GWU. The union wanted him to go on a union-sponsored training course, but management wanted to provide an in-company course and refused to permit him to have time off work with pay to attend the union course. It was held by the EAT that the employers were not acting unreasonably in refusing him time off work to go on the union course. The provisions in regulation 4(2) were for such training as may be reasonable in all the circumstances. It was therefore necessary to consider all the circumstances, including the Code of Practice. The approval of a course by the trade union was a factor to be taken into account, but (unlike s.168 of the Trade Union and Labour Relations (Consolidation) Act 1992 which relates to time off work for training in trade union duties) the Safety Representative and Safety Committees Regulations do not require that the course must be approved by the TUC or by the trade union. If the course provided by the employer was adequate, and contained all the necessary material, including the trade union aspects of safety, then it could be perfectly proper for the employer to insist that the safety representative went on the in-house course.

5.132   Whether it is reasonable for a safety representative to have time off work for training depends on whether, looked at overall, it is reasonable for him to attend for training. It does not depend on management's view of what is reasonable. In *Gallagher v Drum Engineering Co Ltd*, two management members of a safety committee were sent on a training course dealing with the impending introduction of the COSHH Regulations and a third manager was due to go on another course. The union wanted to send three of its members who were on the safety committee to a course run by the TUC, but the company refused to permit this, although they were prepared to allow one union member to go. The applicant, one of those refused permission, applied to an employment tribunal alleging a breach of the Safety Representatives and Safety Committees Regulations, and his claim was upheld. There was no unreasonable expense involved, no operational problems arose out of allowing three union representatives to attend the course and the union members had a large part to play in applying the regulations. In all the circumstances, the employment tribunal thought that it was reasonable to allow the applicant time off work with pay to attend the TUC sponsored course.

5.133   In determining whether it is reasonable in the circumstances to have time off work with pay, the employer's decision is to be judged by standards of reasonableness which are similar to those used in unfair dismissal cases. For example, in *Scarth v East Hertfordshire District Council*, a safety representative applied for time off work, with pay, to attend a training course specifically designed for local government representatives. The request was refused, because the manager who made the decision thought it was not suitable, even though he had not seen the syllabus. Three days later he saw the syllabus, and granted the applicant three days' leave with pay. An employment tribunal held that at the date he made his decision, the manager had not acted reasonably because he had not seen the syllabus for the course. Further, the figure of three days' pay had been "plucked out of the air" without any particular reason. Thus it was held that the applicant had been unreasonably refused time off work, and her claim for a further three days' pay was upheld.

5.134   The Code of Practice also gives guidance on the contents of a safety training syllabus. Basic training should provide for an understanding of the role of a safety representative, of safety committees, and of trade union policies and practices in relation to:
- (a) the legal requirements relating to health and safety at work
- (b) the nature and extent of workplace hazards, and of the measures necessary to eliminate or minimise them
- (c) the health and safety policy of the employer, and the organisations and arrangements necessary to fulfil these policies.

5.135   In addition, they will need to develop new skills, including how to carry out a safety inspection, how to make use of basic sources of legal and official information, etc.

5.136   A safety representative is entitled to go on a specialised training course in order to become familiar with hazards. In *Howard v Volex Accessories Division*, the applicant, who was a safety representative, found that the work involved coming into contact with lead and various chemicals. She applied for time off work to attend a TUC course on chemical hazards. Management refused the request because they took the view that they were doing everything that could be done by way of investigating and checking hazards. She decided to use two of her holiday days to go on the course, and then made a claim to an employment tribunal under regulation 4(2). The employment tribunal thought that she was entitled to learn more about the chemical and other hazards at work and that the TUC course would help her to acquire that knowledge. It was held that she was entitled to be paid for attending the course and she was also awarded £50 compensation for the loss of her two days' holiday.

5.137   However, it may be inappropriate for a newly appointed safety representative to seek to go on a specialist training course before he has had his initial basic training (*Knight v Shell UK Ltd*).

5.138   If there are more safety representatives in the organisation than are warranted by the genuine safety needs of the firm, then the employer may well be justified in refusing time off work with pay in particular circumstances, because such time off will not be "necessary for the purpose of..." the performance of their functions as safety representatives (*Howard & Peet v Volex plc*).

5.139   The HSE has published an ACOP and guidance on the regulations, L87: *Safety representatives and safety committees (The Brown Book)*.

Non-employees as safety representatives

5.140   The regulations specify that if the safety representatives have been appointed by the British Actors' Equity Association or the Musicians' Union, it is not necessary that they shall be employees of the employers concerned. This is because such people are performers in theatres, etc which are not owned by their employer, and are generally itinerant workers.

Health and Safety (Consultation with Employees) Regulations 1996

5.141   However, EC Directive 89/391/EEC (the "Framework Directive") applies to all employees, whether in recognised trade unions or not. Consequently, it became necessary to enact the Health and Safety (Consultation with Employees) Regulations 1996, which extend the consultation provisions to all employees not merely those who belonged to trade unions.

5.142   Under the regulations, the employer has two choices with respect to those employees who are not represented by safety representatives under the 1977 regulations. He can either consult with the employees directly or consult with one or more persons of any group of employees who were elected for the purposes of consultation, and who are referred to as "representatives of employee safety". There is no provision in the regulations as to how the employer shall organise the election but this, apparently, is not necessary (*R v Secretary of State for Trade & Industry, ex parte Unison*).

5.143   The employer shall thus consult those employees (or the representatives), in good time, on matters relating to their health and safety at work and, in particular, with regard to:
   (a) the introduction of any measure at the workplace that would substantially affect the health and safety of those employees
   (b) his arrangements for appointing, or nominating, competent persons to assist him in undertaking the measures needed to ensure compliance with statutory requirements, and to implement evacuation procedures (as required by the Management Regulations, regulations 7(1) and 8(1)(b))
   (c) health and safety information he is required to provide to employees under any statutory requirement
   (d) the planning and organisation of any health and safety training he is required to provide
   (e) the health and safety consequences for those employees of the introduction of new technologies into the workplace.

5.144   If the employer consults with employees directly, he must make available such information as is necessary to enable them to participate fully and effectively in the consultation. If the employer consults with representatives of employee safety, he must make available such information as is necessary to enable them to carry out their functions, and information contained in any records kept by virtue of RIDDOR which relates to the workplace or the group of employees represented by those representatives. However, the employer is not bound to disclose certain information (see paragraph 5.121).

5.145   Representatives of employee safety are entitled to:
   (a) make representations to the employer on potential hazards and dangerous occurrences at the workplace which affect the group represented

(b) make representations on general matters affecting health and safety at work of the group represented

(c) represent the group of employees in consultations with health and safety inspectors.

5.146   Representatives of employee safety are entitled to have time off work for training in respect of their functions, the employer paying for reasonable costs incurred (including travel and subsistence) and to have time off work with pay to perform their functions as such. They have the usual protections under the Employment Rights Act 1996 (see paragraph 5.165).

5.147   A representative of employee safety is entitled to be paid when carrying out his functions or being trained, the amount being calculated under Schedule 1 of the regulations (ie normal pay, average hourly pay or a figure of average hourly earnings which is reasonable in all the circumstances). A complaint may be made to an employment tribunal that an employer has failed to permit the representative of employee safety to take time off to perform his functions or go for training, or has failed to pay him. The complaint must be presented within three months, and if the complaint is well founded, the employment tribunal will make a declaration to that effect, and award such compensation as is thought to be just and equitable, or the amount due.

5.148   A representative of employee safety is entitled not to have action short of dismissal taken against him by way of penalising him for, or deterring him from, performing his functions as such, and it will be an unfair dismissal to dismiss him for participating reasonably in any consultations with the employer.

5.149   The HSE has published an ACOP to accompany these regulations, L95: *A guide to the Health and Safety (Consultation with Employees) Regulations 1996.*

Safety committees

5.150   The Safety Representatives and Safety Committees Regulations lay down (regulation 9) that the employer must establish a safety committee if requested to do so in writing by two union safety representatives. In order to do this, he must consult with safety representatives who made the request and with the representatives of any recognised trade union whose members work in the workplace in respect of which he proposes to establish the committee. The duty is one of consultation, not negotiation or agreement, so that actual composition of the committee is a matter for the employer to determine. However, he must establish the committee within three months of the request. He must also post a notice stating the composition of the committee and the workplace covered by it, and the notice shall be posted in a place where it may easily be read by the employees.

5.151 Section 2(7) of HSWA states that the function of the safety committee shall be to keep under review the measures taken to ensure the health and safety at work of employees and such other functions as may be prescribed. Apart from this vague generalisation, neither the regulations nor the Code of Practice give any further indication as to its functions. However, the Guidance Notes give some very helpful information. The HSC believe that the detailed arrangements necessary will evolve from discussions and negotiations between the parties, who are best able to determine the needs of the particular workplace. Since the circumstances of each case will vary a great deal, no single pattern is possible.

5.152 Certain guides may be followed. The safety committee should have its own separate identity and not have any other function or tasks assigned to it. It should relate to a single establishment although group committees can play an additional role. Finally, its functions should be clearly defined. A suggested brief for the committee might go along the following lines:

(a) a study of the trends of accidents, dangerous occurrences and notifiable diseases, so that recommendations may be made to management for corrective action to be taken

(b) the examination of safety audit reports, to note areas where improvements can be made

(c) consideration of reports and factual information from the enforcing authority

(d) the consideration of reports made by the safety representatives

(e) assisting in the development of safety rules and safe systems of work

(f) an evaluation of the effectiveness of the safety content of employee training

(g) monitoring of the adequacy of health and safety communication and publicity

(h) acting as a link between the company and the enforcing authority

(i) evaluating the safety policy and making recommendations for its revision.

5.153   Safety committees are not specifically empowered to deal with welfare matters, though there is nothing to prevent this happening should the parties so decide.

Membership of the committee

5.154   The aim should be to keep the membership reasonably compact, with adequate representation from all interested parties. Management representatives should include persons involved in health and safety matters, eg works engineers, works doctor, safety officer, etc and there should be seen to exist some form of mechanism for the consideration and implementation of the recommendations by senior management. The committee must contain sufficient expertise to evaluate problems and come up with solutions. Outside specialists may be made ex officio members. There is no requirement that safety representatives should be members of the committee but it would clearly be desirable to have some representation, depending on the numbers involved. There is no provision for time off work to be paid for attendance at the meetings of the committee, but this should be obvious. It is also desirable that a senior member of the company attends the meetings and plays a leading role, eg the company chairman or a board director.

Meetings

5.155   The safety committee should meet on a regular basis, as frequently as necessary, depending on the volume of business. The date of the meetings should be notified well in advance, and provision should be made for urgent meetings. An agenda should be drawn up, minutes kept, with action taken noted. Probably the most important function of the committee will be to monitor action taken on any recommendations made.

Safety committees in non-unionised workplaces

5.156   The HSC has issued some guidance on safety committees in those premises where there is no recognised independent trade union. Since there is no formal trade union machinery, and no legal requirement to set up a committee, the initiative will presumably come from management. Again, there should be adequate representation of appropriate management skills, and the employee representatives should be chosen by their fellow employees. In cases of difficulty, the HSE will give further guidance.

Enforcement of the regulations

5.157   A safety representative may present a complaint to an employment tribunal that:
(a) the employer has failed to permit him to take time off for the purpose of performing his functions as a safety representative or to permit him to go on a training course, or
(b) the employer has failed to pay him for his time off.

5.158   The complaint must be presented within three months from the date when the failure occurred or, if it was not reasonably practicable to do so within that time, within such further period of time as the employment tribunal considers to be reasonable. If the employment tribunal upholds the complaint that the employer has failed to permit him to have time off, a declaration to that effect shall be made. Additionally, the employment tribunal may make an award of compensation to be paid by the employer to the employee, which shall be of such amount as the tribunal considers to be just and equitable in all the circumstances, having regard to the employer's default in failing to permit the employee to have the time off, and to any loss suffered by the employee as a result of that failure. The compensation awarded would normally be a modest amount, for it will be rare that an employee actually suffers any loss. In *Owens v Bradford Health Authority* a trade union appointed as a safety representative a man who was within a year of retirement. He applied to go on a training course, but the employers refused, as they did not think it was reasonable for a safety representative so near to retirement to go on a training course. The employment tribunal upheld the employee's complaint, and awarded him £50 compensation. It is the prerogative of the trade union to make the appointment and a refusal to send someone on a training course because he was near to retirement was not justified.

5.159   If the complaint is that of a failure to pay for the time off work, and it is upheld by the employment tribunal, an award of the amount due to be paid will be made.

5.160 The enforcement of the other duties in the Act and the regulations is the responsibility of the appropriate enforcing authority. Thus if the employer fails to consult with the safety representatives, as required by s.2(4), or fails to set up a safety committee as required by s.2(7), or fails to provide the necessary information as required by regulation 7, he will be in breach of the law and thus commits a criminal offence. HSC has issued Guidance Notes on how HSE should attempt to deal with the enforcement of these matters. In three cases, they will not go to immediate enforcement, but will try other means. These are:

(a) HSE must be satisfied that all voluntary means have been explored, including the taking of advice from or using the services provided by the Advisory Conciliation and Arbitration Service (ACAS)

(b) if there is some doubt as to whether or not the trade union has made a valid appointment as a safety representative for example, the employer may allege that the trade union is not recognised by him; this problem might be resolved by using the services of ACAS

(c) if the problem relates to time off work, or a failure to pay, the specified remedy of using the machinery of the employment tribunal should first be explored.

5.161 Enforcement by the HSE might be appropriate in other cases, for example:

(a) if the trade union or safety representative complain that the employer is not carrying out his obligations after full use has been made of any consultative machinery or disputes procedure

(b) where the employer is refusing to acknowledge the existence of the safety representative who has been validly appointed

(c) where the employer refuses to make particular information available, or refuses to provide particular facilities to enable the safety representative to perform his functions

(d) where the employer has refused or failed to set up a safety committee after being requested to do so under regulation 9.

5.162 Since the employer will be in breach, and is "contravening one or more of the relevant statutory provisions" it is possible that instead of prosecuting for such breaches, the inspector may issue an improvement notice under s.21. To date, this tactic does not appear to have been necessary. Indeed, it is a credit to all concerned that the implementation of the provisions relating to safety representatives has, despite original fears, proceeded with great smoothness.

5.163 Also in force are the Offshore Installations (Safety Representatives and Safety Committees) Regulations 1989, which require the election of safety representatives by the whole workforce (but who cannot represent more than 40 employees) and a mandatory safety committee. There are a number of other differences between these regulations and the 1977 regulations.

Employment protection in health and safety cases

5.164 The Offshore Safety (Protection against Victimisation) Act 1992 gave protection against dismissal (or action short of dismissal) to safety representatives and members of safety committees who worked on offshore installations, and it was intended that such protection should be extended throughout industry. However, the Act was defective, in that it only applied to safety representatives who were appointed by recognised trade unions, whereas EC Directive (89/391/EEC) (the Framework Directive) requires that such protection should be given to all persons with health and safety responsibilities.

5.165 Consequently, the Act was repealed by the Trade Union Reform and Employment Rights Act 1993, and new rights were inserted into what is now the Employment Rights Act 1996. This Act provides that an employee has the right not to be subjected to any detriment (s.44) or be dismissed (s.100) on the grounds that:
  (a) having been designated by the employer to carry out activities in connection with preventing or reducing risks to health and safety at work, he carried out (or proposed to carry out) any such activities, or
  (b) being a representative of workers on matters of health and safety at work, or a member of a safety committee (whether under statutory or voluntary procedures) he performed (or proposed to perform) any functions as a representative or committee member, or
  (c) the employee took part in consultation with the employer in an election of representatives of employee safety.

5.166 The above provisions will clearly protect an employee who is a safety assistant (appointed under the Management of Health and Safety at Work Regulations 1999, see above) as well as safety representatives and safety committee members, whether appointed by independent trade unions, or elected by the work force, or nominated or appointed by the employer in non-union situations.

5.167   The protection for safety representatives is confined to those workers who are employees. In *Costain Building & Civil Engineering Ltd v Smith*, the claimant was an independent engineering consultant who worked for various agencies who supplied labour to building contractors. He was sent by an agency to work at a site being developed by Costain Building, and was appointed safety representative by a trade union in respect of work carried out at the site. After writing several critical safety reports, Costain Building informed the agency that they did not want him to work there any more. He claimed he had been unfairly dismissed for health and safety reasons. An employment tribunal upheld his claim, but the decision was reversed on appeal by the EAT. His contract was with the agency, and he was not an employee of Costain Building. The union's appointment of him as a safety representative was clearly ineffective in law. The protection afforded by s.100 of ERA was confined to those people who were employees.

5.168   The statutory provisions afforded to safety representatives do not confer on them a licence to be irresponsible, and are not designed to give blanket immunity. Thus if a safety representative acts in respect of matters which are not within the area of the workplace for which he is a representative, or acts outside the laid down procedure, or acts in bad faith, then it my be that he is not pursuing a genuine health and safety matter, but is pursuing a personal agenda in order to embarrass the employer. In such circumstances, he may be disciplined as appropriate (*Shillito v Van Leer (UK) Ltd*). Equally, the manner in which he performs his duties may be such as to take him outside the scope of his health and safety activities. This is a question of fact for the employment tribunal to decide (*Goodwin v Cabletel UK Ltd*). But if the safety representative is acting within his remit as such, he will not lose legal protection even if he goes "over the top", for he is entitled not to be overawed by management whilst exercising his proper functions (*Bass Taverns Ltd v Burgess*).

5.169   However, the statutory protection afforded to health and safety representatives, whilst designed to ensure that they are not disadvantaged because they exercise their functions, does not confer any advantage. Thus, in a redundancy exercise, they are entitled to have their performance assessed on the work they do under their normal contractual obligations, and the employer should not take into account the way they perform their health and safety functions. Indeed, to do this would amount to a positive discrimination in their favour, but discriminatory against other employees. The statutory protection is neutral (*Smiths Industries Aerospace & Defence Systems v Rawlings*).

Protection for employees in health and safety cases (Employment Rights Act 1996, s.100)

5.170   In addition, every employee will have the right not to be subjected to any detriment, or be dismissed, if:

(a) being at a place where there was no safety representative or safety committee (or where there was, but it was not reasonably practicable to go through those channels) he brought to the employer's attention, by reasonable means, circumstances connected with his work which he reasonably believed were harmful (or potentially so) to health or safety, or

(b) in circumstances of danger which he reasonably believed to be serious and imminent and which he could not reasonably be expected to avert, he left (or proposed to leave) or refused to return to (while the danger persisted) his place of work or any dangerous part of his place of work, or

(c) in circumstances of danger which he reasonably believed to be serious and imminent, he took (or proposed to take) appropriate steps to protect himself or other persons from danger.

5.171   The "other persons" (mentioned above) are not just employees, but can be members of the public. In *Masiak v City Restaurants Ltd* a chef claimed he was dismissed because he refused to cook food which he believed to be unfit for human consumption. It was held that s.100(1)(e) did not limit the class of persons at risk to danger only to fellow employees, and the claim was remitted back to an employment tribunal for a decision on the merits.

5.172   Whether the steps were appropriate is to be judged by reference to all the circumstances, including his knowledge and the facilities and advice he had at the time. But if it was negligent for the employee to act as he did, action taken against him by the employer would not be a detriment or unfair dismissal, as the case may be.

5.173   In *Harris v Select Timber Frames Ltd*, the employee made a complaint about health and safety standards at his employment, which resulted in a visit from an HSE inspector. He was due to be examined by an Employment Medical Advisor, but shortly before the date of the examination he was dismissed. The employment tribunal thought that in the circumstances he had been dismissed because he had raised the issue of health and safety, and his dismissal was therefore unfair.

5.174   The employment tribunals have considered a number of issues arising out of the protections given by s.100 of ERA, for example, complaints by drivers about a possible breach of the Drivers Hours Regulations, poor working conditions, lifting of heavy loads, confrontational representations made by employees who are not designated health and safety representatives, and action taken by employees to protect members of the public. An unusual case is *Harvest Press Ltd v McCaffrey*, where an employee walked out from his job because of the abusive and threatening behaviour of a colleague. Management interviewed the person responsible, but did not seek the claimant's version of events. It was held that the claimant had a reasonable belief that he was in serious and imminent danger. Section 100 was not confined to dangers which arise from the work or work premises, but covered any danger, no matter how it arose, including the actions or omissions of fellow employees. On the facts, he had been dismissed, and the dismissal was automatically unfair.

5.175   However, in order to claim the statutory protection, it must be shown that the employee's belief that there was a health or safety problem was based on reasonable grounds. Thus in *Kerr v Nathan's Wastesavers Ltd*, the applicant was employed to drive a van collecting bags of waste from different locations. One day he refused to drive the van, because he believed that it would become overloaded. He was dismissed, and claimed that the dismissal was unfair. It was accepted that he reasonably believed that the van would be overloaded by the time he finished his collections, and hence honestly believed that the circumstances were potentially harmful. However, he had failed to take into account the practice whereby drivers who found that their vehicles might be overloaded could return to the depot, or telephone to arrange for another vehicle to be sent. Thus he did not have reasonable grounds on which to sustain that belief, and hence his claim was dismissed by the employment tribunal and the Employment Appeal Tribunal (EAT).

5.176 In *Barton v Wandsworth Council*, the applicant was employed as an ambulance driver. His job involved transporting patients, who had severe physical and mental disabilities. He was accompanied by an escort on each occasion. However, the escorts were not experienced or trained properly, and the applicant made several complaints about the problems he was experiencing, pointing out the risks which were being run. Management felt that the applicant was being aggressive and overbearing, and suspended him pending an investigation. He was eventually given a five year warning about his behaviour, although following an internal appeal, this was reduced on appeal to two years. He claimed that the disciplinary action constituted a detriment. The employment tribunal upheld his complaint. He genuinely believed that the matters he complained about represented a serious and imminent danger to himself and to his patients. There was nothing unreasonable about his beliefs, for there had been a number of unfortunate incidents, and management had failed to address the problem with any sense of urgency. Finally, by transferring him to another centre, suspending him from work (with a consequent loss of overtime working) and imposing a two year final warning, his employer had caused him to suffer a detriment.

5.177 There is an implied term in the contract of employment that the employer will take reasonable steps to ensure the safety of his employees. Thus if an employer fails to address genuine fears or investigate legitimate complaints, this could amount to a fundamental breach of contract by the employer, entitling the employee to resign and claim that he was constructively dismissed.

5.178 The aggrieved employee may bring a claim in an employment tribunal within the usual period of three months. In addition, if he is dismissed, the interim relief procedures will be available, in which case a claim must be brought within seven days.

5.179 Under the Public Interest Disclosure Act 1998, (sometimes referred to as the "Whistleblowers Act") protection is given to workers (a wider term than employees) who make a "protected disclosure" in certain circumstances. They will have the right not to suffer a detriment (ERA, s.47A) not to be dismissed (ERA, s.103A) and not to be made redundant (ERA, s.105(6A)) because they made a protected disclosure.

As with all automatically unfair dismissals, no qualifying period of employment is required, and workers over the age of 65 may bring a claim.

5.180   A protected disclosure is one made by a worker which tends to show that:
  (a) a criminal offence has been, is being or is likely to be committed
  (b) a person has failed, is failing or is likely to fail to comply with a legal obligation
  (c) a miscarriage of justice has occurred or is likely to occur
  (d) the health or safety of any individual is being endangered
  (e) the environment has been, is being or is likely to be damaged
  (f) any of the above matters have been or are likely to be concealed.

5.181   The person making the disclosure must do so in good faith to his employer or other person in respect of whose conduct the above matters relate. However, there can be no protected disclosure in respect of legal privilege or confidentiality between client and professional advisor.

5.182   If disclosure is made to someone other than the employer, to be protected, the person making the disclosure must do so in good faith, reasonably believe the information is substantially true, and the disclosure must not be made for the purpose of personal gain. Thus disclosure could be made to a relevant regulatory body, or a legal adviser, or other responsible person. The worker must also believe that he will suffer a detriment if he makes the disclosure to the employer, or that the evidence will be destroyed or concealed, or he has already disclosed the information to his employer. In all the circumstances, it must be reasonable for him to make the disclosure. Thus, regard will have to be paid to the identity of the person to whom the disclosure was made, the seriousness of the matter, whether action was taken by the employer as a result of any previous disclosure, and whether the worker has complied with any procedure laid down by his employer.

Safety officers

5.183   Under the Management of Health and Safety at Work Regulations 1999 (see paragraph 5.4) every employer shall appoint one or more competent persons to assist him in undertaking the protective and preventative measures which have been identified in consequence of an assessment as to the measures he needs to take in order to comply with the relevant statutory provisions. There is also a requirement to appoint safety supervisors or competent persons to ensure compliance with statutory requirements under certain regulations, eg the Ship Building and Ship-repairing Regulations 1960, the Diving at Work Regulations 1997, the Ionising Radiations Regulations 1999, and a planning supervisor under the Construction (Design and Management) Regulations 1994. No formal standards of training are laid down, the obligation is merely to ensure that he has sufficient time to discharge his duties efficiently, has the experience and expertise necessary to carry out those duties, and the authority to perform his duties. The Transport of Dangerous Goods (Safety Advisers) Regulations 1999 require those who transport dangerous goods by road, rail or inland waterway will have to appoint vocationally qualified safety advisors.

5.184   There are also a number of statutory provisions which require an employee to be "qualified" or "trained", and other provisions require that certain things may only be done by or under the supervision of a "competent person" (see paragraph 5.191). These phrases are usually left undefined, and it may well be that the burden is on the employer to show in any given case that the person who performed the task in question was qualified, trained or competent, as the case may be. The possession of some formal Certificate or qualification would no doubt assist in discharging this burden but it may also be shown that the person concerned has pursued some approved course of training or instruction, as well as possessing practical experience of the work.

5.185   The existence of a safety officer, with details of his functions and powers, would be one of the things an employer would refer to in the written statement of his general policy on health and safety at work, as required by s.2(3) of HSWA, being part of the organisation and arrangements in force for the carrying into effect of that policy.

5.186   The relevant professional organisation for safety officers is the Institution of Occupational Safety and Health (IOSH), which was formed in 1953, and has over 20,000 members. The Institution's examining body is the National Examination Board in Occupational Safety and Health (NEBOSH). Two qualifications may be awarded:

(a) *Certificate*: this examination comprises two written papers (Identifying and Controlling Hazards, and Management of Safety) and a practical test; this course is suitable for those who have a part-time involvement in occupational health and safety

(b) *Diploma*: this course comprises five papers (Risk Management, Health and Safety Law, Occupational Health and Hygiene, Safety Technology and Case Study).

5.187   A new two-part National Diploma in Occupational Safety and Health was phased in from September 1997, replacing the former National Diploma. The new syllabus comprises five modules, the second part of the Diploma course dealing with subjects in greater depth. Part I of the course will satisfy Level 3 of the National Vocational Qualification and Scottish Vocational Qualification in Occupational Health and Safety Practice. Part II of the course will satisfy Level 4.

5.188   A person who has passed the Diploma Part II and has the appropriate period of professional experience may apply to be admitted as a member of IOSH. There are several grades of membership, depending on a person's qualifications and experience.

5.189   There are about 50 educational and training establishments throughout the country which offer Certificate or Diploma courses.

5.190   The Occupational Health and Safety Lead Body and the Employment Occupational Standards Council have now merged to form the Employment National Training Organisation. This body will be responsible for the development and marketing of vocational qualifications and standards of competence in occupational health and safety.

"Competent person"

5.191   A number of legislative provisions require that certain types of work (inspections, testing, assessments, etc) shall only be done by a "competent person" but the phrase is rarely defined and little guidance is given as to the abilities or expertise which are required. Some help may be obtained from an ACOP (eg see ACOP on Control of Asbestos at Work Regulations 1987, etc) but the provisions are usually in very general terms. The Management of Health and Safety at Work Regulations 1999 (see paragraph 5.4) provide that a person shall be regarded as competent "where he has sufficient training and experience or knowledge and other qualities to enable him properly" to do the task in question. However, the ACOP for Pressure Systems and Transportable Gas Containers Regulations 1989 (now revoked) did contain a very detailed definition of a competent person. In practice, whether or not a person is competent will be determined by the courts retrospectively in any particular case (see *Brazier v Skipton Rock*).

5.192   It is clear that the obligation is on the employer to select a competent person and to ensure that either he is trained in the relevant tasks to be performed or that he receives the necessary training. Full information must be given of the tasks to be performed, and all necessary facilities. A competent person is one who has the necessary theoretical and practical knowledge and has the technical and practical experience to carry out the task, such experience being matched to the complexity of the work and the degree of the risk. The statutory provision itself may indicate what is required. Thus, if a statute requires an "inspection", this is something less than an "examination"; it may be that the latter should be carried out by someone with appropriate technical qualifications, whereas the former need not be (see *Gibson v Skibs*).

5.193   However, the appointment of a "competent person", though evidence that the employer is attempting to meet statutory responsibilities, does not, by itself, prove that those responsibilities have in fact been met. The employer's duty is to meet his statutory and common law obligations, by actually adopting measures to ensure the health and safety of his employees. If those measures are not adopted, the fact that a competent person was appointed will not, by itself, absolve the employer from responsibility (see *Bell v Department of Health and Social Security*).

5.194   One would expect a competent person to be able to produce some evidence of his claim to be such, as well as the requisite experience. He would be expected to display the qualities which an ordinary member of his profession would have, but the law "does not require of a professional man that he be a paragon, combing the qualities of a polymath and prophet" (per Lord Justice Bingham, in *Eckersley v Binnie and Partners*).

Safety consultants

5.195   As indicated (see paragraph 5.26) every employer shall appoint one or more persons to provide health and safety assistance. In most cases, the ideal appointment will be made in-house, from persons who are familiar with the firm, its organisation, products, hazards and problems, etc. If no such person is readily available, a suitable person may be trained into the job. Sometimes specialist in-house knowledge will need to be supplemented by reference to external sources, eg trade associations, professional organisations, etc.

5.196 However, there will obviously be occasions when a suitable external consultant will be needed, and, in such circumstances, the employer must be quite clear of the precise nature of the need, and the role to be played. A formal consultancy agreement should be drawn up, with a detailed brief and defined objectives. Responsibilities should be determined, time scales laid down, performance monitored, fees agreed, and so on. The choice of consultant will more likely be determined by the nature of the problem, but, before an appointment is made, appropriate checks should be made on the applicant's qualifications, experience, references, etc. Once the appointment is made, the consultant will presumably make an initial review of the problems being faced, prepare a report on this, and suggest how he proposes to tackle them. Ideally, he should work towards the termination of his consultancy agreement, either by permanently resolving the problem, or putting in place proper procedures to prevent the problem from recurring, or training sufficient in-house staff in how to deal with the problem.

Occupational health services

5.197 The Management of Health and Safety at Work Regulations 1999 (see paragraph 5.23) require an employer to provide employees with such health surveillance as is appropriate having regard to the risks to their health and safety identified by the risk assessment which has been carried out, but this does not give rise to a general legal obligation to provide medical services at the place of work (but see Health and Safety (First Aid) Regulations 1981, Chapter 6). Many employers engage trained medical personnel to ensure the immediate treatment of injuries or illnesses which may occur during the employment, carry out pre-employment screening, investigate existing or potential medical hazards, or generally to provide a health care service for the benefit of employees. Occupational health services, by their very nature, are usually found in large firms, although there is a recent trend for smaller firms to pool together their resources and run a joint scheme. Sometimes the impetus comes from the need to reduce the incidence of accidents or ill health and consequently reduce the number of days lost through absenteeism. In other cases, the service may be part of the company's philosophy to provide additional welfare services on the premises for the use of all employees. Whatever the motive, occupational health services are on the increase.

5.198   Doctors and Registered General Nurses (RGNs) who practise occupational health may obtain their associateship of the Faculty of Occupational Medicine (AFOM) from a recognised institution. Doctors may obtain a Diploma in Industrial Health (DIH) or an MSc in Occupational Medicine. Nurses may obtain a Certificate or Diploma in Occupational Health Nursing (OHNC or OHND).

5.199   The relationship between works doctors (or nurses), management, trade unions, the individual and his own family doctor is a complex one, for problems of confidentiality and conflicting interests may arise.

CHAPTER 6

Health and safety regulations

6.1   In this Chapter we shall consider the more important health and safety regulations brought into force under the Health and Safety at Work, etc Act 1974 (HSWA). The use of regulations, as a means of laying down health and safety standards, enables changes in the legal requirements to be implemented by a procedure which is cheaper, speedier and less time consuming than that which would have to be adopted if changes had to be made by Acts of Parliament. All regulations are now subject to a prior consultation process, so that the views of all interested parties (industry, trade unions, pressure groups, etc) can be taken into account. The requirements of EU Directives are also often implemented via regulations in this way.

Workplace (Health, Safety and Welfare) Regulations 1992

6.2   The objective of these regulations is to implement most of the requirements of Directive (89/654/EEC), while the remaining requirements will be dealt with by other legislative provisions (eg on fire precautions). It is also thought that some requirements of the Directive are adequately dealt with by existing British law, and no changes are proposed in these areas (eg first aid). However, other existing legislation, though adequate, is not comprehensive enough, because it only applies to certain defined premises (eg factories, offices, shops and railway premises, etc). Thus most of these provisions will have been repealed or revoked, to be replaced by the new comprehensive provisions which will apply to all workplaces. The regulations are accompanied by an Approved Code of Practice with guidance, L24: *Workplace health, safety and welfare.*

6.3   The regulations took effect in two stages. With regard to workplaces (including any modifications, extensions or conversions) which were in use prior to 1 January 1993, a three year lead-in period was allowed to enable employers to comply with the legal requirements, and, in respect of those premises only, the "old law" (contained in the Factories Act and Offices, Shops and Railway Premises Act) remained applicable. That period has now expired, and thus the regulations are now fully in force. So far as premises first used on or after 1 January 1993, the regulations have to be complied with from that date.

6.4   The regulations apply to all workplaces, ie any premises (which are not domestic premises) which are made available to any person as a place of work, including any place within the premises to which a person working has access while at work, and any room, lobby, corridor, staircase, road or other place used as a means of access to or egress from the workplace, or where facilities are provided for use in connection with the workplace, other than a public road.

6.5   The application of the regulations is, therefore, very wide. They will apply not only to the traditional factories, offices and shops, but also to schools, hospitals, theatres, common parts of shared buildings, private roads on industrial estates, hotels, nursing homes, etc in fact almost anywhere where people work other than domestic premises (homeworkers are thus not covered by the regulations).

6.6   There are, however, certain statutory exceptions, where the regulations will not apply, or where only limited compliance is required. These are as follows:

    (a) means of transport, including ships, aircraft, trains and road vehicles, although regulation 13 (below) will apply when these places are stationary inside a workplace or when a vehicle is not on a public road

    (b) mines, quarries and other sites where minerals are being explored or extracted, including offshore sites and installations (these workplaces have their own separate legislation)

    (c) sites where building operations or works of engineering construction are being carried out; if construction work is being carried on within a workplace, the site will be excluded if it is fenced off, otherwise the Construction Regulations and the Workplace Regulations will both apply

    (d) so far as temporary sites are concerned, the welfare provisions of the Regulations (regulations 20–25, below) will apply "so far as is reasonably practicable"; a temporary site is one used for a short period or infrequently, eg a fairground

    (e) so far as agriculture and forestry work is concerned, regulations 20–22 (below) apply so far as is reasonably practicable.

6.7   In general, the regulations place duties on employers in respect of workplaces under their control and where their employees work. In addition, duties are placed on controllers of premises in respect of matters within their control. For example, the owner of a multi-occupancy building will be responsible for the common provision of services and facilities (toilets, ventilation plant, etc) thus extending the legal obligations set out in s.4 of HSWA (see paragraph 3.82).

6.8   A breach of the regulations may give rise to civil and/or criminal liabilities.

Maintenance of workplace, and of equipment, devices and systems (regulation 5)

6.9   The workplace, and the equipment, devices and systems shall be maintained (including cleaned as appropriate) to an efficient state, in efficient order and in good repair.

6.10   This regulation applies to equipment, devices and systems, a fault in which is liable to result in a failure to comply with other regulations. Examples of equipment, devices and systems include mechanical ventilation systems, emergency lighting, fencing, fixed equipment used for cleaning windows, powered doors, escalators and moving walkways, etc.

6.11   The ACOP points out that regular maintenance shall be carried out at suitable intervals, dangerous defects remedied, and a suitable record kept.

Ventilation (regulation 6)

6.12   Effective and suitable provision shall be made to ensure that every enclosed workplace is ventilated by a sufficient quantity of fresh or purified air. Any plant used shall include an efficient device which gives a visible or audible warning of any failure. Certain enclosed workplaces are excluded from the regulation (see regulation 6(3)).

6.13   Additional information on compliance with this regulation is given in the ACOP and guidance.

Temperature in indoor workplaces (regulation 7)

6.14   During working hours, the temperature in all workplaces inside buildings shall be reasonable. A method of heating shall not be used which results in the escape into the workplace of fumes, gas or vapour which may be injurious or offensive. A sufficient number of thermometers shall be provided.

6.15   The ACOP suggests that the temperature should provide reasonable comfort without the need for special clothing. It should be at least 16°C unless the work involves severe physical effort, when it should be at least 13°C. These temperatures do not apply to workplaces where lower maximum room temperatures are required by law. The ACOP does not specify a maximum temperature, but this too must be reasonable (see·HSWA s.2(2)(e)). Thus, if there is an exceptional heat wave, a reasonable temperature must still be observed.

Lighting (regulation 8)

6.16   Every workplace shall have suitable and sufficient lighting, which, so far as is reasonably practicable, shall be by natural light. Sufficient emergency lighting shall be provided in any room where persons are exposed to danger if artificial lighting fails.

6.17   The ACOP points out that lighting should also be placed at places of particular risk, eg pedestrian crossing points on traffic routes, dazzling lights and glare should be avoided, and light fittings should not cause a hazard. Lights should not be permitted to become obscured, they should be replaced, repaired or cleaned as necessary.

Cleanliness and waste materials (regulation 9)

6.18   Every workplace, and the furniture, furnishings and fittings therein shall be kept sufficiently clean. Surfaces of floors, walls and ceilings shall be capable of being kept sufficiently clean. So far as is reasonably practicable, waste materials shall not be allowed to accumulate except in suitable receptacles.

6.19   The ACOP states that floors and indoor traffic routes should be cleaned at least once each week. If dirt or refuse is not in suitable receptacles, it should be removed daily.

Room dimensions and space (regulation 10)

6.20   Every room where persons work shall have sufficient floor area, height and unoccupied space for purposes of health, safety and welfare. It will be sufficient compliance in a workplace which is not a new workplace, conversion or extension, and which, immediately before 1 January 1993, was subject to the provisions of the Factories Act 1961, if the workplace complies with the provisions which were contained in s.2 of the Factories Act, ie 11m^3 for each person (ignoring space more than 4.2m from the floor, see Schedule 1, Part 1 to the regulations).

6.21   The ACOP adopts the standard of 11m^3 for each person, although it suggests ignoring space which is more than 3m high when making this calculation. There are exceptions in certain employment where space is limited, eg retail sales kiosks, attendants' shelters, etc. The number of persons who may work in a room at any particular point in time will also depend on the space taken up by furniture, equipment, etc.

Workstations and seating (regulation 11)

6.22   Every workstation shall be so arranged that it is suitable for the person at work and for any work likely to be done there. A workstation which is out of doors shall be so arranged that:
   (a) so far as is reasonably practicable, it provides protection from adverse weather
   (b) it enables any person at the workstation to leave it swiftly or be assisted in the event of an emergency
   (c) it ensures that any person at the workplace is not likely to slip or fall.

6.23   If a substantial part of the work can be done while the person at work is seated, then a suitable seat shall be provided. The seat must be suitable for the person and for the operations to be performed. A suitable footrest shall be provided where necessary.

6.24   The ACOP states that workstations should be so arranged that each task can be carried out safely and comfortably. The worker should have adequate freedom of movement, spells of work carried out in cramped conditions should be limited, seating should provide adequate support for the lower back, and so on.

Condition of floors and traffic routes (regulation 12)

6.25   Workplace floors and surface traffic routes shall be so constructed that they are suitable for the purposes. The floor or surface shall not have a hole or slope, or be uneven or slippery so as to expose a person to a risk to his health or safety and shall have effective means of drainage as appropriate. Suitable and sufficient handrails and guards shall be provided on all traffic routes which are staircases.

6.26   The ACOP gives some practical advice on the construction of floors, stairs, etc and pays particular attention to hazards from spillages and contamination by liquids. Appropriate control measures should be taken.

Falls or falling objects (regulation 13)

6.27   So far as is reasonably practicable, suitable and effective measures shall be taken to prevent any person falling a distance likely to cause personal injury, and any person being struck by a falling object likely to cause personal injury. If there is an area where there is a risk of these events happening, this shall be indicated where appropriate. Every tank, pit or structure which contains a dangerous substance shall be securely fenced or covered if there is a risk of a person falling in.

6.28   The ACOP recommends that secure fencing should be provided wherever possible at any place where a person might fall 2m or more, although this standard is lowered if there are factors which might increase the risk of serious injury. Fixed ladders should not be provided if it would be practicable to install a staircase. Further advice is given on roof work, tanks, pits, etc which contain dangerous substances, stacking and racking, loading and unloading vehicles, scaffolding, etc.

Windows, and transparent or translucent doors, gates and walls (regulation 14)

6.29   Every window, transparent or translucent surface in a wall, partition, door or gate shall, where necessary for reasons of health or safety, be of safety material or protected against breakage. It shall also be appropriately marked.

6.30   The HSC has recently approved a change in paragraph 147 of the ACOP so as to clarify more precisely the factors to be taken into account when assessing whether it is necessary, for reasons of health or safety, for transparent or translucent surfaces to be made of a safety material or be adequately protected against breakage.

Windows, skylights and ventilators (regulation 15)

6.31   Windows, skylights or ventilators shall not be opened, closed or adjusted in a manner which exposes any person performing such an operation to a risk to his health or safety. Nor must they pose a risk to health and safety when open.

Ability to clean windows, etc safely (regulation 16)

6.32   All windows and skylights in a workplace shall be of a design or so constructed that they may be cleaned safely.

Organisation, etc of traffic routes (regulation 17)

6.33   Every workplace shall be organised in such a way that pedestrians and vehicles can circulate in a safe manner. Traffic routes shall be suitable for the persons or vehicles using them, in sufficient number, in suitable position and of sufficient size. (For existing workplaces, this duty shall be complied with "so far as is reasonably practicable".) Suitable measures shall be taken to ensure that pedestrians or vehicles may use traffic routes without causing danger to persons at work nearby, and there is sufficient separation between vehicles and pedestrians. Traffic routes shall be suitably indicated.

6.34   The ACOP gives considerable advice on how safe traffic routes may be achieved. A safe circulation of movement of persons and vehicles requires a suitable combination of the physical layout and safe system of use.

Doors and gates (regulation 18)

6.35   Doors and gates shall be suitably constructed, and fitted with any necessary safety devices. Sliding doors or gates shall have a device to prevent them from coming off tracks during use, an upward opening door or gate shall have a device to prevent it falling back, a powered door or gate shall have a suitable and effective feature to prevent it causing injury by trapping any person, and shall be capable of being operated manually (unless it opens automatically if the power fails), and a door or gate which is capable of being pushed from either side shall provide, when closed, a clear view of the space close to both sides.

Escalators and moving walkways (regulation 19)

6.36 Escalators and moving walkways shall function safely, be equipped with any necessary safety device, and fitted with one or more emergency stop controls which is easily identifiable and readily accessible.

Sanitary conveniences (regulation 20)

6.37 Suitable and sufficient sanitary conveniences shall be provided at readily accessible places. They shall be adequately ventilated and lit, kept in a clean and orderly condition, and separate rooms containing conveniences shall be provided for men and women, except where each convenience is in a separate room the door of which is capable of being secured from the inside.

6.38 So far as workplaces which were in use prior to 1 January 1993 are concerned, and which were subject to the provisions of the Factories Act 1961, it is sufficient compliance if the sanitary conveniences consist of at least one water closet for use by females only for every 25 females, and one for every 25 males (see Schedule 1, Part 2 of the regulations).

Washing facilities (regulation 21)

6.39 Suitable and sufficient washing facilities, including showers if required by the nature of the work for health reasons, shall be provided at readily accessible places. These shall be provided in the immediate vicinity of sanitary conveniences (whether or not provided elsewhere) and include a supply of clean hot and cold or warm running water. Soap or other means of cleaning and towels or other suitable means of drying shall be provided. The rooms shall be sufficiently ventilated and lit, kept clean and orderly, and have separate facilities for men and women, except where they are provided in a room which is capable of being secured from inside.

6.40 The ACOP specifies the minimum number of sanitary conveniences and washing stations which should be provided and deals with, in particular, remote workplaces and temporary work sites.

Drinking water (regulation 22)

6.41 An adequate supply of wholesome drinking water shall be provided for all persons at work in the workplace. This shall be at readily accessible places and be conspicuously marked by an appropriate sign. A sufficient number of suitable cups or other drinking vessels shall be provided, unless the supply is from a jet from which persons can drink easily.

Accommodation for clothing (regulation 23)

6.42   Suitable and sufficient accommodation for clothing shall be provided for clothing not worn during working hours, and for special clothing worn at work which is not taken home. The accommodation must be in a suitable location, and where facilities to change clothing are required by regulation 24 (below) suitable security must be provided. There must be separate accommodation for clothing worn at work where necessary to avoid risks to health (or damage to the clothing), and, so far as is reasonably practicable, the accommodation must allow or include facilities for drying clothing.

Facilities for changing clothing (regulation 24)

6.43   Suitable and sufficient facilities shall be provided for any person at work in the workplace to change clothing where the person has to wear special clothing for the purpose of work, and he cannot, for reasons of health or propriety, be expected to change in another room. Separate facilities for men and women shall be provided where necessary for reasons of propriety.

6.44   In *Post Office v Footitt* it was held that "special clothing" was not restricted to clothing which is worn only at work, but could include clothing worn while travelling to and from work, as well as at work (such as a uniform). Further, the concept of propriety is not confined to gender separation, and that to require one female to undress or dress in the presence of another may offend against the principles of propriety. That many women would not object to changing in the presence of others of the same sex did not absolve the employer from providing facilities for those who may prefer privacy.

Facilities for rest and to eat meals (regulation 25)

6.45   Suitable and sufficient rest facilities shall be provided at readily accessible places. In the case of new workplaces, extensions or conversions, where necessary for reasons of health or safety, one or more

221

rest rooms shall be provided. In other cases, a rest room or rest areas may be provided. Where food is eaten in a workplace which would otherwise become contaminated, suitable facilities for eating meals shall be provided.

6.46 Rest rooms and rest areas shall include suitable arrangements to protect non-smokers from discomfort caused by tobacco smoke. Suitable facilities shall be provided for any person at work who is a pregnant woman or nursing mother to rest.

6.47 Suitable and sufficient facilities shall be provided for persons at work to eat meals, where meals are eaten regularly in the workplace.

6.48 The ACOP suggests that suitable seats should be provided as appropriate, eating facilities should be kept clean to a suitable hygiene standard, and general advice is further given on compliance with this regulation.

Exemption certificates (regulation 26)

6.49 The Secretary of State for Defence may, in the interests of national security, exempt the armed forces and visiting armed forces from the requirements of the regulations, subject to conditions and a time limit.

Repeals and revocations (regulation 27 and Schedule 2)

6.50 The following statutory provisions have been repealed in respect of new premises (see paragraph 6.3), as from 1 January 1993:
  (a) Factories Act 1961, ss.1–7, 18, 29, 57–60, 69
  (b) Offices, Shops and Railway Premises Act 1963, ss.4–16
  (c) Agriculture (Safety, Health and Welfare Provisions) Act 1956, ss.3, 5, 25(3)(6).

6.51 Some 36 regulations and Orders, dating from 1906 onward, have also been revoked, either in whole or in part, from the same date, in respect of new premises.

6.52 In respect of existing premises (see paragraph 6.3) the above repeals and revocations took effect from 1 January 1996.

Provision and Use of Work Equipment Regulations 1998

6.53   The Provision and Use of Work Equipment Regulations 1992 were passed to implement Directive 89/655/EEC on the minimum health and safety requirements for the provision and use of work equipment at the workplace. These regulations have now been revoked and replaced by the Provision and Use of Work Equipment Regulations 1998 (PUWER), which implement Directive 95/63/EC, and generally extend the scope of the 1992 regulations to include mobile, self-propelled and remote controlled work equipment, lifting equipment, and power presses. In consequence, s.19 of the Offices, Shops and Railway Premises Act 1963 was repealed, and some 12 sets of regulations revoked, including the Power Presses Regulations 1965, Abrasive Wheels Regulations 1970, and the Woodworking Machines Regulations 1974. The 1992 Regulations repealed a number of familiar legal provisions, including ss.12–16, 17, and 19 of the Factories Act 1961, s.17 of Offices, Shops and Railway Premises Act 1963, and some 17 sets of regulations (in whole or in part) were revoked. The new regulations are accompanied by a Code of Practice and Guidance Notes (L22: *Safe use of work equipment*).

6.54   To some extent there is an overlap between PUWER and provisions which implement a number of EC product Directives, including the Supply of Machinery (Safety) Regulations 1992 (as amended). These "Supply" Regulations (listed in Schedule 1 to PUWER) impose obligations on manufacturers and suppliers of work equipment to meet essential health and safety requirements (in line with s.6 of HSWA) and work equipment which is able to satisfy those requirements will to that extent be exempt from some of the specific requirements of PUWER, contained in regulations 11–19 and 22–29.

6.55   There is also an overlap between PUWER and a number of other legislative provisions. The general rule to be adopted is that compliance with specific legal requirements will be sufficient to comply with more general requirements. For example, regulation 19 of PUWER requires isolation from sources of energy, but, so far as electrical power is concerned, the specific requirements of regulation 12 of the Electricity at Work Regulations 1989 would be the more appropriate legal rule to follow.

Application of the regulations

6.56 The regulations impose obligations on every employer in respect of work equipment provided for use by an employee at work, and also impose obligations on self-employed persons, and persons who have control to any extent of work equipment to the extent of that control. Duties are also placed on those who use, supervise or manage the use of work equipment or the way work equipment is used. Generally speaking, the regulations do not apply to a ship's work equipment, but they do apply to offshore installations. A breach of the regulations may give rise to civil and/or criminal liabilities.

6.57 Work equipment is defined as "any machinery, appliance, apparatus, tool or installation for use at work (whether exclusively or not)" (this definition differs materially from the definition in the 1992 regulations). The courts have adopted a very wide and liberal approach to the meaning of "work equipment", including materials used in cleaning processes (*Ralston v Greater Glasgow Health Board*), a ship (*Coltman v Bibby Tankers Ltd*), a flagstone (*Knowles v Liverpool City Council*), and a bolt (*Kelly v First Engineering Ltd*). Work equipment is "in use" when there is any activity involving work equipment and includes starting, stopping, programming, setting, transporting, repairing, modifying, maintaining, servicing and cleaning.

6.58 The main provisions of the regulations are as follows.

Suitability of work equipment (regulation 4)

6.59 Work equipment shall be so constructed or adapted as to be suitable for the purpose. When selecting work equipment, every employer shall have regard to the working conditions and to the risks to the health and safety of persons which exist in the premises or undertaking in which that work equipment is to be used, and any additional risk posed by the use of that equipment. Work equipment shall be used only for operations for which, and under conditions for which, it is suitable.

6.60 The ACOP and Guidance Notes point out that the risk assessment carried out under the Management of Health and Safety at Work Regulations 1999 (see paragraph 5.8) will help employers to select work equipment and assess its suitability for particular tasks. Ergonomic risks should be taken into account, and work equipment installed, located and used in such a way as to reduce risks to users and other workers. Energy and substances used or produced must be supplied and removed in a safe manner. If mobile work equipment has a combustion engine, there must be sufficient air of good quality.

Maintenance (regulation 5)

6.61   Work equipment shall be maintained in an efficient state, efficient working order and in good repair. Maintenance logs shall be kept up to date. This regulation imposes an absolute obligation. In *Stark v Post Office* the plaintiff was employed as a delivery postman by the Post Office. He suffered serious injuries when, in the course of his employment, the front brake stirrup of his delivery bicycle broke, with the result that he was thrown over the handlebars. The employers were held liable. It was their duty to ensure that the work equipment was maintained in an efficient state, in efficient working order, and in good repair, and they were thus in breach of their statutory duty.

6.62   The Guidance Notes state that maintenance should only be done by competent persons. Equipment should be checked frequently, maintenance management techniques used, and maintenance logs, if used, should be kept up to date.

Inspection (regulation 6)

6.63   Where the safety of work equipment depends on the installation conditions, it must be inspected before being put into service for the first time, or after assembly at a new site or location, to ensure that it has been installed correctly and is safe to operate. If work equipment is exposed to conditions causing deterioration which is liable to result in dangerous situations, it must be inspected at suitable intervals, to ensure that health and safety conditions are maintained, and that deterioration can be detected and remedied in good time. Records of such inspections shall be kept.

6.64   The purpose of the inspection is to identify whether the equipment can be operated, adjusted, and maintained safely, and that any deterioration can be detected and remedied. The ACOP suggests that the extent of the inspection required will depend on the potential risks.

Specific risks (regulation 7)

6.65   If the use of work equipment is likely to involve a specific risk, the use shall be restricted to those persons who have been specifically designated to use it. Repairs, modifications, maintenance or servicing of work equipment shall be restricted to those persons who have been specifically designated to perform such operations. Such persons shall be given adequate training in the operations in question.

6.66   The ACOP states that risks shall be controlled (a) by eliminating the risk, or (b) control measures, or (c) implementing safe systems, and providing information, instruction and training.

Information and instruction (regulation 8)

6.67   Employers shall ensure that all persons who use work equipment, including those who supervise or manage the use of work equipment, have available adequate health and safety information, and, where appropriate, written instructions. This includes information and instructions on the conditions in which, and the methods by which, work equipment may be used, any foreseeable abnormal situations likely to occur and the action to be taken if such a situation were to occur, and any conclusions to be drawn from experience in using the work equipment. The information and instructions shall be readily comprehensible.

6.68   The Guidance Notes point out that it is for the employer to decide whether the information should be given in writing or verbally, taking into account whether there are unusual or complicated circumstances, the degree of skill of the workers involved, their experience and training, the degree of supervision and the complexity and length of the particular job. Supervisors and managers need access to information and written instructions, which should be presented to workers in clear English or other languages where necessary. Special considerations should be given to workers with language difficulties or with disabilities which may make it difficult for them to understand what is required.

Training (regulation 9)

6.69   Employers must ensure that all persons who use work equipment, and employees who supervise or manage the use of work equipment, have received adequate training for the purposes of health and safety, any risks which such use may entail, including the precautions to be taken.

6.70   The Guidance Notes point out that the requirements for adequate training will be determined by the nature of the job requirements and the work equipment. Special attention should be paid to the needs of young persons. The ACOP draws attention to the need to train drivers of self-propelled equipment and chainsaw operators.

Conformity with Community requirements (regulation 10)

6.71   It is the duty of an employer to ensure that an item of work equipment has been designed and constructed in compliance with any enactment which implements EC Product Directives (a list of the relevant regulations is set out in Schedule 1). Work equipment first provided after 31 December 1992 that is able to satisfy those requirements will not be covered by regulations 11–19 and 22–29 of these regulations.

6.72   The Guidance Notes point out that employers should ensure that work equipment complies with any legislation which implements any relevant legislation (in particular those provisions set out in Schedule 1 to the regulations), if necessary by checking to see if there is the CE marking, and ask for a copy of the EC Declaration of Conformity.

Dangerous part of machinery (regulation 11)

6.73   Employers shall take effective measures to prevent access to any dangerous part of machinery, or to stop the movement of any dangerous part of machinery before any part of a person enters a danger zone. This can he achieved by fixed guards or protection devices, or jigs, holders, pushsticks, etc where it is practicable to do so, but where or to the extent it is not, then the provision of information, instruction, training or supervision. Guards and protection devices shall be suitable for the purpose, of good construction, sound material and adequate strength, be maintained in an efficient state, not give rise to any increased risk to health or safety, not easily bypassed or disabled, be situated at sufficient distance from the danger zone, not unduly restrict the view of the operating cycle of the machinery (where such view is necessary), be so constructed that operations to fit replacement parts and maintenance work can be carried out without having to dismantle the guard or protection device.

6.74 Again, the risk assessment should identify the hazards from machinery, and determine what risk reduction measures are needed. Attached to the Guidance Notes is Appendix 2, which sets out various requirements for guards and protective devices.

Protection against specified hazards (regulation 12)

6.75 Where certain specified hazards are likely to occur, measures shall be taken to ensure that exposure is prevented, or adequately controlled, by measures other that the use of personal protective equipment, as well as by minimising the effects of the hazard and reducing the likelihood of it occurring. The specified hazards are:
  (a) articles or substances falling or being ejected from the work equipment
  (b) rupture or disintegration of parts of work equipment
  (c) work equipment catching fire or overheating
  (d) the unintended or premature discharge of any article or substance which is produced, used or stored in the work equipment, or
  (e) the unintended or premature explosion of work equipment or any article or substance produced, used or stored in it.

6.76 However, this regulation does not apply where the following regulations apply, ie Ionising Radiations Regulations 1999, Control of Asbestos at Work Regulations 1987, Noise at Work Regulations 1989, Construction (Head Protection) Regulations 1989, Control of Lead at Work Regulations 1998, and Control of Substances Hazardous to Health Regulations 1999.

6.77 In general, the risk assessment will identify the likely hazards, eg material falling from equipment, or being ejected, pieces of equipment breaking away, overheating, explosions due to pressure build-up, etc. The primary aim is to prevent the occurrence, but if this is not possible, steps must be taken to reduce the risks. Thus the discharge or ejection of materials intentionally, or inevitably (eg sawdust from woodworking, grit-blasting of castings) is not prohibited as such, but risks must be controlled.

High and very low temperature (regulation 13)

6.78   Where work equipment, or articles or substances produced, used or stored in work equipment, is at a very high or very low temperature, protection must be afforded so as to prevent injury to any person by burn, scald or sear.

6.79   The Guidance Notes point out that although engineering methods should be considered first, other forms of protection may be necessary, eg warning signals, alarms, personal protective equipment, etc.

Starting controls (regulation 14)

6.80   Controls which require a deliberate action (except normal cycles of automatic devices) shall be provided for starting work equipment, or controlling changes in speed pressure, etc where a change results in a greater risk to health and safety. It should not be possible to start or change speed except by a deliberate action on a control, although this does not apply to re-starting or changing operating condition as a result of the normal operating cycle of an automatic device.

6.81   The Guidance Notes state that controls should be designed and positioned so as to prevent inadvertent or accidental operation.

Stop controls (regulation 15)

6.82   Readily accessible stop controls shall be provided which will bring the work equipment to a safe condition in a safe manner, if necessary, for reason of health and safety, to a complete stop, and sources of energy switched off. Stop controls shall act in priority to other controls.

Emergency stop controls (regulation 16)

6.83   Work equipment shall be provided with readily accessible emergency stop controls, unless this is not necessary by reason of the nature of the hazard, and the time taken to come to a complete stop using other controls.

Controls (regulation 17)

6.84   All controls must be clearly visible and identifiable, and not in a position which exposes the operator to a risk to his health or safety. The control operator must be able to ensure from the position of control that no person is in a place where he would be exposed to any risk to his health or safety, as a result of the operation of the control, but where this is not reasonably practicable, the systems of work shall be effective to ensure that when work equipment is about to start, no person is in any such place, or, where this is not reasonably practicable, audible, visual or other suitable warnings are given. Any person who is in a place where he would be exposed to a risk as a result of stopping or starting work equipment shall have sufficient time and suitable means to avoid the risk.

Control systems (regulation 18)

6.85   Control systems shall be safe, and fault or damage must not create an additional or increased risk to health or safety. Control systems must not impede the operation of any stop or emergency controls.

Isolation from sources of energy (regulation 19)

6.86   Where appropriate, work equipment must be provided with suitable means to isolate it from all its sources of energy, and reconnection must not expose any person to any risk.

Stability (regulation 20)

6.87   Work equipment shall be stabilised or clamped where necessary for purposes of health or safety.

Lighting (regulation 21)

6.88   Suitable and sufficient lighting, which takes into account the operations to be carried out, shall be provided at any place where a person uses work equipment.

Maintenance operations (regulation 22)

6.89 Appropriate measures shall he taken to ensure that, so far as is reasonably practicable, maintenance operations shall be carried out while the work equipment is shut down, or otherwise carried out without exposing persons to risk. Appropriate measures shall also be taken to ensure that a person carrying out maintenance is not exposed to risk to his health or safety.

Markings (regulation 23)

6.90 Work equipment shall be marked in a clearly visible manner, with any marking appropriate for reasons of health and safety.

Warnings (regulation 24)

6.91 Warnings or warning devices shall be provided, where appropriate for reasons of health or safety. Warnings shall be unambiguous, easily perceived and easily understood.

Mobile work equipment (regulations 25–30)

6.92 There are detailed requirements in respect of mobile work equipment (including fork-lift trucks and self propelled work equipment). Steps shall be taken to minimise the risk of roll-over, by stabilising the equipment, or providing structures or devices which give protection. Fork-lift trucks shall be adapted or equipped to reduce the risk to safety from overturning. Steps shall be taken to prevent unauthorised persons from starting self-propelled work equipment, minimising the consequences of collision, provide braking devices, and ensuring the driver's vision is adequate. Remote controlled self-propelled work equipment shall stop automatically once it is out of its control range, and have features to guard against the risks of crushing or impact.

Power presses (regulations 31–35)

6.93 There are detailed provisions for power presses (excluding power presses detailed in Schedule 2). Power presses, guards and protection devices shall be thoroughly examined when put into service for the first time, to make that it has been installed correctly, is safe to operate, and any defect remedied. Further thorough examinations shall take place every 12 months where there are fixed guards, or every 6 months in any other case. Power presses shall not be used after setting, re-setting or adjustment of its tools, unless every guard and protection device has been tested while in position by a person who is competent or undergoing training under the supervision of a competent person. A certificate of inspection and testing must be signed. A person making a thorough inspection shall notify the employer forthwith of any defect which could become a danger to persons, and make a report of the thorough examination, containing the information set out in Schedule 3. (See also the Approved Code of Practice and guidance, L112: *Safe use of power presses.*)

Lifting Operations and Lifting Equipment Regulations 1998

6.94   These regulations give effect to certain provisions of Directive 89/665/EEC as amended by Directive 95/63/EC, and deal with the particular risks posed by the provision and use of lifting equipment and the management of lifting operations. Existing sector-based legislation on this topic has been repealed, including 17 sets of regulations (in whole or in part) and ss.22, 23, and 25–27 of the Factories Act 1961. The regulations are accompanied by an Approved Code of Practice, L113: *Safe use of lifting equipment.*

6.95   The regulations impose duties on employers in respect of lifting equipment provided for use at work, and also to self-employed persons and to persons who have control to any extent of lifting equipment to the extent of their control. Generally speaking, they do not apply to a ship's work equipment, which is generally covered by merchant shipping legislation.

6.96   The main provisions of the regulations are as follows.

Strength and stability (regulation 4)

6.97   Lifting equipment shall be of adequate strength and stability for each load.

6.98   The Guidance Notes point out that particular attention should be paid to mounting or fixing points, and account should be taken of any combination of destabilising forces.

Lifting equipment for lifting persons (regulation 5)

6.99   Lifting equipment must ensure that a person cannot be crushed, trapped, struck or fall from the carrier, and, if it is not possible to have a suitable device to prevent the risk of the carrier falling, the carrier must have an enhanced safety coefficient rope or chain, which is inspected by a competent person every working day.

6.100   The ACOP suggests that the lift car should be fully enclosed when in use, and the floor of any carrier should be slip-resistant.

Positioning and installation (regulation 6)

6.101   Lifting equipment must be positioned or installed in such a way as to reduce the risk of the lifting equipment (or a load) striking a person, or from a load drifting, falling freely or being released unintentionally, and is otherwise safe.

6.102   The ACOP states that the positioning of lifting equipment should be such as to minimise the need for loads to be lifted over people. If a load moves along a fixed path, there should be a suitable and substantial enclosure; if the lifting equipment moves along a fixed path (less than two metres above the ground level) barriers or gates should be provided, to prevent a person being endangered by the underside of the lifting equipment or any fitting attached to it.

Marking of lifting equipment (regulation 7)

6.103   Machinery for lifting loads shall be clearly marked to indicate their safe working loads, including safe working loads for each configuration.

6.104   The Guidance Notes point out that a "safe working load" is a value or set of values based on the strength and/or stability of the equipment when lifting. Guidance is also given on handling safe working loads which vary in accordance with the configuration.

Organisation of lifting operations (regulation 8)

6.105   Every lifting operation must be properly planned by a competent person, appropriately supervised, and carried out in a safe manner.

6.106   The ACOP points out that the person planning the operation should have adequate practical and theoretical knowledge and experience of planning lifting operations. The risk assessment should reveal the risks, identify the resources required, the procedures and responsibilities. Measures should be taken to prevent lifting equipment from tilting, overturning, moving or slipping. If lifting equipment is to be used in the open air, meteorological conditions should be considered, and lifting operations halted if the integrity of the equipment could be affected, or persons exposed to danger.

Thorough examination and inspection (regulation 9)

6.107   Before lifting equipment is put into service for the first time, it must be thoroughly examined for any defect (unless it has not been used before and has an EC declaration of conformity). There must be a thorough examination after installation, and if it is likely to be exposed to conditions causing deterioration, thoroughly examined every 6 months if used for lifting persons, otherwise every 12 months, and also whenever exceptional circumstances have occurred which are likely to jeopardise its safety.

6.108   The Guidance Note states that the thorough examination should be by a competent person, who is independent and impartial, so that an objective decision can be made. Deterioration (which can take place for a number of reasons, such as wet, abrasive or corrosive environments) should be detected, and there should be a further examination when a significant change or circumstances has occurred (eg an accident, change of use, long period of disuse, etc).

Reports and defects (regulation 10)

6.109   A person making a thorough examination shall notify the employer of any defect in lifting equipment, make a report containing the information set out in Schedule 1 which shall be sent to the employer and any person from whom the equipment was hired or leased, and, if there is a defect involving an existing or imminent risk of serious personal injury, send a copy of the report to the relevant enforcing authority. Once notified of a defect, the employer shall not use the lifting equipment until the defect is remedied

Keeping of information (regulation 11)

6.110   If the employer has an EC declaration of conformity, he shall keep it for so long as he operates the equipment. The length of time other reports shall be kept will depend on the purposes for which they were made, which generally will be either until the employer ceases to use the equipment or for two years in other cases.

Personal Protective Equipment at Work Regulations 1992

6.111   These regulations are designed to implement Directive 89/656/EEC on the Minimum Health and Safety Requirements for the Use of Personal Protective Equipment at the Workplace. They came into force on 1 January 1993. They should be considered along with the Personal Protective Equipment (EC Directive) Regulations 1992, as amended which implement the Personal Protective Equipment Product Directive (89/686/EEC) dealing with the quality and marking of personal protective equipment (PPE).

6.112   There are in existence a number of health and safety regulations made under HSWA relating to PPE, ie Control of Lead at Work Regulations 1998, Ionising Radiations Regulations 1999, Control of Substances Hazardous to Health Regulations 1999, Noise at Work Regulations 1989, Construction (Head Protection) Regulations 1989, and Control of Asbestos at Work Regulations 1987, as amended. These regulations will continue in force, although they have been modified slightly so as to conform with the new regulations.

6.113   On the other hand, there are a large number of pre-HSWA regulations which deal with PPE, and most of these have been revoked (including the familiar Protection of Eyes Regulations) as they are no longer necessary. Certain legislative provisions which deal with specialised subjects (eg docks, electricity, construction and offshore installations) are retained, and are complemented by the new regulations. Also, the new regulations do not apply to the master or crew of a seagoing ship, to ordinary clothes or uniforms which do not specifically protect the health and safety of the wearer, portable devices for detecting risks and nuisances, PPE used for protection while travelling on a road, equipment used during the playing of competitive sports or an offensive weapon used for self-defence or deterrence.

6.114   PPE is defined as being all equipment (including clothing affording protection against the weather) which is intended to be worn or held by a person at work and which protects him against one or more risks to his health or safety. The Guidance Notes (L25: *Personal protective equipment at work*) suggest that PPE includes protective clothing (aprons, waterproof clothes, gloves, safety footwear, safety helmets, high visibility waistcoats, etc) and protective equipment (eye protectors, life jackets, respirators, underwater breathing apparatus and safety harnesses). Ordinary working clothes and protective clothing used for the purpose of hygiene would not be included.

6.115   The Personal Protective Equipment (EC Directive) Regulations 1992, as amended implement the EC PPE Product Directive and, where appropriate (after 30 June 1995), PPE will have to bear the CE marking. However, PPE obtained before these Regulations came into force may continue to be used as long as it remains suitable for the purpose.

6.116   A breach of the regulations may give rise to civil and/or criminal liabilities.

Provision of personal protective equipment (regulation 4)

6.117   Every employer shall ensure that suitable PPE is provided to his employees who may be exposed to a risk to their health or safety while at work, except where and to the extent that such risk has been adequately controlled by other means which are equally or more effective. A similar obligation is imposed on self-employed persons in respect of their own activities.

6.118   PPE shall not be suitable, unless:
  (a) it is appropriate for the risk involved and the conditions at the place where exposure to the risk may occur
  (b) it takes account of the ergonomic requirements and the state of health of the wearer
  (c) it is capable of fitting the wearer correctly (if necessary after adjustment)
  (d) so far as is practicable, it is effective to prevent or adequately control the risks involved without increasing overall risk
  (e) it complies with any enactment which implements relevant EU Directives applicable to that item of PPE.

6.119   The Guidance Notes suggest that PPE should be regarded as a "last resort". Engineering controls and safe systems of work should first be considered, so that risks are controlled or prevented at source. PPE should be readily available, and generally supplied to employees on an individual basis, although there may be circumstances where it can be shared (eg if required for only a limited period).

6.120   No charge may be made for the provision of PPE (HSWA, s.9, see paragraph 3.113), even if the employer permits the use by the employee outside working hours.

6.121   When considering the provision of PPE, it is important to bear in mind the need to avoid "overkill". For example, if there is a noise hazard, the protection must match the volume of noise which is hazardous, but not eliminate harmless (or even useful) noise, for this could result in a greater hazard being created. An employee who wears every single item of protective clothing provided by his employer would probably resemble someone from outer space, and is likely to be a positive menace to himself and to others.

6.122   PPE must be suitable for each employee to use or wear, for the legal duty is owed to them as individuals, not collectively (*Paris v Stepney Borough Council*).

6.123   The legal problems involved in enforcing the use of PPE will be examined in Chapter 9.

Compatibility of personal protective equipment (regulation 5)

6.124   Every employer shall ensure that where the presence of more than one risk makes it necessary for his employee to wear or use simultaneously more than one item of PPE, such equipment is compatible and continues to be effective against the risks in question. A similar obligation is placed on self-employed persons.

Assessment of personal protective equipment (regulation 6)

6.125   Before choosing PPE, employers (and self-employed persons) shall ensure that an assessment is made in order to determine whether the PPE he intends to provide is suitable. The assessment shall include:
  (a) risks which have not been avoided by other means
  (b) the definition of the characteristics which the PPE must have in order to be effective
  (c) a comparison of the characteristics of the PPE available with those needed to avoid the risk.

6.126   Employers (and self-employed persons) shall review any such assessment if they have reason to believe that it is no longer valid, or if there has been a significant change in the matters to which it relates. If any changes are required as a result of the review, these shall be made.

6.127   The Guidance Notes (Appendix 1) give a specimen risk survey table which may be used to determine whether or not PPE is required. There is also considerable advice given on the selection, use and maintenance of PPE in widely different circumstances.

Maintenance and replacement of personal protective equipment (regulation 7)

6.128   Every employer shall ensure that any PPE provided to his employees is maintained in an efficient state, in efficient order, in good repair and is replaced or cleaned as appropriate. A similar obligation is placed on self-employed persons.

6.129   The Guidance Notes suggest that PPE should be examined when issued, before it is used or worn, and it should not be used or worn if found to be defective or unclean. A sufficient stock of spare parts should be available, and maintenance programmes should include, where appropriate, cleaning, disinfection, examination, repair, testing and record keeping. Manufacturers' maintenance schedules and instructions should normally be followed.

Accommodation for personal protective equipment (regulation 8)

6.130   Every employer shall ensure that appropriate accommodation is provided for PPE when it is not being used.

6.131   The Guidance Notes point out that accommodation may be simple, as long as it is appropriate. It should protect PPE from contamination, loss or damage.

Information, instruction and training (regulation 9)

6.132   Where PPE is provided, employers shall ensure that the employee is provided with such information, instruction and training as is adequate and appropriate to enable the employee to know:
   (a) the risks which the PPE will avoid or limit
   (b) the purpose for which, and the manner in which the PPE is to be used, and

(c) any action to be taken by the employee to ensure that it remains in an efficient state, in efficient working order and in good repair.

6.133   The information and instructions given will not be adequate and appropriate unless it is comprehensible to the persons to whom it is provided.

6.134   The Guidance Notes point out that the extent of the training will vary with the complexity of the equipment. Training should be both theoretical and practical, and its duration and frequency will depend on the individual circumstances. Refresher training should be considered if necessary.

Use of personal protective equipment (regulation 10)

6.135   Every employer shall take all reasonable steps to ensure that any PPE provided to his employees is properly used.

6.136   Every employee shall use PPE provided to him in accordance with the training given to him and the instructions respecting its use. Self-employed persons shall also make full and proper use of PPE. Employees and self-employed persons shall take all reasonable steps to ensure that PPE provided is returned to the accommodation provided for it after use.

Reporting loss or defect (regulation 11)

6.137   Every employee who has been provided with PPE shall forthwith report to his employer any loss or obvious defect.

Exemption certificates (regulation 12)

6.138   The Secretary of State for Defence may exempt the armed forces and visiting armed forces from the regulations, subject to conditions and/or limitations of time.

Extension outside Great Britain (regulation 13)

6.139   The regulations apply to offshore installations, pipelines within territorial waters and areas designated under the Continental Shelf Act 1964 (see paragraph 1.127).

Repeals, revocations and modifications (regulation 14)

6.140   The regulations revoke some 20 old regulations dealing with personal protective equipment, repeal s.65 of the Factories Act 1961, and modify six regulations (see paragraph 6.112) so that they harmonise with the new law.

Manual Handling Operations Regulations 1992

6.141   These regulations are designed to implement Directive 90/269/EEC on the minimum health and safety requirements for the manual handling of loads. They are accompanied by Guidance Notes (L23: *Manual handling*), and came into force on 1 January 1993.

6.142   Accidents caused by manual handling of loads account for some 25% of all reportable accidents. The cost to industry in terms of lost time, compensation payments, etc and the cost to the State by way of medical attention, social security benefits, etc is huge. Accidents of this nature occur in all types of employment and to all categories of workers. Previous legislation had a somewhat limited application, and was usually framed in a general manner. Some specific industries did have actual weight limits, but these were neither effective nor justifiable, because they failed to take into account individual capabilities.

6.143   Consequently, the new Regulations have repealed a number of statutory provisions, including Factories Act 1961, s.72, Offices, Shops and Railway Premises Act 1963, s.23(1), and Agriculture (Safety, Health and Welfare Provisions) Act 1956, s.2. In addition, the Agriculture (Lifting of Heavy Weights) Regulations 1959 were revoked, as was regulation 55 of the Construction (General Provisions) Regulations 1961.

Application of the regulations

6.144   The regulations apply to all employers in respect of their employees at work, including offshore installations, pipelines, etc (see paragraph 1.127). They also apply to self-employed persons in respect of their own activities. However, they do not apply to the master or crew of a seagoing ship.

6.145 The phrase "manual handling operations" is defined as any transporting or supporting of a load (including the lifting, putting down, pushing, pulling, carrying or moving) by hand or by bodily force. A "load" includes any person or animal. However, an injury does not include any contact with a corrosive or toxic substance.

6.146 A breach of the regulations may give rise to civil and/or criminal liability.

Duties of employers (regulation 4)

6.147 Every employer shall, so far as is reasonably practicable, avoid the need for his employees to undertake any manual handling operations which involve a risk of their being injured.

6.148 Where this is not reasonably practicable, the employer shall make a suitable and sufficient assessment of all such manual handling operations, taking into account the factors which are specified in Schedule 1 to the regulations, and considering the associated questions.

6.149 It should be noted that the regulations impose an almost unqualified duty to assess and reduce the risk of injury, as well as to provide employees with information about manual handling operations (*Swain v Denso Marston Ltd*). Thus a failure to carry out a manual handling assessment, or to train employees in safe lifting techniques can make an employer liable for back injuries suffered in consequence of lifting moderately heavy loads (*Stone v Commissioner of Police for the Metropolis*).

6.150 In *Hawkes v London Borough of Southwark* the plaintiff had to carry a heavy door (weighing 72 lbs), up a flight of stairs. Whilst trying to manoeuvre round a half-landing, he was knocked off balance, and fell injuring his ankle. The Court of Appeal held that it was not reasonably practicable to avoid doing the lifting other than by manual handling, and so a proper risk assessment should have been carried out by the employer. This would have revealed that there was a risk of injury, the risk was slight (there had been no previous similar accidents), but the cost of reducing that risk (by providing a second worker to assist) was also small. Thus the risk was not insignificant in relation to the cost to the employers of reducing the risk to the lowest level reasonably practicable, and they were held liable for damages.

6.151   The factors and the questions to be taken into account are as follows.

Factors to be taken into account	Questions

1. The tasks	Do they involve:
	– holding or manipulating loads at distances from the trunk?
	– unsatisfactory bodliy movement or posture, especially:
	  (a) twisting the trunk?
	  (b) stooping?
	  (c) reaching upwards?
	– excessive movement of loads, especially:
	  (a) excessive lifting or lowering of loads?
	  (b) excessive carrying distrances?
	– excessive pushing or pulling of loads?
	– risk of sudden movement of loads?
	– frequent or prolonged physical effort?
	– insufficient rest or recovery periods?
	– a rate of work imposed by a process?

2. The loads	Are they: – heavy? – bulky or unwieldy? – difficult to grasp? – unstable, or with contents likely to shift? – sharp, hot or otherwise potentially damaging?
3. The working environment	Are there: – space constraints preventing good posture? – uneven, slippery or unstable floors? – variations in level of floors or work surfaces? – extremes of temperature? – conditions causing ventialtion problems or gusts of wind? – poor lighting conditions?
4. Individual capability	Does the job: – require unusual strength, height, etc?

	– create a hazard to those who might reasonbly be considered to be pregnant or to have a health problem?
	– require special information or training for its safe performance?
5. Other factors	Is movement or posture hindered by personal protective equipment or by clothing?

6.152 Thus, having regard to those factors, and the answers to the questions posed, the employer shall take appropriate steps to reduce the risk of injury to those employees to the lowest level reasonably practicable.

6.153 The employer shall also provide general indications and precise information (where it is reasonably practicable to do so) on the weight of the load, and the heaviest side of any load whose centre of gravity is not positioned centrally. The assessment which has been carried out shall be reviewed if there is reason to believe that there has been a significant change in the operations, and such revisions made as are appropriate in the circumstances.

6.154 The Guidance Notes which accompany the regulations are extremely informative, and will repay detailed study. It is noted that the regulations set no specific requirements such as weight limits. Instead, they focus on the needs of the individual, based on a range of relevant factors which are used to determine the risk of injury, and indicate the remedial action which should be taken. It is pointed out that the aim of the regulations is to prevent injury to any part of the body, and thus account must be taken of the external properties of the load (eg slipperiness, sharp edges, etc) as well as its weight, size, bulk, etc. Hazards from the contents of the load (eg corrosive substances) are not generally covered, although this should be considered under other appropriate legislation, (eg COSHH regulations, etc). The load may be animate or inanimate, but generally will not be a tool or instrument.

6.155 The first task of the employer is to avoid manual handling where possible and where this is not possible the next task is to make an assessment, taking into account the matters already mentioned. Proper records should be kept, and any evidence which reveals an indication of a relationship between manual handling and illhealth (eg absenteeism due to some form of back injury) should be noted. Employees and safety representatives should be involved in redesigning the systems of work, loads should be reduced to manageable size or otherwise made risk free, and the capabilities of each employee assessed.

Duties of employees (regulation 5)

6.156   Each employee while at work shall make full and proper use of any system of work provided for his use by his employer in compliance with the latter's duty to take appropriate steps to reduce the risk of injury.

6.157   This duty should be read together with the employee's duty under s.7 of HSWA. Also of relevance is regulation 14 of the Management of Health and Safety at Work Regulations 1999 (see paragraph 5.53), which requires employees to use appropriate equipment provided.

Exemption certificates (regulation 6)

6.158   The Secretary of State for Defence may, in the interests of national security, exempt the armed forces and visiting armed forces from the requirements of certain parts of the regulations, subject to conditions and/or time limits.

Health and Safety (Display Screen Equipment) Regulations 1992

6.159   These regulations are designed to implement Directive 90/270/EEC on the minimum health and safety requirements for work with display screen equipment. They are accompanied by Guidance Notes, L26: *Display screen equipment at work.*

6.160   Currently, there are no other legislative provisions on this topic, other than the general duties laid down by HSWA. However, the advent of modern technology in this field has brought in its wake a number of health and safety problems, including musculo-skeletal injuries, visual fatigue and mental stress. Such illnesses are not an inevitable consequence of working with display screen equipment, but the introduction of sound ergonomic techniques can reduce the incidence.

6.161 However, there is no scientific evidence that visual display units (VDUs) pose any hidden health risk to the user (in particular to pregnant women) and generally VDUs have been given a clean bill of health following a number of investigations, including a recent study by the National Radiation Protection Board.

Application of the regulations (regulation 1)

6.162 The term "display screen equipment" refers to any alphanumeric or graphic display screen, regardless of the display process involved. The Guidance Notes state that this definition covers cathode ray tube and liquid crystal displays. As well as the typical office visual display terminals, non-electronic display systems such as microfiche are covered, but not screens used to show television or films, unless the main purpose is to display text, numbers and/or graphics.

6.163 The regulations are generally for the benefit of every person "who habitually uses display screen equipment as a significant part of his normal work." Clearly, the interpretation to be given to the words "habitually uses" and "significant part" is going to be crucial. The Guidance Notes suggest that a person will be covered by the regulations if most or all of the following criteria apply:
  (a) whether the individual has to depend on the display screen equipment to do his job, because alternative means are not readily available for achieving the same results
  (b) whether the individual has no discretion in using it
  (c) whether the individual has had special training and/or particular skills in the use of the equipment
  (d) whether the individual normally uses the equipment for continuous spells of an hour or more at a time on a more or less daily basis
  (e) whether the fast transfer of information is an important requirement of the job
  (f) whether the performance requirements of the system demands high level of attention and concentration.

6.164 The Guidance Notes give a list of examples of persons who are definitely users, eg word processing pool worker, data input operator, air traffic controller, and so on. Some possible users would be airline check-in clerks, customer support officers at a building society, depending on the circumstances. Persons who would not be users include receptionists who only use display screens occasionally.

6.165   Portable laptops will be exempt from the regulations if they are not in prolonged use, but if portable equipment is habitually used by a user as a significant part of normal working, the regulations may well apply. In any case, various safety considerations can still apply to laptop users, bearing in mind such problems as cramped working conditions (trains, aeroplanes), unsuitable seating and desks, inadequate lighting (dimly lit hotel rooms), etc. Risk assessments and proper training techniques can help to avoid problems arising.

6.166   Generally, the regulations are for the protection of two classes of persons, namely "users" and "operators". The former will be an employee, whether working at his employer's workstation, a workstation at home, or at another employer's workstation. Risks to homeworkers must be assessed, regardless of whether or not the workstation is provided by the employer. The term "operator" refers to a self-employed person who habitually uses display screen equipment as a significant part of his normal work.

6.167   The regulations also cover "the workstation", which means the actual display screen equipment, optional accessories, peripheral equipment (disk drive, telephone, modem, printer, chair, desk, etc) and the immediate environment.

6.168   The regulations do not apply to:
    (a) drivers' cabs or control cabs for vehicles or machinery
    (b) display screen equipment on board a means of transport
    (c) display screen equipment mainly intended for public use
    (d) portable systems not in prolonged use
    (e) calculators, cash registers or any equipment having a small data or measurement display
    (f) window typewriters.

6.169   A breach of the regulations may give rise to civil and/or criminal liability.

Analysis of workstations (regulation 2)

6.170   Every employer shall perform a suitable and sufficient analysis of those work-stations which:
    (a) (regardless of who has provided them) are used for the purposes of his undertaking by users, or

(b) have been provided by him and are used for the purposes of his undertaking by operators

for the purpose of assessing the health and safety risks to which those persons are exposed in consequence of that use.

6.171   The assessment shall be reviewed if the employer has reason to believe it is no longer valid, and if revisions are required as a result, these shall be made. Risks which have been identified shall be reduced to the lowest extent reasonably practicable.

6.172   The Guidance Notes state that in simple and obvious cases, there is no need to record the assessment, ie if no significant risks are indicated. However, records are useful to ensure continuity and accuracy, and to check on risk reduction methods. The views of the individual users are an essential part of any assessment. Remedial action should be taken when risks are disclosed, especially postural problems, visual problems and fatigue and stress.

Requirements for workstations (regulation 3)

6.173   In respect of workstations first put into service on or after 1 January 1993, the employer shall ensure that the requirements which are laid down in the Schedule to the regulations are met. For workstations which were already being used on 31 December 1992, these requirements had to be met not later than 31 December 1996.

6.174   The Schedule requires that attention should be given to all the factors which might affect the health and safety of the user or operator, including:
(a) the display screen (monitor)
(b) the keyboard
(c) the work desk or work surface
(d) environmental requirements, such as space, lighting, reflection and glare, noise, heat, radiation and humidity
(e) interface between the computer and operator or user, etc.

6.175   The Guidance Notes provide some useful advice on compliance with these requirements.

Daily work routine of users (regulation 4)

6.176   Every employer shall so plan the activities of users at work in his undertaking that their daily work on display screen equipment is periodically interrupted by such breaks or changes in activity as reduce their workload at that equipment.

6.177   The Guidance Notes suggest that spells of intensive screen work should be broken by activities which do not require broadly similar use of the arms or hands, or which are not equally visually demanding. Further guidance is given on the taking of rest breaks, which should be designed to prevent the onset of fatigue.

Eyes and eyesight (regulation 5)

6.178   This regulation is for the benefit of users (ie employees) and persons who are to become users in the undertaking in which they are employed. The employer shall ensure that such persons are provided (at their request) with an appropriate eye and eyesight test, to be carried out by a competent person. Such tests shall be carried out at regular intervals. Also, where a user experiences visual difficulties from using display screen equipment, the employer shall arrange such a test.

6.179   Further, every employer shall ensure that each user employed by him is provided with special corrective appliances, eg glasses, appropriate for the display screen work being done by the user where:
   (a) normal corrective appliances cannot be used, and
   (b) the result of any eye and eyesight test the user has had under this regulation shows such provision to be necessary.

6.180   This is probably the most important provision in the regulations, but its limitations should be noted.

6.181   (1) The regulation applied only to employees who were users at the date when the regulations came into force, ie 1 January 1993, and (thereafter) to any employee who is a non-user and who is to become a user. There is no obligation to provide tests and/or appliances to prospective employees, although once they are employed as users, there would be an obligation if they experienced visual difficulties caused by the work (it is submitted that the legal interpretation given by the Guidance Notes on this regulation is not correct, and should therefore be treated with caution).

6.182   (2) The special corrective appliances need only be supplied where normal corrective appliances cannot be used. The Guidance Notes suggest that only a small minority of the working population would need the special appliances. Anti-glare screens, VDU spectacles, etc are not included within this category. The employer's liability is to pay for the cost of a *basic* appliance necessary for the display screen work.

Provision of training (regulation 6)

6.183   Every employer shall ensure that each user (and a person about to become a user) shall receive adequate health and safety training in the use of the workstation on which he is required to work, and also when the workstation is substantially modified.

6.184   The Guidance Notes point out that the purpose of training in health and safety requirements is to minimise the risks of musculo-skeletal injuries, visual fatigue and mental stress. The aspects of training which should be covered are outlined.

Provision of information (regulation 7)

6.185   Every employer shall ensure that operators and users at work in his undertaking are provided with adequate information about:
  (a) all aspects of health and safety relating to their workstations, and
  (b) the measures taken by the employer to analyse the workstation (under regulation 2 above) and the measures taken to comply with the requirements of regulation 3 and the Schedule.

6.186   Further, every employer shall provide users (ie his employees) with adequate information about the measures he has taken to periodically interrupt the work activity (regulation 4), to provide eye and eyesight testing (regulation 5) and to provide training (regulation 6).

Exemption certificates (regulation 8)

6.187   The Secretary of State for Defence may, in the interests of national security, exempt home forces and visiting armed forces from the requirements of the regulations, subject to conditions and any limits of time.

Control of Lead at Work Regulations 1998

6.188   These regulations came into force on 1st April 1998, and are designed to give greater protection to the health of workers exposed to lead. The 1980 regulations have been revoked, as have 10 other regulations which deal with the use or manufacture of lead products, and the production of pottery. Also repealed are ss.74, 128, 131 and 132 of the Factories Act 1961. COP2: *Control of Lead at Work* has been updated and gives employers practical advice on how to comply with the new law.

6.189   As with the previous regulations, the objective is to protect the health of workers who are exposed to lead dust, fume or vapour by controlling and reducing the amount of absorption to an absolute minimum level, and to monitor the amount of lead absorbed by a worker so that he or she may be removed or temporarily suspended from work before health is adversely affected. The new regulations also give effect to parts of Directive 82/605/EEC (on the protection of workers from risks relating to exposure to metallic lead and its ionic compounds at work) and Directive 80/1107/EEC (on the protection of workers from the risks relating to exposure to chemical, physical and biological agents at work).

Duties of the employer (regulation 3)

6.190   The regulations place a number of duties on an employer in respect of his employees. In addition, the employer shall, so far as is reasonably practicable, be under a like duty in respect of any other person, whether at work or not, who may be affected by the work carried on by the employer. Thus, a duty is owed not only to employees and workers, but, for example, to members of an employee's family who may be exposed to significant risks of lead poisoning consequent on the employee's own exposure (see *Hewett v Alf Brown's Transport Ltd*, paragraph 8.57). However, this duty does not apply in respect of medical surveillance to persons who are not his employees (other than employees of another employer who is working under the direction of the first-mentioned employer). Nor do the duties relating to air monitoring and provision of information, instruction and training apply to persons who are not his employees, unless such persons are on the premises where the work is being carried on. The regulations also apply to self-employed persons as if they were both an employer and employee, except the provision relating to air monitoring.

Prohibitions (regulation 4)

6.191 There is an absolute prohibition on the use of glaze (other than leadless glaze or low solubility glaze) in the manufacture of pottery. Further, an employer shall not employ a young person or a woman of reproductive capacity in certain specified occupations in lead smelting and refining processes and lead-acid manufacturing processes (see Schedule 1).

Health assessment (regulation 5)

6.192 In addition to any assessment carried out under regulation 3 of the Management of Health and Safety at Work Regulations 1999 (see paragraph 5.4), the employer shall not carry on any work which is liable to expose any employees to lead at work unless he has made a suitable and sufficient assessment of whether the exposure of any employees to lead is liable to be significant. Exposure will be significant if:
 (a) the employee is liable to he exposed to a concentration of lead in the atmosphere exceeding half the occupational exposure limit for lead, or
 (b) where there is a substantial risk of any employee ingesting lead, or
 (c) where there is a risk of contact between the skin and lead alkyls or other substances containing lead which can be absorbed through the skin.

Prevention and control of exposure to lead (regulation 6)

6.193 Every employer shall ensure that exposure of his employees to lead is either prevented or, where this is not reasonably practicable, adequately controlled by means of appropriate control measures. So far as is reasonably practicable, these objectives shall be achieved by control measures other than the provision of personal protective equipment (PPE). However, if notwithstanding the control measures, exposure to lead is likely to be significant, the employer shall provide his employees with suitable and sufficient clothing and, if the control measures do not prevent or adequately control exposure to airborne lead, the employer shall also provide suitable respiratory protective equipment. PPE shall comply with the requirements of the Personal Protective Equipment (EC Directive) Regulations 1992, or be of a type approved by the HSE.

6.194   The employer must ensure that control measures, PPE, or other thing or facility provided is properly used or applied. Further, every employee shall make full and proper use of any control measure, PPE or other facility provided, and shall take all reasonable steps to ensure that it is returned after use to any accommodation provided. If he discovers a defect, he shall report it forthwith to the employer.

Maintenance, etc of control measures (regulation 8)

6.195   The employer shall ensure that control measures provided by him are maintained in a clean condition, in an efficient state, in efficient working order, and in good repair. If engineering controls are used, these shall be thoroughly examined and tested, at least every 14 months in the case of local exhaust ventilation plants, at suitable intervals in any other case. Respiratory equipment (other than the disposable variety) shall be thoroughly examined and tested as appropriate, at suitable intervals. Records of testing and examinations shall be kept for five years. Protective clothing which is contaminated by lead shall be kept within the employers premises, except when sent for cleaning, when it shall be sent in suitable closed containers, to a suitably equipped laundry.

Eating, drinking and smoking (regulation 7)

6.196   Every employer shall take such steps as are adequate to ensure, so far as is reasonably practicable, that his employees do not eat, drink or smoke in any place which is, or liable to be, contaminated with lead. This does not prohibit the use of proper drinking facilities which are required for the welfare of employees who are exposed to lead, as long as the facilities are not contaminated. Employees are forbidden to eat, drink or smoke in any such contaminated place.

Air monitoring (regulation 9)

6.197   Where employees are liable to receive a significant exposure to lead, the employer shall monitor the concentration of lead in the air, in accordance with EC standards set out in Directives 82/1605/EEC and 80/1107/EEC. In principle, the monitoring shall be carried out every 3 months, but the period may be increased to 12 months (except for exposure to lead alkyls) where:

(a) there has been no material change in the work or conditions of exposure since the last occasion of monitoring, and

(b) the lead in the air for each group of workers or work area has not exceeded 0.10 mgm^{-3} on the two previous occasions on which monitoring was carried out.

6.198   The employer shall keep a suitable record of any monitoring carried out, and the records, or a suitable summary, shall be kept for at least five years.

Medical surveillance (regulation 10)

6.199   Every employer shall ensure that each of his employees who is or liable to be exposed to lead is under suitable medical surveillance by an appointed doctor or an employment medical advisor, where:

(a) the exposure of the employee to lead is or is liable to be significant (ie where any employee is liable to he exposed to a concentration of lead in the atmosphere exceeding half the occupational exposure limit for lead, or where there is a substantial risk of an employee ingesting lead, or where there is a risk of contact between the skin and lead alkyls or other substance containing lead which can be absorbed through the skin), or

(b) the appointed doctor or employment medical advisor certifies that the employee should be under such surveillance.

6.200   Medical surveillance shall commence either before an employee starts work, or within 14 days of such commencement. It shall further be carried out at intervals of not more than 12 months. Biological monitoring shall also he carried out in respect of young persons and women of reproductive capacity at intervals not greater than three months, and for other employees at least every six months (see Schedule 2).

6.201   Adequate health records of the results of such surveillance shall be made and maintained and kept for a least 40 years from the date of the last entry. If the medical surveillance is carried out on the employer's premises, the employer shall ensure that suitable facilities are made available.

6.202   An employee shall, when required to do so by his employer, and at the cost of his employer, present himself during his working hours for such medical surveillance, and shall furnish the relevant doctor with such information concerning his health as the doctor may reasonably require. For the purpose of carrying out his functions, the doctor may inspect any workplace or any records kept for the purpose of these regulations. In respect of every female employee whose exposure to lead is liable to be significant, the employer shall ensure that the doctor makes an entry in the health record indicating whether she is of reproductive capacity.

6.203   Where the doctor certifies by an entry in the health record of any employee that, in his professional opinion, that employee should not be engaged in work which exposes him to lead, or should only be so engaged under specified conditions, the employer shall not permit the employee to he engaged in work which exposes him to lead, except in accordance with the conditions, if any, specified in the health record. Once the entry has been cancelled by the doctor, the employee may resume such workings.

6.204   Either the employer or the employee may appeal to HSE for a review of the decision by the doctor (a) that the employee is a female of reproductive capacity, or (b) that the employee should not be engaged in work which exposes him to lead. The result of that review will be entered into the health record.

Action levels (regulation 2)

6.205   When the blood-lead concentration for any employee equals or exceeds the appropriate action level, the employer shall take steps to determine the reasons for the high level of lead in blood, and shall, so far as is reasonably practicable, give effect to measures designed to reduce the blood-lead concentration of that employee to a level below the action level.

6.206   The appropriate action levels are a blood-lead concentration of:
   (a) in respect of a woman of reproductive capacity, 25µg/dl
   (b) in respect of a young person, 40µg/dl
   (c) in respect of any other person, 50µg/dl.

Suspension levels (regulation 2)

6.207   The appropriate suspension levels are now as follows:

(a) a blood-lead concentration of:
   (i) in respect of a woman of reproductive capacity, 30μg/dl
   (ii) in respect of a young person, 50μg/dl
   (iii) in respect of any other employee, 60μg/dl, or
(b) a urinary lead concentration of:
   (i) in respect of a woman of reproductive capacity, 25μPb/g creatinine
   (ii) in respect of any other employee, 110μPb/g creatinine.

6.208   If the blood-lead concentration or urinary lead concentration reaches the appropriate suspension level, the employer shall ensure than an entry is made in the health record of the employee by a relevant doctor. The doctor will certify whether in his professional opinion the employee should be suspended from any work which is liable to expose that employee to lead. If the doctor does not so certify, he may specify the conditions under which the employee may continue to be employed in such work.

Information, instruction and training (regulation 11)

6.209   Every employer who undertakes work which is liable to expose any of his employees to lead shall provide that employee with such information, instruction and training as is suitable and sufficient for him to know:
(a) the risks to health created by such exposure, and
(b) the precautions which should be taken.

6.210   The employer shall also provide the employee with:
(a) information on the results of any monitoring of exposure to lead carried out under regulation 9 (above), and
(b) information on the collective results of any medical surveillance undertaken in accordance with regulation 10 (above), in a form which prevents it from identifying and particular person, and
(c) an explanation of the significance of the above information.

6.211   The employer must also ensure that any person (whether or not his employee) who carries out any work in connection with the employer's duties under these regulations has the necessary information, instruction and training.

Application of the regulations

6.212   The regulations apply to offshore workings covered by the Health and Safety at Work Act 1974 (Application Outside Great Britain) Order 2001 (as amended) but do not apply to the master or crew of a sea-going ship. The HSE may issue exemption certificates, subject to conditions.

Safety notices

6.213   There are a number of legislative provisions which require the display of notices relating to issues of safety and/or health. These include the following:
  (a) Coal and Other Mines (Managers and Officials) Order 1956, which requires a danger sign around dangerous areas
  (b) Stratified Ironstone, Shale and Fireclay Mines (Explosives) Regulations 1956, which require warning notices when shot firing is being carried out
  (c) Miscellaneous Mines (Explosives) Regulations 1959, which require notices warning that shot firing is about to commence
  (d) Gravel and Sand Quarries (Overhanging) (Exemption) Regulations 1958, which require warning notices where there is danger from falls
  (e) Ionising Radiations Regulations 1999 require the designation and demarcation of controlled areas
  (f) Highly Flammable Liquids and Liquefied Petroleum Gases Regulations 1972 require various notices warning persons of the presence of flammable liquids, and prohibiting smoking near such liquids
  (g) Control of Substances Hazardous to Health Regulations 1999 require notices to be affixed to premises when certain fumigation is to be carried out, and removed when the premises are safe to enter
  (h) The Noise at Work Regulations 1989 require ear protection zones to be demarcated and identified by means of specific signs.

6.214   The Health and Safety Commission (HSC) recently conducted a review of all the legal requirements relating to the display of posters and health and safety information, with the result that ss.138–139 of the Factories Act were repealed, and some 53 regulations revoked without replacement (Health and Safety Information for Employees

(Modifications and Repeals) Regulations 1995), on the ground that they no longer fulfilled any necessary health and safety function, and could distract attention from the employer's duties under more modern legislative provisions to provide information for employees and others.

Health and Safety (Safety Signs and Signals) Regulations 1996

6.215 In order to implement Directive (92/587/EEC) on the minimum requirements for the provision of health and/or safety signs at work (which standardises signs throughout the EU) these regulations came into force in 1996, and signs which are lawfully in use prior to that date must now comply with regulations.

6.216 The Safety Signs Regulations 1980 have been revoked.

6.217 Regulation 4 of the new regulations provides that where a risk assessment carried out by the employer under regulation 3 of the Management of Health and Safety at Work Regulations 1999 (see Chapter 5) indicates that notwithstanding that he has adopted all appropriate techniques for collective protection, and measures, methods or procedures used in the organisation of work, he cannot avoid or adequately reduce risks to employees, except by the provision of appropriate safety signs to warn or instruct employees of the nature of the risks and measures to be taken against them, then he shall provide and maintain any safety sign set out in Schedule 1 of the new regulations, or ensure that such a sign is in place, and also ensure, so far as is reasonably practicable, that the appropriate hand signal or verbal communication described in Schedule 1 is used. If there are risks in connection with the movement of traffic (including risks to pedestrians) then the appropriate sign prescribed under the Road Traffic Regulation Act 1984 may be used.

6.218 It is permissible to use illuminated signs and acoustic methods as well as hand signals. Signs are required for fire exits and fire-fighting equipment, and road traffic signs are to be used in respect of roads within the workplace.

6.219 An employer must ensure that comprehensible and relevant information on the measures to be taken in connection with safety signs is provided to each of his employees, and that employees receive suitable and sufficient instruction and training in the meaning of safety signs and the measures to be taken in connection with safety signs.

6.220   Safety signs are to be regarded as the last resort in the hierarchy of control measures for health and safety at work, and should be used when there is an absence of any reasonable or suitable alternative.

6.221   There are five categories of signs, each with its own distinctive shape and colour.

Prohibitory signs

6.222   These will be circular with a red border and diagonal line over a black symbol on a white background. It is meant to indicate the prohibition of the depicted activity, eg "No Smoking".

Warning signs

6.223   These will be triangular in shape with a black border and symbol on a yellow background. It will denote the presence of the depicted danger in the area when the sign is displayed, eg "Caution".

Mandatory signs

6.224   These will be circular on a blue background with symbols in white. These will indicate specific instructions that must be obeyed, where there is an obligation to use safety equipment, eg "Hearing protection must be worn".

Emergency signs

6.225   These will be square or rectangular (depending on the size of the text or symbol) and will consist of a green background with white symbols. These will denote some safety consideration, eg "first aid post".

Fire-fighting signs

6.226   These will be rectangular or square, with a white pictogram on a red background.

6.227   As to shape, colour, placing and intrinsic features, etc safety signs must comply with the minimum requirements set out in Schedule 1 to the regulations. The safety signs above may be used.

Examples of safety signs and their meanings

Prohibitory signs: Round with white background and red border and cross bar. Symbols must be black and placed centrally on the background without obliterating the cross bar. The signs mean that something must not be done, as follows:

No smoking

Smoking and naked
flames forbidden

No access for
pedestrians

Do not extinguish
with water

Not drinkable

No access for
unauthorised persons

No access for
industrial vehicles

Do not touch

Warning signs: Triangular with a yellow background and a black border. The symbol, placed centrally, must be black. These signs warn of a particular hazard as follows:

Flammable material
or high temperature

Explosive material

Toxic material

Corrosive material

Radioactive material

Overhead load

Industrial vehicles

Danger: electricity

General danger

Laser beam

Oxidant material

Non-ionising radiation

Strong magnetic field

Obstacles

Drop

Biological risk

Low temperature

Harmful or irritant material

Mandatory signs: Round with a blue background and white symbol. These signs state what protective equipment must be worn, as follows:

Eye protection
must be worn

Safety helmet
must be worn

Ear protection
must be worn

Respiratory equipment
must be worn

Safety boots
must be worn

Safety gloves
must be worn

Safety overalls
must be worn

Face protection
must be worn

Safety harness
must be worn

Pedestrians must
use this route

General mandatory sign
(to be accompanied where
necessary by another sign)

261

Emergency signs: Square or oblong with white symbols on green background. These signs indicate safe conditions such as first-aid posts or emergency routes.

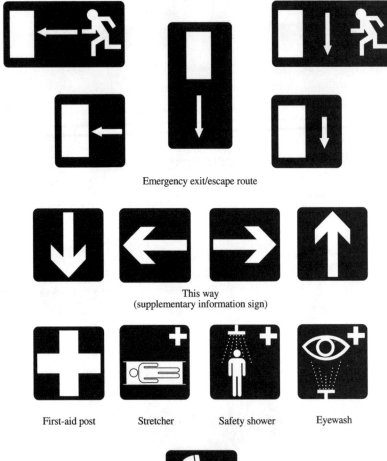

Emergency exit/escape route

This way
(supplementary information sign)

First-aid post   Stretcher   Safety shower   Eyewash

Emergency telephone for first-aid or escape

Fire-fighting signs: Rectangular or square shape with a red background and white symbol.

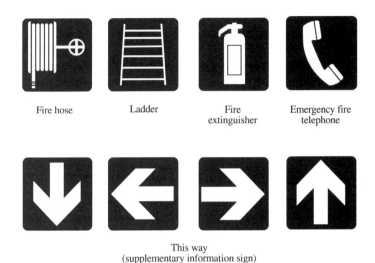

Fire hose   Ladder   Fire extinguisher   Emergency fire telephone

This way
(supplementary information sign)

Health and Safety (Information for Employees) Regulations 1989

6.228 These regulations dispense with the need to display abstracts of the Factories Act and Offices, Shops and Railway Premises Act, and instead require all employers to display a poster or distribute a leaflet entitled *Health and Safety Law What You Should Know*, informing employees in general terms about the requirements of health and safety law. These can be obtained from HSE Books. Employers must also inform employees of the local addresses of the appropriate enforcement authority (either the Health and Safety Executive (HSE) or the local authority) and the Employment Medical Advisory Service (EMAS).

6.229 A new version of the poster *Health and Safety Law* must be used after July 2000.

6.230 The Health and Safety Information for Employees (Modifications and Repeals) Regulations 1995 have revoked a number of statutory requirements to display health and safety information, in particular those made with reference to specific industrial processes under s.139 of the Factories Act 1961. It was thought that these requirements no longer fulfilled any useful health and safety function. The new regulations also permit an employer to dispense with the current *Health and Safety Law* poster and, subject to HSE approval, permit the display or use of a particular form of poster or leaflet designed for a particular employment. The employer would have to show that:

(a) there was a clearly defined industry or group of employees
(b) there was a clear demand for the alternative poster, and
(c) that the poster would satisfy the same requirements as the basic poster, and that the benefits would justify the development costs.

Dangerous Substances (Notification and Marking of Sites) Regulations 1990, as amended

6.231   These regulations require the notification and marking of sites where there is a total quantity of 25 tonnes or more of dangerous substances present at the site. A dangerous substance is any substance which is dangerous for carriage within the meaning of the Carriage of Dangerous Goods (Classification, Packaging and Labelling) and Use of Transportable Pressure Receptacles Regulations 1996. There must be notification to the fire authority and to the enforcing authority, with the specified information. Safety signs must be displayed which give adequate notice to firemen that a dangerous substance is present and access and location markings displayed.

Notification of Installations Handling Hazardous Substances Regulations 1982

6.232   These regulations require a person who stores, manufactures, processes, uses or transfers a specified minimum quantity of substance which is defined in the regulations as being hazardous to supply relevant information to the HSE. This will enable the HSE to define priorities in their inspection programme, notify local planning authorities so as to assist in development control, give necessary advice to emergency services and enable all persons concerned to be made aware of special hazards involved.

6.233   The notification must state the name of the person making it, the address of the site, the area of the site, the date when the activity will commence, a general description of the activity, the name of the local planning authority, and the name and the maximum quantity of each hazardous substance likely to be on the site. The information must be given at least three months before the commencement of the activity.

6.234 Regulations made under the Planning (Hazardous Substances) Act 1990 limit the quantity of hazardous substances which may be kept, until the appropriate authority has had an opportunity to assess the risks of an accident, and the likely consequences for the inhabitants of surrounding areas.

Control of Major Accident Hazards Regulations 1999

6.235 Growing public concern in the UK, Europe and indeed throughout the world following a number of industrial disasters has led to demands for more stringent control over the use and storage of dangerous substances which, if uncontrolled, could lead to major personal and environmental damage. The major accidents which took place at Flixborough, Seveso, Mexico City, Bhopal, etc have highlighted the need not only to reduce the likelihood of such occurrences in the future, but also to establish co-ordinated emergency plans in the event of such major accidents. Thus the Control of Major Accident Hazard Regulations 1999 lay down a comprehensive new set of control systems with the aim of preventing major accidents, or mitigating the consequences should one occur.

6.236 These new regulations are designed to impose certain requirements with respect to the control of major accident hazards arising out of the presence of dangerous substances. Although they follow the same fundamental principles as the Control of Industrial Major Accidents Hazards Regulations 1984 (now revoked), there are some significant changes, which stem largely from the implementation of Seveso II Directive (96/82/EC).

6.237 The regulations apply to an establishment where certain dangerous substances are present in the specified quantities (see Schedule 1 of the regulations). The old distinction between storage and use has been abolished, different materials with similar hazards are to be aggregated (even if the individual quantities of each are below the thresholds), and materials classified as being dangerous to the environment are now included. The general duties apply to all operators who control establishments where the dangerous substances are present in the specified quantities. Additional duties (regulations 7–14 below) apply to the so-called top-tier operators, ie where the dangerous substances are in quantities equal to or in excess of the amounts specified in column 3 of Parts 2 and 3 of Schedule 1.

6.238   The basic obligation is on the operator to take all measures necessary to prevent major accidents and limit their consequences to persons and the environment (regulation 4). The "operator" is the person who is in control of an establishment or installation. Regulation 5 requires the operator to prepare and keep a document setting out his policy with respect to the prevention of major accidents, designed to guarantee a high level of protection for persons and the environment by appropriate means, structures and management systems, taking into account the principles set out in Schedule 2. If there is a modification of the establishment or installation, the processes carried on there, or nature or quantity of dangerous substances which could have significant repercussions, the operator shall review and revise the major accident prevention policy document.

6.239   Regulation 6 provides that prior to the start of construction of an establishment (or prior to the start of the operation of the establishment, as the case may be) the operator shall send to the competent authority (the HSE or Environment Agency or Scottish Environment Protection Agency) a notification, containing the prescribed particulars. Details must also be sent of any significant increase in the quantity of dangerous substances, any significant change in the nature or physical form of substances so notified, the processes employing them, or changes in other information previously notified.

6.240   Regulation 7 provides that in respect of top-tier sites, the operator must also send to the competent authority (HSE and the Environment Agency) a safety report, containing the relevant information specified in Schedule 4, and shall not start construction of an establishment or commence operations until the competent authority has sent its conclusions. The safety report must be reviewed every five years, or as necessary if new facts or new technical knowledge become available, or if there has been a change in safety management systems. A similar revision of the safety report shall take place if there is a modification of the establishment or installation, or the process carried on, or the nature or quantity of dangerous substances, any of which could have significant repercussions with respect to the prevention of major accidents or the limitation of the consequences of major accidents to persons or to the environment.

6.241   The operator of a top-tier site must also prepare an emergency plan adequate for securing the containment and control of incidents, so as to minimise the effects, and to limit damage to persons, the environment and property, implementing measures necessary to protect persons from the effects of major accidents, communicating the necessary information to the public and to the emergency services and authorities concerned in the area, and providing for the restoration and clean-up of the environment following a major accident (regulation 9 and Schedule 5). The plan will also give the names or positions of persons authorised to set emergency procedures in motion, co-ordinate on-site mitigatory action, and other information prescribed in Schedule 5. Local authorities, in whose area there is an establishment shall also prepare an off-site emergency plan (regulation 10). Emergency plans shall be reviewed at least every three years, and revised when necessary. The local authority, emergency services and operator shall endeavour to reach agreement as to how off-site emergency plans are to be tested (regulation 11).

6.242   The operator of an establishment shall ensure that persons who are likely to be in an area likely to be affected by a major accident occurring are provided with information (without their having to request it) on safety measures at the establishment and on the requisite behaviour in the event of a major accident occurring (regulation 14).

6.243   The regulations also specify the functions of the competent authority, which will be the HSE, Environment Agency or Scottish Environment Protection Agency (regulations 17–22). The competent authority will examine safety reports, and can prohibit the operation of an establishment or installation if the measures for the prevention or mitigation of major accidents are seriously deficient. The authority will also have an ongoing system of inspection of establishments and control measures and, if a major accident has been notified, obtain all relevant information from the operator, ensure that urgent, medium and long-term measures proven necessary are taken, make a full analysis of the accident and collect any appropriate information, ensure that the operator takes remedial action, make recommendations for the future, and in the event of certain types of accidents, notify the European Commission, together with specified information.

Dangerous substances

6.244   After being in force for less than a year, the Chemicals (Hazard Information and Packaging) Regulations 1993 (CHIP 1) were revoked, and replaced by the Chemicals (Hazard Information and Packaging for Supply) Regulations 1994 (CHIP 2), which came into force on 31 January 1995. The main change is the removal from CHIP 1 of the carriage requirements covering the conveyance of chemicals by road and rail, which are now to be found in the Carriage of Dangerous Goods by Road Regulations 1996 and the Carriage of Dangerous Goods by Rail Regulations 1996 respectively. A number of other minor amendments were made in order to comply with recent EU Directives, particularly in relation to the supply requirements, such as advertising and child resistant closures and tactile danger warnings for certain products so as to alert purchasers who are blind or partially sighted. CHIP 2is accompanied by an Approved Code of Practice (ACOP). Further amendments were made to CHIP 2 in 1996, 1997 and 1998 with a view to ensure that users of dangerous chemicals are provided with adequate information about the hazards, so that people and the environment can be protected. The Approved Supply List was enlarged in 1999, giving agreed hazard classification and labelling requirements for about 2500 substances. It was updated again in 2000, when certain requirements and information were revised with respect to 168 dangerous substances via the sixth edition of the Approved Supply List.

6.245   A "supplier" is a person (including an importer) who supplies a dangerous substance or preparation for use at work. Three obligations are imposed.
1. The supplier must classify the chemical in accordance with one of the categories specified in Schedule 1 to the regulations, ie explosive, oxidising, extremely flammable, highly flammable, flammable, very toxic, toxic, harmful, corrosive, irritant, carcinogenic, mutagenic, toxic to reproduction, and dangerous to the environment. Such classification will identify the properties of the substance or preparation that would be hazardous during normal use. For each category, a symbol letter is to be given. In order to make a classification, reference should be made to the Approved Supply List.

2. The supplier must provide a safety data sheet, to the recipient, no later than the receipt by him of the product. This must contain such information as to enable the recipient to take necessary measures relating to health and safety at work and for the protection of the environment. The safety data sheet shall deal with the following headings: identification of the substance or preparation and company, composition/information on ingredients, hazards identification, first aid measures, fire-fighting measures, accident release measures, handling and storage, exposure controls/personal protection, physical and chemical properties, stability and reactivity, toxicological information, ecological information, disposal considerations, transport information, regulatory information, and other information. The safety data sheet shall be dated, and revised if significant new information becomes available. A copy of the revision shall be sent to all recipients who have received the substance or preparation within the previous 12 months. The HSE has produced a leaflet, *Why do I need a data sheet?*

3. The supplier must ensure that the substance or preparation is in a package which is suitable, prevents the contents from escaping, and is itself made from materials which will not be adversely affected. If it has a replaceable closure, it must be capable of being repeatedly resealed without permitting the contents to escape. The receptacle must be labelled with the following information; name, address and telephone number of the supplier, name of the substance, an indication of the danger with a corresponding symbol, risk phrases, safety phrases and the EEC or EC number (if any). A breach of any of the provisions of regulations 5–14 of CHIP 2 may be actionable in civil as well as criminal proceedings. However, in criminal proceedings, the supplier may be able to raise the defence that he took all reasonable precautions and exercised all due diligence to avoid the commission of the offence.

6.246   The Notification of New Substances Regulations 1993 (NONS) implement the Dangerous Substances Directive (92/32/EEC) together with CHIP 2 and require the notification of a new substance to be reported to HSE and the Department of the Environment, together with information concerning the substance. The competent authority will then be able to carry out a risk assessment, and make a judgment on the level of concern. In exceptional cases control measures may be imposed.

Reporting of Injuries, Diseases and Dangerous Occurrences Regulations 1995

6.247 The Reporting of Injuries, Diseases and Dangerous Occurrences Regulations 1995 (RIDDOR) came into force on 1 April 1996. The aim is to revise and simplify the previous RIDDOR 85 Regulations, to which a number of changes have been made.

6.248 Reporting shall be done by the "responsible person". Usually, this will be the employer, or someone acting on his behalf, although more specific persons are identified as being responsible for reporting in mines, quarries, offshore and diving activities.

1. The following incidents must be reported forthwith by the quickest practicable means (usually this will be by telephone) and a report sent to the relevant enforcing authority on the approved form within 10 days:
   (a) where any person dies as a result of an accident arising out of or in connection with work
   (b) where any person at work suffers a major injury (defined below) as a result of an accident arising out of or in connection with work
   (c) where a person not at work suffers an injury as a result of an accident arising out of or in connection with work, and that person is taken to a hospital for treatment in respect of that injury
   (d) any person not at work suffers a major injury as a result of an accident arising out of or in connection with work at a hospital (excluding accidents arising from medical or dental treatment)
   (e) any dangerous occurrence (defined below).
2. The following injuries must be reported as soon as practicable, and a report sent to the relevant enforcing authority within 10 days on the approved form: where a person is incapacitated for work of a kind which he might reasonably be expected to do, for more than three consecutive days (excluding the day of the accident but including days which would not have been working days), because of an accident arising out of or in connection with work.
3. Where an employee, as a result of an accident at work, has suffered an injury reportable under 1(a), (b) or (e) above, which is the cause of his death within one year from the date of the accident, the employer shall inform the relevant enforcing authority in writing of the death as soon as it comes to his knowledge, whether or not it was previously reported.

4. Where a person at work suffers from any of the occupational diseases specified in Schedule 3 of the regulations, and the work involved one of the activities specified in the corresponding entry, the responsible person shall forthwith send a report to the relevant enforcing authority on an approved form. However, he need only do this if he has received a written statement prepared by a registered medical practitioner diagnosing the disease as one of those specified in Schedule 3.

5. Also reportable are incidents arising out of the supply or distribution or installation of gas, failures in railway signalling and railway accidents, and accidents and occurrences, etc on offshore installations.

6. Road accidents are only reportable if:

   (a) a person was killed or injured as a result of exposure to a substance being conveyed on the vehicle

   (b) a person was engaged in, or was killed or injured as the result of the activities of another person who was engaged in work connected with the loading or unloading of any article or substance onto or off the vehicle

   (c) a person was engaged in, or killed or injured as a result of, the activities of another person engaged in work on or alongside a road, being work concerned with the construction, demolition, alteration, repair or maintenance of the road (or markings or equipment thereon), or verges, fences, hedges or boundaries of the road, or pipes or cables on, under, over or adjacent to the road, or buildings or structures adjacent to or over the road

   (d) a person was killed or injured as a result of an accident in connection with the movement of a vehicle on a road which also involved a train.

7. Not reportable are deaths or injuries which arise from medical treatment or examinations carried out by a registered medical practitioner or registered dentist. Nor is it necessary to report an occupational disease identified during health surveillance.

6.249   A major injury (see above) is defined as:

   (a) any fracture, other than to the fingers, thumbs or toes

   (b) any amputation

   (c) dislocation of the shoulder, hip, knee or spine

   (d) loss of sight (whether temporary or permanent)

(e) a chemical or hot metal burn to the eye, or any penetrating injury to the eye

(f) any injury from an electric shock or electric burn leading to unconsciousness or requiring resuscitation or admission to hospital for more than 24 hours

(g) any other injury leading to hypothermia, heat-induced illness, or unconsciousness, or requiring resuscitation, or admission to hospital for more than 24 hours

(h) loss of consciousness caused by asphyxia or by exposure to a harmful substance or biological agent

(i) acute illness or loss of consciousness caused by the absorption of any substance by inhalation, ingestion or through the skin

(j) acute illness resulting from exposure to a biological agent or its toxins or infected material.

6.250 A list of dangerous occurrences (see above) is contained in Schedule 2 of the regulations. These include incidents involving the collapse or overturning of lifting machinery (or the failure of any load-bearing part), the failure of pressure systems, failure of freight containers, incidents connected with overhead electric lines, electric short circuits or overloads which result in the stoppage of plant for more than 24 hours, incidents involving explosives, release or escape of biological agents, malfunctioning of radiation generators, malfunctioning of breathing apparatus while in use or being tested prior to use, incidents relating to diving operations, the collapse of scaffolding, train collisions, and incidents connected with wells, pipelines, fairground equipment, and the carriage of dangerous substances by road, the collapse of a building or structure, an explosion or fire, the escape of flammable substances, and the escape of any substance likely to cause injury, death or any other damage to the health of any person. There are specific definitions dealing with dangerous occurrences in mines, quarries, transport systems and offshore installations.

6.251 It should be noted that the term "accident" now includes non-consensual physical violence done to a person at work. Thus an assault on an employee is now reportable (subject to the above provisions). Also included now are suicides on "relevant transport systems".

6.252 The HSE has published a guide (L73: *A Guide to the Reporting of Injuries, Diseases and Dangerous Occurrences Regulations 1995* (RIDDOR)) and a free leaflet on the new regulations *(Everyone's Guide to RIDDOR "95)*, and new simplified accident reporting forms have been drawn up. The relevant form (F2508 for accidents and F2508A for diseases) must be sent to the local office of the HSE or to the environmental health office of the local authority, as appropriate.

6.253   HSE, together with local authorities, has set up a new single Incident Contact Centre (ICC), to which all work-related health and safety incidents can be reported, as an alternative to local HSE or local authority offices. Users may telephone or fax their reports, or send by e-mail electronic copies of RIDDOR report forms, or continue to use and send completed Forms F2508. Reports may be sent by post to Incident Contact Centre, Caerphilly Business Park, Caerphilly, CF83 3GG. Telephone reports should be made to tel: 0845 300 9923. Fax reports should be made to fax: 0845 300 9924. E-mail reports should be sent to riddor@natbrit.com.

Obtaining further information

6.254   Once having received a report, the HSE can, with the approval of the Commission, require further information about the reported incident. This may be further details about the circumstances which gave rise to the incident, details about the plant (including its design), details of safety systems, qualification experience and training of staff, protection arrangements, tests, levels of exposure, etc.

Keeping records

6.255   Employers are required to keep records of all events reported under the regulations. No specific design is required, and the records may be in the form of photocopies of accident report forms, or an accident book, or stored on a computer. All that is necessary is to comply with the requirements laid down in Schedule 4. In the case of a notifiable disease, the information must contain the occupation of the person affected, the name or nature of the disease, and the date of its diagnosis. In the case of a reportable accident or dangerous occurrence, the record must contain the date and time of the incident, the name, occupation and nature of any injury, the place where the injury or dangerous occurrence happened and a brief description of the circumstances.

Defences

6.256 If a person is prosecuted for an offence under the regulations, it will be a defence for him to show that he was not aware of the event which he was required to report or notify, and that he had taken all reasonable steps to have all such events brought to his notice.

Health and Safety (First Aid) Regulations 1981

6.257 The Health and Safety (First Aid) Regulations came into force on 1 July 1982. Four statutory provisions were repealed (Factories Act s.61, Mines and Quarries Act s.115 (in part), OSRPA s.24, and Agriculture (Safety, Health and Welfare Provisions) Act s.6(1)(4). In addition, some 42 regulations and orders were revoked in whole or in part, and thus the new Regulations, (as amended), supported by an Approved Code of Practice and Guidance Notes, are now the main source of legal rules on this subject.

6.258 The regulations lay down three general requirements. First, an employer shall provide, or ensure that there are provided, such equipment and facilities as are adequate and appropriate in the circumstances for enabling first aid to be rendered to his employees if they are injured or become ill at work. A similar obligation applies to a self-employed person to enable him to render first aid to himself while he is at work.

6.259 Second, an employer shall provide (or ensure that there is provided) such number of suitable persons as is adequate and appropriate in the circumstances for rendering first aid to his employees if they are injured or become ill at work. A person shall not be regarded as being suitable for this purpose unless he has undergone:
   (a) such training and has such qualifications as the HSE may approve for the time being in respect of that case, and
   (b) such additional training, if any, as may be appropriate in the circumstances of that case.

6.260 However, where such a person is absent in temporary and exceptional circumstances, it is sufficient compliance if another person has been appointed to take charge of the situation relating to an injured or ill employee who will need help from a medical practitioner or nurse, and who is also in charge of the equipment and facilities. Further, where, having regard to the nature of the undertaking, the number of employees at work and the location of the establishment, it would be adequate and appropriate to appoint someone to take charge of the situation and equipment and facilities (who may not necessarily be trained or qualified as above), the employer meets the legal requirements by making such appointment.

6.261   Third, the employer shall inform his employees of the arrangements that have been made in connection with the provision of first aid, including the location of equipment, facilities and personnel.

First aid Approved Code of Practice and Guidance Notes

6.262   The original Approved Code of Practice has now been revoked, and a new Code, supplemented by extensive Guidance Notes, came into force in March 1997. It was thought that the old Code was too prescriptive, and thus many of its provisions have been moved into Guidance Notes (L74: *First aid at work*), so as to achieve greater flexibility.

Assessment

6.263   The first step is for the employer to make an assessment of the first aid needs appropriate to the circumstances of each workplace. This should take into account factors such as:
  (a) workplace hazards and risks
  (b) the size of the organisation
  (c) the organisation's history of accidents
  (d) the nature and distribution of the workforce
  (e) the remoteness of the site from emergency services
  (f) the needs of travelling, remote and lone workers
  (g) employees working on shared or multi-occupied sites
  (h) annual leave and other absences of first aiders and appointed persons.

6.264   There is no requirement that the assessment shall be in writing, but it is suggested that it is advisable to do so. Appendix 1 to the regulations contains a checklist for assessing whether additional provisions should be made.

6.265   The assessment will reveal the appropriate steps for the employer to take in the circumstances. Thus, if there is a comparatively low risk to health and safety, the employer will only need to provide a clearly identified and well-stocked first aid container, and appoint a person to look after the first aid arrangements and take charge in emergencies. However, if the assessment reveals particular risks, eg if there are hazardous substances or dangerous tools or equipment, the employer will need to consider that sufficient number of trained first aiders are always available, that they are trained in special procedures dealing with identifiable hazards, that local emergency services are informed of the site where hazardous substances or dangerous processes are used or carried on, and that first aid rooms are provided. The assessment will also note that there may be different requirements in different parts of the establishment, that there may be employees who are potentially at greater risk (disabled persons, trainees, young persons, etc) problems arising from working patterns (shift work, night work, etc) distances involved, the type of first aid or medical assistance that may be needed and so on. Like all assessments, the first aid assessment should be reviewed and, if necessary, revised periodically in the light of experience and new knowledge.

Personnel

6.266 First aiders should be provided in sufficient numbers and at appropriate locations. The ACOP suggests that where 50 or more employees are employed, at least one first aider should be provided unless the assessment justifies otherwise. However, there are no hard and fast rules; a small organisation, with comparatively low health and safety risks, may not need a first aider, but will need an appointed person. A high-risk organisation, or where there are scattered sites, might need additional first aiders. The employer must make an appropriate judgement in the light of all the circumstances.

6.267 A person should be selected to be a first aider, depending on his reliability, skills and aptitude, and on his ability to absorb knowledge, develop new skills and cope in emergencies. His normal duties should be such that he is able to respond immediately and rapidly to an emergency. He should hold a valid certificate of competence in first aid work (issued by an organisation approved by the HSE), be given time off work for training and refresher courses, and be put in touch with suitable sources of advice.

6.268 An appointed person is not necessarily a qualified first aider, but he should be given instruction on how to look after the first aid equipment and, as a minimum, should know what to do in emergency situations.

Equipment and facilities

6.269 The minimum level of first aid equipment is a well-stocked and properly identifiable first aid container (with a white cross on a green background). These should be easily accessible and, if possible, near to hand-washing facilities. There is no mandatory list of contents, but the assessment should reveal any special requirements. The container should contain a leaflet giving guidance on first aid, individually wrapped sterile adhesive dressings, sterile eye pads, triangular bandages, safety pins, unmedicated wound dressings and disposable gloves. The contents of the container should be checked regularly and restocked after use. Additional material that may be needed may be stored separately, as long as they are available for use if required. Travelling first-aid kits should be provided where necessary.

6.270 A suitable first aid room should be provided when the assessment identifies such a need. Again, it should contain essential first aid equipment and facilities and, if possible, should be reserved exclusively for the purpose of providing first aid. It should have a couch, be kept clean and tidy, be positioned near to a point of access for transport to hospital and display a notice on the door advising of the names, locations, etc of first aiders, with information on how they are to be contacted.

Information for employees

6.271 Employees must be informed of the nature and location of first aid facilities and first aiders. New employees may be given this information on an induction course. Suitable first aid notices and information concerning the location of first aiders should be displayed, with special attention being paid to the need to inform employees who are visually impaired or have language difficulties.

Control of Asbestos at Work Regulations 1987 (as amended)

6.272 These regulations, amended in 1992 and 1998, apply not only to the asbestos product manufacturing industry, but to persons whose work involved exposure, in particular, those in building-related trades, eg demolition, maintenance, repair and refurbishment, etc. Before any such work commences, the employer must identify the type of asbestos involved, draw up a plan of work, and carry out an adequate assessment of the exposure. Both the plan of work and the written assessment must be kept at any place where the work is being carried out. The work is to be done in accordance with the plan. Until the contrary is shown, the employer must assume that the material concerned is a more hazardous form of asbestos fibre, ie crocidolite or amosite, and thus take more stringent precautions on exposure limits.

6.273   Employees who are liable to be exposed to asbestos are to be given adequate instruction and training (at suitable intervals) so that they are aware of the risks from asbestos, and the precautions which should be observed. Employers shall prevent employees from being exposed to asbestos, but where this is not reasonably practicable, reduce exposure to the lowest reasonably practicable level. This may be done by using some other substance, or by the provision suitable respiratory protective equipment which will reduce the exposure to as low as is reasonably practicable, and in any event below the control limits. Control measures and respiratory protective equipment must be kept in a clean and efficient state, efficient working order, regularly examined and tested. Appropriate records shall be kept for five years.

6.274   If a significant quantity of asbestos is likely to be deposited on an employee's clothing, adequate and suitable protective clothing must be provided. Employers must prevent the spread of asbestos, and the places where asbestos was used must be kept clean and thoroughly cleaned when the work is completed. There must be facilities for washing, changing clothing and separate storage for personal and protective clothing and respiratory protective equipment must be provided.

6.275   Indeed, there have been a number of successful common law claims (see Chapter 8) brought not only by workers who worked with asbestos, but also by persons who contracted asbestos-related illnesses after being exposed to asbestos dust on the clothing of employees who worked with asbestos.

6.276   **Note:** Respiratory protective equipment and protective clothing must comply with relevant EU "product" Directives as implemented in the UK.

6.277   The regulations lay down a new action level of exposure, above which it is necessary to notify the HSE of the work being carried on, 14 days in advance of commencement. Records of air monitoring results must be kept for 40 years where the exposure is such that a health record is required under regulation 16, or for 5 years in any other situation. Health records must be kept, and health surveillance should be carried out where appropriate (regulation 16). In addition, two Approved Codes of Practice associated with the regulations have been issued (L27: *The control of asbestos at work* and L28: *Work with asbestos insulation, asbestos coating and asbestos insulating board*).

6.278 In addition to the 1987 Regulations, asbestos is also controlled by several other statutory instruments. The Asbestos (Licensing) Regulations 1983 (as amended) deal with the licensing of asbestos removal contractors who are concerned with asbestos insulation and asbestos coating. The holders of any such licence must ensure that their employees are medically examined. Employers who were not licenced (because they were using their own employees on their own premises) are under a duty to control exposure to the lowest level reasonably practicable. The Asbestos (Prohibitions) Regulations 1992 prohibit the spraying of asbestos and certain other processes, and were amended in 1999 so that there is now an almost complete ban on the importation and the supply or use of asbestos (including chrysotile). The Asbestos Products (Safety) Regulations 1985 prescribe labelling requirements on the supply of products which contain asbestos, and prohibit the supply of products which contain chrysotile or amosite.

6.279 The Control of Asbestos in the Air Regulations 1990 implements Directive 87/217/EEC on the prevention and reduction of environmental pollution by asbestos. There is a limit value for the discharge of asbestos into the air during the use of this substance, and regular measurements must be made from plants to which the regulations apply. There are controls on environmental pollution by asbestos resulting from the working of products or demolition of buildings, structures and installations containing asbestos.

Ionising Radiations Regulations 1999

6.280 There are two types of radiation: ionising and non-ionising radiation. The more dangerous type of ionising radiation comes from X-rays and other radioactive material. (Non-ionising radiation can stem from laser beams, arc-welders, infra-red and ultra-violet sources, microwave ovens, etc) The effect of ionising radiation exposure will vary according to the dose and exposure time, but it is accepted that serious illnesses and even death can result, as well as damage being caused to a person's genetic structure, causing stillbirths and malformation in newly born children. The exposure limits at present adopted in this country are those recommended by the International Commission on Radiological Protection, and those limits vary with the area of the body exposed. However, there appears to be no valid proof that the thresholds recommended are in fact safe and any radiation exposure must therefore be regarded as being potentially damaging. Proper shielding is therefore essential (principally by the use of lead material), the equipment must be properly maintained so as to prevent leakage, radiation film badges should be worn at all times when there is a likelihood of exposure in order to measure the amount (or a dosimeter used), and whole body counts should be made when there is a danger that an affected person may have absorbed or ingested radiation.

6.281   The Ionising Radiation Regulations 1999 supersede and consolidate the Ionising Radiation Regulations 1985 and the Ionising Radiation (Outside Workers) Regulations 1993. The regulations implement in part Council Directives 96/29/Euratom, 90/641/Euratom and 97/43/Euratom, which generally lay down basic safety standards for the protection of health workers and the general public against the dangers arising from radiation, particularly in relation to medical exposure. The regulations apply to employers, employees, self-employed persons and trainees.

6.282   A radiation employer (ie a person who in the course of business carries out work with ionising radiation) shall not carry out certain specified practices (use of x-rays and accelerators) without prior authorisation from HSE, unless the practice is of a type which has been approved by HSE. Before carrying out certain specified work with ionising radiation for the first time, the radiation employer must notify HSE, and provide specified particulars. Before commencing work with radiation, the employer shall make a risk assessment of the hazards likely to arise from that work, for the purpose of identifying the measures he needs to take to restrict the exposure of an employee or other person to ionising radiation. Hazards with the potential to cause a radiation accident need to be identified, and the nature and magnitude of the risks evaluated. All reasonable practicable steps shall be taken to prevent an accident, or limit the consequences should one occur, and employees must be provided with the information, instruction and training and the equipment necessary, to restrict their exposure to radiation.

6.283 Every radiation employer shall take all necessary steps to restrict so far as is reasonably practicable the extent to which his employees and other persons are exposed to ionising radiation, by means of engineering controls, design features, safety features and warning devices. These must be properly maintained with thorough examination and tests carried out at suitable intervals. Personal protective equipment shall be provided where appropriate. Pregnant women must not be exposed to a dose which exceeds lmSv. An investigation shall be carried out if any employee receives a dose in excess of 15mSv for the first time in any calendar year.

6.284 Radiation employers must consult with suitable radiation protection advisers, (except in respect of work specified in schedule 1). Employees must be given suitable information and instruction so that they know the risks to health from exposure, and the precautions which should be taken. Controlled or supervised areas shall be designated, and local rules set down in writing. Employees who are likely to receive a dose in excess of 6mSv shall be designated as classified persons, and an assessment made and recorded of all doses likely to be significant. Dose records shall be kept until the employee reached age 75 or for 50 years from when they are made. Outside workers shall be provided with a radiation passbook, with particulars kept up to date. Classified persons and employees who receive an over-exposure shall be under adequate medical surveillance, with a health record kept. If an appointed doctor or employment medical adviser certifies that an employee shall not be engaged in work with ionising radiation, the employer shall not permit him to do so.

6.285 If a radiation employer suspects that any person has received an over-exposure he shall immediately investigate, and notify HSE, the employer of the employee (where appropriate) and the appointed doctor or employment medical adviser.

6.286 Employees must not knowingly expose themselves or any other person to ionising radiation, to a greater extent than is reasonably necessary, shall make full and proper use of any personal protective equipment, report defects to his employer, and ensure that personal protective equipment is returned after use to accommodation provided.

If he has reasonable cause to believe that he has received an exposure, he will notify his employer forthwith.

6.287 The regulations and the Approved Code of Practice and Guidance (L121) also deal with arrangements for the control of radioactive substances, articles and equipment, the approval of dosimetry services by HSE, and a new criteria of competence for individuals or organisations who wish to act as radiation protection advisers.

6.288 The Ionising Radiation (Medical Exposure) Regulations 2000 lay down basic measures for the protection of individuals against the dangers of ionising radiation in respect of medical exposure. Duties are imposed on an employer (which term refers to any natural or legal person who, in the course of trade, business or other undertaking, carries out medical exposures at a given radiological installation), to ensure that the practitioner or operator protects persons undergoing medical exposure, whether as part of:
- (a) their own medical diagnosis or treatment, or
- (b) occupational health surveillance, or
- (c) a health screening programme, or
- (d) a voluntary medical, diagnostic or therapeutic research programme, or
- (e) medico-legal procedures.

6.289 The Regulations require the employer to lay down procedures and written protocols for standard radiological practices, establish recommendations for referral criteria, quality assurance programmes, diagnostic reference levels, and dose constraints. Practitioners and operators must undertake continuous training after qualification, and comply with the employer's procedures.

Electricity at Work Regulations 1989

6.290 The Electricity at Work Regulations 1989 replaced a range of inflexible and out-of-date legislation with a comprehensive and systematic set of main principles covering electrical safety in all work activities. They apply to work on or near electricity. They are supported by two Approved Codes of Practice relating to mines and quarries, and a Memorandum of Guidance for other workplaces. Some of the regulations contain absolute requirements, so that civil liability (based on the tort of breach of statutory duty) is retained, but so far as a criminal prosecution is concerned, it will be a defence for the accused to show that he used "due diligence".

6.291 In a number of ways, the new regulations differ from the approach taken by the previous law. There is no voltage threshold, no exemption for electrothermal operations, or for testing and research. The regulations apply in all circumstances where it is necessary to avoid danger, defined as meaning a risk of injury. This, in turn, means "death or personal injury from electrical causes, fire or explosion associated with the transmission, rectification, conversion, conduction, distribution, control, storage, measurement or use of electrical energy." Consequential or indirect injuries due to electrical malfunction are not generally included.

6.292 The regulations impose duties on employers and self-employed persons in relation to matters within their control. Further, employees are under a duty to comply with the provisions insofar as they relate to matters within their control, and they are also under a duty to co-operate with their employer so far as is necessary to enable the duties to be carried out. Persons who have control of non-domestic premises (see HSWA, s.4) come within the regulations because they will be either employers or self-employed persons.

6.293 Electrical systems must, so far as is reasonably practicable, be constructed and maintained so as to be safe, as must be the work activity and the adequacy of protective equipment. There is an absolute duty not to exceed the strength and capability of electric equipment so as to cause danger. If there are adverse or hazardous environmental circumstances, exposure is limited to that which is reasonably foreseeable. There are provisions relating to insulation, protection, placing and earthing of conductors, and installing switches or other devices in neutral conductors. Excess current protection must be efficient and suitably located, and there must be provision for cutting off the supply and isolating it.

6.294 Working space, means of access and lighting shall be adequate, so as to prevent injury.

6.295 Probably the most significant feature of the regulations is the general prohibition on live working. This will only be permitted if *all* three of the following conditions are met:

(a) it is unreasonable in all the circumstances for the system to be dead

(b) it is reasonable in all the circumstances for the work to be carried out live, and

(c) suitable precautions are taken to prevent injury.

6.296   There are no specific age restrictions on those who work with electricity, but those who do this type of work must have sufficient technical knowledge and experience to prevent danger and avoid injury, and if they do not have such expertise, they must be supervised as appropriate, having regard to the nature of the work.

6.297   The regulations apply to offshore installations (Offshore Electricity and Noise Regulations 1997).

Noise at Work Regulations 1989

6.298   Although it has long been recognised that excessive noise levels at work could cause deafness (boiler-makers' deafness was well known in the 19th century) it is only in comparatively recent times that the law has begun paying attention to the problem. It is now accepted that excessive exposure to noise levels in excess of 90dB(A) will cause permanent damage to a person's hearing, as will exposure to louder impact noises (explosions, hammer guns, etc). However, not every deaf person can complain of the hazards of his occupation, for there are other causes of deafness, including presbyacusis, which is brought on by old age. Since noise is a common feature of everyday living, it cannot be assumed that occupational noise is the sole cause of deafness.

6.299   Occupational deafness was not given serious treatment by the authorities until the mid-1960s, when the various scientific evidence began to percolate through to industry. Several legislative provisions were enacted to deal with specific problems, eg the Woodworking Machines Regulations 1974, the Agriculture (Tractor Cabs) Regulations 1974, as amended, the Offshore Installations (Construction and Survey) Regulations 1974, and the Offshore Installations (Operational Safety, Health and Welfare) Regulations 1976. The Department of Employment issued a Code of Practice in 1972, and it occasioned little surprise when the EU passed a Directive in 1986 (86/188/EEC). Following on this, the Noise at Work Regulations 1989 were enacted.

6.300   The regulations also apply to offshore installations (Offshore Electricity and Noise Regulations 1997).

6.301   The regulations require action to be taken at three noise exposure levels, namely (a) 85dB(A) (first action level), (b) 90dB(A) (second action level) and (c) 200 Pascals (peak level for impact noise).

6.302   There is a general obligation on the employer to reduce the risk of hearing damage to the lowest level reasonably practicable. If the daily personal noise exposure is likely to be 85dB(A) or above, a noise assessment must be made by a competent person. Workers must be given adequate information, instruction and training about the risks to hearing, how the risk is to be minimised and personal ear protection must be provided on request. However, at this level, there is no obligation on the employer to ensure that they are used and no obligation on the worker to use them.

6.303   More stringent provisions apply if the noise levels are 90dB(A) or above. Ear protection zones should be marked with notices, ear protectors which comply with relevant EU "product" Directives should be provided to those exposed to the noise and, so far as is reasonably practicable, exposure to noise shall be reduced by means other than ear protectors. Employees shall use such protectors (or other protective equipment) and report defects to the employer. Manufacturers and suppliers are required to supply adequate information on the generation of noise by the product. The HSE may grant exemptions, particularly when the use of ear protectors may create a risk which outweighs the risk of hearing damage, or if the employer has adequate arrangements for ensuring that the average level over the whole working week will be below 90dB(A).

6.304   The chart below shows a summary of the legal requirements.

Action required where $L_{EP,d}$ is likely to be [1]:	below 85dB(a)	85dB(A) (first AL)	90dB(A) (second AL) [2]
Employers' duties			
General duty to reduce risk Risk of hearing damage to be reduced to the lowest level reasonably practicable (reg 6)	√	√	√

Assessment of noise exposure
Noise assessments to be made by   √   √
competent person (reg 4)
Record of assessments to be kept un-   √   √
til a new one is made (reg 5).

Noise reduction
Reduce exposure to noise so far as is   √
reasonably practicable by means
other than ear protectors (reg 7).

Provision of information to workers
Provide adequate information, in-   √   √
struction and training about risks to
hearing, what employees should do
to minimise risk, how they can obtain ear protectors if they are exposed
between 85 and 90dB(A), and their
obligations under the regulations (reg
11).
Mark ear protection zones with no-   √
tices, so far as is reasonably practicable (reg 9).

Ear protectors
Ensure so far as is practicable that
protectors are:
• provided to employees who ask for   √
them (reg 8(1))
• provided to all exposed (reg 8(2))   √
• maintained and repaired (reg   √   √
10(1)(b))
• used by all exposed (reg 10(1)(a))   √
Ensure so far as is reasonably practi-   √
cable that all who go into a marked
ear protection zone use ear protectors
(reg 9(1)(b)).

Maintenance and use of equipment
Ensure so far as is practicable that:

• all equipment provided under the regulation is fully used, except for the ear protectors provided between 85 and 90dB(A) (reg 10(a))	√	√
• all equipment is maintained (reg 10(1)(b))	√	√

Employees' duties

Use of equipment
So far as is practicable:

• use ear protectors (reg 10(2))		√
• use any other protective equipment (reg 10(2))	√	√
• report any defects discovered to the employer (reg 10(2))	√	√

Machine makers' and suppliers' duties

Provision of information

Provide information on the noise likely to be generated (reg 12)	√	√

Notes: (1) The dB(A) action levels are values of daily personal exposure to noise (LEP).
(2) All the actions indicated at 90dB(A) are also required where the peak sound pressure is at or above 200 P.

6.305 The problem of noise at work can be tackled in four ways. First, by reducing the noise at its source. This involves new design techniques, new technology, new materials, etc. Consultations can take place with manufacturers (reminding them of their obligations under s.6 of HSWA). The level of 90dB(A) is a somewhat arbitrary level which it was thought could be afforded by industry, bearing in mind the cost of replacing existing machinery, but it is not a safe standard in absolute terms, and ideally, a level not exceeding 85dB(A) should be aimed at.

6.306 Second, noise reduction techniques can be implemented. This may involve isolating the source of the noise, so that workpeople are unaffected by it, or blanketing walls and ceilings with noise absorbing materials which will have the effect of reducing noise levels, and so on.

6.307 Third, ear protection should be provided, appropriate to the dangers present. This can be achieved by ear plugs, ear muffs, helmets, etc but it is important that the correct protection is provided in each case, depending on the level of noise present. The object must be to reduce harmful sound, not sound itself, for it is essential to retain the latter (eg as a warning of danger, or to receive instructions, etc). Ear plugs should initially be fitted by a qualified person (occupational nurse, etc) otherwise the selection of a wrong size may render the protection ineffective. Ear muffs must be comfortable to wear, aesthetically acceptable to the wearer and must not interfere with the work or other protective equipment.

6.308   Fourth, exposure time to excessive noise can be reduced by allowing rest periods in rest rooms away from the noise, or operating a rota system.

6.309   The civil remedy in respect of occupational deafness is a claim for compensation based on common law negligence (see *Berry v Stone Manganese and Marine Ltd*). The existence of a duty of care is now well recognised, and while a failure to provide the necessary precautions will clearly amount to a breach of that duty, there is some room for argument as to the duty to compel, exhort or propagandise in order to ensure that they are used. An employee may not readily realise the insidious nature of the danger of working without the precautions or the fact that he may suffer permanent damage. Something more positive is required from the employer than the passive duty to provide ear muffs, plugs, etc. It also follows that if an employee fails to use the precautions after being instructed in their proper use, any compensation awarded can be reduced in respect of his contributory conduct. Compensation awards have been awarded in the region of £4000–£8000, depending on the extent of the deafness (see *Smith v British Rail Engineering Ltd*). Any claim must be brought within three years from the damage (Limitation Act 1980), but since deafness is a process which takes place over the years, an affected person may not know in the early stages of the nature or extent of the damage caused.

6.310   The Social Security (Industrial Injuries) (Prescribed Diseases) Regulations 1985 (as variously amended) enable a worker to obtain industrial injuries disablement benefit (see paragraph 8.94) if he suffers from occupational deafness. The worker must have been employed in the prescribed occupation for more than 10 years, and he must suffer from an average hearing loss of at least 50 decibels in both ears. In at least one ear, the loss must be due to noise at work.

Pressure Systems Safety Regulations 2000

6.311 These regulations re-enact, with amendments, the Pressure Systems and Transportable Gas Containers Regulations 1989, which have consequently been revoked. Also repealed were ss.34–38 of the Factories Act 1961. The regulations apply to plant containing a "relevant fluid"(eg all steam systems, and a gas or fluid which has a vapour pressure greater than 0.5 bar above atmospheric pressure), which is used or intended to be used at work. The requirements or prohibitions imposed by the regulations on employers in respect of his employees also extend to a self-employed person in respect of his own activities at work. Requirements or prohibitions which are imposed on designers, manufacturers, importers or suppliers of components only extend to those matters for which such persons had within their control.

6.312 Designers, manufacturers, importers or suppliers of any pressure system or any article intended to be a component of a pressure system, must ensure that the system or article is properly designed, and constructed from suitable material. The design should be such that all necessary examinations can be carried out, and, if there is means of access to the interior of a pressure system, access must be without danger. All necessary protective devices shall be provided. Designers and suppliers must provide written information concerning the design, construction, examination, operation and maintenance of pressure systems or articles intended to be a component. Manufacturers shall ensure that the pressure vessel has attached to it the manufacturer's name, a serial number, date of manufacture, standard to which the vessel was built, the maximum allowable pressure, the minimum allowance pressure (other than atmospheric) and the design temperature.

6.313 The installer of a pressure system shall ensure that nothing about the way it was installed gives rise to danger or impairs the operation of any protective device or inspection facility, and the user shall not operate the system until he has established the safe operating limits, and drawn up a written scheme for periodic examination by a competent person. The user will ensure that the competent person does in fact examine the system in accordance with the scheme, and the competent person shall make a written report of such examination as soon as is practicable after the examination. If the competent person is of the opinion that the pressure system will give rise to imminent danger unless certain repairs or modifications are carried out, he will make a report to that effect, and send a copy to the local enforcing authority. The user shall not operate the system until the appropriate repairs, modifications or changes have been made.

6.314   The user of a pressure system will keep records of the last report made by the competent person, as well as previous reports if they contain information which will assist in assessing whether the system is safe to operate.

6.315   In proceedings for an offence under the regulations, it will be a defence to prove that the commission of the offence was due to the act or default of another person, and that all reasonable precautions were taken and due diligence exercised in order to avoid the commission of the offence. The regulations are accompanied by an Approved Code of Practice (L122).

Control of Substances Hazardous to Health Regulations 1999 (COSHH)

6.316   The Control of Substances Hazardous to Health Regulations 1999 (COSHH), which revoke and replace the 1994 regulations (as amended), are designed to protect workers against the risks of exposure to substances considered to be hazardous to health, the use of which arises out of or in connection with work undertaken under the control of the employer. The COSHH regulations are designed to implement a number of EC Directives, and extend to offshore oil and gas installations.

6.317   The major change in the 1999 regulations is the removal from the Schedules of the list of substances assigned maximum exposure limits (MELs), thus avoiding the need to frequently amend the regulations. MELs will still be legally binding, but the list will appear in HSE's publication EH40 *Occupational Exposure Limits,* which is revised annually. Also published will be occupational exposure standards (OESs). MELs are generally assigned to substances which may cause serious health problems (eg cancer, occupational asthma, etc) for which there is no known "safe" level of exposure, or, if it does exist, control to that level is not reasonably practicable. OESs can be set at a level so that daily inhalation will not damage the health of workers exposed, based on current scientific knowledge.

6.318 The regulations are accompanied by a new Approved Code of Practice, which will consolidate the previous ACOP, together with the ACOPs on carcinogens and biological agents.

6.319 Apart from certain specified substances emissions, such as asbestos, lead, ionising radiations and those used in mining activities, all of which have their own specific legislative provisions, COSHH applies to all substances which are hazardous to health. A substance is hazardous if it is a potential cause of harm; whether there is a risk from the substance will depend on the circumstances in which it is being used or controlled. Thus a substance with a low hazard can have a substantial risk if poorly controlled, whereas the most hazardous substance can have a low risk if adequately controlled. COSHH does not apply to flammable or explosive substances, which convey a risk to safety rather than to health.

6.320 As well as placing duties on employers in respect of their employees, like duties apply, so far as is reasonably practicable, in respect of any other person, whether at work or not, who may be affected by the work carried on by the employer, except in relation to health surveillance. The duties relating to monitoring, providing information and training also do not apply to non-employees, unless they are on the premises where the work is being carried out.

6.321 The use of certain substances for certain purposes is prohibited (see Schedule 2), as is the importation of certain substances and articles. The supply of those substances or articles is also prohibited.

6.322 COSHH defines a substance as being hazardous to health if it is:
  (a) a substance listed in Part 1 of the Approved Supply List as dangerous for supply within the meaning of the Chemicals (Hazard Information and Packaging for Supply) Regulations 1994 (as amended) (see paragraph 6.244) which is very toxic, toxic, harmful corrosive or irritant, or
  (b) a substance for which HSC has approved a maximum exposure limit or an occupational exposure standard, or
  (c) a biological agent, or
  (d) dust of any kind, when present at substantial concentrations in the air (as defined), or
  (e) a substance (not mentioned above) which creates a hazard to the health of any person which is comparable to the hazards created by the above-mentioned substances.

6.323   Regulation 6 states that an employer shall not carry on any work which is liable to expose any employees to a substance hazardous to health unless he has made a suitable and sufficient assessment of the risks created by that work to the health of those employees and of the steps that need to be taken to eliminate or reduce those risks in accordance with the requirements of the regulations.

6.324   Thus the first step is to make an assessment of the risk. This is done by identifying the hazardous substance, considering the circumstances in which it is being used, assessing the likelihood of exposure, contact, etc identifying the harmful effects identifying the form of the hazardous substance, eg solid, liquid, gas and so on. The assessment is essentially a practical exercise to ascertain what actually happens in the workplace. This involves asking a great number of questions, ie from suppliers, manufacturers, trade and/or professional organisations, medical and other experts and so on. It means consultation with all levels in the work force in order to ascertain what they are actually doing and what risks they are exposed to. It means looking at all substances which are used by the work force, an assessment not only of the risks attendant on the work activity, but also those risks which can arise after the work activity ceases. It means checking on labels, information supplied, records of previous incidents, examination of trade data, HSE Guidance Notes and other published documentation. It means consideration of accidental leakage, spills or unexpected discharges. The length of exposure may be just as important as the amount of exposure.

6.325   It is submitted that all assessments should be done in writing, so that information gleaned can be followed through, omissions noted and dealt with, and comparisons made with past and future assessments.

6.326   If an employer fails to enquire from a supplier of the hazards present in a substance, with the result that an employee suffers an injury or illness, the employer will be liable for a breach of the regulations as well as common law negligence (*Ogden v Airedale Hospital*). The burden of proof to show that sufficient steps were taken to prevent deleterious exposure is on the employer (*Bilton v Fastnet Highlands Ltd*).

6.327   Regulation 7 then provides that every employer shall ensure that exposure of employees to substances hazardous to health is either prevented or, if this is not reasonably practicable, adequately controlled. So far as is reasonably practicable, the prevention or control shall be secured by means other than the provision of personal protective equipment. However, if these measures do not prevent or adequately control exposure then, in addition the employer shall provide the employees with such suitable personal protective equipment as will adequately control their exposure and which complies with the Personal Protective Equipment (EC Directive) Regulations 1992. Measures must be taken to reduce the level of exposure, so far as is reasonably practical, and in any case to below the maximum exposure limit, and if an occupational exposure standard has been approved it must not be exceeded or if it. is the employer must determine why and take appropriate action. If respiratory protective equipment is provided, these shall be suitable and of a type or standard approved by the HSE.

6.328 Thus control of the exposure to the hazard may be done in a number of ways. Primarily, the hazardous substance should be removed or replaced by a safer substance or the processes changed to avoid using the substance. In some circumstances, it may be possible to enclose the process, or use extraction equipment, or ventilation. Finally, safe working systems and handling procedures, including the provision of personal protective equipment, should be considered.

6.329 Regulation 8 requires employers to take all reasonable steps to ensure that control measures and personal protective equipment shall be properly used or applied. Employees are also under a duty to make full and proper use of them, and to report any defect to the employer. Control measures and personal protective equipment shall be maintained in an efficient state and in good repair. Local exhaust ventilation plant must be tested and thoroughly examined at least every 14 months, and other controls at suitable intervals. Records of such tests and examinations shall be kept for five years.

6.330 Regulation 10 requires employers to monitor exposure to substances hazardous to health, and to keep suitable records. If these records are representative of the personal exposures of identifiable employees, they must be kept for 40 years but, in any other case, they need to be kept for 5 years. Regulation 11 provides that employees who are exposed to substances which are hazardous to health shall undergo health surveillance where appropriate (see Schedule 5). Health records shall be kept for at least 40 years.

6.331 Employers must provide employees with such information, instruction and training as is suitable for the employees to know the risks to health created by the exposure, and the precautions to be taken. In particular, the employee (or his representative) shall be informed forthwith if monitoring shows that the maximum exposure limit has been exceeded (regulation 12).

6.332   In any criminal proceedings brought in respect of an alleged contravention of the regulations, it shall be a defence for any person to prove that he took all reasonable precautions and exercised all due diligence to avoid the commission of the offence.

6.333   There is little doubt that the COSHH regulations are one of the most significant developments in UK law since the introduction of the Health and Safety at Work, etc Act in 1974. They apply to all employers and require the introduction of pro-active safety policies. They are also in line with many of the changes made to UK law following the adoption by the EU of a number of directives on health and safety (see Chapter 10). The HSE has published a number of documents which may be used for guidance.

Metrication

6.334   All unmetricated health and safety legislation (apart from certain offshore legislation) must now be expressed in metric units of measurement (see Health and Safety (Miscellaneous Provisions) (Metrication, etc) Regulations 1992, which implement Directive 80/181/EEC. However, special provision has been made for the measurement of temperature and humidity in humid textile factories, where use is made of wet and dry bulb temperatures. The regulations also harmonise the flash-point test measures in the Petroleum (Consolidation) Act and supporting regulations with the Chemicals (Hazard Information and Packaging for Supply) Regulations 1994 (as amended).

Construction industry

6.335   Section 127 of the Factories Act 1961 applies the relevant provisions of that Act to building operations and works of engineering construction undertaken by way of trade or business, or for the purpose of any industrial or commercial undertaking and to any line or siding used in connection therewith which is not part of a railway. The relevant provisions are:

(a) Part II relating to explosive or inflammable dust, etc (s.31)
(b) Part V (formal investigation of accidents and cases of disease)
(c) Part X with respect to general registers and the preservation of records and registers (ss.140, 141)
(d) Part XI relating to certain duties of district councils (s.153)
(e) Part XII relating to offences (ss.155–171)
(f) Part XIII (ss.172, 174)
(g) Part XIV (ss.175, 176).

6.336 The main source of legal rules relating to health and safety in the construction industry are the following regulations which are currently in force:
(a) Construction (Head Protection) Regulations 1989
(b) Construction (Design and Management) Regulations 1994
(c) Construction (Health, Safety and Welfare) Regulations 1996.

6.337 In addition, there are a number of relevant regulations which were passed in order to comply with EC Directives on type examination certificates of approval. These include:
(a) Construction Plant and Equipment (Harmonisation of Noise Emission Standards) Regulations 1988 (as amended)
(b) Falling Object Protective Structure for Construction Plant (EC Requirements) Regulations 1988
(c) Roll-over Protective Structures for Construction Plant (EC Requirements) Regulations 1988.

Construction (Head Protection) Regulations 1989

6.338 The Construction (Head Protection) Regulations 1989 are designed to give protection to persons who work on construction sites, which are defined as being works of building operations and engineering construction. Employers must provide and maintain head protection and replace it whenever necessary. An identical obligation lies on self-employed persons. The head protection must be suitable, ie conform to British Standard 5240 (or equivalent), be compatible with the work or activity and comply with relevant EU "product" Directives. Head protection must be worn at all times during construction work unless there is no risk of injury to the head from falling objects. Employers, self-employed persons and employees who control others (eg foremen) must ensure that the head protectors are worn. A person who has control of a site may make rules governing when and where helmets shall be worn. Such rules shall be in writing, and brought to the attention of those affected by them.

6.339   Sikhs are exempted from the requirements of the regulations at any time when they are wearing their turbans while working on construction sites and thus they cannot be required to wear safety helmets in such circumstances (Employment Act 1989, s.11). In consequence, an employer will not be liable to tort in respect of any injury or damage caused because he failed to comply with the statutory duty. A Sikh who is injured because of failure to wear the safety helmet will only be able to recover damages to the extent the injury or damage would still have occurred had he been wearing a safety helmet.

Construction (Design and Management) Regulations 1994

6.340   These regulations implement (with minor exceptions) Directive 92/57/EEC on the minimum safety and health requirements at temporary or mobile construction sites, and came into force on 31 March 1995.

6.341   An Approved Code of Practice (ACOP), L54: *Managing construction for health and safety* and other guidance documents have been issued by HSE, to assist all concerned to understand their obligations under the regulations, and to give guidance on actions to be taken.

Application of the regulations

6.342   The regulations (other than regulation 13 — duties of designers, see below) do not apply to construction work which is not notifiable, and where the largest number of persons at work at any one time is less than five.

Appointment of planning supervisor

6.343   Every client is required to appoint a planning supervisor, who must give notice of the project to the HSE unless it is not notifiable. A project is notifiable if the construction phase will last longer than 30 days, or will involve more than 500 person days of construction work. The following particulars shall be given as soon as they are known or can be reasonably ascertained.

1. Date of forwarding the particulars.
2. Exact address of the construction site.
3. Name and address of client.
4. Type of project.
5. Name and address of planning supervisor.
6. Declaration of appointment signed by the planning supervisor.
7. Name and address of principal contractor.
8. Declaration of appointment signed by the principal contractor.
9. Planned starting date.
10. Planned duration of the construction phase.
11. Estimated maximum number of people at work on the site.
12. Planned number of contractors.
13. Name and address of any contractors already chosen.

Duties under the regulations

6.344   The regulations place duties on five parties involved in construction work, namely:
   (a) the client
   (b) the designer
   (c) the planning supervisor
   (d) the principal contractor
   (e) other contractors.

(a) Duties of the client

6.345   The client is any person for whom a project is carried out. Regulation 6 requires the client to appoint a planning supervisor and a principal contractor (who can be the same person provided he is competent to carry out both functions). The client must be reasonably satisfied that the person he intends to appoint as a planning supervisor is competent to perform his functions under the regulations. The client must also be satisfied that the planning supervisor has allocated adequate resources to enable him to perform his functions. The client shall not permit the construction phase of any project to commence unless a health and safety plan has been prepared. He must also make sure that the planning supervisor is provided with all information relevant to his functions relating to the state or condition of the premises on which construction work is to start. The client must take reasonable steps to ensure that the safety file is available for inspection.

(b) Duties of the designer (regulation 13)

6.346 No person shall arrange for a designer to prepare a design unless he is reasonably satisfied that the designer is competent to prepare that design, and that he has allocated adequate resources to meet the requirements of regulation 13. The designer must take reasonable steps to ensure that the client is aware of his own duties and of any practical guidance issued by the Health and Safety Commission (HSC).

6.347 In *R v Paul Wurth SA* it was held that this duty (under regulation 13(2)(a)(i) only applied to a designer within the meaning of regulation 2(1)(a), who prepares a design and not to a person who arranges for a person under his control to prepare a design. Nor did the act of approving a design constitute the preparation of the design. However, the Construction (Design and Management) (Amendment) Regulations 2000 nullified the effect of this decision, by introducing a new definition of designer, to mean a person who carries on a trade, business or other undertaking in connection with which he prepares a design. The reference to a person preparing a design includes a reference to an employee or other person at work under his control. Thus the duty under regulation 13(2) applies to a person where an employee or other such person prepares a design.

6.348 The designer must ensure that any design he prepares includes design considerations which are adequate, having regard to the need:
   (a) to avoid foreseeable risks to the health and safety of any person working or cleaning in or on the structure, or any person who might be affected by the activities of a person at work
   (b) to combat at source risks to health and safety of any person working or cleaning on or in the structure, or any person who might be affected by the activities of a person at work
   (c) to give priority to measures which will protect all persons at work (or cleaning or affected as above) over measures which will only protect each individual person carrying out such work; in other words, general health and safety precautions, which protect everyone, are to be preferred to individual precautions.

6.349 The designer must also ensure that the design includes adequate information about any aspects of the structure or materials used which might affect the health or safety of any person working, cleaning or other person affected by the work, and he must co-operate with the planning supervisor so far as is necessary to enable each of them to comply with the relevant statutory provisions.

(c) Duties of planning supervisor

6.350   No client shall appoint any person as a planning supervisor unless the client is reasonably satisfied that the person he intends to appoint is competent to perform the functions as a planning supervisor in respect of that project, and that he will allocate adequate resources to enable him to perform his functions as such.

6.351   The planning supervisor must ensure that the designer has met the above-mentioned legal requirements, that there is any necessary co-operation between designers, give appropriate advice to the client and contractor, ensure that a health and safety file is prepared, completed, reviewed as necessary and delivered to the client at the end of the work (regulation 14).

6.352   The planning supervisor must also ensure that a health and safety plan has been prepared before the contractor starts work (regulation 15). The plan shall contain the following information:
  (a) a general description of the construction work
  (b) the time within which the project is intended to be completed
  (c) that he, and the designer, are competent, and that adequate resources will be allocated
  (d) information which the contractor needs in order to keep the safety plan up to date.

(d) Duties of principal contractor

6.353   The principal contractor:
  (a) shall take reasonable steps to ensure co-operation between all contractors on the site so as to enable the statutory provisions to be complied with
  (b) shall ensure that every contractor and every employee at work complies with the rules contained in the health and safety plan
  (c) shall take reasonable steps to ensure that only authorised persons are allowed on the site
  (d) shall ensure that the particulars given in the notice to the HSE under regulation 7 (above) are displayed in a readable condition in a place where they can be read by any person at work on the construction site
  (e) shall provide the planning supervisor with any information

which it is reasonable to believe would be included in the health and safety file but which the planning supervisor does not have (regulation 16).

6.354 The principal contractor is also required to given reasonable directions to any contractor in order to ensure compliance, and to include in the health and safety plan, health and safety rules, which must be in writing, and brought to the attention of those who may be affected by them. Every contractor must be provided with comprehensible information on risks to the health and safety of the contractor, his employees or other persons under the contractor's control, and also take steps to ensure that the contractor has provided his employees with information as required by regulation 10 of the Management Regulations (see paragraph 5.37), and has provided those employees with appropriate training as required by regulation 13(2)(b) of those regulations.

(e) Duties of contractors

6.355 Every contractor shall:
  (a) co-operate with the principal contractor insofar as it is necessary to enable each of them to comply with the various statutory provisions
  (b) provide the principal contractor with any information in his possession which might affect the health and safety of any person at work or any other person affected by such work
  (c) comply with any directions given to him by the principal contractor including health and safety rules
  (d) ensure that the notification of the project given under regulation 7 (above) is displayed where it can be read by any person at work on the site
  (e) comply with any rules applicable to him in the health and safety plan
  (f) promptly provide the principal contractor with any information in relation to any death, injury, condition or dangerous occurrence which the contractor is required to report under RIDDOR
  (g) promptly provide the principal contractor with any information which the contractor has, which the principal contractor does not have, but needs to provide to the planning supervisor.

Exclusion of civil liability

6.356   The regulations do not confer any right of action in any civil proceedings, other than regulation 10 (a client shall ensure, so far as is reasonably practicable, that the construction phase of any project does not start unless a health and safety plan has been prepared) and regulation 16(1)(c) (the principal contractor shall take reasonable steps to ensure that only authorised persons are allowed into any premises where construction work is being carried on).

Construction (Health, Safety and Welfare) Regulations 1996

6.357   These regulations came into force in September 1996, and are designed to implement the outstanding provisions of Directive 92/57/EEC on the minimum health and safety requirements at temporary and mobile sites. The Regulations are intended to "modernise, simplify and consolidate" existing legislation, and do not contain any particularly new obligations, apart from some minor details. The Regulations are objective-setting and risk-based, rather than prescriptive, although there will be no lowering of existing standards. Thus, terms such as "suitable and sufficient" replace precise details and measurements. A risk assessment should always be first carried out (as required by the Management of Health and Safety at Work Regulations 1999). The new regulations are to be considered together with the Construction (Design and Management) Regulations 1994. Guidance Notes are available from HSE (HSG150: *Health and safety in construction*).

6.358   Three sets of regulations have in consequence been revoked. These are:
   (a) Construction (General Provisions) Regulations 1961
   (b) Construction (Working Places) Regulations 1966
   (c) Construction (Health and Welfare) Regulations 1966.

6.359   The Construction (Lifting Operations) Regulations 1961 have been revoked and replaced by the Lifting Operations and Lifting Equipment Regulations 1998 (see paragraph 6.94).

Definitions (regulation 2)

6.360   The regulations apply to construction sites, which are any place where the principal activity carried on is construction work. This latter term is extensively defined, including construction, alteration,

301

conversion, fitting out, commissioning, renovation, repair, upkeep, redecoration or other maintenance (including high-pressure water cleaning), decommissioning, demolition or dismantling of a structure.

6.361 The definition also includes preparatory work (eg site clearance and excavation), the assembly of prefabricated elements, the removal of a structure or of any product or waste resulting from the demolition or dismantling of a structure; and the installation, commissioning, maintenance, repair or removal of services (electrical, gas, compressed air, hydraulic, telecommunications or computer services) which are normally fixed to or within a structure.

Application (regulation 3)

6.362 The regulations therefore apply to construction work carried on by a person at work, but not to any workplace on a construction site which is set aside for purposes other than construction work.

Persons upon whom duties are imposed (regulation 4)

6.363 It shall be the duty of every employer, every self-employed person, and every person who has control of the way construction work is being carried on to comply with the Regulations insofar as they affect him, or any person at work or under his control, or relate to matters which are within his control. It is also the duty of every employee to comply with the Regulations insofar as they relate to the performance of or the refraining from an act by him. Every person at work shall co-operate with any other person upon whom a duty is imposed so far as is necessary to ensure that duty is performed or complied with. Every person at work shall also report any defect of which he is aware and which may endanger the health or safety of himself or others.

Safe places of work (regulation 5)

6.364 There shall be, as far as is reasonably practicable, safe access to (and egress from) every place of work, and to every other place provided for the use of any person while at work. These accesses shall be without risks to health and properly maintained. Every place of work shall, so far as is reasonably practicable, be made and kept safe for, and without risks to the health of, any person at work there. Suitable and sufficient steps must be taken to ensure that no person gains access to any unsafe access or place of work, except persons who are engaged in making the place safe, and that all practical steps have been taken to ensure that person's safety while engaged in that work. There shall be, so far as is reasonably practicable, sufficient working space, having regard to the nature of the work being carried on.

Falls (regulation 6)

6.365   Suitable and sufficient steps shall be taken to prevent, so far as is reasonably practicable, any person falling. If a person is liable to fall a distance of two metres or more, then suitable and sufficient guard-rails, toe-boards, barriers or other means of protection shall be provided, and these must comply with the requirements of Schedules 1 and 2 to the regulations. Working platforms shall be provided where necessary in the interests of safety and, in certain circumstances, suitable personal suspension equipment (complying with Schedule 3) may be provided. Ladders shall not be used as a means of access to and from work unless it is reasonable to do so, having regard to the nature of the work and its duration, and the risks from using a ladder. The installation or erection of scaffolding shall be carried out only under the supervision of a competent person.

Fragile material (regulation 7)

6.366   Suitable and sufficient steps must be taken to prevent any person falling through any fragile material. Platforms, coverings or other means of support must be provided if a person would be liable to fall two metres or more.

Falling objects (regulation 8)

6.367   Where necessary to prevent danger to any person, suitable and sufficient means shall be taken to prevent, so far as is reasonably practicable, the fall of any material or object. If it is not reasonably practicable to do so, steps must be taken to prevent any person from being struck by any falling material or object which is likely to cause injury. Neither material nor objects shall be thrown or tipped from a height that is liable to cause injury. Materials and equipment must be stored in such a way as to prevent danger to any person.

Stability of structures (regulation 9)

6.368   All practicable steps shall be taken to prevent the accidental collapse of new or existing structures due to the construction work. Buttresses or temporary supports or structures used to support a permanent structure shall be erected or dismantled only under the supervision of a competent person.

Demolition or dismantling (regulation 10)

6.369   Suitable and sufficient steps shall be taken to ensure that the demolition or dismantling of any structure is planned and carried out in such a manner so as to prevent, so far as is reasonably practicable, risk of danger to any person.

Explosives (regulation 11)

6.370   Explosive charges shall be used or fired only if suitable and sufficient steps have been taken to ensure that no person is exposed to the risk of injury from the explosion, or from projected or flying material caused thereby.

Excavations (regulation 12)

6.371   All practicable steps shall be taken to ensure that new or existing excavations, which may be in a temporary state of weakness or instability due to the carrying out of construction work, do not collapse accidentally. Suitable and sufficient steps shall be taken to prevent any person being buried or trapped by a fall or dislodgement of any material. Steps must be taken to prevent any risk of injury arising from any underground cable or other such subterranean services.

Cofferdams and caissons (regulation 13)

6.372   Every cofferdam or caisson shall be of suitable design and construction, of suitable and sound material and of sufficient strength, and shall be properly maintained. The construction, installation, alteration or dismantling of a cofferdam or caisson shall take place only under the suspension of a competent person.

Prevention of drowning (regulation 14)

6.373   If construction work is such as to involve a risk of drowning in water or other liquid to any person, then suitable and sufficient steps shall be taken to prevent this happening, so far as is reasonably practicable. Suitable rescue equipment shall be provided and maintained. If any person is conveyed to or from work by water, safe transport shall be provided; any such vehicle shall be of suitable construction, properly maintained, under the control of a competent person, and not overloaded.

Traffic routes (regulation 15)

6.374   Construction sites shall be so organised that, so far as is reasonably practicable, pedestrians and vehicles can move safely without risks to health. Traffic routes must not cause danger, doors or gates intended to be used by pedestrians must be so positioned so as to enable pedestrians to see any approaching vehicle or plant; if vehicles and pedestrians cannot be separated, other means of protection must be provided. Loading bays must have at least one exit point for the exclusive use of pedestrians, and a separate gate provided if it is unsafe to use a gate intended primarily for vehicles. A vehicle shall not be driven on a traffic route unless, so far as is reasonably practicable, that traffic route is free from obstruction and permits sufficient clearance. Suitable traffic signs shall be used where necessary for reasons of health and safety.

Doors and gates (regulation 16)

6.375   Where necessary to prevent the risk of injury to any person, doors and gates shall be fitted with suitable safety devices. Sliding doors, etc shall have a device that prevents them coming off their track during use; upward-opening doors, etc shall have a device that prevents them falling back; powered doors, etc shall have suitable and effective features which prevent them causing injury by trapping persons, and they must be capable of being opened manually if the power fails.

Vehicles (regulation 17)

6.376   Suitable and sufficient steps shall be taken to prevent the unintended movement of any vehicle. Where any person may be endangered by the movement of any vehicle, suitable and sufficient steps shall be taken to ensure that the person having control of the vehicle shall give warning to any person liable to be at risk. Vehicles shall be driven, operated, towed and loaded in a safe manner, and persons shall not be permitted to ride on a vehicle or remain on it during the loading or unloading of loose material otherwise than in a safe place provided. If a vehicle is being used for excavating or handling (including tipping) materials, suitable and sufficient steps shall be taken to prevent it from falling into any pit or water, or overrunning the edge of any embankment or earthwork.

Prevention of fire (regulation 18)

6.377 Suitable and sufficient steps shall be taken to prevent, so far as is reasonably practicable, the risk of injury to any person arising from fire, explosion, flooding, or any substance liable to cause asphyxiation.

Emergency routes and exits (regulation 19)

6.378 Where necessary in the interests of health and safety, a sufficient number of suitable emergency routes or exits shall be provided to enable persons to reach a place of safety in the event of danger. These shall lead as directly as possible to a safe area. They shall be kept free from obstruction, and shall be provided having regard to the type of construction work, the number and location of places at work on the site, the plant and equipment being used, the number of persons likely to be present, and the physical and chemical properties of substances or materials likely to be on the site. Emergency routes or exits shall be indicated by suitable signs.

Emergency procedures (regulation 20)

6.379 Where necessary in the interests of health and safety, suitable and sufficient arrangements shall be prepared and implemented for dealing with any foreseeable emergency, including the evacuation of the site. Steps shall be taken to ensure that every person to whom they apply shall be familiar with them, and the arrangements shall be tested at suitable intervals.

Fire detection and fire-fighting (regulation 21)

6.380 Construction sites shall have suitable and sufficient fire-fighting equipment and fire detectors and alarm systems, all of which shall be suitably located. They shall be properly maintained, examined and regularly tested to ensure that they remain effective. Fire-fighting equipment shall be easily accessible, and persons at work instructed in the correct use. It shall be indicated by suitable signs.

Welfare facilities (regulation 22)

6.381   Any person in control of a construction site, and every employer and self-employed person (with respect to any person under his control), shall ensure that there are suitable and sufficient sanitary conveniences, washing facilities, an adequate supply of wholesome drinking water, accommodation for clothing, changing facilities and rest facilities. These must comply with the more detailed requirements set out in Schedule 6.

Fresh air (regulation 23)

6.382   Every workplace or approach thereto shall have sufficient fresh or purified air to ensure that it is safe and without risks to health. Any plant used for this purpose shall include an effective device to give a visible or audible warning of failure.

Temperature and weather protection (regulation 24)

6.383   Suitable and sufficient steps shall be taken to ensure, so far as is reasonably practicable, that during working hours the temperature of any indoor place of work is reasonable for the purpose for which the place is used. Every place of work outdoors shall be so arranged that, so far as is reasonably practicable, it provides protection from adverse weather, having regard to, among other things, any protective clothing or equipment provided.

Lighting (regulation 25)

6.384   There shall be suitable and sufficient lighting for every place of work, including traffic routes, and this shall be, so far as is reasonably practicable, by natural light. Artificial lighting shall not be such as to adversely affect or change the perception of any sign or signal provided.

Good order (regulation 26)

6.385   Every construction site shall, so far as is reasonably practicable, be kept in good order, and every part used as a place of work shall be kept in a reasonable state of cleanliness. The perimeter shall be identified by suitable signs. Timber or other materials shall not have protruding nails. Such nails shall not be allowed to remain in a place where they may be a source of danger to any person.

Training (regulation 28)

6.386 Any person who carries out any activity involving construction work where training, technical knowledge or experience is necessary to reduce the risks of injury to any person shall possess such training, knowledge or experience, or be under the supervision of a person who has such training, knowledge or experience as may be appropriate, having regard to the nature of the activity.

Other matters

6.387 The Schedules to the Regulations set out further matters in great detail, including requirements for guard-rails, etc working platforms, personal suspension equipment, means for arresting falls, requirements for ladders, welfare facilities, places of work that require inspection, particulars to be included in inspection reports, and various other minor amendments.

Confined Spaces Regulations 1997

6.388 The Confined Spaces Regulations 1997 came into force on 28 January 1998, and implement part of Directive 92/57/EEC on minimum safety and health requirements on temporary or mobile construction sites. Various relevant items of legislation are in consequence repealed or revoked, including s.30 of the Factories Act 1961 and parts of certain regulations relating to processes which involved working in confined spaces, including ship-building, agriculture, breathing apparatus, etc.

6.389 The new regulations define a confined space as being any place, including chamber, tank, vat, silo, pit, trench, pipe, sewer, flue, well or similar space in which, by virtue of its enclosed nature, there arises a reasonably foreseeable specified risk. The "specified risks" are risks of:
- (a) serious injury to any person at work arising from a fire or explosion
- (b) the loss of consciousness of any person at work arising from an increase in body temperature, or the loss of consciousness or asphyxiation of any person at work arising from gas, fume, vapour or lack of oxygen
- (c) drowning of any person at work arising from a free flowing solid or the inability to reach a respirable environment due to entrapment by a free flowing solid. "Free flowing" solid means any substance consisting of solid particles and which is of, or is

capable of being in, a flowing or running consistency, including flour, grain, sand, sugar or other similar material.

6.390   The duty to ensure compliance with the regulations is placed on the employer, in respect of any work carried out by his employees, and to ensure compliance, so far as is reasonably practicable in respect of any work carried out by persons other than his employees, insofar as the provisions relate to matters which are within his control. Self-employed persons are under similar obligations with respect to their own work carried out by other persons.

Work in confined spaces (regulation 4–5)

6.391   No person at work shall enter a confined space to carry out work for any purpose unless it is not reasonably practicable to achieve that purpose without such entry. If such entry is necessary, no person shall enter or carry out any work in or (except in an emergency) leave a confined space otherwise than in accordance with a system of work which, in relation to any specified risks (see above) renders that work safe and without risks to health. A person shall not enter or carry out work in a confined space unless suitable and sufficient arrangements have been prepared for the persons in the event of any emergency, whether or not arising out of specified risk. Those arangments must also reduce the risks to the health and safety of any person required to put rescue arrangements into operation, and include the provision and maintenance of resuscitation procedures.

Exceptions

6.392   The regulations do not apply to activities on sea-going ships, work below ground in mines, and diving operations. The HSE may also grant exemption certificates, subject to certain stringent conditions, if satisfied that the health and safety of persons who are likely to be affected by the exemption will not be prejudiced in consequence.

6.393   The regulations are supplemented by an Approved Code of Practice and Guidance Notes, L101: *Safe work in confined spaces*. In particular, the ACOP emphasises the need for a risk assessment to be carried out under regulation 3 of the Management of Health and Safety at Work Regulations 1999 (see paragraph 5.8), and details a wide range of risks which are commonly associated with work in confined spaces.

CHAPTER 7

Particular health and safety issues

Employment of women

7.1 All restrictions on the hours of work which women may work have now been abolished, as well as most of the restrictions on the type of work they may perform (Employment Act 1989, ss.4–9 and Schedules 1 and 2). The remaining restrictions are as follows.

1. Under the Maternity and Parental Leave Regulations 1999 (regulation 7), a woman shall not be permitted to work by her employer during the period of two weeks beginning with the date of her confinement, and a breach of this provision is punishable by a fine not exceeding level 2 on the standard scale. Also, a woman must not be employed in a factory within four weeks of childbirth (Factories Act 1961, Schedule 5; Public Health Act 1936, s.205).

2. Under the Control of Lead at Work Regulations 1998 (see paragraph 6.188), a woman of reproductive capacity is prohibited from being employed in certain processes and activities involving lead and lead products. These are as follows.
    (a) in lead smelting and refining processes:
    – work involving the handling, treatment, sintering, smelting or refining of ores or materials containing not less than five per cent of lead fire
    – the cleaning of any place where any of the above processes are carried out
    (b) in lead-acid battery manufacturing processes:
    – the manipulation of lead oxides
    – mixing or pasting in connection with the manufacture or repair of lead batteries
    – the melting or casting of lead
    – the trimming, abrading or cutting of pasted plates in connection with the manufacture or repair of lead-acid batteries
    – the cleaning of any place where any of the above processes are carried out.

3. The Ionising Radiations Regulations 1999 (see paragraph 6.280) set lower dose limits for exposure to ionising radiation for women who are still of reproductive capacity, and for pregnant women, than the limit set for men.

4. There are restrictions on the employment of pregnant women as
aircraft flight crew, air traffic controllers, and on merchant ships
while at sea (Air Navigation Order 1995; Merchant Shipping (Medical
Examination) Regulations 1983).

7.2   Indeed, it is lawful to discriminate against a woman insofar as
it is necessary to comply with the above restrictions (Employment Act
1989, s.4).

7.3   As a general rule, it can be stated that the critical exposure of a
pregnant woman to deleterious substances is not so much in terms of
the quantity or amount, but in the timing of exposure. The first six
weeks of pregnancy when the foetus is being formed (and when
possibly the woman might not even know she is pregnant) might well
be the most critical time of all, together with the last three months of
pregnancy when the brain of the foetus is being formed. An American
organisation — the National Institute of Occupational Safety and Health
(NIOSH) — has issued guidelines which may usefully be followed
when a woman is exposed to potentially harmful substances. These
cover (a) when a pregnant woman may continue to work, (b) when she
may continue to work but with environmental modifications to
accommodate her working and (c) when she should not work at all.
Similar guidance is available from the Society for Occupational
Medicine.

Maternity rights

7.4   The Employment Rights Act 1996 (ERA) provides that a woman
employee who is pregnant has a number of statutory rights.

7.5   First, if, on the advice of a registered general practitioner or
midwife or health visitor, she has made an appointment to attend an
ante-natal clinic, she has the right not to be unreasonably refused time
off work to attend. She must produce documentary evidence of such an
appointment (though not for the first appointment), and she is entitled
to be paid at her appropriate hourly rate (ERA, s.55).

7.6   Second, she may be suspended from work on maternity
grounds where, in consequence of:
   (a) any   requirement   imposed   by   an   enactment   (including
       regulations), or
   (b) any recommendation in an Approved Code of Practice (ACOP)

she is entitled to be suspended because she is pregnant, has recently given birth, or is breast-feeding a child (ERA, s.66).

7.7 The Suspension from Work (on Maternity Grounds) Order 1994 (as amended) specifies regulation 16–18 of the Management of Health and Safety at Work Regulations 1999 to be the relevant statutory provision for the purpose of s.66. There are thus two grounds for maternity suspension:

(a) if the risk assessment of women of child-bearing age (see paragraph 5.62) reveals a risk which cannot be avoided, the employer shall, if it is reasonable to do so, and would avoid such risks, alter her working conditions or hours of work; if it is not reasonable to do so (or if doing so would not avoid the risk) the employer shall suspend her from work for as long as is necessary to avoid such risk (regulation 16 of the Management Regulations). However, the employer is not required to take any such action unless the woman informs him, in writing, that she is pregnant, or has given birth within the previous six months, or that she is breastfeeding (regulation 18).

(b) where a new or expectant mother works at night, and a certificate from a registered general practitioner or midwife shows that it is necessary for her health or safety that she should not be at work for any period of such work, the employer shall suspend her for as long as is necessary (regulation 17).

7.8 These provisions were considered by an employment tribunal in *Hickey v Lucas Services*, where, following a finding of dissatisfaction with the applicant's performance, she was told that she had to transfer to work as a stores assistant in a warehouse. She discovered that she was pregnant, and because the new work would have involved her lifting heavy objects, she was advised by her doctor that this could constitute a risk to her health and to the health of her unborn child. Consequently, she went off work sick and was paid statutory sick pay. She complained to an employment tribunal that she should have received her full pay, as she had been effectively suspended from work on maternity grounds, and was thus entitled to her usual remuneration under s.68 of the ERA. Her claim was upheld. The employers had not carried out a risk assessment as required by the Management Regulations, and, had they done so, they would have realised that the risks to her health could not be avoided by preventative or protective measures. Thus they should have altered her working conditions or suspended her on full pay under ss.66–67 of the ERA.

7.9   Before suspending the woman from work under the above provisions, the employer, where he has suitable alternative work for her, must offer her such work. The work must be suitable for her and appropriate in the circumstances, and the terms and conditions, if they differ from those which normally pertain to her work, must not be substantially less favourable than those which previously applied (ERA, s.67). Otherwise, she is entitled to be paid her normal remuneration, unless she is offered suitable alternative employment which she unreasonably refuses (s.68).

7.10   Third, irrespective of her period of continuous employment, she is entitled to have 18 weeks' ordinary maternity leave, during which time she is entitled to the benefit of her terms and conditions of employment (except remuneration). Her absence cannot commence earlier than the 11th week prior to the expected week of childbirth (Maternity and Parental Leave Regulations 1999).(The Government is currently consulting on a number of changes to maternity rights, including extending the maternity leave period to one year, increasing the paid maternity leave period to six months, increasing the length of parental leave available to the parents of disabled children, and so on.)

7.11   Fourth, a woman who is pregnant may be entitled to receive Statutory Maternity Pay, which is paid by her employer, who then recoups the amount from the national insurance contributions which are paid to the Inland Revenue (Social Security (Contributions and Benefits) Act 1992, ss.164–171). If she does not qualify for SMP because she lacks the relevant period of continuous employment, she may be entitled to a Maternity Allowance, payable by the Department of Social Security.

7.12   Fifth, s.99 of the Act provides that it will be unfair to dismiss an employee if the reason was:
   (a) that she is pregnant, or any reason connected with her pregnancy, or
   (b) that her maternity leave period is ended by a dismissal and the reason for this was because she has given birth to a child, or
   (c) that she took maternity leave, or
   (d) because before the end of her maternity leave period she produced a medical certificate stating that she would be

incapable of work after the end of that period, and she was dismissed within four weeks from the end of her maternity leave period whilst her medical certificate was current, and the reason for the dismissal was that she had given birth to a child or was for any other reason connected with her having given birth to a child, or

(e) that she was liable to be suspended from work on maternity grounds (above), or

(f) that her maternity leave period ended for reason of redundancy, and she was not offered alternative employment where there was a suitable vacancy (see s.77).

7.13   Sixth, a woman who has been continuously employed for one year prior to the 11th week prior to the expected week of childbirth is entitled to additional maternity leave of absence up to 29 weeks from the actual week of confinement.

7.14   It will also be recalled (see paragraph 6.46) that under the Workplace Regulations suitable rest facilities for pregnant and breast-feeding workers shall be provided.

7.15   The HSE has issued some guidance documents, HSG122: *New and expectant mothers at work: a guide for employers* and *Infection risks to new and expectant mothers: A guide for employers* (ISBN 0 7176 1360 7).

7.16   It is generally accepted that English law would not provide a remedy for any injury suffered to a foetus while *en ventre sa mère*, there being no duty owed in tort and no statutory duty applicable. The thalidomide tragedy highlighted this problem, and the Congenital Disabilities (Civil Liability) Act 1976 was passed. It was intended to be a temporary measure, pending legislation consequent on the report of the Pearson Commission, but as the recommendations of the latter are unlikely to be the subject of Parliamentary action in the foreseeable future, the Act remains.

7.17   It provides that a child who is born disabled as a result of any breach of duty (whether through negligence or breach of statutory duty) to either parent, will be able to bring a civil action against the person responsible. In practice this will mean that if something happens to a woman while she is pregnant which results in her child being born disabled, the child will have a separate right of action. Since the Limitation Act 1980 does not apply to a minor (ie one under the age of

18) he may be able to bring a claim any time within three years from attaining his majority, ie potentially 21 years after the event which caused the disability. There must be a breach of duty to the child's parent, but it is not necessary that the parent be injured. The disability may be something which happened to either parent which prevents the mother from having a normal child, or an injury to the mother while she is pregnant, or an injury to the foetus during pregnancy.

7.18 If the person responsible would have been liable to the parent, he is liable to the child. The child must be born alive, for there is no duty to the foetus as such. It is not relevant that the person responsible knew that the woman was pregnant, as long as a duty was owed to her. Thus if a woman is working with a chemical which causes her to have a disabled child as a result of ingesting minute particles, an action will lie against the employer by the child.

7.19 This can cause some concern among those employers who regularly use chemicals, for there are a number of substances which are suspect so far as pregnant women are concerned, eg vinyl chloride, benzene, mercury, lead, etc. Molecules of almost any substance can pass through the placenta, and therefore any woman may, by ingesting, inhaling, or through skin absorption, pass a deleterious ingredient into her baby.

7.20 The Act poses problems for employers who have to balance delicately between the law against sex discrimination on the one hand and liability to unknown potential plaintiffs on the other.

Working alone

7.21 There are some situations where there is a serious risk to a person if he is injured while working alone, because he is unable to summon help.

7.22 There are a number of legal provisions which specify systems of working which require more than one person. These include:
 (a) Work in Compressed Air Regulations 1996
 (b) Diving at Work Regulations 1997
 (c) Control of Substances Hazardous to Health Regulations 1999
 (d) Carriage of Explosives by Road Regulations 1996
 (e) Electricity at Work Regulations 1989.

7.23 There are other provisions which require work to be done "under the immediate supervision of a competent person" or similar wording, which would suggest that the work, although carried out by one person, must be done in the presence of another.

7.24 The Health and Safety Executive (HSE) has produced a leaflet, *Working alone in safety*, to which reference may be made. The CBI has also published a guidance document on the subject.

Working abroad

7.25 An employer may send an employee to another country to work, perhaps for a temporary period, and the question then arises as to the employer's duty to ensure the employee's health and safety. Since the duty is to take reasonable care, and does not involve an absolute guarantee, the circumstances of each case must be considered. In *Cook v Square D Ltd*, the plaintiff worked for the defendant company. Part of his duties took him to Saudi Arabia, where he worked on premises of a reputable oil company. Also working on the site was a reputable main contractor. The plaintiff was working in a computer control room, the floor of which consisted of large tiles. One of these tiles had been lifted by the main contractor, and the plaintiff tripped and injured his knee. He claimed damages from his employers arguing that they had been negligent. A High Court Judge found in his favour, arguing that his employers had not taken proper steps to ensure his safety, but this decision was reversed by the Court of Appeal. It was noted that both the occupier of the premises and the main contractor were reputable companies, and it was not for the defendants to advise them of the need to take precautions against the type of hazard which caused the plaintiff's injury. Further, it was stated that "the suggestion that the home-based employer has any responsibility for the daily events of a site in Saudi Arabia has an air of unreality."

7.26 Nonetheless, it was suggested that if an employee is being sent to a foreign site to work there for a considerable period of time, an employer may be required to inspect the site and satisfy himself that the occupiers are conscious of their obligations concerning the health and safety of people working there.

7.27 Although an employer is required to take out compulsory insurance for the benefit of his employees (see paragraph 4.1) there is no duty to do so in respect of employees who are working abroad. Nor need an employer advise an employee to take out his own insurance cover. In *Reid v Rush & Tompkins Group plc*, the claimant worked for the defendants in Ethiopia. He received severe injuries in a road accident which was the fault of the other driver, for whom the defendants had no responsibility. The claimant was unable to recover damages from the other driver, as there was no third party insurance in Ethiopia, and so he sued his employers in the UK. His statement of claim was struck out. The employer owed no duty to inform or advise on the potential danger of suffering economic loss in the form of uncompensated injuries.

Working at heights

7.28   About two-fifths of all serious injuries at work are caused by workers falling from a height, and such falls are the commonest cause of fatalities. The proper planning of working premises and systems of work would obviate the need for certain types of work (maintenance, servicing, etc) to be done in circumstances where there is a risk of falls, and plant and equipment should be installed with the problem in mind. The Construction (Design and Management) Regulations 1994 (see paragraph 6.349) place specific duties on designers and architects to ensure that health and safety features are considered at the earliest stage of a project, and these features must be applied during all subsequent stages of the project up to completion.

7.29   There are a number of statutory provisions which specifically address the problem in certain industries, including:
  (a) Docks Regulations 1988 (regulation 7)
  (b) Shipbuilding and Ship-repairing Regulations 1960 (regulations 25–30)
  (c) Construction (Health, Safety and Welfare) Regulations 1996 (regulation 6)
  (d) Lifting Operations and Lifting Equipment Regulations 1998.

7.30   The main provision (which does not override the above specific provisions) is now contained in the Workplace (Health, Safety and Welfare) Regulations, regulation 13 (see paragraph 6.27) supplemented by the Approved Code of Practice (ACOP) and Guidance Notes, L24: *Workplace, health, safety and welfare.*

7.31   There are a number of ways the risks of falling from heights can be prevented. First, there is the provision of adequate information about the nature of the risk and the precautions to be taken. There should be clear and accurate instructions given about safe systems of work and safety rules to be followed. Employees should be thoroughly trained not only in the nature of the work to be done, but also in how to do the work safely. Competent supervisors should ensure that safe working practices are followed.

7.32   Second, there should be proper planning in the use and provision of proper access equipment. Included in this category are ladders, scaffolding, mobile towers, or powered equipment, each of which has its own hazard if proper care is not taken in the use or maintenance.

7.33   Third, access to areas where employees may fall can be restricted by the use of fencing, covers for tanks and pits, guard rails, toe boards, barriers, etc.

7.34   Fourth, fall restraint equipment should be provided if there is no other suitable alternative method of preventing a fall. This includes harnesses (with suitable anchor points) safety nets, safety belts, etc.

7.35   Foresight of the risk can, more often than not, reduce or eliminate the risk totally.

Immigrant workers

7.36   There is no evidence to suggest that immigrant workers are more prone to accidents than any other group of employees, although since immigrants tend to be employed in those industries where there are greater dangers, obviously they may have a higher than average accident rate. The problem must be tackled by means of adequate training and language and cultural factors must be taken into account. Safety instructions may have to be prepared in the language of the worker concerned and signs and posters which need little translation should be used to indicate the hazards and/or the precautions to be taken. Several health and safety regulations, eg Management of Health and Safety at Work Regulations 1999 require employers to provide employees with "comprehensible" information, which implies that account should be taken of language difficulties. The HSE publishes several of its guidance notes in a wide range of languages. In *James v Hepworth and Grandage Ltd* the employers put up a notice which stated that spats should be worn. Unknown to them, the claimant could not read English and he was injured through not wearing spats. His claim for compensation failed. He had observed other workmen wearing spats and his failure to make any enquiries about them led to the conclusion that he would not have worn them anyway. However, this case cannot be regarded as authority for the proposition that an employer fulfils his legal duty by merely drawing attention to a precaution (see Chapter 8) and if there is a risk of a more serious injury, greater steps must be taken to ensure the use of protective clothing, etc. Further, in *Hawkins v Ian Ross (Castings) Ltd* an employee was injured partly because he was working alongside an immigrant who had a limited command of English and who misunderstood a warning shout. The court held that in such circumstances, a higher standard of care is required on the employers when considering the layout of the work and the steps to be taken to avoid accidents.

7.37   Language barriers may not be used as a device to exclude immigrants from employment and attempts to impose language tests have resulted in allegations of racial discrimination. The problem will no doubt be with us for many years, for although we tend to equate immigration with the influx from Asian or African countries, under article 48 of the Treaty of Rome the free movement of workers throughout the European Union is guaranteed, and an influx of non-English speaking workers from Europe cannot be excluded. Training for safety officers may well include some form of instruction in foreign languages in the not-too-distant future.

7.38   The Race Relations Act 1976 makes it unlawful to discriminate on grounds of colour, race, nationality, ethnic or national origins, in the recruitment, employment or dismissal of any person.

7.39   The Asylum and Immigration Act 1996 (s.8) makes it a criminal offence to employ a person who has not been granted leave to enter or remain in the United Kingdom, or who is subject to a condition prohibiting employment.

Sick building syndrome

7.40   Sick building syndrome is a convenient term which is sometimes used to describe certain mild symptoms, somewhat similar to the common cold, together with headaches, low concentration, and a general feeling of irritability and lethargy. It is usually associated with office work, and the symptoms tend to disappear when away from the building. It has nothing to do with illnesses generally associated with more specific hazards, nor to identifiable physical conditions brought on by environmental factors. It is not a recognised illness and its causes are unknown. Its presence is likely to be indicated by an increase in absenteeism, reduced efficiency and a general lowering of morale.

7.41   If sick building syndrome is suspected, the first step should be to ensure that all the requirements of the Workplace (Health, Safety and Welfare) Regulations have been complied with, together with the advice given in the Approved Code of Practice (ACOP). Consultation with employees may reveal their concerns, and possibly lead to a reorganisation of job factors, office design or the changing of furnishings and fittings, etc. Cleaning, ventilation, mild pollutants in the atmosphere (tobacco smoke, unpleasant smells from various sources, etc) should be attended to. Redecoration, designed to create a warm, friendly atmosphere, may also assist.

7.42   The HSE has produced a Guidance Document, HSG132: *How to deal with sick building syndrome: Guidance for employers, building owners and building managers* to which reference may be made.

Smoking at work

7.43   There are a number of specific prohibitions on smoking whilst at work, usually when there is a health or safety hazard (see paragraph 9.15). In the absence of a legal requirement to prohibit smoking the topic is somewhat emotive, there being a conflict between an individual's "right" to smoke, and the equal "right" of non-smokers to breathe unpolluted air. There is some evidence that it is possible for people to be affected by passive smoking, but there is no legal decision in this country which takes the matter very far. It has been suggested that the employer's duty under s.2 of HSWA includes a duty to protect workers from the effects of passive smoking, but again there is no legal authority on the point.

7.44   There is an employment tribunal decision to the effect that an employee who was forbidden to smoke was entitled to resign and claim constructive dismissal *(Watson v Cooke, Webb & Holton Ltd)* but there appear to be special facts in the case which led the employment tribunal to hold that the employers had broken a fundamental term of Mrs Watson's contract of employment by imposing a new term without any discussion and consultation. Another employment tribunal held that an employee does not have a contractual right to smoke *(Rogers v Wicks &*

Wilson Ltd), and it is suggested that this is the correct approach. It would be unusual for there to be an express contractual term to this effect and to imply a contractual term that an employee has the right to smoke is stretching the implied term theory too far.

7.45   This view was confirmed by the Employment Appeal Tribunal in the recent case of *Dryden v Greater Glasgow Health Board*. Here, the Board operated a "no smoking" policy in all areas except a "smoking" coffee room and a smoking area in the canteen. After extensive consultations it was decided to ban smoking altogether in all the Board's premises, and three months' notice of the ban was given to all employees. Counselling and support was offered to those employees who wished to give up smoking. The applicant, who was a lifelong smoker, found that she could only smoke if she left the Board's premises, but this was difficult for her to do in view of the time constraints. Three days after the commencement of the ban, she resigned and claimed constructive dismissal. It was held that the right to smoke was not a contractual term, but a personal habit. The fact that the Board had, in the past, provided her with facilities for smoking did not imply that those facilities were needed by her to enable her to perform her contractual duties, and therefore the withdrawal of the facility did not break an implied term of the contract that it was necessary to give business efficacy to the contract. Further, the Board had not broken the implied term of trust and confidence which must exist between employer and employee, for they had handled the matter as sympathetically as possible with full consultation.

7.46   The problem can be handled by tactful consultations, education and agreement. Due notice of a "no smoking" ban should be given and prospective employees informed of the employer's policies. If possible, special smoking areas may be created away from the workplace, smokers and non-smokers could be segregated, counselling and medical advice/assistance provided for inveterate smokers and non-smokers recruited for vacant posts.

7.47   There is an implied term in every contract of employment that an employee will not be required to work in unreasonable conditions (*Concord Lighting v Willis*) and to require an employee to work in a confined space with habitual smokers may be regarded as being unhealthy as well as unpleasant. Further, if an employer permits smokers to smoke in work areas where non-smokers work, he may be in breach of his duty under s.2(2)(e) of HSWA, which requires him to provide and maintain a working environment which is reasonably safe and without risks to health — there is some evidence that passive smoking can be a cause of certain illnesses. It follows that an employee who feels that the employer has broken that implied term may resign and claim constructive dismissal. Such a claim was upheld by the Employment Appeal Tribunal in *Waltons & Morse v Dorrington*, where the applicant shared a room with other employees, some of whom smoked, but in premises which were well ventilated. She was asked to move to another part of the building near to several heavy smokers, and when she complained, she was told that there was nothing which could be done about the situation. She therefore resigned, and her claim for unfair dismissal was upheld. The employers had broken the implied term in the contract of employment that she would not be required to work in an environment which was unhealthy.

7.48 It will be recalled that under the Workplace (Health, Safety and Welfare) Regulations 1992 (see paragraph 6.46), rest rooms and rest areas shall include suitable arrangements to protect non-smokers from discomfort caused by tobacco smoke.

7.49 In a recent decision (R(I) 6/91), a Social Security Commissioner held that a woman who was obliged to inhale smoke from fellow workers' cigarettes was entitled to a declaration that she had suffered an accident arising out of and in the course of her employment (see paragraph 8.93). It was stated that in the ordinary case an injury caused by "passive smoking" would not constitute an "accident", but in this particular case the claimant suffered from asthma and she was able to document six occasions when the sudden inhalation of cigarette smoke caused her a sharp pain in her lungs and severe breathlessness for several days. Thus, on each of those days she had suffered personal injury within the meaning of the Social Security Act 1975.

7.50 On the other hand in *Sparrow v St Andrews Homes Ltd* a nurse who worked in a residential home claimed that she had to give up her work because she suffered from asthma caused by passive smoking. In the particular circumstance of the case, it was held that the employers had done all they could to ensure a safe system of work. The requirement for an employer to take into account a worker's susceptibilities had to be kept within bounds, and the judge was not convinced, on the balance of probabilities, that the passive smoking caused the appellant's asthma. The employers were not liable for common law negligence (see Chapter 8).

7.51   The HSC has produced an Approved Code of Practice on Passive Smoking at Work, but at the time of writing it has not received Ministerial approval. The obstacle appears to be the application of the Code to the hospitality industry (pubs, hotels, etc) where employers would be faced with disproportionate costs in order to overcome the effects of smoke when compared with other workplaces. The HSC is currently considering this matter.

Drug abuse

7.52   Generally, it is not the concern of an employer what an employee does outside working hours, but this rule may not necessarily apply if those actions have some effect or impact on work activities. There are a number of telling signs which may indicate whether an employee is having a drug problem, including frequent absenteeism, poor performance, erratic behaviour, lateness, repetitive minor illnesses, etc. Management can be trained in recognition techniques, although it may be advisable to have assistance from the police when it comes to training in identifying the actual substances. Once the signs have been recognised, help by way of counselling, medical examinations, etc can be offered.

7.53   However, it is always better to pre-empt a problem before it arises than to have to deal with it after it has caused difficulties. The first step is to have a clearly worded policy statement, drawn to the attention of all employees, setting out the employer's prohibition on having illegal substances on the premises, and noting that employees who take such substances outside working hours will be disciplined if their actions (a) have a deleterious effect on work performance, or (b) bring the employer's business into disrepute.

7.54   In cases of minor infringements of the company's rules on the taking or possession of drugs, the disciplinary procedure should be invoked and warnings, etc given, but in serious cases, stronger measures should be taken.

7.55   Thus, in *Mathewson v RB Wilson Dental Laboratories Ltd*, the applicant, during his lunch break, purchased a small amount of cannabis for his own use, but was arrested by the police. His employers dismissed him because they felt that they could no longer employ a person who was using drugs. They also thought that he might adversely influence younger members of staff. An employment tribunal held that his dismissal was fair, and this was upheld on appeal. The decision to dismiss fell within the range of reasonable responses of a reasonable employer.

7.56 It is an offence under the Misuse of Drugs Act 1971 for an occupier knowingly to permit the possession of certain controlled drugs on his premises. Thus, if an employee is known to possess drugs on his person, it may be a ground for dismissal (*Mathewson v RB Wilson Ltd* above).

Alcohol at work

7.57 Similar considerations apply to alcohol abuse. These matters are best dealt with by a clearly defined policy statement or in the works/staff rules.

7.58 As a general rule, an employer owes no duty of care towards an employee to prevent him consuming an excess amount of alcohol which results in the employee suffering an injury or even death, although the normal duty of care would arise if it is necessary to provide medical care and/or assistance should he collapse whilst at work (*Barrett v Ministry of Defence*).

7.59 The HSE has published a guidance document, *Don't mix it — a guide for employers on alcohol at work*.

Policies for alcohol and drug abuse

7.60 There are many employment positions where it is inherently unsafe for employees to take unlawful drugs or excessive quantities of alcohol. Airline pilots, lorry drivers, employees who work with dangerous substances or machinery are but a few examples. No one would care to be operated on by a surgeon whose breath smelt of drink; no one would care to be a passenger in a vehicle driven by an individual who has been taking cocaine.

7.61 The first problem for the safety conscious employer who wishes to stamp out substance abuse, and ensure safety for employees and for others, is that of detection. It cannot be sufficient to rely on the suspicions (however well founded), of supervisors, managers, etc. Should disciplinary action (including dismissal) take place, the employee will doubtless plead innocence. The fact that the supervisor thought that the employee's breath smelt of alcohol will be challenged; seeing an employee staggering about will be put down to a trip or stumble. Employment tribunals require solid proof and are not always consistent. They are not likely to be sympathetic to precipitous actions, even those taken for the best of motives.

7.62 Currently, the main method of detection is by the taking of blood or urine samples. These are intrusive, and require the services of an expert, such as a doctor or occupational nurse who is skilled in taking and handling the sample. If the testing is done on a substantial scale, there must be secure procedures, so that there can be no doubt that samples have not been mixed up.

7.63 Finally, the employee must consent to the taking of a blood or urine sample. To do this without such consent would be an assault, and the person responsible could incur criminal penalties. If the employee refuses to give consent, the employer may possibly need to consider disciplinary proceedings. The action taken will also depend on the status of the individual, ie whether an employee, a sub-contractor or an employee of a sub-contractor. These are difficult issues which do not admit of ready answers.

7.64 However, there are a number of common law and statutory provisions to which the employer must pay attention, including the Health and Safety at Work, etc Act 1974, the Misuse of Drugs Act 1971, the Transport and Works Act 1992, the various regulations outlined in Chapters 5 and 6, as well as the common law duties. Thus, as well as criminal liabilities for permitting an employee to work who has had an excess of alcohol or who is known to be taking unlawful drugs, civil liabilities may also exist if an accident occurs and someone (not necessarily the drug or alcohol user) is injured. There is also the adverse effect on the employer's business to consider, should an incident attract publicity, depending, of course, on the nature of that business.

7.65 There is some scope to argue that the employer should treat the matter as a health problem, rather than institute disciplinary proceedings against the employee concerned. In other words, the employee should be encouraged to seek medical assistance rather than face dismissal. This sympathetic approach may work if the health and safety risks involved are not likely to be very great, or if no dangerous incident has happened. However, it is unlikely to be a satisfactory solution if drink or drugs can be seen to have caused an accident or injury, and employment tribunals generally will take a fairly robust approach to claims of unfairness made by the person responsible. Nevertheless, forethought and prevention is the preferable approach.

7.66 Modern science has come up with one solution which could well be of considerable assistance to employers wishing to take a firm stand on drug and alcohol abuse. Oral fluid testing is a technique which is simple to use, and accurate in its results. A specially treated pad is used to collect fluid from all areas of the mouth until the swab is saturated. This can then be tested to give an almost instant reading of the level of alcohol and/or drugs present in the subject's system. It can be used by anyone with a minimum of training, and is reliable and effective.

7.67 However, employers must be aware of the need to follow proper procedures. Ideally, there should be full consultation with representatives of trade unions or other employee representatives of safety, although the agreement of such bodies is not essential. Each employee should be asked, in advance, to sign a consent form, agreeing to undergo such tests on a random basis, either before starting work, during work or immediately after ceasing work. Specific persons should be nominated to operate the testing procedures, and disciplinary proceedings which follow should be fair and consistent. There should also be warnings that severe disciplinary action (including dismissal) will follow if the employee is found to have used unlawful drugs and/or has been drinking alcohol. The level of tolerance must be related to the activity and the risks. Thus, whereas zero tolerance may be the benchmark for airline pilots who are about to commence duty, or lorry drivers who are about to drive their vehicles (or who have been driving, etc), perhaps a more lenient approach may be taken in the case of an office worker or someone whose activities are unlikely to cause injury.

7.68 A major difficulty will arise if the employee refuses to sign such consent form. The employee may seek to invoke the provisions of the Human Rights Act 1998 (see paragraph 1.129). Article 8 of the European Convention states that "Everyone has the right to respect for his private and family life ......" and the employee may argue that what is done in non-working hours is no concern of the employer. This may be true, but if what an employee does impinges on the employer's business, different considerations would apply. Article 8 specifically excludes from that right actions taken in accordance with the law, in the interests of public safety and for the protection of health and morals. Thus the employee's argument is unlikely to succeed — but can the employer enforce the consent form by taking disciplinary action against recalcitrant employees? There is no direct legal authority on the point, but it is submitted that if consultation and persuasion do not succeed, and if the employer can show a genuine concern for the safety and health of others, or that there would be an adverse effect on the business should an incident occur, it is likely that disciplinary action, including dismissal, will be held to be fair. For new employees, the matter should be made part of the contractual obligations entered into, to remove this potential issue altogether.

Other illnesses

7.69   There are a number of contagious diseases which call for special consideration if contracted by an employee or, indeed, in appropriate circumstances, when an employee comes into contact with an infected person during the course of his employment. These include hepatitis, HIV/AIDS, herpes, tuberculosis, sexually transmitted disease, typhoid, rubella, chicken pox, etc. A full assessment of the health risks should be made, in consultation with medical advisors, and consideration should be given to a period of suspension so as to minimise the risks revealed.

7.70   There are some occupations where employees are particularly vulnerable, eg health workers, laboratory workers, and those in contact with animals or animal products, etc (see Directive 90/679/EEC).

7.71   Certain occupational diseases are reportable under the Reporting of Injuries, Disease and Dangerous Occurrences Regulations 1995. For a disease to be reportable, the person at work (including a self-employed person) must be suffering from a disease specified in column 1 of Part II of Schedule 3 of the regulations, and the work must involve one of the corresponding activities in column 2. However, the disease is only reportable in the case of an employee if the responsible person receives a written statement from a registered medical practitioner diagnosing the disease as one of those specified.

Acts of violence against employees

7.72   Recent studies have indicated that acts of violence against employees whilst carrying out their employment duties are on the increase, and the matter is clearly becoming a factor in health and safety policies. Such acts may be committed by fellow employees, customers or third parties. So far as acts perpetrated by employees are concerned, these should be dealt with within the confines of the disciplinary procedures (see paragraph 9.42), and generally an employee would be left to pursue his own legal remedies, either criminal or civil, for assault.

7.73   The possibility of an employee suffering an act of violence whilst at work should be included in the risk assessment. There may be organisations where there is no history of such acts, but if it can be shown that the risk is not negligible, either in that particular type of industry or because of special features of the organisation, ways of avoiding or mitigating against such acts should be considered. Employees particularly at risk include those who handle cash in isolation (eg all-night petrol stations, rent collectors in certain housing estates), those who come into contact with violent people who are affected by drink or drugs (eg social workers, carers), those who have to deal with dissatisfied customers or complainants (eg clerks in Benefits Agency offices) those who handle or transport cash or valuables (eg cashier, diamond merchants) and so on.

7.74   So far as acts committed by others are concerned, the general test of the conduct of the reasonable employer has to be applied and the question posed, has the employer taken reasonable care to see that his employees are not exposed to the risk of injury, even by criminals? The employer must take precautions against risks which he knows of or which he ought to know. Thus in *Houghton v Hackney Borough Council* a rent collector, employed by the defendants, was attacked while collecting rents on a housing estate. He alleged that the council had been negligent in failing to take proper precautions to protect him from injury. On the facts of the case, his claim for damages failed. The council had taken a number of precautionary steps, such as arranging for an estate porter to be around when rents were being collected, inviting the police to keep a watchful eye on the estate, and arranging for the claimant to be collected by car in order to take all the monies to the bank. In the circumstances, it was not negligent.

7.75   There are some employments where the risk of being assaulted is not a negligible one, for example, when dealing with violent offenders or mentally disturbed people. This does not mean that the employee voluntarily accepts the risk of being injured (see paragraph 8.61), and the employer must still exercise reasonable care to ensure appropriate protection and assistance (see *Michie v Shenley and Napsbury General Hospital Management Committee*).

7.76   It should finally be noted that if the employer fails to institute the necessary precautions to protect an employee from violence, the employee may resign his employment, and claim constructive dismissal (see paragraph 9.33).

7.77   Although there are no statutory provisions on this subject, reference may be made to s.2(1) of HSWA (see paragraph 3.25) and the Management of Health and Safety at Work Regulations 1999 (see paragraph 5.8) which require an employer to make an assessment of the risks to the health and safety of employees to which they are exposed whilst at work, and arrangements for dealing with that risk must be put into effect. As has been noted, these provisions do not give rise to civil liability (see paragraph 5.6).

7.78   Once the risk has been determined, appropriate measures can be taken. The working environment can be changed as appropriate, systems of work can be monitored and made safe, security measures can be introduced, and appropriate training given on how to counter acts of violence, or the effects thereof.

7.79   An act of violence at work which causes an injury to an employee is now reportable under the Reporting of Injuries, Diseases and Dangerous Occurrences Regulations 1995 (see paragraph 6.247).

Homeworkers

7.80   There is a growing tendency for more and more employees to work from home, where the work can be done this way efficiently. From the employer's point of view, there is a saving in working space and overheads, the employee gains by having to avoid spending time and money travelling, and can enjoy any relevant home comforts. The use of computers and other modern communication aids means that there can be an immediate exchange of information; employees working from home are no less in touch than employees who work on the employer's premises.

7.81   Nonetheless, the employer's responsibility for the health and safety of his employees, particularly as set out in s.2(2) of the Health and Safety at Work, etc Act 1974 (HSWA), still exists in respect of homeworkers, and such employees should not be disregarded by those concerned with health and safety. As always, the first step is to carry out a risk assessment (see paragraph 5.8), with particular attention to the potentially unusual and/or unexpected problems which could arise. For example, employees who work in a home environment could have their working area or equipment affected by children, or visitors, etc. Ideally, segregation from the rest of the house would avoid many problems (eg in a separate room which was locked, or keeping work equipment in a locked cupboard, etc) but if this is not possible, steps must be taken to ensure that neither the employee nor others who come into his house are adversely affected by any work activity. Equipment used by the worker must also meet the statutory requirements (see Chapter 6), and this applies not only to the technology used (computers, machines, etc) but also to ordinary items such as desks and chairs, even though these are initially provided by the employee.

7.82   Electrical equipment generally must comply with the requirements of the Electricity at Work Regulations 1987 (see paragraph 6.290), any hazardous substances used or provided must be assessed and identified under the COSHH regulations (see paragraph 6.316) and training and instruction given as appropriate. The Health and Safety (Display Screen Equipment) Regulations 1992 (see paragraph 6.159) will be of particular importance, and the employer must ensure that, for example, the desks, chairs, etc supplied by the employee are suitable, and do not give rise to any risks. Other relevant legislation which will need to be considered includes provisions relating to first aid, reporting of accidents, etc.

7.83   Similar considerations apply to those employees who work in someone else's home. There is a growing army of professional carers who provide various services in the homes of the elderly, sick and disabled. Such carers are frequently at risk in relation to back injuries (when lifting or trying to move patients) violence (dealing with the mentally disturbed people who have been discharged into the community), simple domestic hazards (caused by the untidy nature of the premises), and so on. A full risk assessment is necessary, together with whatever training and supervision may be found necessary in the circumstances. If the risk assessment identifies a potential problem, appropriate precautions should be taken, eg the provision of personal security alarms, ensuring that employees are accompanied, training given in self-defence methods, the provision of a breakdown recovery service (for employees who may become stranded in vehicles) or mobile telephones, and so on.

7.84 The HSE has issued a Guidance Note, *Homeworking: Guidance for employers and employees on health and safety.*

Bullying at work

7.85 One of the more frequent causes of stress and other work-related illnesses arises from bullying at work, which would normally, but not necessarily, stem from the actions by senior members of the workforce. Frequently, this is caused by some form of interpersonal conflict, and can take a number of different forms, apart from physical violence. Subtle forms of bullying can take place when someone in authority deliberately withholds essential information or makes belittling remarks; unwarranted criticism, public humiliation, unnecessary threats, veiled hints of inadequacies, and generally undermining confidence are other examples which can have an adverse reaction on the person bullied (see, eg, *Hetherington v Darlington Borough Council*). The end result can be an increase in work-related illnesses, causing absenteeism, low morale, poor performance and possibly accidents. The problem is probably more widespread than is generally realised.

7.86 A pro-active personnel policy is needed to deal with the problem. Frequently, the bully will be unaware of the effect of his or her actions, and while it may be difficult to change a person's personality, training in man-management may be indicated. A complaints procedure may be set up, complaints investigated and appropriate action taken. Counselling can be provided for those affected, and monitoring procedures put in place. As pressures increase for more output and greater efficiency in working practices, the consequences of bullying at work should be faced up to, and should not be dismissed as mere incidents of over-sensitivity on the part of alleged neurotic employees.

7.87 There appears to be some increase in awareness of a problem caused by "bullying" at work, which may have a sexual implication, although not always confined to such. To permit or tolerate this sort of behaviour may have health and safety implications under s.2(1) of HSWA, as well as a claim for constructive dismissal (see *Harvest Press Ltd v McCaffrey*, see paragraph 5.174).

Disabled employees

7.88   The Disability Discrimination Act 1995 was passed with the avowed intention of preventing the discrimination against disabled persons. The Act, which is now fully in force, is supported by a Code of Practice and Guidance Notes. All these provisions will have to be borne in mind when considering most of the problems that are dealt with in the remaining parts of this Chapter.

Definition of disabled person

7.89   A person will be regarded as being disabled for the purposes of the Act if "he has a physical or mental impairment which has a substantial long-term adverse effect on his ability to carry out normal day-to-day activities" (s.1), but the provisions of the Act may also apply to persons who have had a disability in the past (s.2 and Schedule 2). Thus, for example, a person who has had a history of mental illness is not to be discriminated against because of this. But a propensity to future illness (eg a person with Huntington's chorea gene) will not come under the Act's protection until he develops some symptoms of the illness. The fact that a person cannot lift heavy objects does not mean that he has a disability, if he can lift everyday objects *(Quinlan v B&Q)*.

7.90   It is the effect of the impairment that must be substantial, not the severity of impairment. Thus a person with dyslexia may only have a moderate impairment, but it could have a substantial effect on his day-to-day activities. The Guidance Notes state that account should be taken of the time taken to carry out an activity, the way it is carried out, the cumulative effects of the impairment, and the effect of behaviour and of the environment. Minor impairments which, taken together, have a cumulative effect, can lead to a substantial impairment.

7.91   The disability may be physical or mental; the impairment is to be taken as affecting normal day-to-day activities if it affects a person with regard to mobility, manual dexterity, physical co-ordination, continence, ability to lift, carry or move objects, hearing, eyesight, memory, ability to learn or understand, or perception of physical danger. The impairment will have a long-term effect if it has lasted, or will last, for at least 12 months, or is likely to have a life-time effect. Where the impairment ceases, it is to be treated as continuing if the effect is likely to recur. A severe disfigurement is also included in the definition, but not if as a result of tattoos or piercing of the body for decorative or other non-medical purpose.

7.92   The phrase "normal day-to-day activities" is not defined, but the Guidance Notes emphasise that it is not intended to include activities that are normal only for a particular group of persons, eg sportsmen or musicians.

7.93   If a person has a progressive condition (eg cancer, multiple sclerosis, muscular dystrophy or HIV), which has an effect, but not a substantial adverse effect, he will come within the Act if the condition is likely to result in him having such an impairment. Addiction to alcohol, nicotine or other substances (not stemming from the result of the administration of medically prescribed drugs or other medical treatment) does not amount to an impairment. But an impairment caused by such addiction (eg liver damage) will fall within the Act. Seasonal allergic rhinitis (eg hay fever) will not amount to an impairment, unless it aggravates the effect of another condition.

7.94   A mental impairment will come within the Act, although this must arise from a clinically well-recognised illness (see Guidance Notes). But conditions such as pyromania, kleptomania, tendencies to physical or sexual abuse of other persons, exhibitionism and voyeurism are all excluded.

7.95   There is a danger of adopting a stereotype approach to disabled persons. Only a relatively small proportion of the disabled community are visually disabled, ie in wheelchairs, or carrying white sticks or other aids. The vast majority of disabled persons have a physical or mental disability which may not be immediately obvious, and will only come to light when they fail to do that which a non-disabled person can do. Thus in deciding whether a claimant's impairment is substantial, a purposive approach should be taken by the employment tribunal, having regard to the Guidance Notes and the Code of Practice issued by the Secretary of State. The focus of the Act is on the activities which the claimant cannot do (or can only do with difficulty), rather on the things he can do. "Substantial" means "more than minor or trivial" rather than "very large" (*Goodwin v Patent Office*). But the list of examples in the Guidance Notes are illustrative, not exhaustive. In *Vicary v British*

Telecommunications, the employers had relied largely on the opinion of their medical officer who was of the opinion that the claimant's disabilities were not substantial, and did not affect her normal day-to-day activities, a conclusion which the employment tribunal appeared to adopt. On appeal it was held that a medical expert is entitled to express an opinion based on observation and examination, but it was for the employment tribunal to make this finding of fact, based on their own assessment of the evidence.

Discrimination against disabled workers (s.4)

7.96   It will be unlawful for an employer to discriminate against a disabled person:
  (a) in the arrangements made for determining to whom he should offer employment
  (b) in the terms on which he offers employment, or
  (c) by refusing to offer, or deliberately not offering, employment.

7.97   Further, it will be unlawful to discriminate against a disabled person:
  (a) in terms and conditions of employment
  (b) in opportunities for promotion, transfers, training or any other benefit, or
  (c) by dismissing him or subjecting him to any detriment.

What is discrimination? (s.5)

7.98   A person discriminates against a disabled person if:
  (a) for a reason which relates to the person's disability, he treats him less favourably than he treats others to whom that reason does not apply, and
  (b) he cannot show that the treatment is justified.

7.99   In *Clark v TDG Ltd t/a Novacold*, the Court of Appeal held that the less favourable treatment does not turn on a like-for-like comparison of the disabled person and of others in similar circumstances, and thus it was not appropriate to make comparisons of the cases in the same way as the Sex Discrimination Act and the Race Relations Act. The comparison is to be made with others to whom the reason for the treatment does not apply, even if their circumstances are different from the disabled person. Thus to dismiss a person who is absent from work for a long time because of sickness is less favourable treatment when compared with the non-dismissal of a worker who is still performing his work.

7.100 It will also amount to discrimination if an employer fails to make reasonable adjustments to the premises or disabled person's working conditions (see below) and if he cannot show that the failure to comply with the legal requirements is justified.

7.101 It will be noted that the burden of proof is on the employer to show that the less favourable treatment is justified, but the reason must be both material to the circumstances of the particular case and substantial. Depending on the circumstances, one may assume that less favourable treatment is capable of being justified if:
  (a) the disabled person is not suitable for employment
  (b) the disabled person is less suitable for employment than another person, and that other person is given the job
  (c) the nature of the disabled person's disability significantly impedes the performance of any of his duties, or
  (d) in the case of training, the nature of the disabled person's disability would significantly reduce the value of the training.

7.102 However, each individual circumstance must be taken into account. One should not assume that all blind persons are unable to type or use computers. A person who is off work sick because of a disability is not to be dismissed solely for that reason, if his level of absenteeism is not substantially less than other employees. Blanket concern for health and safety requirements should not over-ride the need to consider the individual circumstances of a disabled person.

7.103 Discriminatory treatment will be justified if it arises from performance related pay, eligibility for and contributions to occupational pension schemes, and permits for incapacitated persons under the agricultural wages legislation (see Disability Discrimination (Employment) Regulations 1996).

Duty of employer to make adjustments (s.6)

7.104 Where any arrangements made by the employer, or any physical feature of premises occupied by him place the disabled person at a substantial disadvantage in comparison with persons who are not disabled, it will be the duty of the employer to take such steps as it is reasonable in all the circumstances for him to take in order to prevent the arrangement or feature having that effect.

7.105   The following are examples of the steps which an employer may have to take:
(a) make adjustment to premises
(b) allocating some of the disabled person's duties to another person
(c) transferring him to fill an existing vacancy
(d) altering his working hours
(e) assigning him to a different place of work
(f) allowing him to be absent during working hours for rehabilitation, assessment or treatment
(g) giving him, or arranging for him to be given, training
(h) acquiring or modifying equipment
(i) modifying instructions or reference manuals
(j) modifying procedures for testing or assessment
(k) providing a reader or interpreter
(l) providing supervision.

7.106   Whether it will be reasonable for an employer to take any particular step will depend on:
(a) the extent to which taking the step would prevent discrimination
(b) the extent to which it is practicable for the employer to take the step
(c) the financial and other costs which would be incurred by the employer in taking the step, and the extent to which it would disrupt any of his activities
(d) the extent of the employer's financial and other resources
(e) the availability to the employer of financial or other assistance with respect to the taking of that step.

7.107   The exact nature of an employer's duty to make "reasonable adjustments" is specified further in a Code of Practice. An employer will not be required to make the best adjustment possible, nor to adapt workplaces to make them accessible in anticipation of employing a disabled person at some future time. Further, an employer will not be expected to reallocate key functions of the job, nor to provide items which a disabled person could reasonably be expected to have already for his personal use.

7.108   Numerous cases have now been heard in the employment tribunals and the Employment Appeal Tribunal (EAT) alleging disability discrimination, and generally a purposive approach is being taken. Thus whether a person is disabled within the meaning of the Act is an objective fact, and does not depend on the knowledge of the employer. The decision in *O'Neill v Symm & Co Ltd*, which held that an employer does not discriminate against a disabled person if he has no knowledge of the disability was disagreed with by another division of the EAT in *H J Heinz Ltd v Kendrick*. Section 5 of the Act does not require the employer to have knowledge of the disability, although the absence of knowledge may be highly relevant to the issue of justifiability under s.5, or as to the steps to make a reasonable adjustment under s.6. Similarly, whether there is a duty to make reasonable adjustments, and whether a failure to make adjustments can be justified are also objective facts, and the employment tribunal can substitute its own views for those of the employer (*Morse v Wiltshire County Council*).

7.109 An employer cannot be expected to make reasonable adjustments if he does not know the employee has a disability (*Ridout v TC Group*), and the adjustments must be related to the job, not to personal services required by the disabled person (eg going to the toilet, see *Kenny v Hampshire Constabulary*).

7.110 The Disability Discrimination (Employment) Regulations 1996 deal with the situation where the employer needs to obtain the consent of another person before he can make alteration to the premises.

7.111 The Code of Practice is comprehensive, and gives advice on all aspects of the nature of discrimination, recruitment, employment arrangements (including steps to make reasonable adjustments), and generally setting up management systems to avoid discrimination. The Code can be taken into account should an action be brought in an employment tribunal.

Exclusions

7.112 The above requirements will not apply where an employer has fewer than 15 employees (Disability Discrimination (Exemption for Small Employers) Order 1998). Employees employed by an associated employer are not be counted for this purpose (*Hardie v CD Northern Ltd*).

7.113 Also, the employment provisions of the Act do not apply to members of the Armed Forces, prison officers; firefighters; employees who work wholly outside Great Britain; employees who work on ships, aircraft or hovercraft; policemen; and other members of the constabulary.

Remedies

7.114   A complaint of disability discrimination may be made to an employment tribunal, who have the same powers as those which exist for complaints of race or sex discrimination. The time limits are the same, and there is a questionnaire procedure.

Disability Rights Commission (DRC)

7.115   This body was created by the Disability Rights Commission Act 1999, and given powers and functions similar to the Commission for Racial Equality and the Equal Opportunities Commission. The DRC will work towards the elimination of discrimination against disabled persons, promote equalisation of opportunities, take such steps as it considers appropriate with a view to encouraging good practice in the treatment of disabled persons, and keep the workings of the Disability Discrimination Act 1995 under review. The Commission may make proposals or give advice to the Minister or any other government agency as to the practical application of the law, and undertake (or arrange for support of) the carrying out of research or the provision of advice or information.

7.116   The Commission may prepare Codes of Practice (which must be approved by the Secretary of State and laid before Parliament) in order to give practical advice to employers and other service providers, give assistance to persons who propose to bring claims for unlawful discrimination, carry out formal investigations, and issue non-discrimination notices.

Repeals

7.117   The requirements contained in the Disabled Persons (Employment) Act 1944 that an employer should employ 3% of employees who are disabled (the quota system) have been repealed.

Employment

7.118   Under the Companies Act 1985, Schedule 7, every directors' report relating to a financial year shall contain a statement describing the policy of the company throughout that year for:
  (a) giving full and fair consideration to applications for employment made by disabled persons, having regard to their particular aptitude and abilities
  (b) continuing the employment of, and the arranging of appropriate training for, employees of the company who have become disabled persons during the period when they were employed by the company, and
  (c) the training, career development and promotion of disabled persons employed by the company.

7.119   The regulations apply to every company which employs on average more than 250 employees throughout the year in question. It is hoped that the new legal requirements, by throwing a spotlight of publicity on the problem, will encourage more companies to provide job opportunities for disabled persons.

To act reasonably

7.120   Once a disabled person has been taken into employment, he can of course be dismissed on health or safety grounds, but there is a high burden on the employer to show that he made a full appraisal of all the facts, and in particular that he searched around for suitable alternative employment before contemplating dismissal (see *Milk Marketing Board v Grimes*, see paragraph 9.59). The employer must familiarise himself with the job, the disability and the hazard *(Littlewood v AEI Cables)*, and extra efforts must be made to accommodate a disabled person. In *Cannon v Scandecor*, when the applicant, who was registered disabled, was employed it was recognised that her output would not be too high. She then had a series of illnesses and a car accident, and when she returned to work her daily output was that which she had previously achieved in an hour. She was dismissed, but this was held to be unfair. Much too short a period had elapsed between her return to work and her dismissal, and sufficient time had not been allowed in order to enable her to make a full recovery. She should have been given a reasonable trial period, and then, if her output had not reached her previous performance, her dismissal would have been fair.

7.121   It has been held that the failure to place a disabled person on a short list for interview did not, by itself, indicate that the employer had discriminated unlawfully, for frequently there are a large number of applicants for a particular job, and it is inevitable that only a limited number of applicants can be called for interview. In another case, an employee developed multiple sclerosis and it was held that the employer acted unreasonably in dismissing him without taking heed of a report from a neurologist, who thought that the employee's prospect of working should be assessed on a "try and see" basis. By and large, the employment tribunals appear to be applying the same tests under the new Act towards the dismissal of a disabled person as they did before the Act came into force, ie did the employer act reasonably in dismissing this employee for the reason put forward? (see *Pascoe v Hallen & Medway*). Therefore, a consideration of alternatives, proper consultation, a review of attendance and performance, providing additional support facilities, obtaining a full and up-to-date medical report are all steps which a reasonable employer would take.

7.122   It will thus be evident that employers who take on a disabled person have a special responsibility to do more than they would normally do to give him a period of time in which to reach acceptable standards. Some companies meet the problem by excluding disabled employees from departmental budgets, so as to ensure that they are not regarded as a drain or millstone by management seeking to reach targets. Certainly, a great deal can be done and although safety hazards must not be ignored, these are not always insuperable obstacles. There is no substitute for a careful assessment of the nature of the work, the risks associated with it and a measured judgment based on an investigation into the nature of the disability matched against the risks involved.

7.123   Clearly, disabled persons will always pose special problems so far as health and safety matters are concerned. Deaf persons will not always be able to hear fire alarms or warning cries, blind persons will not find their way to escape routes, physically disabled persons will not be able to react with the necessary speed to emergency situations, and so on. Since the duties owed by an employer to his employees are personal to each employee, special attention should be paid to these problems when disabled persons are involved.

7.124   Even so, there must come a point in time when safety factors

341

will override all other considerations, although the duty of the employer is to act reasonably when handling employees who have any type of disability. Usually this will mean taking medical advice and looking round for suitable employment. In *McCall v Post Office*, the applicant, unknown to his employers, suffered from epilepsy. He was employed as a cleaner, but had several fits which were of short duration. The personnel department took medical advice and were told that he should be employed in a "no risk" area. Unfortunately there was no suitable vacancy and he was dismissed. This was held to be fair. On medical advice the employee had to be moved to a safe area, and as there was none available it was in his interests and in the interests of other employees that he be dismissed.

Work-related upper limb disorders

7.125   This is a generic term for a group of musculo-skeletal injuries which affect the muscles, tendons, joints and bones usually in the hand or arm or shoulder, and is generally caused or aggravated by repetitive work. A variety of illnesses can result, including tenosynovitis, tendinitis, carpal tunnel syndrome, epicondylitis capullitus, peritendinitis, spondylosis bursitis, etc. From a legal point of view, an employee who suffers from this complaint may be able to sue for a breach of statutory duty and/or for common law negligence (see Chapter 8). For example, in *McSherry v British Telecommunications plc* the claimant worked as a data processing officer. Her job was to key telephone meter readings into a computer controlled data system. She would be expected to reach a speed of some 13,000 key depressions an hour, and her work was regularly monitored to ensure that she maintained this speed. After doing this for about four years she began to feel pain in her hands, wrists, arms and shoulders, and her doctor diagnosed bilateral tenosynovitis (tennis elbow). It was established that these symptoms were attributable to the nature of the work. The main cause was poor postural positioning, due to unsuitable chairs and a modesty panel beneath her desk, which prevented her from stretching her legs. It was held that the employers were liable for a breach of statutory duty under the Offices, Shops and Railway Premises Act 1963 (OSRPA), s.14 (failure to provide suitable seating together with a footrest) and for common law negligence (failure to foresee that the sort of posture adopted by the plaintiff would, in the course of time, be likely to cause serious musculo-skeletal injury).

7.126   Although there is well-documented evidence of the disorder existing in specific industries and processes it is now acknowledged that work-related upper limb disorders (WRULD) can occur in any particular occupation, and is therefore not confined to a particular sector of industry or commerce. Indeed, many of the more recent cases of claims for compensation appear to arise as a result of modern technology.

7.127   A failure by management to respond adequately to the dangers of WRULD can have a number of consequences, eg high levels of sickness and absenteeism, reduced output, complaints by employees of pain, poor-quality work, civil claims for compensation and, ultimately, a prosecution for failing to comply with s.2(1) of the Health and Safety at Work, etc Act 1974 and/or health and safety regulations (eg Health and Safety (Display Screen Equipment) Regulations 1992).

7.128   There are a number of possible causes of WRULD, including awkward posture, (affecting the hand, wrist, shoulder or body), repeated forceful movements (usually by the hands or arms), frequent repetitive movements (eg keyboard work) and so on. Prevention techniques include:
(a) a recognition of the risk
(b) identifying the cause
(c) removing the risk by redesigning the work using ergonomic techniques, providing suitable tools, introducing adequate rest breaks in the work, teaching correct postures, introducing job rotation, and so on.

7.129   The first step is to identify whether or not the problem exists. An initial assessment should be carried out, which should reveal the nature and extent of WRULD in the workplace. If further action is needed, a more detailed assessment should be undertaken with a view to seeking solutions. These can be achieved in a number of ways, which vary from making minor adjustments to a major overhaul of the systems of work and/or equipment and materials used. Finally, as with every risk assessment, there should be a periodic review of the action taken, and further remedial steps implemented, as required.

7.130   A phrase frequently used to describe certain musculo-skeletal illnesses is "repetitive strain injury" (RSI), but there is considerable controversy over the use of the term, and disagreement between medical practitioners as to whether or not such an illness actually exists.

In *Mughal v Reuters Ltd* the plaintiff spent at least 50% of his time typing on a keyboard. He received no advice on working posture, the need to take breaks, the importance of keeping his wrists parallel to the keyboard, nor for the need to have his eyes at a proper angle to the screen. He then transferred to another job with the same firm, doing similar work. After a month he felt tingling and numbness in his fingers and hands, which then moved up his forearm. For two years thereafter he consulted a number of medical practitioners, and eventually a consultant physician diagnosed tenosynovitis. However, another consultant neurologist was unable to find any clinical symptoms. The employee brought a claim for damages against the employers alleging they had been negligent (see para 8.18). Although the judge accepted that there was a well-known condition called tenosynovitis, with a defined pathology and cause, he held the term "repetitive strain injury" was meaningless, and had no place in the medical books. Its use could only lead to speculation and confusion. Any resultant pain could arise from psychological or emotional disturbance. Further, the judge held that there had been no breach of duty by the employers. Each keyboard operator employed by them had to establish a comfortable position by trial and error, and the employers had fulfilled their legal duty by providing British Standards equipment.

7.131   However, there has always been a disagreement within the medical profession as to whether RSI had organic or psychogenic causes, and the existence of RSI was consequently accepted in a number of other legal cases (eg *Bettany v Royal Doulton (UK)* Ltd). There have also been a number of substantial out-of-court settlement of RSI claims. On the other hand, the existence of RSI was doubted by the House of Lords in *Pickford v Imperial Chemical Industries*.

7.132   In this case, the claimant worked for ICI as a secretary from 1984. In 1986, she estimated that she spent 50% of her time typing, the remaining time being spent on various other secretarial duties. By 1988 she estimated that she spent 75% of her time typing. However, she was able to plan her own workload. She then experienced a strange feeling on the back of her hands, and went to see her doctor, who could find nothing wrong. She was referred to an orthopaedic surgeon, who said that her symptoms were work related, but there was nothing he could do for her. She contacted the Repetitive Strain Injury Association, who referred her to several specialists, only one of whom suggested that the injury might be psychological in origin. Her works doctor suggested that she should be redeployed, but after working for three days as a filing clerk her hands became sore and painful, and she could not continue with that work. There being no other work available for her, her employment was eventually terminated. She issued a writ for damages, claiming that she had contracted prescribed industrial disease PDA4 in the course of her employment as a secretary (PDA4 is defined in the Social Security (Industrial Injuries) (Prescribed Diseases) Regulations 1985 as being "cramp of the hand or forearm" caused by any repetitive movements, which might arise from "any occupation involving prolonged periods of handwriting, typing, or other repetitive movements of the fingers, hand or arm, eg typists, clerks and routine assemblers..."). She claimed that the illness was organic in origin caused by excessive typing without being advised to have rest periods, and that the defendants were negligent in not giving her any instructions about the need to have rest breaks.

7.133 The trial judge held that PDA4 may have an organic or psychogenic cause, but he was not satisfied, on the evidence, that the claimant's cramp was organic in origin. He further held that it was not reasonably foreseeable, considering the amount of typing the claimant did, that she was likely to suffer from PDA4, that she could intersperse her typing with other secretarial work, and that the defendants were not negligent in failing to advise her to take rest pauses from typing. Her claim was therefore dismissed. On appeal, the Court of Appeal reversed the decision, and held that the defendants were liable for negligence.

7.134 On a further appeal, the House of Lords reversed the decision, and restored the finding of the trial judge that the defendants had not been negligent. Because PDA4 is a condition which is not easily identifiable, and not well understood, great caution should be exercised before laying down a duty that warnings of the risks to health should be given, because these could do more harm than good, and might even bring about the very condition it was designed to prevent. Nor was it the practice in the industry to give any such warnings, other than advice to see the works doctor in the event of experiencing unusual pain or discomfort. The employers had carefully taken steps to advise all their word processor operators of the need to have correct hand positions when typing, and to have breaks and rest pauses. Bearing in mind that the claimant did not work all the time on typing, and that she could intersperse her typing with other work, it was not foreseeable that she would suffer this particular injury.

7.135   It was stated in the House of Lords that the term "repetitive strain injury" was a familiar expression, but medical experts agree that that as a medical term it is unhelpful. It covers so many conditions that it is of no diagnostic value as a disease.

7.136   Nonetheless, it is likely that diffuse work related upper limb disorder can be caused by repetitive work carried out under intense pressure, with insufficient work breaks and poor arm posture. If the judge thinks that the case for psychogenic cause has not been proven, it follows that there must be a physical cause, and the employer could well be liable (*Alexander v Midland Bank plc*).

7.137   It would appear that "RSI" is a somewhat loose and vague description of a complaint which may have a psychogenic cause, or may be physical. A term which is sometimes used, non-specific arm pain (NSAP) is perhaps more descriptive and accurate. It is often stress-related, for in many cases no muscular, tendon or neurological abnormality can be found. In other cases, magnetic resonance scans have revealed reduced median nerve movement in the carpal tunnel, suggesting some form of nerve entrapment. Some doctors have defined RSI as a cumulative trauma disorder which results from the over-repetitive use of the muscles in the fingers, hands, arms and shoulders. Certainly there are a number of occupations where it is recognised that repetitive use of the fingers and hands, etc will produce symptoms which are clearly related to the occupation (musicians, keyboard operators, packers, machine operators, etc). It would seem that compensation claims will have to rely on the factual and medical evidence that can be adduced in each case.

Vibration white finger

7.138   Vibration white finger (VWF) disorder is caused by a constriction of the blood supply to the fingers, due to working with vibrating tools, such as pneumatic drills, hammers, etc. In the vast majority of cases it does not prevent a person from continuing to work, although it may cause considerable discomfort, particularly in cold conditions. The precise causes of the injury are not clear and thus it is not possible to lay down specific safe exposure limits.

7.139   The first recorded civil action for damages in respect of VWF was in 1946 (*Fitzsimmons v Ford Motor Co Ltd*) where a successful claim was brought under the Workman's Compensation Act. Later claims floundered because it could not be shown that the employer had been in breach of a duty to take reasonable care or because the trivial nature of the problem did not warrant preventative measures (eg *Joseph v Ministry of Defence*). Employers were entitled to follow the recognised and generally accepted practice, and there was nothing in the literature to make them aware of any danger (see *Walker v Wafco Automotive Ltd*). Further, even if an employee had been warned of the risk, he would still have continued to work. However, more recently, a number of claims for damages have succeeded, for the illness is now widely recognised, and appropriate precautionary measures can be taken (see *Shepherd v Firth Brown Ltd*).

7.140   In a recent case (*Armstrong v British Coal Corporation*) the defendants did carry out some investigation into the existence of VWF in the coal industry. Although it was discovered that there were some employees who had the complaint, they failed to carry out a wider investigation. The judge held that had they done so, they would have realised by 1973 that there was a problem which needed to be addressed, and would have set up a system of preventative measures. A compensation fund of some £500 million has been created for the benefit of thousands of former coal miners who were found to be suffering from VWF.

7.141   A useful summary of the legal and medical background of VWF, with a guide on the assessment of compensation, can be found in a decision of the Northern Ireland High Court in the case of *Bowman v Harland & Wolffe plc*. The HSE has produced a Guidance Note on hand-arm vibration (HSG88: *Hand-arm vibration*).

7.142   Under the Supply of Machinery (Safety) Regulations 1992, suppliers must provide information on vibration levels from hand held tools and hand guided machinery which produce a vibration level of a magnitude exceeding the prescribed level.

7.143   VWF is now a prescribed disease for certain categories of workers under the Social Security (Industrial Injuries) (Prescribed Diseases) Regulations 1985.

Acquired Immune Deficiency Syndrome (AIDS)

7.144   Acquired Immune Deficiency Syndrome (AIDS) is caused by a virus which attacks the body's natural defence system, thus leaving it vulnerable to a number of infections and cancer. However, not all those who have the Human Immunodeficiency Virus (HIV) develop AIDS, although medical statistics on the extent of the disease are still in their infancy. At the present time there is no known cure. The HIV virus can only be transmitted through sexual intercourse with an infected person, by being inoculated with infected blood or (possibly) by drinking breast milk from an infected person and by sharing infected needles. There is no evidence at present to suggest that the virus can be transmitted in any other way and certainly not by other physical contact with an infected person. This means that there is no grounds for refusing employment to a person who has the virus and the fact of infection is not a ground for dismissal.

7.145 However, there are some groups who are clearly at risk. These include doctors, nurses, dentists and others who, by the nature of their work, could come into contact with blood, etc and face the possibility of infection through a cut or accidental injection. These persons must take additional precautions in order to reduce the risk. Many employers have issued policy statements which as well as indicating a refusal to discriminate against someone who has the virus, state the counselling services and other support which will be available.

Epileptics

7.146 Reconciling safety with social responsibility is one of the more difficult tasks of recruitment officers, and it is essential that judgments be made on the basis of informed opinion. This is particularly true of epilepsy, about which there is a great deal of ignorance. There is no reason in principle why an epileptic cannot be employed in most types of work, provided a full appraisal is made of the situation. Epilepsy does not conform to a single pattern; it varies in type, frequency, severity and timing. A candidate for a job who has all the necessary qualifications and experience should not be excluded from consideration on the ground of epilepsy without a full investigation, in which, of course, medical assessment would be invaluable.

7.147 A person who has a history of epilepsy cannot be permitted to drive a heavy goods vehicle or passenger vehicle (unless free from an attack for two years), or work as a specialist teacher of physical education. Other than these restrictions, objections to appointing an epileptic should be based on sound functional reasons. Once employed, safety considerations obviously become important, and if there is any risk to the employee or to his fellow employees, attempts must be made to find suitable employment where the risks are minimised. In the last resort, however, firmer action must be taken. For example, in *Harper v National Coal Board* the applicant had three epileptic fits in a period of two years. During these fits he was, quite unknowingly, violent to other workers. He was then medically examined, and it was recommended that he be retired on medical grounds, under a mine workers pension scheme. He refused to accept retirement and was dismissed. This was held to be fair. The employers owed a duty to their other employees to ensure their safety as well. The applicant was working alongside other disabled employees and they were clearly at risk.

7.148   Epilepsy is likely to be a long term disability under the Disability Discrimination Act, although this will not necessarily be so if the attacks are infrequent or only occur during sleep. As such, the provisions of that Act will apply, and any less favourable treatment is unlawful unless it can be justified. A full review of the medical evidence, together with a consideration of re-deployment away from areas of potential risk, will be necessary. A number of cases relating to epileptics have been considered by employment tribunals, with varying results (eg *Alexander v Driving Standards Agency, Jewell v Stoke Mandeville Hospital NHS Trust*, etc).

7.149   Advice on the employment of epileptics can be obtained from the British Epileptic Association and the Employment Medical Advisory Service may also be contacted when necessary (see also *McCall v Post Office*, see paragraph 7.124).

Mental illness

7.150   This term encompasses a wide range of medical and psychological problems, but from the point of view of health and safety, an employer has to consider (a) whether to employ someone who has, or who has had, mental illness, (b) if he is employed, what steps should be taken to ensure that he is not a health or safety hazard to himself or to others and (c) whether or not a past or present illness is sufficient ground for dismissal.

7.151   The problem is one of medical evidence, and recruitment should be done in consultation with such specialists as are available (eg company doctor, nurse, etc) so that a full and satisfactory assessment can be made of the illness and the risks involved in employing the applicant. Generally, mental illnesses are of two types, namely psychoneurosis and psychosis. The former is a species of "bad nerves", the latter is more serious and involves a lack of contact with reality. So far as psychoneurosis is concerned, the recovery rate is good, and a person who has had a previous history of this sort of mental illness, but who is now fit and well, is no more likely to have a recurrence of the illness than a person who has no previous history is likely to have a mental breakdown. The prognosis for psychosis, however, is mixed, depending on the severity of the illness and the medical evidence which can be adduced.

7.152   Many companies, while they may be unwilling to take on persons with a history of mental illness, adopt a policy of social responsibility to existing employees and seek to provide suitable employment, rehabilitation units, and encourage the employee to obtain medical treatment. Satisfying work, of course, is a great therapy. The problem is one which requires sympathetic handling, involving the co-operation of all those who can contribute some expertise, as well as employees and management generally. Progress should be monitored, risks assessed, work planned and adequately supervised, and so on. Once the nature of the illness can be established, it may be possible to match it with employment where safety can be observed.

7.153   The fact that an employee "tells a lie" on a job application form and denies that he has ever had any history of mental illness is not, *per se*, grounds for dismissal should the previous history come to light (*Johnson v Tesco Stores Ltd*), but if it can be shown that there is a good, sound, functional reason why the person cannot be employed, it may be fair to dismiss him. In *O'Brien v Prudential Assurance Co Ltd*, when the applicant was interviewed for a job he was given a medical examination and asked specific questions about his mental health. He made no mention of the fact that he had had a long history of mental illness, including psychosis, which necessitated the taking of drugs and a period of hospitalisation. When the truth came to light, the company consulted various medical experts and a decision was taken to dismiss him. He brought a claim for unfair dismissal, but it was held that the dismissal was fair for some other substantial reason. It was the company's policy not to appoint as district agents persons who had long histories of mental illnesses, as the job involved going into people's homes. Clearly, there was a risk that an unpleasant incident could occur which would seriously tarnish the company's image and thus the policy was not an unreasonable one. Had the company been aware of his long history of mental illness he would never have been appointed to the job.

7.154 The greater the risk of a serious incident occurring, the more management should consider dismissing the employee. In *Singh-Deu v Chloride Metals* the applicant was sent home from work after complaining that he felt unwell. His doctor diagnosed paranoid schizophrenia and when the company could not obtain a satisfactory assurance from a specialist that there would not be a recurrence, he was dismissed. This was held to be fair. If he had an attack of this illness during working hours, a catastrophic accident could have happened. There was no other suitable alternative employment for him, and the company could not be expected to wait until an accident occurred before taking some action (see *Spalding v Port of London Authority*).

7.155 The need to exercise caution when dealing with employees who have a mental illness can be seen from the decision of the Employment Appeal Tribunal in *Goodwin v The Patent Office*. The appellant was a paranoid schizophrenic who had auditory hallucinations which interrupted his power of concentration. He was dismissed after complaints from female staff about his disturbing behaviour. An employment tribunal held that he was not a disabled person within the meaning of the Disability Discrimination Act 1995, because it was felt that his impairment did not have a substantial adverse effect on his normal day-to-day activities, as required by s.l(l) of the Act. The Employment Appeal Tribunal upheld an appeal, and remitted the case for rehearing by a fresh tribunal. The appellant was unable to carry on a normal day-to-day conversation with work colleagues, which was evidence that his capacity to concentrate and communicate was adversely affected in a significant manner. The Act is primarily concerned with things the applicant cannot do (or can only do with difficulty) rather than on the things he can do.

7.156 A person has a mental impairment for the purpose of the Disability Discrimination Act if he suffers from a clinically well-recognised illness. If there is any doubt, reference should be made to the World Health Organisation's International Classification of Diseases.

Stress at work

7.157 Whilst most illnesses caused by work activities have a physical pathology, recent research appears to indicate that the somewhat vaguer claims of mental stress or depression can have their origin in the workplace These illnesses can be brought on by excessive working hours, pressures to meet deadlines, poor communications, office politics, uncertainties about job security, lack of guidance and/or training, demands for high standards or increased production, and so on. The end result is sometimes absence from work or even a mental breakdown. At the present time, there is little in health and safety legislation which may be invoked, although, in appropriate circumstances, an affected employee could seek to pursue a claim for damages at common law. For example, in *Petch v Commissioners of Customs and Excise,* the claimant was regarded as being a "high flyer" in the Civil Service, and was promoted on a number of occasions. In 1974 he had a mental breakdown, and on his return to work he was transferred to another post. A few years later, he had another breakdown, and was eventually retired on medical grounds. He claimed that his employers had broken their duty of care towards him (see paragraph 8.18) by failing to prevent his mental breakdown in 1974, and failing to take further steps to prevent his second breakdown. The court accepted that the claimant was a manic depressive, and that his breakdown in 1974 was the result of the workload which had been imposed on him and the various conflicts of personalities which arose with other managers. However, prior to his first breakdown, the employers could not have been expected to have known about this facet of his personality, and indeed, evidence was accepted that he was the last person who would have been expected to break down under work pressure. Since he had shown no sign of stress prior to his breakdown, the employers were not negligent in failing to take steps to prevent it. Further, following his return to work, his employers had transferred him to another department where the work was less stressful, and, following several incidents where he displayed symptoms of hypomania, had tried to get him to take sick leave, and had sought to have him medically examined, which he refused to permit. In the circumstances, the employers had not been negligent, but had handled a difficult situation with care and tact.

7.158 Somewhat different facts led to a different result in *Walker v Northumberland County Council,* where the claimant was an area social services officer. Because of the pressure of work he had a nervous breakdown in 1986, and was off work sick for about three months. On his return, the employers indicated that they would provide additional help for him, but the work continued to grow, and six months later he broke down with stress-related anxiety. He was ultimately dismissed on grounds of permanent illhealth, and he sued his employers for damages in respect of the psychiatric damage he had suffered. His claim succeeded. It was the duty of the employers to consider the risk of a reasonably foreseeable injury occurring, the seriousness of the injury, and the cost and/or practicality of averting that risk (taking into account the employers' resources and facilities). On the facts, the employers had known that the claimant was over-worked, and that he had suffered from one breakdown. Thus there was a reasonably foreseeable risk to his mental health which was significantly greater than that anticipated in the ordinary course of a job of his description. The employers could and should have provided him with additional assistance or restructured his work so as to lighten his workload. Had they done so, on the balance of probabilities, the second breakdown would not have occurred.

7.159 Thus, although there is clearly a duty at common law on an employer to take reasonable care that an employee will not suffer from mental (as well as physical) damage, the extent of the precautionary steps to be taken by an employer may well be determined by the employee's resilience, stability of character, mental strength, and so on, which will clearly vary in each individual employee. The steps taken by the employer will also frequently be determined by the financial and physical resources available. Each case is likely to give rise to complex evidential problems of causation and foreseeability.

7.160 It is thus clear that a duty of care to prevent mental breakdown does exist, and no doubt further cases will be brought under this heading of common law liability in the near future.

7.161 In recent years there has been an increasing awareness of work-related stress syndrome, which has resulted in a new and fertile source of litigation, whether by way of common law claims, claims for constructive or unfair dismissal, or as an aspect of claims for race and/or sex discrimination. Precise statistics are hard to come by, and may well vary from year to year. However, current estimates are that stress-related absenteeism results in the loss of some 90 million working days each year, and that some 182,000 people are affected annually. It is the second largest cause of occupational illness.

7.162   There is no medical or legal definition of stress. It is unlikely that stress, per se, will be regarded as a clinically well recognised illness within the meaning of schedule 1 paragraph 1(1) of the Disability Discrimination Act 1995, though the line dividing it from other mental illnesses, eg depression, is somewhat fine. To come within the Act, there must be an impairment which has a substantial and long term adverse effect on a person's ability to carry out normal day-to-day activities. However, there can be a progression from stress to anxiety, depression, clinical depression, post traumatic stress disorder and other associated mental illnesses, which could well fall within the scope of the Act.

7.163   The causes of stress are many. It can arise as the result of unhappy personal circumstances or from a variety of workplace problems. Sometimes the one may be exacerbated by the other. It can affect employees differently, because some will be more vulnerable than others. For example, one employee may find a boring monotonous job stressful, whereas another may prefer its routine nature. What is acceptable pressure for one person may be unacceptable stress for another. Some may prefer to have control over their work situation, others may find responsibility too much for them. The general low morale in the firm, lack of knowledge of career prospects, inter-personal relationships with fellow employees, conflicts between demands of work and personal factors affecting one's home life, and so on, may all play a part in creating stress which can have an impact on an employee's working life.

7.164   Signs to look for include changes in patterns of behaviour, deteriorating relationships, an increase in drinking, smoking, drug taking, irritability, lateness, absenteeism, poor work performance, trivial complaints, lack of concentration, stammering, and so on. There may also be identifiable physical symptoms, including headaches, visual problems, muscular pains, tiredness, insomnia, etc. Low productivity, high staff turnover, higher accident rates and an increase in customer complaints may also signify the existence of a problem which needs be investigated.

7.165   The risk assessment carried out under regulation 3 of the Management of Health and Safety at Work Regulations should contain an assessment of risks from work-related stress, pressures, etc particularly in occupations which demand that a high level of targets and deadlines are met, or where highly skilled and demanding work needs to be carried out under less than favourable conditions. (According to a recent report, the highest stress occupations were teaching, nursing and management.) The pressures which may be causing stress should be identified, the risks from stress assessed, reasonably practical measures should be taken to alleviate the problem, and the effectiveness of any preventative measures reviewed as appropriate. This will involve checking on morale generally, monitoring absenteeism and lateness, checking on improvements in quality, service and productivity, noting improvements in staff relationships and so on.

7.166 Stress can produce physical symptoms (headaches, tiredness real or imaginary aches and pains), behavioural symptoms (increase in alcohol or smoking, irritability, inability to cope), and psychological problems (feelings of anxiety, depression, paranoia), all of which will result in poor performance, increasing absenteeism, potentially higher rate of accidents, and general inefficiency. The first step in dealing with the problem is to recognise that it exists; the next step is to consider the remedial action which needs to he taken. Finally, measures should be taken to prevent any recurrence, whether in respect of any particular individual, or the whole organisation.

7.167 In order to combat stress at work problems, a stress reduction programme should be considered where necessary. Job ambiguities should be noted, and proper job descriptions issued. There should be adequate training in the job requirements, monotonous work routines eliminated or reduced if possible, team focussed work introduced, and personality conflicts dealt with where possible. Health education may be introduced, and managers trained in effective management skills. Counselling may help, and, in the last resort, medical advice taken or given. A well-structured stress reduction programme should produce a significant reduction in sickness absenteeism, as well as facilitate improvements in organisational efficiency.

7.168 The HSE has produced a booklet, HSG116: *Stress at work: A guide for employers.* HSC has also issued a Discussion Document *Managing Stress at Work,* inviting opinions on what, if anything, should be done to tackle stress at work, in an effort to assess how serious the problem is. However, it has been decided not to produce a Code of Practice on stress, as there are too many problems associated with its clinical diagnosis and prognosis. Nonetheless, in a number of recent cases, substantial awards have been made in out of court settlements, and an increasing number of claims is to be expected in the coming years.

Private vehicles/private equipment

7.169   The fact that an employee used his own private vehicle for the purpose of the employer's business does not exonerate the employer from health and safety responsibilities. There is still a need to ensure that safety training is carried out, and safety procedures put in force. For example, there appears to be an increase in two-wheeled delivery drivers (fast food chains, document exchanges, etc) and steps should be taken to minimise or eliminate road accidents, by ensuring that such vehicles are subjected to regular periodic checks, maintenance carried out, and are taxed, appropriately insured, and roadworthy. Safety procedures require that riders must have suitable experience, delivery times must not be so unrealistic as to put pressure on riders to take risks or ride at excessive speed, and should be capable of being modified in accordance with traffic and weather conditions.

7.170   The recent prosecution of the Royal Mail over the death of a young delivery postal worker focused attention on the need to ensure that permission should be sought and given before vehicles are used on a regular basis for the employer's business. Employers should then carry out the usual risk assessment, and implement appropriate action. This is particularly important if the riders/drivers are young or inexperienced, if vehicles are being used for the purpose for which they may not have been intended (eg carrying heavy or awkward loads) or if they are so old or in such poor condition as to expose the driver/rider or other road users to the risks of an accident.

7.171   Privately owned vehicles are not, by themselves, work equipment within the meaning of the Work Equipment Regulations, and in general are covered by road traffic legislation. However, motor vehicles which are owned by employees but used for the purpose of the employer's business could well come within the scope of the regulations. Additionally, motor vehicles can be "a place of work"(*Bradford v Robinson Rentals*, see paragraph 8.31). Section 2(2)(a) of HSWA requires employers to ensure that plant and systems of work must be maintained, and at common law, a vehicle is "plant"for the purpose of assessing the employer's common law duty of care (see paragraph 8.18). The risk assessment provisions of the Management Regulations must also be considered to be appropriate, in respect of activities involving the use of vehicles whether on or off the public highway.

7.172   Similar principles apply to the use by an employee of his own tools or equipment for the purpose of his employer's business. Risk assessments should be made, appropriate safety policies should be drawn up in accordance with the level of risk assessed, spot checks made to ensure that the tools or equipment are in good working order, maintained as appropriate, and are not likely to be the cause of injury or damage to any person.

Young persons

7.173   The Management of Health and Safety at Work Regulations 1999 (regulation 19) require every employer to carry out a risk assessment before employing a young person (ie one who is below the age of 18). The employer must also ensure that young persons employed by him are protected at work from any risks to their health and safety which are a consequence of their lack of experience, or the absence of awareness of existing or potential risks, or the fact that young persons have not yet fully matured.

7.174   In particular, an employer shall not employ a young person for work:
   (a) that is beyond his physical or psychological capacity
   (b) that involves harmful exposure to agents which are toxic or carcinogenic, or cause heritable genetic damage or harm to an unborn child, or which in any other way chronically affect human health
   (c) involving harmful exposure to radiation
   (d) involving the risk of accidents which may reasonably be assumed cannot be recognised or avoided by young persons owing to their insufficient attention to safety, or lack of experience, or training, or
   (e) in which there is a risk from extreme cold, heat, noise or vibration.

7.175   However, it is permissible to employ a young person in the above work where it is necessary for his training, provided he is supervised by a competent person, and any risks have been reduced to the lowest level that is reasonably practicable.

7.176   There are special provisions in the Working Time Regulations 1998 (see paragraph 5.74) concerning free health assessment for young persons who work at night.

7.177   The Children (Protection at Work) Regulations 1998 deal with the employment of children below the minimum school leaving age. Hitherto, restrictions on the working hours of children were contained in local authority bye-laws, but these are now to be standardised by virtue of provisions in the Children and Young Persons Act 1993 and the Children and Young Persons (Scotland) Act 1937.

7.178   Children have the right to have a two-week break from any work during school holidays, and local authorities will update their bye-laws to include a list of jobs which a 13 year old child may do. No child of that age may do a job unless it is on the list. Any work other than light work is prohibited (light work is work which does not jeopardise a child's safety, health, development, attendance at school or participation in work experience). Local authorities have the power to prohibit the employment of children who are employed in a manner which may be prejudicial to their health, or render them unfit to obtain the benefit of full-time education, and they may also impose restrictions on such employment (Education Act 1996, s.559). Otherwise, children may not be employed below the age of 14, unless they are employed by their parents or guardians in light agricultural or horticultural work on an occasional basis.

7.179   The Children (Performances) Regulations 1968 have been amended so as to extend controls on the employment of children in performances to include sport, advertising and modelling, and a licence must be obtained from the local authority if it is proposed to take a child abroad for these purposes. Further information about the new rules can be obtained from the Education Welfare Office of a local education authority.

Risk assessments

7.180   There are a number of regulations that require an employer (sometimes also a self-employed person) to carry out a risk assessment. The nature of the duty and the obligations to be performed will vary in each case. The Health and Safety Executive (HSE) has produced a leaflet, *Five steps to risk assessment*, which gives useful guidance on this subject. However, whilst a failure to carry out a proper risk assessment may be an offence, in criminal proceedings the prosecutor must specify in what respect the risk assessment is alleged to be inadequate, for making the allegation, by itself, is not sufficient (*Carmichael v Marks & Spencer plc*). In normal circumstances, there will have been a detailed investigation after an accident prior to charges being brought, and thus the prosecutor will have sufficient information to enable the inadequacies of the risk assessment to be identified.

7.181 The importance of carrying out a risk assessment cannot be over-emphasised. There is the obvious benefit of identifying risks and hazards, and thus helping to reduce the incidence of accidents and ill-health. Should an accident occur and no risk assessment has been made, it is likely that a prosecution for breach of the relevant regulations would follow. Additionally, the absence of a risk assessment has been used in the courts and employment tribunals leading to some other heading of legal liability. Three such instances can be cited.

(a) In *Godfrey v Bernard Matthews plc* the claimant had to clean between 800 and 1000 trays in an eight hour shift, with three rest breaks. After a few weeks he was diagnosed as suffering from tenosynovitis, which subsequently developed into reflex sympathetic dystrophy. It was held that the injuries were work-related, and foreseeable. A risk assessment, had it been performed, would have led to some form of job rotation, which may have prevented the injury. Compensation of £212,000 was awarded.

(b) In *Buxton v Equinox Design* the employee developed multiple sclerosis. The employer was advised by the Employment Medical Advisory Service to carry out a risk assessment, but this was not done, and the employee was subsequently dismissed. The employment tribunal upheld his claim for unfair dismissal and disability discrimination, the failure to carry out a risk assessment defeating a defence of justification which had been raised. An award of £7627 compensation was made, although on appeal this matter was remitted to the tribunal for reconsideration, based on what would have been the outcome had a risk assessment been made.

(c) In *Day v T Pickles Farms Ltd* a woman was employed in a sandwich shop. She became pregnant, and the constant smell of food made her feel nauseous at work. She became unfit for work and resigned her employment. The Employment Appeal Tribunal held that she had been discriminated against on grounds of sex, in that she had suffered a detriment because of the employer's failure to carry out a risk assessment, under the Management of Health and Safety at Work Regulations. That obligation applies whenever an employer employs a woman of child-bearing age, as well as when a woman is pregnant. The claim was remitted back to the employment tribunal for reconsideration.

7.182 On the other hand, it is unrealistic to carry out a risk assessment for a mundane everyday task (*Koonjui v Thameslink Healthcare Services*), and an employer will not be liable for an injury if the carrying out of a risk assessment would not have prevented the accident (*Hawkes v London Borough of Southwark*). The following regulations require a risk assessment to be carried out.

7.183 *(1) Control of Lead at Work Regulations 1998* (see paragraph 6.188). The employer shall not carry on any work which is liable to expose employees to lead at work unless he has made a suitable and sufficient assessment of whether the exposure of any employee to lead is liable to be significant. The requirement is without prejudice to the matters set out in regulation 3 of the Management of Health and Safety at Work Regulations 1999 (see paragraph 5.8). The Approved Code of Practice gives further guidance on how the assessment is to be carried out, by whom, and the matters which should be considered, etc.

7.184 (2) *Control of Asbestos at Work Regulations 1987 (as amended)* (see paragraph 6.272). An employer shall not carry out any work which exposes any of his employees to asbestos unless he has made an adequate assessment of that exposure, identifying the type of asbestos, determining the nature and degree of exposure, and setting out the steps to be taken to prevent or reduce this to the lowest level reasonably practicable. The assessment shall be reviewed regularly, and a new assessment substituted, when there is reason to suspect that the existing assessment is no longer valid, or where there is a significant change in the work to which the assessment relates.

7.185 An Approved Code of Practice (ACOP) accompanies the regulations, which spells out the tasks to be performed when making an assessment in greater detail.

7.186 (3) *Control of Substances Hazardous to Health Regulations 1999* (see paragraph 6.316). An employer shall not carry on any work which is liable to expose any employees to any substance hazardous to health unless he has made a suitable and sufficient assessment of the risks created by that work to the health of those employees, and of the steps that need to be taken to meet the requirements of the regulations. The assessment shall be reviewed regularly or if there is reason to suspect that it is no longer valid or there has been a significant change in the work to which it relates, and changes shall be made in the assessment as required.

7.187 A number of Approved Codes of Practice have been issued, and HSE has produced a number of guidance documents.

7.188 (4) *Noise at Work Regulations 1989* (see paragraph 6.298). Whenever any of his employees are exposed to a daily personal noise exposure of 85dB(A) or above (the first action level) or to a level of peak sound pressure of 200 pascals or above (the peak action level) every employer shall ensure that a competent person makes a noise assessment which is adequate for the purpose of identifying which of his employees are so exposed, and providing the employer with such information as will facilitate compliance with his duties under regulation 7 (reduction of noise exposure), regulation 8 (provision of ear protection) regulation 9 (designating ear protection zones) and regulation 11 (provision of information to employees).

7.189 HSE has published Guidance Notes to the regulations (L108: *Guidance on the Noise at Work Regulations 1989*).

7.190 (5) *Management of Health and Safety at Work Regulations 1999* (see paragraph 5.4). Every employer shall make a suitable and sufficient assessment of the risk to the health and safety of his employees to which they are exposed at work, and the risks to the health and safety of persons not in his employment arising out of the conduct by him of his undertaking, for the purpose of identifying the measures which the employer needs to take in order to comply with the requirements and prohibitions imposed on him by any relevant statutory provision. A similar assessment shall be made by every self-employed person. The assessment shall be reviewed by the employer (or self-employed person) if there is reason to suspect it is no longer valid, or there has been a significant change in the matters to which it relates. Where the employer employs five or more employees, he shall record the significant findings of the assessment, and identify any groups of his employees who are especially at risk. A risk assessment should also be made of the fire precautions in the workplace (see paragraph 4.17).

7.191   The ACOP attached to the regulations gives further guidance on the matters to be given attention to when carrying out the assessment, the general principles of risk assessment, and the follow-up with preventative and protective measures.

7.192   (6) *Regulation 16 of the Management of Health and Safety at Work Regulations 1999.* Where an employer employs a woman of child-bearing age and the work is of a kind which could involve risk to her if she were pregnant, or nursing a baby, or involved risk to her baby, from any processes or working conditions, including those specified in Annexes I and II of Directive 92/85/EEC (which sets out a non-exhaustive list of certain physical, biological and chemical agents and certain industrial processes), then the employer shall make an assessment of such risks. If the employer cannot take action under relevant statutory provisions to avoid that risk then, if it is reasonable to do so and would avoid such risks, he shall alter her working conditions or hours of work. If this is not possible, then he shall suspend her from work for so long as is necessary to avoid such risk. An employer is not required to take such action unless the woman informs him in writing that she is pregnant, has given birth to a child within the previous six months, or is breast-feeding. A guidance document accompanies the regulations (see Chapter 5).

7.193   (7) *Regulation 19 of the Management of Health and Safety at Work Regulations 1999.* An employer shall carry out a risk assessment in respect of young persons employed by him, and the assessment shall be reviewed. The assessment will take particular account of:
  (a) the young person's inexperience, immaturity and lack of awareness of risks
  (b) the fitting-out and layout of the workplace and workstation
  (c) the nature, degree and duration of exposure to physical, biological and chemical agents
  (d) the form, range and use of work equipment and the way in which it is handled
  (e) the organisation of processes and activities
  (f) the extent of the health and safety training provided, or to be provided, to young persons
  (g) the risks from agents, processes and work listed in the Annex to

the EC Directive 94/33/EEC (which deals with ionising radiation, work in high-pressure atmosphere, biological and certain chemical agents, certain types of dangerous work connected with explosives, high-voltage electrical hazards, dangerous animals, dangerous gases, where there is a risk of structural collapse, etc). (See Chapter 5.)

7.194   (8) *Manual Handling Operations Regulations 1992* (see paragraph 6.141). Where it is not reasonably practicable to avoid the need for employees to undertake any manual handling operations which involve a risk of their being injured, every employer shall make a suitable and sufficient assessment of all such manual handling operations undertaken by the employees. Then, having regard to the questions specified in Schedule 1 to the regulations (see paragraph 6.151) the employer shall take appropriate steps to reduce the risk of injury to the lowest level reasonably practicable, and take appropriate steps to provide those employees with general indications and precise information on the weight of each load and the heaviest side of any load whose centre of gravity is not positioned centrally. The assessment shall be reviewed when the employer suspects it is no longer valid, or there has been a significant change in the manual handling operations to which it relates, and changes will be made to the assessment as are appropriate in the light of the review.

7.195   The regulations are accompanied by comprehensive Guidance Notes, L23: *Manual handling*.

7.196   (9) *Personal Protective Equipment at Work Regulations 1992* (see paragraph 6.111). Before choosing any personal protective equipment (PPE) required by regulation 4 (see paragraph 6.117) an employer (or self-employed person) shall make an assessment to determine whether the PPE he intends to provide is suitable. The assessment shall consist of:

(a) risks which have not been avoided by other means
(b) the definition of the characteristics which the PPE must have in order to be effective against the above risks, and
(c) a comparison of the characteristics of the PPE with the characteristics of the PPE needed to be effective against those risks.

7.197   The assessment shall be reviewed forthwith if there is reason to suspect that any element of it is no longer valid, or there has been a significant change in the work to which the assessment relates. If, as a result of the review, changes in the assessment are required, these shall be made.

7.198   The regulations are accompanied by detailed Guidance Notes, L25: *Personal protective equipment at work.*

7.199   (10) *Health and Safety (Display Screen Equipment) Regulations 1992* (see paragraph 6.159). Every employer shall analyse the workstations in his undertaking for the purpose of assessing the risks to the health and safety of any user which arise out of or in connection with a person's use of those workstations. Any risks identified by the assessment shall be reduced to the lowest extent reasonably practicable.

7.200   The regulations are accompanied by Guidance Notes (L26: *Display screen equipment work*) which give further information on the form, method and purpose of the assessment.

7.201   (11) *Fire Precautions (Workplace) Regulations 1997* (see paragraph 4.17) require every employer to make an assessment of the fire risk at the place of work, prepare an evacuation plan, train their employees in fire precautions, and keep appropriate records.

7.202   (12) *Genetically Modified Organisms (Contained Use) Regulations 2000* (see paragraph 4.36) require a risk assessment to be carried out before the premises are first used and before undertaking any activity involving genetic modification. The organisms shall be classified, and decisions made about the level of confinement. The assessment shall be reviewed if it is no longer valid, or if there has been a significant change in the activity.

7.203   (13) *Ionising Radiations Regulations 1999* (see paragraph 6.280). Before commencing a new practice involving work with ionising radiations in respect of which no risk assessment has been made, a radiation employer shall make a suitable and sufficient assessment of the risk to any employee and other person, for the purpose of identifying the measures he needs to take to restrict the exposure of that employee or other person to ionising radiation. Work shall not commence with ionising radiations unless the assessment is sufficient to demonstrate that all hazards with a potential to cause a radiation accident have been identified, and the nature and magnitude of the risks to employees and to other persons have been evaluated.

7.204 The HSE is currently undertaking a review of all common provisions relating to risk assessments, with a view to the clarification and simplification of the legal requirements, without in any way lowering existing standards of health and safety.

Health surveillance

7.205 Under the Management of Health and Safety at Work Regulations 1999 (regulation 6) every employer shall ensure that his employees are provided with such health surveillance as is appropriate having regard to the risks to their health and safety which are identified by the risk assessment. The general requirement to introduce health surveillance applies when the assessment reveals an identifiable disease or health condition arising from the work, and there is a reasonable likelihood that the disease or condition will occur under the particular working conditions. A health record should be kept, any symptoms noted and examined by an occupational nurse or doctor, biological monitoring carried out, and techniques developed for detection.

7.206 Under the Control of Substances Hazardous to Health Regulations 1999 (regulation 11) suitable health surveillance is required in respect of employees who are, or who are likely to be, exposed to substances hazardous to health, ie if there is exposure to one of the substances specified in column 1 of schedule 6, and engaged in a process set out in column 2 of that schedule (unless the exposure is not significant) or if the exposure to a substance hazardous to health is such that an identifiable disease or adverse health may be related to the exposure. There must be a reasonable likelihood that the disease or effect may occur under the particular conditions of work, and that there are valid techniques for detecting indications of the disease or the effect. If the exposure is to column 1 of schedule 6 substances and the employee is engaged in column 2 of schedule 6 processes, the health surveillance must include a medical surveillance under the supervision of an employment medical adviser or appointed doctor at intervals of not more than 12 months or at such shorter intervals as may be required.

7.207 Under the Control of Lead at Work Regulations 1998 (regulation 10) every employer shall ensure that each of his employees who is or who is likely to be exposed to lead is under suitable medical surveillance by a relevant doctor, where the exposure is likely to be significant or a relevant doctor certifies that the employee should be under medical surveillance. So far as is reasonably practicable, the medical surveillance shall be carried out before the employee commences any work which gives rise to exposure to lead or in any event within 14 working days, and thereafter at intervals of not more than 12 months or such shorter intervals as the relevant doctor may require. Biological monitoring shall be carried out on employees (except women of reproductive capacity and young persons) every six months unless on two previous occasions the lead in air exposure and blood-lead concentration was below certain limits, in which case the biological monitoring can be carried out once a year. Biological monitoring shall also be carried out at least every three months on women of reproductive capacity and young persons. A relevant doctor is an appointed doctor or an employment medical adviser.

7.208   Under the Ionising Radiations Regulations 1999 (regulation 24) the employer shall ensure that each of his employees to whom the regulation applies is under adequate medical surveillance by an appointed doctor or employment medical adviser for the purpose of determining the fitness of each employee for work with ionising radiations. This regulations applies to classified persons (and persons who are to be designated as classified), employees who have received an overexposure and are not classified persons, and employees who are engaged in work with ionising radiations subject to conditions imposed by an appointed doctor or employment medical adviser. A health record shall be kept (containing the prescribed particulars, see schedule 7) and a copy kept until the person to whom it relates, until that person reached the age of 75, or in any event for at least 50 years from the date of the last entry. If the appointed doctor or employment medical adviser is of the opinion that the employee should not be engaged in work with ionising radiations, the employer shall not permit this (except in accordance with any specified conditions).

7.209   Under the Control of Asbestos at Work Regulations 1987, every employer shall ensure that each of his employees who is exposed to asbestos is under adequate medical surveillance by an employment medical adviser or appointed doctor unless the exposure does not exceed the action level. The employer should also keep a health record, containing approved particulars, which must be kept for 40 years. On reasonable notice being given, an employee is entitled to have access to his health records.

Provision of information, instruction and training

7.210   There are a number of legislative provisions which require, in one form or another, an employer to provide necessary information, instruction and training. These include the Management of Health and Safety at Work Regulations 1999, Personal Protective Equipment at Work Regulations 1992, Health and Safety (Display Screen Equipment) Regulations 1992, Provision and Use of Work Equipment Regulations 1998, Noise at Work Regulations 1989, Control of Substances Hazardous to Health Regulations 1999, Control of Asbestos at Work Regulations 1987 (as amended), Control of Lead at Work Regulations 1998, and the Safety Representatives and Safety Committee Regulations 1977.

7.211   The HSE is currently undertaking a review of all the common provisions on these subjects, with a view to achieving some form of rationalisation.

Keeping records

7.212   Problems can be incurred by anyone who has responsibilities for health and safety within an organisation due to the amount of record keeping which has to be done. In the fullness of time, filing cabinets become overloaded, files misplaced, new personnel have great difficulties in locating previous records, and so on. Doubtless computerised information may alleviate the situation, but storing such information may take time and expertise.

7.213   There are two problems to consider. The first concerns the nature of the records which need to he kept. Clearly, certain documentation is required by law, including employers' liability insurance certificates, fire certificates, safety policies, risk assessments, certain medical and health surveillance records, working time, atmospheric monitoring, records of accidents and diseases, etc. Other documents need to be kept as evidence that certain things have been done, eg minutes of safety committee meetings, inspection systems, maintenance logs, safety rules and procedures, safety audits, requests for information from suppliers, and so on. The value of such documentation will largely be proportionate to the use to which it is put. Collecting statistics, for their own sake, is a pointless exercise. Collecting them for the purpose of showing trends or problems in health and safety procedures can be of value, if positive action is thereby provoked.

Obviously, adequate and complete records will be of great value in proving a point in an employment tribunal or High Court in the event of litigation arising. Many a case has been won or lost on the basis of good or poor records.

7.214 The next problem to arise concerns the length of time such documents need to be kept. Apart from specific statutory requirements (see below), there is no easy solution. A worker who has been injured and who wishes to claim compensation from his employer must generally bring a claim within three years of the accident or injury in question, and to that extent records of any such event could be destroyed once that period has passed. However, the Limitations Act 1980 (see paragraph 8.66) also contains a provision that the court may extend the time for bringing a claim to three years from the date when the employee knew, or ought to have known, that his employer was in breach of an alleged legal duty. Thus certain medical conditions, like bladder cancer, pneumoconiosis, etc asbestosis, may take many years to develop into full blown illnesses, and records going back many years, concerning the nature of the employment (eg was the employee exposes to the alleged hazard) the precautions which were taken (eg was he provided with information, instruction, training, protective clothing, etc) could well have a determinant effect on the outcome of the case. Claims brought before an employment tribunal must normally be brought within three months from the alleged act or default of the employer, but again, the tribunals have a wide discretion in allowing claims out of time if it was not reasonably practicable to have brought the claim earlier. In criminal matters, proceedings in respect of summary offences must be brought within six months from the alleged offence, but "time does not ran against the Crown" and proceedings in respect of an indictable offence may be brought many years after the commission of the alleged offence. The ability to produce records to an HSE inspector, showing that safe systems of work, safe operating procedures, etc were in place, and that the legal requirements relating to training, supervision, provision of information, etc were complied with, may well pre-empt a decision to prosecute, or, alternatively, strongly influence a jury's decision in criminal proceedings.

7.215 Sometimes, relevant information may be requested by an external body, although as a general principle the employer may not necessarily have a legal obligation to provide such information. For example, a request may come from the Benefits Agency for information as to the nature of the work (and/or work processes used) carried out by an employee (or ex-employee) in order that a claim for industrial injuries benefit may be determined, arising out of the use of certain tools or equipment or exposure to certain substances, which are set out in Schedule 1 of the Social Security (Industrial Injuries) (Prescribed Diseases) Regulations 1985 (as amended). On such a claim, the employer is basically a disinterested party.

7.216 Certain legislative provisions require documents or records to be kept for a specified period of time. These include the following.

Statutory provision	Records to be kept	Length of time
Factories Act General Register Order 1973	General register	2 years from the date of the last entry
Social Security (Claims and Payments) Regulations 1979	Accident Book (Form B1510)	3 years from date of an entry
Control of Asbestos at Work Regulations 1987	Health records; Certificate of medical information	40 years
Noise at Work Regulations 1989	Records of risk assessment	Until a further assessment is made
Control of Explosives Regulations 1991	Possession of explosives	3 years from last date of entry
Offshore Installations (Safety Case) Regulations 1992	Safety case	As long as is current
	Audit report, record of action, written statement	3 years from when made
Ionising Radiations (Outside Workers) Regulations 1993*	Issue of radiation passbook	5 years after passbook ceased to be used

	Passbook	5 years after return by outside worker
Reporting of Injuries, Diseases and Dangerous Occurrences Regulations 1995	Record of reportable injuries and dangerous occurrences	3 years from date when made
	Record of diseases	3 years from date when made
Offshore Installations and Pipeline Works (Management and Administration) Regulations 1995	Onshore record of persons working on installation	28 days after ceasing to work
Construction (Health, Safety and Welfare) Regulations 1996	Report of inspection	3 months from completion of work
Work in Compressed Air Regulations 1996	Health record	40 years from date of last entry
	Exposure to compressed air	40 years from date of last entry
Control of Lead at Work Regulations 1998	Record of examinations and tests of control measures and respiratory equipment	5 years from date when made
	Air monitoring	5 years
	Adequate health record	40 years from date of last entry
Provision and Use of Work Equipment Regulations 1998	Reports of power press examinations	2 years from date when made

Lifting Operations and Lifting Equipment Regulations 1998	Reports of thorough examination of lifting equipment	Until employer ceases use of lifting equipment
Employers Liability (Compulsory Insurance) Regulations 1998	Certificate of insurance	40 years
Working Time Regulations 1998	Maximum weekly working time; Exclusion from maximum weekly working time; Length of night work	2 years from date when made
	Health assessment for night workers and young workers	
Control of Substances Hazardous to Health Regulations 1999	List of employees exposed to Group 3 or Group 4 biological agents	10 years from last known exposure or 40 years if exposure may result in infection
	Examination and tests of control measures	5 years from date when made
	Monitoring of specified substances or processes	40 years from personal exposure of identifiable employees
	Health record	40 years from date of last entry
Ionising Radiations Regulations 1999	Dose assessment after accident	50 years (or until the age of 75)

	Health record	50 years (or until the age of 75)
	Examination of respiratory protective equipment	2 years
	Dose record	2 years
Pressure Systems Safety Regulations 2000	Report made by competent person	Until next report
Railways (Safety Case) Regulations 2000	Safety case for train operators	So long as is current
	Reports and records	5 years after made

* These Regulations have been revoked by the Ionising Radiations Regulations 1999, but existing records will still need to be kept.

Disclosure statement in civil claims

7.217 It will be recalled (see paragraph 1.82) that the Woolf reforms of civil procedure has made considerable changes in the way civil litigation is to be conducted in the future. There will be a premium on full and proper disclosure of all relevant matters by both sides (by nature of the claims, the burden will fall largely on the employer), and this will have particular relevance to health and safety documentation.

7.218 It is highly likely that the health and safety manager will have considerable responsibilities under the new system. If an accident or injury occurs, a report should be made in the internal accident report book, Form F2508 (report of injury or dangerous occurrence) should be completed and sent to HSE, the names and addresses of any witnesses obtained, photographs taken as appropriate, and medical certificates and/or medical reports kept. Once a claim has been made, a supervising officer should be appointed (this could well be the person responsible for health and safety management), who will be responsible for gathering together all documentation relating to the claim (including videos, tape recordings, photographs, etc) and signing a disclosure statement. So far as workplace claims are concerned, the suggested standard disclosure is of the following documents:

- Accident entry book
- First aiders report
- Surgery record
- Foreman's/supervisor's accident report
- Safety representative's accident report
- RIDDOR report to HSE
- Other communications between the defendant and HSE
- Minutes of health and safety committee meeting(s) where the incident was considered
- Report to the Department of Social Security (DSS)
- Documents listed above relative to any previous accident or matter identified by the claimant and relied upon as proof of negligence
- Information relating to the earnings of the claimant at the time of the accident.

7.219 The following additional documents should be disclosed as a matter of routine, where applicable.

7.220 Documents produced in order to comply with the Management of Health and Safety at Work Regulations 1999:
  (a) pre-accident risk assessment (regulation 3)
  (b) post-accident risk assessment (ie, on review, regulation 3)
  (c) accident investigation report prepared in implementing the requirements of regulation 5, 7 and 11
  (d) health surveillance records (regulation 6)
  (e) information provided to employees (regulation 10)
  (f) health and safety training records relating to the employee (regulation 13).

7.221 Documents produced in order to comply with the Workplace (Health, Safety and Welfare) Regulations 1992:
  (a) repair and maintenance records (regulation 5)
  (b) housekeeping records (regulation 9)
  (c) hazard warning signs or notices (regulation 17).

7.222 Documents produced in order to comply with the Provision and Use of Work Equipment Regulations 1998:
  (a) manufacturer's specifications establishing suitability (regulation 4)
  (b) maintenance logs and records (regulation 5)
  (c) information and instructions to employees (regulation 8)
  (d) records of adequate training (regulation 9)

(e) notices, signs and documents dealing with controls and control systems (regulations 14–18)

(f) instructions and training documents dealing with maintenance operations (regulation 22)

(g) work equipment markings (regulation 23)

(h) warning signs or devices (regulation 24).

7.223 Documents produced in order to comply with the Personal Protective Equipment Regulations 1992:

(a) assessment of PPE (regulation 6)

(b) maintenance and replacement of PPE (regulation 7)

(c) records of maintenance procedures (regulation 7)

(d) records of tests and examinations of PPE (regulation 7)

(e) records of providing information, instruction and training for PPE (regulation 9)

(f) instructions for using PPE (including manufacturer's instructions) (regulation 10).

7.224 Documents produced in order to comply with the Manual Handling Operations Regulations 1992:

(a) manual handling risk assessment (regulation 4)

(b) post-accident re-assessment (regulation 4)

(c) information given to employees in relation to the load, and heaviest side of the load (regulation 4)

(d) training records in respect of manual handling operations.

7.225 The pre-action protocols also provide lists of other documents which need to be disclosed where other regulations are likely to be in issue, eg Construction (Design and Management) Regulations 1994.

7.226 The above lists are for guidance as to what documents should be disclosed as appropriate in the circumstances, provided, of course, they are in existence. They do not have to be specially created for disclosure purposes. A reasonable and proportionate search should be made for relevant documents, depending on the numbers involved, the complexity of the proceedings, the expense of retrieval, and the significance of them if found. If it is unreasonable to search for certain documents (eg relating to an incident which occurred many years ago) that fact should be stated. The duty is to disclose documents which are in the party's control, and if certain documents have been destroyed, an explanation given. If further documents come to light during the proceedings, they must be produced. Some documents may be privileged and advice should be taken before disclosing them.

7.227 A disclosure statement should then be signed by a representative of the party making the disclosure, containing a list of the documents submitted, and stating:
(a) the extent of the search that has been made to locate documents which he is required to disclose
(b) that he understands the duty to disclose documents
(c) that to the best of his knowledge he has carried out that duty
(d) his official position
(e) why he is an appropriate person to make the statement.

CHAPTER 8

Compensation for injuries at work

8.1   Inevitably, an employee who is injured in the course of employment will seek some form of compensation from the person (if any) who was responsible for those injuries, or look to the state to provide some assistance. If an employee is killed, his dependants will also be seeking some form of financial recompense for themselves. It is this area of the law which in the past has tended to dominate all other considerations of health and safety, as compensation, rather than prevention, became the main function of the law. This attitude prompted the Robens Committee to attempt some shift in the impact of the legislation.

8.2   It is a truism to say that legal decisions reflect the current social and economic forces of the day and this explains some of the changes in judicial attitudes which have taken place from time to time. Further, the impact of state and private insurance schemes (especially employers' liability insurance) has cast a powerful shadow over strict legal reasoning, for there is a natural tendency to seek some way in which the injured employee can be assisted financially, and, after all, if an insurance company had to foot the bill, this could easily be recouped by a minute increase in general premiums. This benevolent attitude even reached employers, and there are many cases where liability is admitted or where valiant attempts were made to admit their own negligence so as to enable an injured employee to obtain compensation (eg see *Hilton v Thomas Burton (Rhodes) Ltd*). But there were limits, too, on judicial credulity, which compelled some judges to hold that they could no longer equate the relationship between employer and employee with that of nurse and imbecile child (Lord Simmonds in *Smith v Austin Lifts Ltd*) or that of schoolmaster and pupil (Devlin LJ in *Withers v Perry Chain Ltd*).

8.3   The basis of the employer's duty towards his employees stems from the existence of a contract of employment. It is an implied term of that contract that the employer will take reasonable care to ensure the safety of his employees (*Matthews v Kuwait Bechtel Corporation*), and an employer who fails to fulfil that duty is in breach of that contract (*British Aircraft Corporation v Austin*). The express terms of the contract must be capable of co-existing with the implied terms. In *Johnson v Bloomsbury*

Health Authority, Dr Johnson was required by his contract of employment to work a basic 40 hour week, and to be "on call" for a further 48 hours each week. He claimed that the number of hours he had to work were intolerable, depriving him of sleep, with consequent depression, stress and anxiety, which could result in the risk of mistakes or inefficient treatment of patients. He sought a declaration that he could not lawfully be required to work for so many hours in excess of his standard working week as would foreseeably injure his health. At a preliminary hearing, the Court of Appeal held that he had established an arguable case to warrant a full trial of the issues. The Court, however, were not unanimous in their views, but it appears that the employer's right to require Dr Johnson to work up to 48 hours "on call" was subject to the implied duty of the employer to take care that the employee's health was not damaged as a result. Further, it was held that it was arguable that the term (that he should work for up to 88 hours a week) was void under the Unfair Contract Terms Act 1977, which prohibits a contract term which excludes or restricts liability for personal injury caused by negligence. Since the offending term could be said to restrict or limit the ambit of the duty of care owed by the employers, the claimant was permitted to proceed with that aspect of his claim.

8.4 However, from the point of view of an injured employee there is little advantage in suing in contract. Practically all modern cases are brought under the law of tort, in particular for the tort of negligence which, since the famous case of *Donoghue v Stevenson* in 1932 consists of three general ingredients, namely (a) there is a general duty to take care not to injure someone whom one might reasonably foresee would be injured by acts or omissions, (b) that duty is broken if a person acts in a negligent manner, and (c) the breach of the duty must cause injury or damage. The existence of a duty-situation between employer and employee has been long recognised, and most of the cases turn on the second point, ie was the employer in fact negligent?

8.5 The liability of the employer may come about in two ways. First, he will be responsible for his own acts of negligence. These may be his personal failures or (since many employers nowadays are artificial legal entities, ie limited companies or other types of corporations) due to the wrongdoings of the various acts of management acting as the *alter ego* of the employer. Second, the employer may be liable vicariously for the wrongful acts of his employees which are committed in the scope of their employment and which cause injury or damage to others.

8.6   Compensation may be obtained under one or more of three headings. The first is for the injured employee (or his personal representatives, if he has died) to bring an action at common law. This will be for either (a) a breach by the employer of a duty laid down by statute, or (b) a breach of the duty owed by the employer at common law to ensure the health and safety of his employees. Frequently, a claim will be presented under both headings simultaneously. With two strings to his bow, it matters not if he wins under either heading, or both. (Of course, if he wins under both, he will only get one lot of damages.) It is regarded as a misfortune if he fails under both headings, for he has then lost his main financial solace. It was the uncertainties of litigation in this area of the law, the difficulties of establishing satisfactory evidential standards in court hearings held years after an incident had occurred, the legal expenses and complexities, and the social injustices caused, which were among the main reasons for the appointment of the Pearson Commission in 1974. Its report, however, did not recommend any major changes in the compensation system.

8.7   The second remedy for an injured employee is the automatic recourse to the National Insurance (Industrial Injuries) scheme operated by the State in one form or another since 1911 (see now the Social Security (Contributions and Benefits) Act 1992), which provide for a pension in respect of an injury at work or a prescribed disease which causes permanent disabilities. This scheme is in addition to the right to sue at common law, although benefits payable will be taken into account when fixing damages. However, the State scheme operates as of right, irrespective of the existence of fault or blame on the part of any person, including the injured worker.

8.8   Third, in appropriate circumstances, there are other schemes which may be resorted to, such as those operated by the Criminal Injuries Compensation Authority, the Motor Insurers' Bureau or (rarely used) the power of the courts to award compensation.

Claims at common law

Breach of statutory duty

8.9   When Parliament lays down a duty for a person to perform, it will usually ensure that there is an appropriate sanction to enforce that duty. This sanction will normally take the form of some sort of punishment in the criminal courts. The further question will thus arise; can a person who has been injured by the failure of another to perform that statutory duty bring a civil action based on that failure? After some hesitation, British courts upheld an action for the tort of breach of statutory duty, although the full extent of legal liability is not entirely settled. There is no automatic presumption that all breaches of statutory duties are actionable in civil courts; it is necessary to examine the purposes and objects of the statute in question, seek the intentions of Parliament (it is now permissible to look at Hansard in order to ascertain those intentions, see *Pepper v Hart*, see paragraph 1.99) and ascertain the class of persons for whose benefit the Act was passed. If the injured party has suffered the type of harm the Act was designed to eliminate, it would not be unreasonable to grant him a remedy in respect of a breach of the statutory duty. The first case in which these propositions were accepted was *Groves v Lord Wimborne*, where a statute provided that an occupier of a factory who did not fence dangerous machinery was liable to a fine of up to £100. A boy employed in the factory was caught in an unfenced cog wheel, and his arm was amputated. It was held that the criminal penalty was irrelevant to civil liability, and the claim for a breach of statutory duty succeeded.

8.10   However, not every breach of statutory duty is actionable (eg see *Richardson v Pitt-Stanley*, see paragraph 4.9), and though the point appears to be well settled so far as health and safety legislation is concerned, there are one or two areas where there may still be an element of doubt. Certain legal problems were encountered when dealing with the welfare provisions of the Factories Act 1961 and the Offices, Shops and Railway Premises Act 1963 (eg see *Ebbs v James Whitson & Co Ltd*), but as those provisions have now been repealed the point need no longer be of concern.

8.11   No civil action may be brought in respect of a breach of the provisions contained in ss.2–8 of HSWA, but if an employee is injured because his employer has failed to observe the requirements of a health and safety regulation, this will amount to the tort of breach of statutory duty, in respect of which the employee may be able to recover damages (eg *Hawkes v London Borough of Southwark*, see paragraph 6.150). This is so in respect of all such regulations, COSHH, Manual Handling, Personal Protective Equipment, Control of Lead, and so on, unless there is a specific exclusion of civil liability (see Management of Health and Safety at Work Regulations 1999, see paragraph 5.4).

Elements of the tort of breach of statutory duty

8.12   The first requirement is that the plaintiff must show that he is within the class of persons for whose benefit the duty was imposed. This will depend entirely on the provision in question. Thus there were provisions in the Factories Act which were designed to protect all persons who work in a factory, whether or not they are the employees of the occupier and whether or not they are doing the employer's work or their own (*Uddin v Associated Portland Cement Manufacturers Ltd*). Other provisions may be more limited in their scope. Thus in *Hartley v Mayoh & Co* a fireman was electrocuted whilst fighting a fire at the defendant's premises. The widow sued in respect of a breach by the defendant of a statutory regulation. Her claim failed. The provisions in question were designed to protect "persons employed" in the premises and the fireman was not within this class of person. In *Reid v Galbraith's Stores* it was held that the provisions of OSRPA did not apply to a customer who was visiting the shop as the Act was concerned with people who work on the premises.

8.13   Insofar as old health and safety regulations are concerned, the right to bring a civil claim in respect of a breach is probably even more circumscribed. Sometimes these will be designed to protect a person who is performing a particular type of work, and a person who is not engaged on that process but who may be injured as a result of a breach of the regulation will not generally be entitled to compensation under this heading. The reason is that in the past it was presumed that Parliament only intended that the power to make regulations shall be exercised within particular limits, and the courts will not therefore go outside those limits. However, the power to make regulations under s.15 of HSWA is not so restricted and thus they may include a wider category of affected persons, as appropriate. It is clear that when regulations are made for the benefit of a particular group of persons, only those who are in that group can take advantage of the statutory protections (*Canadian Pacific Steamships Ltd v Bryers*).

8.14   Second, the injury must be of a kind which the statute was designed to prevent. In *Close v Steel Co of Wales* a workman was injured by a part of dangerous machinery which flew out of a machine. His claim, based on a breach of s.14 of the Factories Act (duty to fence dangerous parts of machinery) failed. The object of s.14 was to prevent the worker from coming into contact with the machine, not to stop the parts of the machine from coming into contact with the worker. The purpose of fencing was not to keep the machine or its products inside the fence.

8.15 The third requirement of the tort is that the defendant must be in breach of that duty. This involves a consideration of the duty imposed, the person upon whom it is placed, and the steps taken to perform that duty. Thus in *Chipchase v British Titan Products Co Ltd*, regulations provided that every working platform from which a person is liable to fall more than 2m (6 feet 6 inches) shall be at least 34 inches wide. A worker fell from a platform which was only 9 inches wide, but which was 6 feet from the ground. The plaintiffs case obviously failed, as there was no breach of duty by the defendant. If the statute or regulations impose absolute duties, then these must be observed irrespective of the inconvenience caused (*Summers & Sons v Frost*), but if these are qualified, eg "so far as is reasonably practicable", etc it is a question of fact in each case as to whether or not the defendant has complied with that standard.

8.16 Finally, it must be shown that the breach of the duty caused the damage. This is the causation rule, which may be illustrated by the decision in *McWilliams v Sir William Arrol & Co Ltd*. Here, the employers provided safety belts for steel erectors on a site. As the belts were not being used, they were taken to another site. A steel erector on the first site fell from a scaffolding and was killed. Although the employers were clearly in breach of their statutory duty to provide the safety belts, they were not liable for damages. Even if they had provided the belts, there is nothing to suggest that this workman (who had never used them before) would have worn them on the day he was killed. Thus, the breach of duty did not cause the damage; it would have occurred anyway.

8.17 But if an injury is caused by the act of the injured employee, which would not have occurred if the employer had performed his statutory duties, then the employer will be liable for damages unless the act of the employee was an unnatural and improbable consequence of the breach. For example, in *McGovern v British Steel Corporation*, the plaintiff was walking along a gangway made from scaffold boards. He saw a toe board which had fallen from the upright position and which was obstructing the walkway. He attempted to pick it up but, because it was jammed, it "whiplashed" causing him to suffer from a slipped disc.

It was held that the employer was liable. The injury was not caused by the employee tripping or falling over the obstruction, but by the employer's breach of duty in failing to remove it. It was natural that the employee should attempt to do this, and the injury was not unforeseeable. Thus the injury was a natural and probable cause of the breach and the conduct of the employee was not such as to break the chain of causation.

Negligence

8.18 At common law the employer is under a duty to take reasonable care for the health and safety of his employees. This duty is a particular aspect of the general law of negligence, which requires everyone to ensure that his activities do not cause injury or damage to another through some act of carelessness or inadvertence (see *Donoghue v Stevenson*, see paragraph 8.4). The court must decide whether the wrongdoer (or tortfeasor) could have reasonably foreseen the injury (whether physical or psychological) to the victim (*Alcock v Chief Constable of Yorkshire*).

The personal nature of the duty

8.19 The duty at common law is owed personally by the employer to his employee, and he does not escape that duty by showing that he has delegated the performance to some competent person. In *Wilsons and Clyde Coal Co v English* the employer was compelled by law to employ a colliery agent who was responsible for safety in the mine. Nonetheless, when an accident occurred, the employer was held liable. Thus it can never be a defence for an employer to show that he has assigned the responsibility of securing and maintaining health and safety precautions to a safety officer or other person. He can delegate the performance, but not the responsibility.

8.20 Further, the duty is owed to each employee as an individual, not to employees collectively. Greater precautions must be taken when dealing with young or inexperienced workers and with new or untrained employees than one might take with more responsible staff. The former may require greater attention paid to their working methods or may need more supervision (*Byers v Head Wrightson & Co Ltd*). In *Paris v Stepney Borough Council* the plaintiff was employed to scrape away rust and other superfluous rubbish which had accumulated underneath buses. It was not customary to provide goggles for this kind of work.

However, the plaintiff had only one good eye, and he was totally blinded when a splinter entered his good eye. It was held that the employers were liable for damages. They should have foreseen that there was a risk of greater injury to this employee if he was not given adequate safety precautions and the fact that they may not have been under a duty to provide goggles to other employees was irrelevant.

8.21 A higher standard of care is also owed to employees whose command of the English language is insufficient to understand or comply with safety instructions, to ensure that as a result they do not cause injuries to themselves or to others. In *James v Hepworth and Grandage Ltd* the employers put up large notices urging employees to wear spats for their personal protection. Unknown to them, one of their employees could not read, and when he was injured he claimed damages from his employer. His claim failed. He had observed other workers wearing spats and his failure to make any enquiries led the court to believe that even if he had been informed about the contents of the notice, he would still not have worn the spats. But with the growth of foreign labour in British factories, the problem is one for obvious concern, especially as immigrants tend to concentrate in those industries which are most likely to have serious safety hazards. The task of the safety officer to ensure the health and safety of such employees is likely to be very onerous in practice (see *Hawkins v Ian Ross (Castings) Ltd*).

8.22 The duty is owed by the employer to his employees, but this latter term is not one which is very precise, and a number of problems have arisen. In *Ferguson v John Dawson & Partners (Contractors) Ltd* a man agreed to work on the "lump", ie as a self-employed bricklayer, but when he was injured, he sued, claiming the employers owed a duty to him as an employee. By a majority, the Court of Appeal upheld his claim, holding that it was the substance of the relationship, not the form, which was the determining factor in deciding whether or not a person was an employee in the legal sense.

8.23 As a general rule, each employer must ensure the safety of his own employees, and is not responsible in his capacity as an employer for the safety of employees of other employers. However, where a number of employees from different firms are employed on one job, there is a duty to coordinate the work in a safe manner (*McArdle v Andmac Roofing Co*).

8.24 The employer's duty of care persists even when an employee is "loaned" to work for another employer. Thus in *Morris v Breavenglen Ltd*, the claimant worked for a firm called Anzac Construction, and during the course of his employment he was permitted to drive a dumper truck, although he was not trained or licensed to do so. He was then sent to work at a prison farmyard, the main contractors being a firm called Sleeman Construction. On being informed that he could drive a dumper truck, he was instructed by Sleeman to dump some soil at a tipping site. While doing this, the dumper went over the edge, and he was injured. It was held that his main employer, Anzac, were liable for damages in respect of injuries received. They still owed him a duty of care under his contract of employment, and were in breach of that duty in failing to ensure that precautions were not taken to prevent the accident from occurring. An employer is not released from his duty of care which exists under the contract of employment merely because the employee is required to work under the direction and control of another employer. By failing to provide him with proper training and instruction in using the dumper truck, and by permitting him to use one when not properly instructed, they had exposed him to an unnecessary risk of injury. In this case, the Court of Appeal drew a distinction between those circumstances when a loaned employee injures himself, and when he injures a third party. In the latter case it is permissible to ascertain whether there had been a transfer of the legal obligations from one employer to the other (see *Mersey Docks and Harbour Board v Coggins and Griffiths (Liverpool) Ltd*) and the issue is usually which of the two employers will be vicariously liable for that injury. But when a loaned employee himself has been injured, either or both employers may be liable, for either or both could be in breach of their common law duties. Thus, in this case, there was no contract of employment between the employee and Sleeman, and thus Anzac, as the employer of the claimant still owed a duty not to expose him to unnecessary risks. If a workman is loaned (together with an expensive piece of equipment, such as a crane) or he is an expert in his job so that the second employer cannot exercise any control over the way the work is done, it will be rare that the courts will infer that the right of control vested in the first employer has been transferred to the second. But if an unskilled workman is loaned, it would be easier to infer that there has also been a transfer of the legal responsibility to the second employer (*Garrad v Southey & Co*) insofar as his activities cause injury or damage to a third party.

The extent of the duty

8.25   The standard of care which must be exercised by the employer is "The care which an ordinary prudent employer would take in all the circumstances" (*Paris v Stepney Borough Council*). The employer does not give an absolute guarantee of health or safety, he only undertakes to take reasonable care and will be liable if there is some lack of care on his part or in failing to foresee something which was reasonably foreseeable. The employee, for his part, must be prepared to take steps for his own safety and look after himself and not expect to be able to blame the employer for everything which happens. In *Vinnyey v Star Paper Mills Ltd*, the claimant was instructed by the foreman to clear and clean a floor area which had been made slippery by a viscous fluid. The foreman gave him proper equipment and clear instructions. The claimant was injured when he slipped on the floor while doing the work, and it was held that the employers were not liable. There was no reasonably foreseeable risk in performing such a simple task, and they had taken all due care. In *Lazarus v Firestone Tyre and Rubber Co Ltd* the claimant was knocked down in the general rush to get to the canteen. It was held that this was not the sort of behaviour which could be protected against.

8.26   If an employer does not know of the danger and could not reasonably be expected to know, in the light of current knowledge available to him, or did not foresee that there was a potential hazard and could not reasonably be expected to foresee it, he will not be liable. In *Down v Dudley, Coles Long Ltd* an employee was partially deafened by the noise which came from a cartridge assisted hammer gun. At the then state of medical knowledge (ie in 1964) a reasonable employer would not have known of the potential danger in using this particular piece of equipment without providing adequate safety precautions and the employer was held to be not liable for the injury. Clearly, with the wide dissemination of literature on noise hazards nowadays, a different conclusion would be drawn on these facts although the general principle of law remains the same.

8.27   Once a danger has been perceived, the employer must take all reasonable steps to protect the employees from the consequences of those risks which have hitherto been unforeseeable. In *Wright Rubber Co Ltd, Cassidy v Dunlop Rubber Co Ltd* the employers used an anti-oxidant known as Nonox S from 1940 onwards. The manufacturers then discovered that the substance was capable of causing bladder cancer and informed the defendants that all employees should be screened and tested. This was not done for some time, and thus the employers, as well as the manufacturers, were held to be liable to the claimants.

8.28   The matter was summarised by Swanwick J in *Stokes v GKN Ltd*:

- (a) the employer must take positive steps to ensure the safety of his employees in the light of the knowledge which he has or ought to have
- (b) the employer is entitled to follow current recognised practice unless in the light of common sense or new knowledge this is clearly unsound
- (c) where there is developing knowledge, the employer must keep reasonably abreast with it, and not be too slow in applying it
- (d) if he has greater than average knowledge of the risk, he must take more than average precautions
- (e) he must weigh up the risk (in terms of the likelihood of the injury and possible consequences) against the effectiveness of the precautions to be taken to meet the risk and the cost and inconvenience.

8.29   Applying these tests, if the employer falls below the standards of a reasonable and prudent employer he will be liable.

The threefold nature of the duty

8.30   Recent cases have stressed that there is only one single duty on the part of the employer, namely to take reasonable care. However, we may conveniently analyse that duty under three categories.

8.31   *Safe plant, appliances, and premises.* First, all tools, equipment, machinery, plant which the employee uses or comes into contact with and all the employer's premises shall be reasonably safe for work. Thus a failure to provide the necessary equipment (*Williams v Birmingham Battery and Metal Co*) or providing insufficient equipment (*Machray v Stewarts and Lloyds Ltd*) or providing defective equipment (*Bowater v Rowley Regis Corporation*) will amount to a breach of the duty. There must be a proper and adequate system of inspection and testing, so that defects can be discovered and reported (*Barkway v South Wales Transport Co*) and then remedied (*Monaghan v WH Rhodes & Son*). In *Bradford v Robinson Rentals*, a driver was required to go on a 400 mile journey during a bitterly cold spell of weather in a van which was unheated and had cracked windows. He suffered frostbite and his employers were held liable for failing to provide suitable plant. Before putting secondhand machinery into use, it should be checked to make sure that it is serviceable (*Pearce v Round Oak Steel Works Ltd*). If unfenced machinery is liable to eject parts of the machine or materials used by the machine, then a failure to erect suitable and effective guards may well constitute negligence at common law (*Close v Steel Co of Wales*) irrespective of any liability for a breach of the Work Equipment Regulations (*Kilgollan v William Cooke & Co Ltd*). If the equipment is inherently dangerous, extra precautions must be taken (*Naismith v London Film Productions Ltd*).

8.32   However, if an employer purchases tools or equipment from a reputable supplier and has no knowledge of any defect in them, he will have performed his duty to take care and cannot be held liable for negligence (see *Davie v New Merton Board Mills*). An employee who was injured in consequence could only pursue his remedy against the person responsible for the defect under the general law of negligence (*Donoghue v Stevenson*). In practice, this would frequently be difficult or impossible. The employee would not have the time or resources to do this; it may be that the negligence was due to the acts of a foreign manufacturer, or stevedores at the docks, etc. In view of these problems, the law was changed with the passing of the Employers' Liability (Defective Equipment) Act 1969. This provides that if an employee suffers a personal injury in the course of his employment in consequence of a defect in equipment provided by his employer for the purposes of his employer's business, and the defect is attributable wholly or partly to the fault of a third party (whether identified or not), then the defect will be deemed to be attributable to the negligence of the employer. Thus, in such circumstances, the injured employee would sue the employer for his "deemed" negligence, and the latter, for his part, would attempt to recover the amount of damages he has paid out from the third party whose fault it really was. Since the insurance company is the real interested party in such matters, it is they, rather than the employer, who will attempt to make such recovery. The Employers' Liability (Compulsory Insurance) Act was also passed in 1969 to ensure that all employers have valid insurance cover to meet personal injuries claims from their employees, and a certificate to this effect must be displayed at the employers' premises (see paragraph 4.1).

8.33   The Employers' Liability (Defective Equipment) Act was considered by the House of Lords in *Knowles v Liverpool City Council,* where the claimant was employed as a "flagger" by the highway authority. He was injured when a flagstone he was handling broke. The flagstone had not been cured properly by the makers. He sued his employers, arguing that the flagstone was "equipment provided by the employer for the purpose of the employer's business", and his claim was upheld. The House of Lords refused to draw a distinction between "equipment" and materials, for to do so would create unjustifiable inconsistencies. There is little doubt that the decision represents a purposive construction of the Act.

8.34   If an employer is aware of any defect in tools, etc which have been purchased from outside he should withdraw them from circulation. In *Taylor v Rover Car Co Ltd* a batch of chisels had been badly hardened by the manufacturers. One had, in fact, shattered without causing an injury, but the rest of the batch were still being used and another chisel shattered, injuring the claimant in his eye. The employers were held liable.

8.35   The employer must also ensure that the premises are reasonably safe for all persons who come on to the premises (under the Occupiers Liability Act 1957–1984) as well as for his employees in particular. In *Paine v Colne Valley Electricity Supply Co Ltd* an employee was electrocuted because a kiosk had not been properly insulated and the employers were held liable. However, it must be stressed that the employer need only take reasonable care, and this is a question of fact and degree in each case. In *Latimer v AEC Ltd* a factory floor was flooded after a heavy storm, and a mixture of oil and water made the floor slippery. The employers put down sand and sawdust, but there was not enough to treat the whole of the factory in this way, and the claimant was injured. The employers were held not liable. The danger was not grave enough to warrant closing down the whole factory (which would have been unreasonable, bearing in mind that the risk was fairly minimal). However, had there been dangers because the structure had been damaged, different considerations would have applied.

8.36   The employer cannot be responsible for the premises of other persons where his employees have to work, but as he still owes to them a duty of care, he must ensure that a safe system of work is laid down.

8.37   *Safe system of work.* Second, the employer is responsible for the overall planning of the work operations so that it can be carried out safely. This includes the layout of the work, the systems laid down, training and supervision, the provision of warnings, protective clothing, protective equipment, special instructions, etc. Regard must be had for the fact that the employee will be forgetful, careless, as well as inadvertent, but the employer cannot guard against outright stupidity or perversity.

8.38   A reasonable employer will frequently be expected to be aware of the existence of risks to health and safety even though they arise out of commonplace activities. In *Pape v Cumbria County Council* the claimant was employed as a part-time cleaner. During her work, she used various chemical cleaning agents. The employer made available rubber gloves, but never advised her to use them, or warned of the dangers of the risks of working without them. She contracted dermatitis and eczema on her hands, which then spread to other parts of her body, and she was forced to give up her employment. She sued for damages. It was held that the employer should have warned her of the dangers arising from the use of chemical cleaning agents, instructed her to use the rubber gloves provided, and taken reasonable steps to ensure that those instructions were carried out. The knowledge of the risk was not so well known to employees that the mere provision of rubber gloves was sufficient performance of the employer's duty of care.

8.39   Examples of a failure to provide a safe system of work abound. In *Barcock v Brighton Corporation*, the claimant was employed at an electric substation. A certain method of testing was in operation which was unsafe and in consequence the employee was injured. The employers were held liable. If there are safety precautions laid down, the employee must know about them; if safety equipment is provided, it must be available for use. In *Finch v Telegraph Construction and Maintenance Co Ltd* the claimant was employed as a grinder. Goggles were provided for this work, but no one told him where to find them. The employers were held liable when he was injured by a piece of flying metal. Whether a system is safe in any particular case will be a question of fact, to be decided on the evidence available.

8.40   The more dangerous the process, the greater is the need to ensure that it is safe. On the other hand, the employer cannot be expected to take over-elaborate precautions when dealing with simple and obvious dangers (*Vinnyey v Star Paper Mills*). A situation which gives rise to some legal difficulties is where the employer provides safety precautions or equipment, but the employee fails or refuses to use or wear them. Is the duty a mere passive one, to provide and do no more? Or is it a more active one, to exhort or even compel their use? It is suggested that the answer to these questions can be summarised in four propositions.

8.41 (1) If the risk is an obvious one, and the injury which may result from the failure to use the precautions is not likely to be serious, then the employer's duty is a mere passive one of providing the necessary precautions, informing the employees of their presence, and leaving it to them to decide whether or not to use them. In *Qualcast (Wolverhampton) Ltd v Haynes* an experienced workman was splashed by molten metal on his legs. Spats were available, but the employers did nothing to ensure that they were worn. The injury, though doubtless painful, was not of a serious nature, and the employers were held not liable.

8.42 Similarly, in *Smith v Scott Bowyers Ltd*, the claimant had been provided with wellington boots to protect against the risk of slipping on a wet floor. The soles of the boots had worn smooth, and he asked for and was given another pair. These also wore smooth but he did not seek a replacement pair. He then slipped on the wet floor and was injured. The trial judge held that the employers were liable, as they had taken no steps to emphasise to employees the importance of wearing boots with soles in good condition, but the decision was reversed on appeal. The employee knew why the boots were provided and he knew they would be replaced if the soles were worn. The Court of Appeal cited with approval a dictum from *Qualcast (Wolverhampton) Ltd v Haynes* that "there may be cases in which an employer does not discharge his duty of care towards his workmen merely by providing an article of safety equipment, but the courts should be circumspect in filling out that duty with the much vaguer obligation of encouraging, exhorting or instructing workmen or a particular workman to make regular use of what is provided."

8.43 However, it is submitted that the employer must not only provide the safety precautions, but also inform the employee of the relevant work risks involved. Thus in *Campbell v Lothian Health Board* the claimant was a cleaner in a hospital. She was provided with rubber gloves, but was not told about the risks from using detergents, or how these risks could be reduced by using the gloves provided. The employers were thus held liable when she contracted dermatitis.

8.44 (2) If the risk is that of a serious injury, then the duty of the employer is a higher one of doing all he can to ensure that the precautions are used. In *Nolan v Dental Manufacturing Co Ltd* a tool setter was injured when a chip flew off a grinding wheel. Because of the seriousness of the injury should one occur, it was held that the employers should have insisted that protective goggles should be worn.

8.45 (3) If the risk is an insidious one, or one the seriousness of which the employee would not readily appreciate, then again, it is the duty of the employer to do all he can by way of propaganda, constant reminders, exhortation, education, etc to try to get the employees to use the precautions. In *Berry v Stone Manganese and Marine Ltd* the claimant was working in an environment where the noise levels were dangerously high. Ear muffs had been provided, but little effort was made to ensure their use. It was held that the workmen would not readily appreciate the dangers of injury to their hearing if they did not use the ear muffs and the employers were liable for failing to take further steps to impress on the claimant the need to use the protective equipment.

8.46 (4) When the employer has done all he can do (and in the context of safety and health, this means doing a great deal), when he has laid down a safe system, provided the necessary safety precautions and equipment, instructed on their use, advised how they should be used properly, pointed out the risks involved if they are not used, and given constant reminders about their use, then he can do no more and he will be absolved from liability. Admittedly, this does not solve the problem, which is how to ensure that employees are protected from their own folly. Various ways of dealing with the enforcement of safety rules will be discussed in Chapter 9.

8.47 If an employee is working on the premises of another, the employer must still take reasonable care for that employee's safety. There may well be some limits to what he can do, but this does not absolve him from doing what he can. In particular, he must ensure that a safe system of working is laid down, give clear instructions as to how to deal with obvious dangers, and tell him to refuse to work if there is an obvious hazard. In *Wilson v Tyneside Window Cleaning Co* the claimant was a window cleaner who had, in the course of his employment over a period of ten years, cleaned certain windows at a brewery on a number of occasions. One day he pulled on a handle, which was rotten, and fell backwards, sustaining injuries. His claim against his employers failed. He knew the woodwork was rotten and he had been instructed not to clean windows if they were not safe. This may be contrasted with *General Cleaning Contractors Ltd v Christmas*, where in almost identical circumstances, the employee succeeded in his claim. The distinction appears to be that in *Christmas*, the employers provided safety belts, but there were certain premises where these could not be used and there was a failure to instruct the employees to test for defective sashes before the work could proceed. Further, the employers could have provided ladders or taken other steps to ensure that the work could be performed safely.

8.48 *Reasonably competent fellow employees.* Finally, if an employer engages an incompetent employee whose actions injure another employee, the employer will be liable for a failure to take reasonable care. In *Hudson v Ridge Manufacturing Co. Ltd* an employee was known for his habit of committing practical jokes. One day he carried one of his pranks too far and injured a fellow employee. The employer was held to be liable. The practical answer in such cases is, after due warning, to firmly dispense with the services of such a person, for he is a menace to himself and to others. On the other hand, an employer will not be liable if he has no reason to suspect that practical jokes are being played, for such acts are outside the scope of the employee's employment, and not done for the purpose of the employer's business (*Smith v Crossley Bros*). In *Coddington v International Harvester Co of Great Britain Ltd* an employee, for a joke, kicked a tin of burning thinner in the direction of another employee. The latter was scorched with flames and in the agony of the moment kicked the tin away so that it enveloped the claimant, causing him severe burns. The employers were held not liable. There was nothing in the previous conduct of the guilty employee to suggest that he might be a danger to others and his act was totally unconnected with his employment.

8.49 If an employer appoints an inexperienced person to perform highly dangerous tasks, he may be liable if through lack of experience another employee is injured (*Butler v Fife Coal Co*).

Proof of negligence

8.50 As a general rule, the burden is upon the claimant in an action to affirmatively prove his case. In other words, he must show that the defendant owed to him a duty to take care, that the defendant was in breach of that duty by being negligent and that as a result of that negligence the claimant suffered damage. To assist him in such an action, there are a number of rules of evidence and procedure, designed to enable each side to clarify the issues in dispute and to avoid surprises at the actual court of trial (see paragraph 7.217). Thus the court may make an order for inspection of the premises or machinery, it can order one party to disclose documents, records, etc to another, it can order that a party should make further and better particulars of his case, and so on. In *Waugh v British Railways Board* the claimant's widow sued for damages, alleging that the defendant's negligence caused the death of her husband. She sought the disclosure of an accident report which was prepared by the defendants partly for the purpose of establishing the cause of the accident and partly to assist their legal advisors to conduct the proceeding before the courts. The defendants resisted the disclosure on the ground of professional privilege, but it was held that the report should be disclosed. A document is only privileged if the dominant purpose of making it in the first place was for the purpose of legal proceedings. If the document had a dual purpose, it would not be covered by professional privilege. The implications of this case in practice can be very wide. Thus if an accident report is made as a result of an employee being away from work for more than three days because of an accident, it will not be privileged. If a safety officer makes a report of an accident, it will also not be privileged. However, once legal proceedings have been commenced, or are imminent, a report prepared for the exclusive use of the company's legal advisors would be privileged.

8.51   Further assistance can be obtained from the inspector under s.28(9) of HSWA which enables him to disclose any factual information about any accident to persons who are a party to any civil proceedings arising from the accident.

8.52   Another rule of evidence which may be of considerable assistance to a claimant is *res ipsa loquitor* (let the facts speak for themselves) (see Chapter 1). This will apply when the circumstances are such that an accident would not have occurred unless there had been some want of care by the defendant. Thus if a barrel of flour fell out of a building and injured a person walking below, the latter would find it extremely difficult to show that someone was negligent (*Byrne v Boadle*). In practice, he would not need to do so. He would invoke the rule *res ipsa loquitor*, barrels of flour do not normally fall out of buildings unless someone was negligent, and thus the burden of proof is thrown back to the other party to show that he had, in fact, taken reasonable care. *Res ipsa loquitor* is a rule of evidence, not a rule of law. It creates a rebuttable presumption that there was negligence. If the presumption is rebutted by evidence then the burden of proof is thrown back to the claimant to prove his claim in the usual way.

Defences to a common law action

8.53   Only one action may be brought against an employer in respect of injuries which arise out of one incident. The claimant, therefore, must plead his case in such a manner that all possible legal headings are covered. Thus, where appropriate, he should claim in respect of a breach of statutory duty and common law negligence, for each is a separate cause of action. The defendant, for his part, must also be prepared to defend each heading where liability is claimed.

8.54   Since there is no automatic right to compensation, the following defences may be raised.

Denial of negligence

8.55   The employer may deny that he has failed to take reasonable care, or claim that he did everything which a reasonable employer would have done in the circumstances (see *Latimer v AEC Ltd*, above). For example, in *Brown v Rolls Royce Ltd* the claimant contracted dermatitis owing to the use of an industrial oil. The employers did not provide a barrier cream on the advice of their chief medical officer, who doubted its efficacy. The employers were held not to be negligent in failing to provide the barrier cream. They were entitled to rely on the skilled judgment of a competent advisor and no more could be expected. Indeed, the medical officer had instituted his own preventative methods, as a result of which the incidence of dermatitis in the factory had steadily decreased.

8.56   An employer can only take reasonable care within the limits of the knowledge which he has or ought reasonably to have. After all, not every firm (particularly the smaller employer) can have available the resources of specialist expertise. Nonetheless, they must pay attention to current literature which may be available, either from their trade or employers' associations or from other sources. In *Graham v Co-operative Wholesale Society Ltd* the claimant worked in a furniture workshop where an electric sanding machine gave off a quantity of fine wood dust. This settled on his skin and caused dermatitis. No general precautions were taken against this, although the manager received all the information which was commonly circulated in the trade. It was held that the employers were not liable. They had fulfilled their duty to take reasonable care by keeping up to date with current knowledge, and were not to blame for not knowing something which only a specialist advisor would have known.

8.57   An employer will not be liable for an injury if he does not owe a duty of care to the injured person. In *Hewett v Alf Brown's Transport Ltd*, the claimant's husband was a lorry driver. He was employed to drive a lorry which contained lead oxide. While working he wore overalls and boots. When he returned home, the claimant would bang the overalls against a garden wall and bang or wipe his boots. While doing this she either inhaled lead oxide powder or came into contact with it. She was subsequently diagnosed as suffering from lead poisoning and sued her husband's employers for personal injuries suffered.

8.58   It was held that the action would be dismissed. It was accepted that if there was a foreseeable risk to the families of an employee from clothing, etc worn by the employee at work which became contaminated, then the employers owed a duty of care to those family members. However, in the circumstances of this case, the claimant's husband had not been exposed to any risk while removing the lead oxide waste from the site, and therefore the employers were not in breach of their duty to the claimant's husband either under the Control of Lead at Work Regulations 1980 or at common law. Consequently, there was no breach of duty to the claimant.

The sole fault of the employee

8.59   If it can be shown that the injury was the sole fault of the employee, again the employer will not be liable. In *Jones v Lionite Specialities (Cardiff) Ltd* a foreman became addicted to a chemical vapour from a tank. One weekend he was found dead, having fallen into the tank. The employers were not liable. In *Brophy v JC Bradfield* a lorry driver was found dead inside a boiler house, having been overcome by fumes. He had no reason to be there and the employers had no reason to suspect his presence. Again, they were not liable. And in *Horne v Lec Refrigeration Ltd* a tool setter had been fully instructed on the safety precautions to be followed when operating a machine, but was killed when he failed to operate the safety drill. The employers were held not liable, even though they were in breach of their statutory duty to ensure secure fencing.

8.60   If the claim is based on a breach of statutory duty, the employee cannot, by his own actions, put his employer in breach and then try to blame the employer for that breach. Provided the employer has done all that the statute requires him to do, ie provided the proper equipment, given training, provided adequate supervision, laid down safe systems, and so on, there will come a point when the injured workman will only have himself to blame. In *Ginty v Belmont Building Supplies Ltd* the claimant was working on a roof. He knew that it was in a defective state and that he should not work without boards. The employer provided the boards for use, but the claimant failed to use them and fell through the roof. It was held that the employers were not liable for his injuries. They had done all they could do, and the accident was the sole fault of the claimant.

8.61   In the nineteenth century the courts were inclined to the view that a worker accepted the risks which were inherent in the occupation and had to rely on his own skill and care, but this view was firmly discounted in the leading case of *Smith v Baker & Sons* and the defence of *volenti non fit injuria* (a person consents to the risk of being injured) is no longer applicable. The fact that the employee knows that there is a risk in the occupation does not mean that he consents to that risk because the employer has been negligent in failing to guard against it. This must apply, *a fortiori*, if the employer is under a statutory duty to guard against the risk. However, if the statutory duty is placed on the employee, and he disregards it, the employer is entitled to raise the defence of *volenti*. In *ICI Ltd v Shatwell*, the Quarries (Explosives) Regulations 1959 provided that no testing of an electrical circuit for shot firing should be done unless all persons in the vicinity had withdrawn to shelter. This duty, which was imposed in order to avoid risks from premature explosions, was laid on the employees. The employers had also prohibited such acts. Two employees were injured when they acted in breach of the regulations and the employers' instructions, and it was held that the employers could successfully raise the defence of *volenti*.

8.62   The payment of "danger money" to certain types of employees (eg stunt artistes) may indicate that there is an inherent risk in the occupation which cannot be adequately guarded against, but the real question to be asked is, was the employer negligent? Further, the Unfair Contract Terms Act 1977 states that a person cannot by reference to a contract term or prominently displayed notice exclude or restrict his liability for death or personal injury resulting from negligence.

8.63   In the 19th century there were reports of unscrupulous employers requiring their employees to sign "blood chits" which effectively excluded the employers from liability for injuries at work. Such signed waivers are virtually unknown today, but a problem does arise when the employer provides all the necessary health and safety precautions and/or equipment, and the employee deliberately refuses to use/wear them. As long as the employer has done all he can do, by way of encouragement, persuasion, provision of information, etc and complied with his common law and statutory duties, the employee would have no come-back if consequently he suffers an injury. An employer should keep any necessary records indicating the efforts made to ensure that compliance, and the employee's responses, and, if sued, plead *volenti non fit ijuria* as a defence.

Causation

8.64   Although the employer may be negligent, it must still be shown that the injury resulted from that negligence. If the injury would have happened had the employer not been negligent, then the breach of the duty to take care has not caused the damage (see *McWilliams v Sir William Arrol & Co Ltd*, see paragraph 8.16). Where a breach of statutory duty is alleged, the same principles apply. In *Bonnington Castings Ltd v Wardlaw* the claimant was subjected to a silica dust in premises where there was inadequate ventilation. It was held that the fact that there was a breach of statutory duty (to provide ventilation, Factories Act, s.4) and the fact that the employee suffered from pneumoconiosis did not by itself lead to the conclusion that the breach caused the injury. There must be sufficient evidence to link the one with the other. However, a more liberal view was taken in *Gardiner v Motherwell Machinery and Scrap Co Ltd* (see paragraph 1.123) where the court took the view that evidential presumptions may arise in such cases.

Contributory negligence

8.65   This defence is based on the Law Reform (Contributory Negligence) Act 1945 which provides that if a person is injured, partly because of his own fault, and partly due to the fault of another, damages shall be reduced to the extent the court thinks fit, having regard to the claimant's share in the responsibility for the damage. This defence is successfully raised in many cases. The employer will argue that even if he were negligent, the employee failed to take care for his own safety, and the court may well decide to reduce the damages awarded. There is no scientific basis for determining the percentage reduction and appeal courts may well take a different view of the apportionment of the blame between the parties.

Limitations of actions

8.66   Any action for personal injury or death must be commenced within three years from the date of the accident (Limitation Act 1980, s.11; Prescription and Limitations (Scotland) Act 1973). This means that the actual writ must be issued within the three year period, although the date of the court hearing may be considerably delayed thereafter. In accident cases the date of the incident is usually ascertainable, but in some circumstances, where the injury is a result of a constant exposure to the hazard, eg noise which causes deafness (*Berry v Stone Manganese and Marine Ltd*) or exposure to dangerous substances which can cause cancer (*Wright Cassidy v Dunlop Rubber Co Ltd*) or pneumoconiosis (*Cartwright v GKN Sankey Ltd*) it is not possible to fix a date, or the claimant will be unaware of the date. In such circumstances, the Limitation Act 1980, s.14 provides that the three year period shall begin to run from the date on which the cause of action accrued or the date when the claimant had knowledge of the fact that the injury was significant and that this was due to the employer's negligence. Knowledge in this connection means actual or constructive knowledge, ie knowledge which the claimant had or ought to have had. For example, if he has received medical advice which indicated an injury, he should know of the likely cause. The Act permits the court to exercise its discretion and allow the action to proceed even though it is outside the limitation period, if it is equitable to do so, having regard to the factors which brought about the delay, the effect it may have on the credibility of witnesses after such a period of time, the disability suffered by the claimant, and whether he acted promptly once he realised that he may have a cause of action having regard to any expert advice he may have received.

8.67   Thus in *Barrand v British Cellophane Ltd* the claimant alleged that he had suffered noise induced deafness through working in excessively noisy conditions between 1958 and 1980. He was aware of his condition from 1982, but did not start his legal action until 1990. The Court of Appeal thought that it was wrong for the trial judge to permit him to proceed with the action. The delay was entirely his fault, the defendants would be substantially prejudiced because of the passage of time, and it would have been inequitable to disapply the usual time limits.

8.68   A different conclusion was reached in *Irshad Ali v Courtlands Textiles Ltd*, where the claimant suffered exposure to excessive noise from 1969 to 1988. It was not until 1991 that he was told that his deafness could be work-related, and he obtained a medical report in 1992 which confirmed this. He issued proceedings in 1995. The trail judge held that his knowledge dated from 1991, and that proceedings were outside the limitation period, but the decision was reversed by the Court of Appeal. The claimant's personal circumstances were relevant. He spoke little English, and could not read or write either in English or his native language. He had no contact with his trade union, and he was thus isolated from potential knowledge. A suspicion that he might have had a cause of action was not enough to confer knowledge on him that he had a cause of action.

Damages

8.69   If an employee is killed in the course of his employment, an action may be brought by his personal representatives for the benefit of the estate of the deceased, under the provisions of the Law Reform (Miscellaneous Provisions) Act 1934. Damages will be awarded under the following heads:
   (a) loss of expectation of life (this is usually a fairly modest sum)
   (b) pain and suffering (if any) up to the time of death
   (c) loss of earnings up to the time of death.

8.70   A further action may be brought simultaneously by his dependants for their own benefit under the Fatal Accidents Act 1976 based on the loss of financial support suffered by, for example, his wife, children or other dependants. Any other money due to the estate is not taken into account, eg personal insurances, pensions payable to the widow, etc but any award made under the 1934 Act will be taken into account. In other words, the one action is brought for the benefit of the deceased estate, the other for the benefit of his family dependants. The two claims are invariably settled together.

8.71 The quantum of damages awarded is frequently a matter of speculation. No amount of money can compensate for the loss of a faculty (arm, leg, eyesight, etc) but the courts must try to do their best and awards will take account of inflation, the permanency of the injury, the effect of earning capacity, additional expenses incurred, and so on.

Rights against insurers

8.72 In normal circumstances, any damages awarded to an injured employee would be paid by the employer's insurance company. If the employer is no longer in business (eg because he has died, gone bankrupt or gone into liquidation, etc) then, provided his liability has been established, it is possible to pursue a claim against the insurance company under the provisions of the Third Parties (Rights against Insurers) Act 1930. But if, at the time of the claim, the employer's liability has not been established, this is not possible. For example, in *Bradley v Eagle Star Insurance Co Ltd*, the claimant claimed that she contracted byssinosis whilst working in a mill from 1933 to 1970. The employer company had been dissolved in 1976, but her claim was not made until 1984. It was not possible to resurrect the company in order to establish liability and hence her claim failed.

8.73 However, by s.141 of the Companies Act 1989 (which amends s.651 of the Companies Act 1985) it is possible to make an application to have a company re-registered and its dissolution declared void. Once this is done the action may be proceeded with in the normal way and if liability is shown, the insurance company (who will in any case be the real defendant) will be obliged to pay any damages awarded.

Vicarious liability

8.74 The tort of vicarious liability arises when one person (who has not committed a wrongful act) is legally liable for the acts of another person which cause injury or damage to a third person. Of course the actual wrongdoer is always personally liable, but in practice he is unlikely to have sufficient financial resources to meet any claim and so the injured party will seek to make the first person vicariously liable.

There are two general circumstances to consider: (a) the liability of an employer for the wrongful acts of his employees which are committed in the course of their employment, and (b) the liability of the employer for the acts of an independent contractor.

8.75 The general principle is that an employer will be liable for the acts of his employee which injure a third party if the employee, when doing the act, was acting in the course of his employment, in the sense that he was doing that which he was employed to do. Thus in *Century Insurance Co v Northern Ireland Road Transport Board*, an employee was the driver of a petrol tanker. While he was discharging petrol at a garage forecourt, he lit a cigarette and the subsequent explosion caused damage to the garage. It was held that the employer was liable. The act (of lighting a cigarette) was a negligent way of doing that which he was employed to do, namely to discharge petrol from the tanker, and he was therefore still acting in the course of his employment.

8.76 The act can be in the course of employment even though the employee was not authorised to do it. In *Kay v ITW Ltd* a fork-lift truck driver found that the path was obstructed by a lorry. Although he was not authorised to do so, he drove it out of the way and in so doing injured a fellow employee. Again, the employer was held liable, for the act was for the purpose of the employer's business.

8.77 If the employer expressly prohibits an employee from doing something, this will not necessarily remove the act from the course of the employment. In *Rose v Plenty* the employer prohibited milkmen from permitting children to ride on milk floats. In breach of this instruction a milkman engaged a young boy to help him deliver and collect milk bottles and as a result of negligent driving by the milkman the boy was injured. It was held that the employer, nonetheless, was liable, for the act (of permitting a boy to ride on the vehicle) was done for the purpose of the employer's business, and hence was still within the scope of employment. But in *Conway v George Wimpey Ltd* the employers issued an instruction to their drivers that no person other than a fellow employee was to be permitted to ride as a passenger in their lorries. In breach of this instruction, a driver gave a lift to a hitchhiker, who was injured following an accident. It was held that the employers were not liable, for the express prohibition had taken the act (of giving lifts) outside the scope of the employment and it had nothing to do with the employers' business.

8.78 If an employee does an act which is unauthorised or prohibited, it has been suggested that the test may well be, would a reasonable man consider that the act was part and parcel of the employee's employment, or was it so divergent from it as to be alien from it? In the former case, the employer would be vicariously liable for the act, in the latter case he would not (see *Harrison v Michelin Tyre Co Ltd*).

8.79 An employee may be acting in the course of his employment even if he is outside working hours or away from the employer's premises. In *Poland v John Parr & Sons* an employee was going home from work when he saw a boy trying to steal property from the employer's lorry. The employee struck the boy a hard blow, causing serious injury. It was held that the employer was liable, for the employee was acting in what he believed to be the employer's interests by protecting his property, even though his methods were somewhat over-enthusiastic.

8.80 But excessive zeal or force may take the act outside the course of the employment. In *Warren v Henley's Garage Ltd* a garage forecourt attendant had a violent argument with a customer and committed an assault on him. The employers were held not liable, for this was not part of his duties and the employee was pursuing a personal vendetta. Similarly, in *Hilton v Thomas Burton (Rhodes) Ltd* some workers were driven to a building site in the firm's lorry. After working for a short time, they made a journey in the lorry to a nearby pub and this was repeated several times during the day. As they were being driven back from the pub the claimant's husband was killed following a road accident, caused by the fault of the driver of the lorry. The employer was held not liable, for it could not be said that while driving to and from the pub the driver was acting in the course of his employment.

8.81 If an employee is travelling to and from work in a vehicle (whether or not provided by his employer) he will be acting in the course of his employment if, at the material time, he is going about his employer's business. The duty to turn up to work must not be confused with being on duty while travelling to work. In *Smith v Stages and Darlington Insulation Co*, the House of Lords laid down a series of propositions.
1. An employee travelling to work is not generally in the course of his employment, but if he is obliged by his contract of employment to

use the employer's transport he will normally be regarded as being in the course of his employment while doing so.

2. Travelling in the employer's time between workplaces, or in the course of a peripatetic occupation will be in the course of employment.

3. Receipt of wages (but not a travelling allowance) will indicate that the employee is travelling in the employer's time and for his benefit and will be in the course of employment, and the fact that the employee has a discretion as to the mode and time of travelling will not generally affect this.

4. An employee travelling in his employer's time from his ordinary residence to a workplace other than his regular place of work or in the course of a peripatetic occupation or to the scene of an emergency will be acting in the course of his employment.

5. A deviation or interruption of the journey (unless merely incidental to the journey) will, for the time being, take the employee out of the course of his employment. Thus if the employee is driving in the course of his employment, and then departs from his normal route, he will be engaged "on a frolic of his own" (*Storey v Ashton*), and once he seeks to rejoin his normal route, it is a question of fact and degree as to whether or not he is in the course of his employment.

6. Return journeys are to be treated on the same footing as outward journeys.

8.82　These propositions are always subject to any express arrangements which may be made between the employer and employee, and do not always apply to salaried employees, with regard to whom the touchstone of payment made in the employee's time is not generally significant.

8.83　An employer is not generally liable for the wrongful acts of an independent contractor. The main difficulty here is to distinguish between an independent contractor and an employee, the former being employed under a contract *for* services, the latter employed under a contract *of* service. However, an employer may be liable (a) if he authorises the act, (b) if the independent contractor is carrying out a hazardous activity over which the employer has some control (see *Holliday v National Telephone Co*), (c) if he co-ordinates or controls the activities of a number of independent contractors (*McArdle v Andmac Roofing Co*) or (d) if he fails to show that he has exercised reasonable care in the selection of a competent contractor (*McTeare v Dooley*).

8.84   The reality of the situation is frequently to decide which insurance company is going to pay the damages. In road accidents, the dispute will usually be between one company holding the employers' liability insurance and another company holding the road traffic insurance; so far as independent contractors are concerned, the dispute will usually be between the insurance companies holding the respective employers' liability insurance. However, there are many situations which occur when one (or neither) of the parties will be insured and liability must be established in accordance with the above principles.

Liability of others

8.85   Hitherto we have considered the liability of an employer for his failure to take reasonable care for the health and safety of his employees. There are, additionally, a number of other people who are not employers, but who may, in the particular circumstances of the case, owe a duty of care to ensure that another person (including, for our purposes, the employees of an employer) is not injured or does not suffer damage. This is merely a further application of the general law of negligence. Sometimes, the injured party will sue the employer and the other alleged wrongdoer jointly, leaving it to the court to apportion blame and responsibility accordingly. For example, in *Driver v William Willett (Contractors) Ltd*, a building contractor engaged a firm of safety consultants to advise on safety requirements and compliance with the relevant regulations. They failed to advise the employers to discontinue the unsafe use of a hoist, with the result that an employee was injured. He sued his employers and the safety consultant. The former were held to be 40% to blame for the accident, the latter 60%. Further, the employers were entitled to recover from the safety consultants the sum which they were liable to pay the injured employee.

8.86   This principle can be extended to other circumstances, eg a main contractor who employs a number of subcontractors (*McArdle v Andmac Roofing*, see paragraph 8.23), manufacturers who fail to provide adequate and meaningful information about the dangers associated with their products (*Cook v Englehard Industries Ltd*), occupiers of premises, and so on. As Lord McMillan stated in *Donoghue v Stevenson* "the categories of negligence are never closed".

Occupiers' liability

8.87   At common law, an occupier of premises owed legal duties to those people who came on to his premises, but the extent of those duties varied in accordance with the legal status which was ascribed to them, ie contractual invitee, invitee, licensee, etc. Because of the unnecessary legal complications which arose, the common law rules were swept away by the Occupiers' Liability Act 1957, which introduced a common duty of care to all lawful visitors (see also Occupiers' Liability (Scotland) Act 1960).

8.88   The Act provides that an occupier is to take such care in all the circumstances as is reasonable to ensure that a visitor will be reasonably safe in using the premises for the purposes for which he was invited or permitted to be there.

8.89   However, it was recognised that a person exercising his calling would be expected to appreciate risks ordinarily incidental to the work (eg a window cleaner, see *General Cleaning Contractors Ltd v Christmas*, see paragraph 8.47). An occupier must expect children to be less careful than adults, and if he puts up some form of warning, this will not discharge his legal duty unless in all the circumstances it is sufficient. As a general rule, an occupier is not liable for the risks which have been created by an independent contractor.

8.90   The position with regard to trespassers was left unaltered by the Act, the common law rule being that the occupier owed no duty of care to such persons. However, in *British Railways Board v Herrington*, the House of Lords held that if an occupier knew that trespassers were on the land, and knew of physical facts in relation to the land which would constitute a serious risk to those trespassers, he would owe a duty to take reasonable steps to enable the trespasser to avoid the danger. Common humanity dictated that the occupier should not ignore the problem.

8.91   Following *Herrington's* case, Parliament passed the Occupiers' Liability Act 1984, which provides that an occupier of premises owes a duty to trespassers if:

   (a) he knows there is a risk because of the state of the premises
   (b) he knows the trespasser will be on the premises, and
   (c) the risk was one which the occupier could reasonably be expected to provide some protection against.

State insurance benefits

8.92   An employed person who is injured at work may make a claim for financial assistance under the scheme which is now contained in the Social Security Contributions and Benefits Act 1992 and the regulations made thereunder. Statutory sick pay will be payable for the first 28 weeks, followed by incapacity benefit under the provisions of the Social Security (Incapacity for Work) Act 1994. Entitlement to incapacity benefit is assessed on the claimant's ability to carry out a range of work-related functions, such as walking, bending, carrying, etc and other mental, sensory and physical activities. A medical assessment, based on a points system, will be made of the claimant's ability to do any kind of work for which a reasonable employer would be prepared to pay a reasonable wage. The right to claim is independent of any right of action which may or may not exist at common law for negligence or breach of statutory duty, or indeed any other remedy, for the state scheme is a form of insurance policy, paid for partly by contributions from the employer and employee. Further, questions of fault, blame, contributory conduct, etc are irrelevant to the issue of claiming benefits, provided the employee is within the scope of the relevant provisions.

Industrial injuries

8.93   The basic outline of the industrial injuries scheme is to provide compensation for a person who suffers a personal injury caused by accident arising out of and in the course of his employment (Social Security Contributions and Benefits Act 1992, s.94), or a prescribed disease or personal injury due to the nature of that employment (s.108). Provided certain criteria are met, a claimant may be able to claim certain benefits.

Prescribed diseases and injuries

8.94   A person who suffers from a prescribed disease or injury, which is a disease or injury due to the nature of the employment, is also entitled to claim benefits under the Act. The disease or injury must be one which has been prescribed as such by the Secretary of State (Social Security (Industrial Injuries) (Prescribed Diseases) Regulations 1985, as variously amended), if he is satisfied that it ought to be treated as a risk of the occupation (and not just a risk common to all employments) and that it is attributable to the nature of the employment (s.108).

8.95   There is a presumption that if the employee works in the prescribed employment and he contracts the prescribed disease or suffers the prescribed injury, the disease or injury will be regarded as being due to the nature of the employment unless the contrary is proved (s.109).

8.96   The Secretary of State may also make special provision by regulations for cases of pneumoconiosis which is accompanied by tuberculosis, emphysema and chronic bronchitis, and for occupational deafness and byssinosis.

Benefits under the Act

8.97   A considerable number of changes have been made to the industrial injuries benefits which were formerly payable under the Social Security Act 1975. Benefits which have been abolished include industrial injury benefit (replaced by incapacity benefit), death benefit, unemployability supplement, and so on. As from 13 April 1995, sickness and invalidity benefits have been replaced by "incapacity" benefit. Claimants receiving either of the two former benefits will be automatically transferred to the new benefit. Special hardship allowance was replaced by reduced earnings allowance and this too is no longer payable in respect of accidents or claims which occur after 1 October 1990. Certain benefits already granted will continue to be paid, but, so far as new claims are concerned, there are only three benefits payable, namely, disablement benefit, constant attendance allowance and exceptionally severe disablement allowance.

8.98   (1) Disablement benefit (s.103). This is payable as a pension if as a result of the relevant accident or prescribed disease there is a loss of a physical or mental faculty amounting to not less than 14%. The assessment of the extent of the disability, and questions as to whether the disability results from the relevant accident or employment are to be determined by the medical authorities. The pension is payable after 15 weeks from the date of the accident.

8.99   (2) Constant Attendance Allowance (s.104). If there is a 100% loss of a faculty, so that the claimant requires constant attendance, a constant attendance allowance is payable.

8.100   (3) If constant care allowance is paid at the maximum rate, and the claimant is likely to be permanently in need of attendance, then exceptionally severe disablement allowance is payable (s.105).

Claims for benefit

8.101   These will be dealt with initially by the local insurance officer. There is a right of appeal from his decision to the local Social Security Appeal Tribunal, to which matters may also be referred by the insurance officer. An appeal will then lie to the commissioner. Certain matters may be referred by the insurance officer direct to the Secretary of State.

8.102   Questions which relate to disablement pensions, such as whether or not the applicant has lost a faculty or the degree of disability are referred to the medical board, with a right of appeal to a medical appeal tribunal.

Other legal remedies

8.103   An employee who is injured by an act which amounts to a criminal offence on the part of some person may find that he is unable to sue his employer for compensation, for the employer will not have broken any legal duty towards him.

8.104   By way of example, we may cite the case of *Charlton v Forrest Printing Ink Co*, where the claimant was a manager at the defendants' works. One of his duties was to collect the wages from the bank. In 1974 there was an unsuccessful attempt to snatch the wages and thus the managing director gave instructions to those who were to collect the wages that they should take precautions, such as varying the route taken each week, using different modes of transport and sending different people. Despite these instructions, a pattern of collection tended to develop. In 1977, when the claimant was returning from the bank, he was attacked by bandits who threw ammonia into his face, causing severe damage to his eyesight. He claimed damages from his employers, arguing that they had failed to take reasonable care for his safety. In the High Court, the judge accepted the argument that although the sum of money involved was only small (£1500), in view of the previous robbery, it would have been reasonable to use a professional security firm for this task and hence the employers were in breach of their common law duty to take sensible precautions to protect employees who were involved in a hazardous task. This decision was reversed by the Court of Appeal. Proper steps had been taken to instruct the employees to vary their methods used for collecting the wages. It was unreasonable to expect the employers to guard against a possibility which would not influence the mind of a reasonable man. Statistics showed that the majority of firms of this size did not employ specialist security firms. Hence, the employers were not negligent. However, Lord Denning went on to point out that the applicant would no doubt have a good claim if he applied to the Criminal Injuries Compensation Board.

8.105   Formerly, a claim for compensation in respect of injuries caused by a criminal offence could be made to the Criminal Injuries Compensation Board, but the Board has now been abolished, and has been replaced by a new Authority, following the enactment of the Criminal Injuries Compensation Act 1995. Under the new scheme, if a person suffers a personal injury directly attributable to a crime of violence, or while trying to arrest an offender, he will be able to receive compensation on a scale laid down in a predetermined tariff, ranging from £1000 to £250,000, according to the nature of the injury. There will also be additional payments for special expenses and loss of earnings or earning capacity, for those who are incapacitated for more than 28 weeks, and dependency and support provisions if death results. The award will initially be made by a claims officer, from whose decision there is a right of appeal to an independent Adjudicator. Certain types of injury, eg traffic accidents, are excluded from the scheme.

8.106   Another type of scheme is operated by the Motor Insurers' Bureau, which was set up in 1969 by an agreement between insurance companies and the Ministry of Transport. If a person suffers death or injury arising out of the use of a motor vehicle, and he is unable to trace the person responsible, or the person responsible is unable to pay compensation (usually because he is uninsured), then the board will accept the liability to compensate the injured party, the damages to be assessed in a like manner as a court applying the normal legal principles would assess. In practice, the bureau nominates an insurance company to accept the risk and the latter will then seek to recover the damages paid (insofar as they are able to do so) from the wrongdoer.

8.107   The Pneumoconiosis, etc (Workers' Compensation) Act 1979 provides for lump sum payments to be made to persons who are disabled by industrial lung diseases (pneumoconiosis, byssinosis and diffuse mesothelioma). The conditions are that the claimant must be entitled to disablement benefit under the Social Security Contributions and Benefits Act 1992 (paragraph 8.98), he must be unable to recover damages from his employer because the latter has gone out of business and no legal action has been brought or compromised. This scheme is an interesting example of the state providing compensation to injured workers in circumstances where tort liability claims would not be met. A similar scheme for victims of pneumoconiosis has been in force on a voluntary basis for coal miners since 1974 and is operated by the National Coal Board.

8.108 Finally, under the Powers of Criminal Courts Act 1973, the criminal courts (including magistrates' courts) are empowered to make an award of compensation to a person who has been injured or suffered any loss or damage as a result of the commission of a criminal offence. This is in addition to any other punishment which the court may impose. The maximum amount of compensation which may be awarded is (currently) £5000. Thus, in strict theory, if an employer was prosecuted for an offence under HSWA or other legislation for an offence which caused personal injury or damage to an employee's property, the latter could apply to the court for a compensation order to be made at the same time. Indeed, the court can make such an order on its own volition. If the injured person subsequently brings civil proceedings, any compensation awarded in the criminal court will be taken into account. Although this is a useful provision for dealing with claims in respect of minor personal injuries, very little use appears to have been made of it.

CHAPTER 9

Enforcing health and safety rules

9.1   The duty to ensure that health and safety policies are observed falls on all those who are involved in the work processes on the employer, management, safety officer, shop steward, safety representative, supervisor, and employees generally. Each must play his own special role in ensuring that health and safety policies are laid down, adequately promulgated, and, perhaps the most important of all, carried out in practice.

9.2   The basis for these duties is the contract of employment, which is essentially mutual agreement. It follows that a breach of contract by either side entitles the other party to pursue whatever remedy is appropriate in the circumstances. Thus, on the one hand, if the employee commits a breach of contract, the employer may terminate the contract and in theory at any rate sue for any damage he has suffered. On the other hand, there is an implied term of the contract that the employer will take reasonable care to ensure the health and safety of his employees while at work (*Matthews v Kuwait Bechtel Corporation*); if he is in breach of that term the employee may "accept" the breach and resign (this is the doctrine of constructive dismissal). If he has suffered damages, he may claim in respect of these. Additionally, if the employer's breach has caused injury, he may sue in tort for a breach of duty imposed by law (see Chapter 8).

Appointment procedures

9.3   Health and safety policies begin with appointment procedures. In theory, the employer should ensure that all his employees are fit and healthy and not suffering from any disability which renders them liable to an accident which would make them a hazard to the safety of themselves or to others. To this aim, pre-employment medicals may be used.

9.4   A medical practitioner retained by an employer to carry out a pre-employment medical assessment owes no duty of care to a job applicant when assessing that person's suitability for employment, because there is no proximity of relationship such as to give rise to a duty of care. Consequently, a disappointed job applicant, who is refused employment as a result of a doctor carrying out an independent medical examination on behalf of an employer, cannot claim damages from that doctor for negligence (*Kapfunde v Abbey National plc*).

9.5   Pre-medical screening must be related to a particular hazard. Judgment must be made on medical and safety grounds, not on the ground of general health. Epileptics can do a useful job of work, depending on the degree of their illness and the nature of the danger they face at work. Disabled employees can do work other than act as car park attendants, if the work is matched to their abilities and care is taken to ensure their safety. Dedication to health and safety does not mean the exclusion of a large section of the population from employment opportunities. The provisions of the Disability Discrimination Act 1995 (see paragraph 7.88) must also be borne in mind by those responsible for making appointments. Thus the object of pre-medical employment must not be to exclude certain people, but to place employees in the appropriate niche.

9.6   Nonetheless, critical situations may require extreme measures. In *Jeffries v BP Tankers Ltd* it was the company's policy not to employ people as radio operators on ships if they had had any history of cardiac disease. They dismissed a radio officer who had suffered a heart attack, even though he had made an excellent recovery. His dismissal was held to be fair, for the policy was one which had to be rigorously enforced for reasons which the employers were satisfied were necessary.

9.7   Health considerations are equally relevant. In *Panesar v Nestlé Co. Ltd* the claimant, who was a Sikh, enquired about a job with the respondents. He was told that there was a company rule prohibiting beards, and since he was not prepared to shave off his beard he was not interviewed for the job. He claimed that he had been unlawfully discriminated against on grounds of race (see Race Relations Act 1976, s.4). It was conceded that he had been indirectly discriminated against, in that the proportion of applicants of his race who could comply with the requirement that they should not wear a beard was smaller than the proportion of applicants from other racial groups (Race Relations Act, s.1(1)(b)). However, the requirement or condition was capable of being justified on grounds other than race, namely hygiene considerations and his claim failed before the employment tribunal, the EAT and the Court of Appeal. It should be noted that it would be discriminatory on grounds of race to refuse employment to (or to dismiss from employment) a Sikh who refuses to wear a head protection helmet on a building site, as long as he is wearing a turban (see paragraph 6.339).

Works rules

9.8   A rule book is a valuable source of information and guidance, and should in particular lay down precise rules concerning all aspects of health, safety and welfare. The contents of the rule book should be incorporated into the contract of employment, they should be updated in accordance with developments and experience and should be contained in a booklet which can be retained by the employee. Somewhat strangely, s.1 of the Employment Rights Act 1996 (which requires employers to give to their employees written particulars of their terms and conditions of employment) includes a requirement to provide information relating to disciplinary and grievance procedures, but specifically states that this does not apply to rules, disciplinary decisions, grievances or procedures relating to health or safety at work. This exclusion is even more surprising when it is realised that health and safety matters probably constitute the biggest single cause of disciplinary problems. It is to be hoped that this gap in the law is remedied in the near future. However, the Code of Practice issued by the Advisory Conciliation and Arbitration Service (ACAS) entitled *Disciplinary Practice and Procedures in Employment* states that "When drawing up rules the aim should be to specify clearly and concisely those necessary for the efficient and safe performance of work."

9.9   Particular attention should be paid to publicising the contents of the rule book to new employees on some form of induction course. Those rules which are mandatory can be highlighted and disciplinary procedures and sanctions which will follow a breach can be spelt out. Attention can be paid to ways of communicating the rules to immigrant employees and others whose command of English is less than perfect, so that they are unable to plead ignorance. Records can be kept of when and how the rules were communicated to each individual concerned.

9.10   Rules which relate to health and safety are designed to protect employees individually and collectively and should therefore contain sanctions in the event of a breach. The matter was expressed forcefully by Stephenson LJ in *Bux v Slough Metals Ltd*, when he said "The employer must make the law of the land the rule of the factory". In other words, the employee should be informed as to the legal requirements and warned that he is breaking the law if he fails to wear or use the precautions provided, for which he can be prosecuted. He can also be warned that he faces disciplinary action or even dismissal if he acts in breach of the safety rules or the legal requirements.

9.11   To achieve consistency in procedure, certain principles must be observed. First, the rules must be promulgated. This means that they must be brought to the attention of the employees in a suitable form. It is no longer regarded as being sufficient to post rules on a notice board or hide them in the personnel office. In *Pitts v Rivertex Ltd*, the employee was dismissed for breaking a works rule, a copy of which could be found on the notice board. It was held that if a rule was so important that a breach would be visited by instant dismissal, it should have been expressly communicated to all the employees concerned.

9.12   Second, rules must be reasonable. An employer may impose his own standards, but they must have a sound functional basis and not be old-fashioned, out-of-date or based on prejudice. In *Talbot v Hugh M Fulton Ltd* the applicant was dismissed for having long hair in breach of the company's rules. The dismissal was held to be unfair. Management did not specify the length of hair which was acceptable, it was not shown that long hair was a safety hazard and the rule did not appear to apply to women with long hair. Clearly, it was an act of prejudice against the hair style of the day. By contrast, we can cite *Marsh v Judge International*, where a youth had hair which was two feet six inches long, reaching down to his waist. The factory inspector told the employers that they would be prosecuted if the youth caught his hair in any machinery and was injured, and so, after due warnings to cut his hair (which he ignored) the youth was dismissed. This was held to be fair. The rule, in the nature of an instruction, was perfectly reasonable and in the interests of safety. It follows that an employer can lay down suitable safety standards provided they are functional and reasonable (*Singh v Lyons Maid Ltd*).

9.13   Third, the rules must be consistently enforced. If a rule is generally disregarded, or no severe sanction is imposed for a breach, then it may be unfair to act on it without giving some indication that there was to be a change in enforcement policy. Thus in *Bendall v Paine and Betteridge* the applicant had been employed for fifteen years. From time to time he was told to put out a cigarette he was smoking, as there was a fire risk. One day, he was summarily dismissed for smoking and this was held to be unfair. In the past he had been warned without it being brought home to him that he was risking instant dismissal. He should have been given a final, written warning before he was dismissed.

9.14 Health and safety rules should therefore be drawn up in accordance with the hazards perceived. This requires a careful assessment of the likely risks, based on the nature of the firm, its processes, the workforce, and all other relevant considerations. The following are some examples of the more common rules which should be considered.

Smoking

9.15 If there is a risk of fire (*Bendall v Paine and Betteridge*) or a health hazard (*Unkles v Milanda Bread Co*), clear rules should be laid down informing employees that anyone caught smoking in the prohibited area will be instantly dismissed. Areas where smoking is permitted should be clearly defined. Additionally, the employer must pay attention to the statutory provisions which prohibit smoking. These include:

(a)	Celluloid Regulations 1921	no person shall be allowed to smoke in any room in which celluloid is manufactured, manipulated or stored
(b)	Control of Lead at Work Regulations 1998	an employer shall take such steps as are adequate to ensure that employees do not smoke in any place which is or likely to be contaminated with lead; there is also a prohibition on employees smoking in any place which an employer has reason to believe is contaminated with lead
(c)	Manufacture of Cinematograph Film Regulations 1928	no person shall take any smoking materials into any room in which cinematograph film is manufactured, repaired, manipulated or used
(d)	Cinematograph Film Stripping Regulations 1939	no smoking materials shall be allowed in any part of the premises

(e)	Highly Flammable Liquids and Liquefied Petroleum Gases Regulations 1972	no smoking shall be permitted when flammable liquids are present. The occupier shall take all reasonable practicable steps to ensure compliance, including the display of a clear and bold notice
(f)	Factories (Testing of Aircraft Engines and Accessories) Special Regulations 1952	no smoking shall be allowed in any place where aircraft engines are being tested
(g)	Control of Asbestos at Work Regulations 1987 (as amended)	employees should not smoke in any "designated asbestos area"
(h)	Gas Safety (Installation and Use) Regulations 1998	no person shall smoke in any area designated as a controlled area
(i)	Ionising Radiations Regulations 1999	no employee shall smoke in any area designated as a controlled area
(j)	Magnesium (Grinding of Castings and other articles) Special Regulations 1946	no smoking shall be permitted within 20 feet of certain processes or in any room where magnesium dust is being kept, or smoke when handling magnesium dust
(k)	Explosives Act 1875, s.10	smoking is prohibited
(l)	Control of Substances Hazardous to Health Regulations 1999	smoking is prohibited in areas contaminated by carcinogens.

9.16 Several other relevant statutory provisions were repealed by the COSHH Regulations. For the introduction of a "No Smoking" policy, see paragraph 7.43. Note also the Workplace (Health, Safety and Welfare) Regulations 1992 which require that rest rooms and rest areas shall include suitable arrangements to protect non-smokers from discomfort caused by tobacco smoke (see paragraph 6.46).

Eating and drinking

9.17   The following provisions prohibiting the partaking of food or drink are in force:

(a)	Control of Lead at Work Regulations 1998	an employee shall not eat or drink in any place which he has reason to believe to be contaminated by lead
(b)	Control of Asbestos at Work Regulations 1987 (as amended)	employees should not eat or drink in any "designated asbestos area"
(c)	Ionising Radiations Regulations 1999	no employee shall eat or drink in any area designated as a "controlled area"
(d)	Control of Substances Hazardous to Health Regulations 1999	eating and drinking is prohibited in areas contaminated by carcinogens

Fighting

9.18   This can lead to a serious accident occurring, and the rule should lay down that anyone caught fighting will be subject to disciplinary proceedings. It cannot be right to state that fighting will lead to instant dismissal; after all, if two people are fighting, one may be merely defending himself, or the one who started the fight may have been provoked. A careful investigation of the circumstances is therefore called for. Further, two people may be fighting in a no-risk area, which may invoke a disciplinary sanction less than dismissal. The rule, therefore, should indicate the discretionary power of management. In *Taylor v Parsons Peebles Ltd*, the applicant had been employed for twenty years by the company before he was dismissed after he was involved in a fight. It was the company's policy to dismiss automatically any employee who deliberately struck another employee. The employment tribunal held that the dismissal was fair, because the policy was applied consistently and the other employee who was fighting was also dismissed. On appeal, the decision was reversed by the EAT. In determining whether a decision to dismiss was reasonable, the proper test was not the employer's policy, but what the reaction would be of a reasonable employer in the circumstances. The employers' rules of conduct must be considered in the light of how it would be applied by a reasonable employer. Taking into account the fact that the employee had been employed for twenty years with no serious disciplinary record against him, a reasonable employer would not have applied the rigid sanction of automatic dismissal. In other words, the employer must be consistent in his procedures, but flexible in his punishment. He must consider the gravity of the offence, and the circumstances of the offender. The employee must always be given at least an opportunity to plead mitigating circumstances, although the weight to be attached to such a plea is for the employer to decide, bearing in mind the gravity of the incident. In the *Taylor* case, because the employers had applied a policy consistently without taking into account relevant factors, the dismissal was unfair. However, it was also held that the employee had contributed towards his dismissal, and compensation was reduced by 25%.

Drunkenness

9.19   If an employee is found to be drunk on the premises or to have been drinking alcohol, it may be good policy to escort him off the premises, for the fact of drinking *per se* may not be sufficient to warrant dismissal (*McGibbon v Gillespie Building Co*). However, disciplinary proceedings should normally be instituted. If the drunkenness is such as to cause or constitute a serious safety hazard, different considerations would apply. In these circumstances, the matter should be dealt with as a serious disciplinary offence and the procedure should be activated immediately. In *Abercrombie v Alexander Thomson & Son* the claimant was found to be in an intoxicated state while in charge of a crane. A decision was taken to dismiss him, but this was not implemented until two weeks had elapsed, during which time he was permitted to carry on working. The dismissal was held to be unfair. By delaying the taking of action, the employers had condoned the offence.

9.20   A person who has symptoms of alcoholism should not be put through the disciplinary procedure immediately. Rather, his condition should be treated as an illness, and medical advice should be sought as to his condition and the likelihood of recovery or obtaining treatment.

9.21   There are some statutory provisions which also need to be borne in mind. These include the Work in Compressed Air Regulations 1996 (no person employed shall consume alcohol whilst in compressed air).

There are a number of regulations which prohibit the consumption of food and drink whilst engaged in certain processes, and these could certainly cover drinking alcohol (see above).

Skylarking

9.22 The dangers from employees who indulge in horseplay or skylarking have already been noted (see Chapter 8 and see *Harrison v Michelin Tyre Co Ltd*), and the rules should state that such conduct will not be tolerated. Employees, particularly the young or inexperienced, should be given final written warnings, indicating that any repetition will result in instant dismissal. In *Hudson v Ridge Manufacturing Co Ltd* the plaintiff was injured as a result of a prank played upon him by an employee who was known for horseplay. The employers were held to be liable. It was stated that "If a fellow workman by his habitual conduct is likely to prove a source of danger to his fellow employees, a duty lies fairly and squarely on the employer to remove the source of danger."

Breach of safety rules

9.23 Again, this will be dealt with in accordance with the hazard incurred. In *Martin v Yorkshire Imperial Metals* the claimant tied down a lever on an automatic lathe with a piece of wire. This had the effect of bypassing the safety device, for the machine could only be used if the operator used both hands. It was held that his dismissal was fair. He knew that he would be dismissed if he neglected to use the safety device. In *Ashworth v John Needham & Sons* the claimant acted in flagrant breach of safety rules by putting a fence around a hole in the ground instead of replacing a plate. After the matter had been discussed with the company's safety officer and a trade union official he was dismissed. This was held to be fair, as a serious accident could have happened.

Failure to use safety equipment

9.24 Again, the gravity of the consequences should be a factor which determines the severity of the sanction and the rules should be flexible enough to deal with this situation. Thus in *Frizzell v Flanders* the employee was provided with a gas mask while working in a tank. He was seen working without the mask and was dismissed. This was held to be fair. It was essential to enforce rigorously the use of safety equipment. On the other hand, in *Henry v Vauxhall Motors Ltd* the employee discovered that his safety helmet was missing. He was provided with another one which, he claimed, was uncomfortable. He therefore worked without the helmet and persisted in his refusal after being instructed to wear it by the foreman. He was dismissed, but this was held to be unfair. There was no proper enquiry into the reasons for his refusal. Nonetheless, the employment tribunal thought that he had contributed substantially to his dismissal and reduced his compensation award by 60%.

Hygiene observance

9.25   It may be necessary to enforce standards of hygiene because there is a risk of contamination to the product or a health hazard to employees. For example, in *Gill v Walls Meat Co*, the claimant, who was a Sikh, was employed to work with open meat. He did not have a beard at the time he commenced employment, but at some later stage he grew a beard. He was subsequently told that he could not be employed on that particular job whilst wearing his beard, but he refused to shave it off. He was offered alternative employment where he would be permitted to have his beard, but he refused and was dismissed. This was held to be fair. Similarly, the rules should provide that employees who have been suffering from or in contact with a contagious disease should be encouraged to report to the appropriate medical advisor before commencing work to ensure that they are "clear" and do not transmit the disease or illness to other employees or do not cause contamination of the product. Personal hygiene is also important. In *Singh v John Laing & Sons* a company rule provided that anyone misusing the toilet facilities would be liable to instant dismissal. The applicant was seen urinating in a room he had been instructed to clean and he was thus dismissed. This was held to be fair. He knew of the rule, had a good command of English and could offer little by way of explanation. After all, employers are legally bound to maintain toilet facilities in clean and proper condition and thus it is not wrong to enforce high standards of hygiene (*Singh v Elliotts Bricks*).

Health generally

9.26   In some circumstances, general ill health must be reported and noted, so as not to cause a hazard. In *Singh-Deu v Chloride Metals Ltd* the employee worked in a lead smelting factory where it was essential to remain alert in view of the dangerous processes which were being carried on. He was sent home by the works doctor after complaining of feeling unwell. He visited his own doctor who diagnosed paranoid schizophrenia. He was then examined by a specialist, after which he attempted to return to work. However, the works doctor would not allow him to return unless the specialist gave an assurance that there would be no recurrence of the illness. This assurance was not forthcoming and so he was dismissed, as the works manager, mindful of the inherently dangerous processes being carried on in the lead factory, was not prepared to take the responsibility of allowing him back at work. The dismissal was held to be fair. It was not reasonable to continue to employ him in a delicately balanced job which called for a high degree of concentration. The effect of a relapse on the claimant and on others could have been devastating had a mistake or error been made. A similar result was reached in *Balogun v Lucas Batteries Ltd* where the claimant, who was working with lead, suffered from hypertension. Medical evidence clearly indicated that this type of work can be harmful, especially to those who have an existing predisposition to certain types of illnesses, including hypertension. Efforts were made to find him alternative work, but there was no suitable job and he was dismissed. This was held to be fair. His continued employment constituted a risk to himself and to others.

9.27   However, an employee with a health problem may well have a long-term disability within the meaning of the Disability Discrimination Act 1995, and the employer may be under a duty to make reasonable adjustments so as to enable the disabled employee to do his work safely (see paragraph 7.104). A careful risk assessment should be carried out, and ways of enabling the employee to continue in employment without being a risk to himself or others should be investigated, before dismissal is contemplated.

Vandalism

9.28   An employee who misuses the company's property or interferes with anything provided for the use of employees generally can be disciplined. This is especially true if there is an interference or misuse of anything provided for health, safety and welfare, for there is also a breach of s.8 of HSWA. In *Ferodo Ltd v Barnes* an employee was dismissed after the company decided he had been committing an act of vandalism in the lavatories. The employment tribunal decided that the dismissal was unfair, as they were not satisfied that in fact the employee had committed this act. This was reversed on appeal. It is not the duty of the employment tribunal to re-try the case. It was their duty to see that management acted reasonably and as long as there had been a fair and proper investigation, the employment tribunal should not substitute their judgment for that of management.

Neglect

9.29 An employee who is incompetent or neglectful in his work may cause some damage to the work processes and the matter should be regarded as a disciplinary problem. The first duty of management is to ensure that the employee has been trained properly, supervised adequately, has sufficient support staff and sufficient facilities to do the job in question. An employee who is suffering from irredeemable incompetence can be offered alternative employment, failing which a dismissal will be fair. If he is suffering from neglectful incompetence, he should be warned, in accordance with the gravity of the case. However, if the neglect is of such a dangerous nature that there is the likelihood of serious injury to persons or damage to property, then the matter becomes a health and safety issue and can be dealt with as such. This could result in a disciplinary sanction which is appropriate to the case, and even dismissal. In *Taylor v Alidair Ltd*, an airline pilot landed his aeroplane in a manner which caused some concern and consternation among the rest of the crew and passengers. After a full investigation it was decided that he had been negligent and he was dismissed. This was held to be fair. There are some activities the consequences of which are so serious and grave that it is not possible to risk a repetition. Nor does it matter if the neglect causes a risk of injury to fellow employees or to the public or customers of the employer. Thus if an employee fails to follow the prescribed safety checks (*Wilcox v HGS*) or the work is done in a negligent manner which creates a risk (*McGibbon v Gillespie Building Co*) he may be dismissed.

Sleeping on duty

9.30 Whatever may be the position in other work situations, it has always been recognised that safety considerations must be regarded as being paramount. In *Jenkins v British Gypsum Ltd* the claimant was employed on the night shift checking and taking the temperature of a gas-fired kiln. He was found asleep on duty and was dismissed, even though there was no specific rule to cover this situation. Nonetheless, his dismissal was held to be fair. It was essential for him to monitor the temperature regularly as a safeguard, and the fact that he had to be aroused in order to do his work constituted gross misconduct. "Alertness is essential from the safety angle", commented the employment tribunal.

Training

9.31   Since the employer is under an obligation to train his employees in safety and health matters, and since also the employee is obliged to co-operate with the employer in the performance of the statutory duties, an employee who refuses to be trained may be fairly dismissed. In *Minter v Willingborough Foundries Ltd* the claimant was a nurse employed at the employer's factory. There were complaints about her standards of medical care and she was asked to go on a training course, but she refused. Subsequently, there were further complaints and she was again asked to undertake further training, and again she refused. Because the employers were concerned about their obligations under HSWA, she was dismissed. The EAT upheld the finding of the employment tribunal that the dismissal was fair. The course would not have involved her in any expense or inconvenience and she did not give an adequate explanation for her refusal.

Other dangerous practices

9.32   No list of actions which are to be the subject of disciplinary sanctions can be exhaustive and each employer must try to complete the list in accordance with his own situation, as well as covering the unexpected. Thus, it should be fairly obvious that it is an extremely dangerous practice to light a bonfire near to flammable material (*Bussey v CSW Engineering Ltd*) or to fire air guns whilst at work, even though this is during the lunch hour (*Shipside (Ruthin) Ltd v T&GWU*), to smoke in a wood and paint shop *Bendall v Paine and Betteridge)*, to walk out, leaving a high pressure steam boiler on (*Gannon v JC Firth Ltd*), to drive a vehicle without being qualified to do so, or to drive a vehicle so badly that the brakes overheat (*Potter v WJ Rich & Sons*) are all examples of conduct capable of attracting disciplinary sanctions, including dismissal. The list can be extended almost indefinitely.

Enforcing safety rules: action by the employee

9.33   If there is an actual injury to an employee, he can, of course, pursue whatever remedy is available to him at common law (see Chapter 8). If there is a threatened injury, the situation is more delicate. Since it is an implied term of the contract of employment that the employer will ensure the health and safety of his employees, the employer will be in breach of contract if he fails to take the necessary steps. In these circumstances, the employee will accept the breach, and resign, but, in law, since he was entitled to resign by virtue of the employer's conduct, it is the employer who has "dismissed" the employee. In technical terms, even though the employee has resigned, he may bring a claim for "constructive dismissal", and, provided he has the requisite period of continuous employment (or is asserting a statutory right, for which no period of continuous employment is required), he can bring his claim before the employment tribunal for compensation. For example, in *British Aircraft Corporation v Austin* the employee asked her supervisor for a pair of prescription safety glasses. After waiting several months, during which time she heard nothing further, she resigned and claimed constructive dismissal. Her claim succeeded. It was an implied term of the contract that the employers would ensure her safety, and by failing to investigate her request and provide the necessary safety precaution they had broken the contract. It will be noted at this stage that the inaction was the fault of the supervisor, yet it was the employer who was held responsible.

9.34   A constructive dismissal claim does not need to be based on an actual injury (see *Knight v Barra Shipping Co Ltd*); the fear of the possibility is sufficient. In *Keys v Shoefayre Ltd* the employee worked in a shop which was robbed in the daytime by a gang of youths. The manager was asked by the employee to do something about the security of the premises, but he replied that there was nothing he could do. A further daytime robbery took place, and the employee resigned and claimed constructive dismissal on the ground that the premises were no longer safe to work in. Her claim succeeded. The employers were obliged to take reasonable steps to operate a safe system of work and to provide safe premises. The employment tribunal thought that it might have been possible to install a telephone, or to employ a male assistant, etc.

9.35   However, the contractual obligation of the employer is no higher than the duty owed in tort, which is to take reasonable care only. The employer does not guarantee absolutely the safety of his employees. In *Buttars v Holo-Krome Ltd* the employee was injured when a blank flew out of a machine and struck his safety glasses. A lens broke and injured his eye. When he returned to work he asked for a guard to be fitted to the machine, but the employers claimed it was safe. He resigned and claimed constructive dismissal, but the claim was rejected. The accident had been reported to the factory inspector who agreed that the machine was safe and proposed to take no further action on the incident. There was no duty on the part of the employer to fence, for this duty does not apply to parts of the machine or materials used by the machine which fly out (*Nicholls v F Austin (Leyton) Ltd*). The accident was a freak one, it was not usual to fit guards on this type of machine. In these circumstances, the employment tribunal thought that the employers had not broken the contract, and hence there was no constructive dismissal.

9.36 The fact that an employee genuinely believes that his health and safety is at risk will not, by itself, support a claim for constructive dismissal. In *Wojcik v Amtico Co Ltd* the claimant suffered a minor back injury while working on a machine. He did not take the matter further, either with his health and safety representative or with the safety committee. He asked to be supplied with a back support, but the company's medical officer advised against this, arguing that the medical evidence indicated that this would do more harm than good. The company arranged for the machine to be examined by a consultant engineer and, following a report, made some minor adjustments to it. The employee subsequently resigned, claiming that he had been constructively dismissed, alleging that the employer had broken the implied term of trust and confidence, by failing to take seriously his concerns about the safety of the machine. An employment tribunal dismissed his claim, stating that he had become obsessed with the whole matter. Health and safety concerns had been largely theoretical, and very minor. The employers had taken the complaint seriously, modifying the machine following the receipt of the consultant's report, and acted as a responsible employer. In the circumstances, the employer had not broken any implied term of trust and confidence.

9.37 More difficult is the situation where the employee responds to the employer's breach by action other than resignation. In *Mariner v Domestic and Industrial Polythene Ltd*, some workers discovered that the temperature in the workplace was 53°F. There was no fuel left for heating, as the employer had allowed his supplies to run down in anticipation of the warmer weather. The workers therefore went home, and the following day, when they reported for work, they were dismissed for going on strike. At that time, a complaint of unfair dismissal, brought about because a person is taking part in a strike or other industrial action could not normally be entertained by the employment tribunal (Trade Union and Labour Relations (Consolidation) Act 1992, s.238) but, in this case, the employment tribunal decided that the workers had not been on strike for they had not withdrawn their labour in breach of their employment contracts. It was the employer who was in breach, for he had allowed the temperature to fall below the statutory minimum and there is an implied term in the contract of employment that the employer will perform his statutory obligations. If he fails to do so, the employees are merely responding to the breach, not acting themselves in breach.

9.38 It is sound practice for an employee to take matters up with the appropriate level of management before taking the drastic step of resignation, but there appears to be no legal reason why he should do so, for the fact that the employer is in breach of contract should be sufficient (*Seligman and Latz Ltd v McHugh*). Thus in *Graham Oxley Tool Steels Ltd v Firth*, the employee had to work in a small bay near to an open door. The only heating came from a radiant heater fixed to the ceiling. One day, when the weather was very cold, she was kept waiting outside the entrance to the premises and eventually she decided to go home. She subsequently resigned and claimed constructive dismissal. She had made no previous complaint about the cold working conditions, although a subsequent visit from the factory inspector revealed that the temperature was 49°F. Her claim for unfair dismissal succeeded. The employer was in breach of his obligation to provide a proper working environment and the failure to do so constituted a fundamental breach of contract which entitled her to resign.

9.39 Nonetheless, a well-drawn-up grievance procedure which is incorporated into the contract may prove to be a useful method of preventing claims of this nature, particularly in respect of those "innocent" breaches, about which the employer knows nothing, or which were accidental or unintentional. Thus an employee who fails or refuses to use that procedure may find that he is not entitled to claim constructive dismissal, or, if he does succeed, he may find that his compensation award is reduced, on the ground that by failing to adopt the grievance procedure, he contributed towards his own dismissal, or failed to mitigate against his loss.

9.40 A claim based on constructive dismissal must be tested by employment tribunals in accordance with the principles of employment law relating to the reasonableness of the employer's conduct, not in accordance with the principles of health and safety law relating to the employer doing something so far as is reasonably practicable. In *Dutton & Clark Ltd v Daly* the employee worked in the office of a building society agency. The employers had installed protective safety devices, including screens, partitions and alarm buttons. However, the premises were subjected to two armed robberies in a space of two months and the employee resigned. She claimed that the safety measures were inadequate and that she was too frightened to work in the premises, and she alleged that by failing to provide adequate security the employers were in breach of a fundamental term of the contract which entitled her to resign and claim that she had been dismissed. An employment tribunal upheld her claim, but on appeal the EAT remitted the case to another tribunal for further consideration. The test to be applied is whether the safety precautions which were taken were those which a reasonable employer would have taken. This duty is not as high as ensuring safety so far as is reasonably practicable.

9.41 It is interesting to note that the original test, formulated in *Western Excavating (EEC) Ltd v Sharp* by the Court of Appeal was has the employer broken the contract? The more modern approach appears to be, did the employer evince an intention to break the contract? This is slightly different, and employees who imagine that minor things which go wrong in their daily employment automatically give them a right to claim constructive dismissal should be cautioned about such a false assumption. Further, it must be borne in mind that while constructive dismissal is, in law, a "dismissal", it is not necessarily an unfair dismissal (*Industrial Rubber Products v Gillon*).

Enforcing safety rules: action by the employer

9.42 Safety rules can be enforced within the context of existing disciplinary procedures. These may be drawn up by management, in consultation with the trade unions or work force if possible, without their co-operation or agreement if necessary. Details should be given to each employee explaining the steps to be followed, the sanctions which may be applied in accordance with the gravity of the case and the method of appeal. Further reference should be made to the *ACAS Code of Practice on Disciplinary Procedure and Practice*.

9.43   A disciplinary procedure should have five characteristics.

9.44   (1) There must be a full and proper investigation into the incident. This should be undertaken as soon as possible (*Abercrombie v Alexander Thomson & Son*), and consideration should be given to a short period of suspension (with or without pay, in accordance with the contract and/or procedure) pending such investigation.

9.45   (2) The offender must be told of the charge against him. It is no bad thing to put this in writing, particularly if his command of English is weak, or the charge is a serious one, so that he can obtain advice from any available source.

9.46   (3) He should be given an opportunity to state his case, to plead that he didn't do it, or if he did, it was not his fault, or if it was, there were mitigating circumstances which ought to be taken into consideration, etc.

9.47   (4) He is entitled to be represented by a single companion (ie a trade union official or a fellow worker), see Employment Relations Act 1999, ss.10–15.

9.48   (5) He should be given the right of appeal, to a level of management not previously involved in the decision-making process.

9.49   Obviously, the nature of the disciplinary procedure will vary with the size and resources of the firm. One does not expect the same formalities in a small firm as might exist in a large firm. Equally, the sanction which will be imposed will depend on the nature and seriousness of the offence, the circumstances of the individual, and so forth. The purpose of disciplinary sanctions is to improve the conduct of the offender, to deter others from doing the same or similarly wrongful acts, and to protect the individual, other employees, the public and ultimately, the employer. Thus no simple pattern emerges; sometimes the sanction will be corrective in nature, sometimes it will be designed to encourage others not to break the rules. The gravity of the sanction will reflect the objectives to be achieved. In the case of a minor offence, a minor sanction will be imposed, such as a warning, which may be verbal. A repetition of the offence, or a different kind of offence, or a serious offence, would be dealt with by a written warning, which should detail the offence, warn as to the consequences which may flow from a repetition of the offence, or any other offence of a similar or dissimilar nature. A very serious offence should be dealt with by a final warning, or by dismissal.

9.50 No matter how serious the breach, how dangerous the practice, nor how strong the evidence is, an employer must always carry out a proper investigation into the incident, give the employee an opportunity to respond to any allegations made, and take account of any mitigating circumstances, before dismissing an employee. A failure to do so will invariably lead to a finding that the dismissal was unfair, despite whatever merits the decision would otherwise have. An employment tribunal may decide to reduce any compensation award on the grounds of contributory conduct, but they are not bound to do so (*OCS Cleaning Scotland Ltd v Oag*).

9.51 Depending on the nature of the offence and the circumstances of the offender, other sanctions might be imposed. Thus, consideration could be given to a period of suspension without pay (provided the disciplinary procedure confers this power), a transfer to other work, or even a "fine" (eg if an employee is failing to use safety equipment), which has been agreed as a recognised type of punishment (perhaps with the proceeds going to an appropriate charity).

Dismissal

9.52 The final power left to the employer is to dismiss the employee. This may be done for a number of reasons.

9.53 First, the circumstances may be so serious that a dangerous situation was created which put the employee or others at risk of serious injury. There are some activities where the degree of safety required is so high, and the consequences of a failure to achieve those standards so potentially serious, that a single departure from them could warrant instant dismissal. For example, in *Taylor v Alidair Ltd* (see above) it would be totally unrealistic to give the pilot a final warning saying "If you land your aeroplane in such an incompetent manner again we will dismiss you", etc. The driver of an express train, the scientist in charge of a nuclear power station, the driver of a vehicle carrying a dangerous chemical, etc must all display the highest standards of care. In *Wilcox v*

HGS, the employee was employed as a converter, changing gas appliances from town gas to natural gas. He was instructed that before he left premises he had to undertake a mandatory safety check, but he failed to do so and was dismissed. The dismissal was held to be fair by the employment tribunal, although on appeal the case was remitted for reconsideration. If, as he alleged, the employers had persistently ignored the safety regulations, then such acquiescence was a relevant factor to be taken into account in determining whether or not a final warning should have been given.

9.54   Second, an employee may be in serious risk of injury to himself. In *Finch v Betabake (Anglia) Ltd* an apprentice motor mechanic was found to have defective eyesight. A report from an ophthalmic surgeon stated that the lad could not be employed without undue danger to himself and to others and he was therefore dismissed. This was held to be fair. The fact that the employee is willing to take a risk that he may be injured is irrelevant, for the employer may expose himself to civil or criminal liabilities by continuing the employment (*Marsh v Judge International*).

9.55   Third, the situation may arise where the employee's physical condition is such that it amounts to a health or safety hazard. This must be handled carefully; there must be a full investigation, preferably backed with medical reports, there should be consultation with the employee and alternative employment should be considered. In *Spalding v Port of London Authority*, the employee failed a medical examination after it was discovered that he was suffering from deafness. It was recommended that he worked with a hearing aid, but this did not prove to be satisfactory and he was dismissed. This was held to be fair; the company's medical standards were not unnecessarily high, and were justified in order to ensure the safety of the employee and his fellow employees. In *Yarrow v QIS Ltd* the employee was dismissed after it was discovered that he was suffering from psoriasis. Because he had to work with radiography equipment, he was subject to the Ionising Radiation (Unsealed Sources) Regulations, which made it unsafe for him to be employed. This dismissal too was held to be fair. The employers were in danger of breaking the law if they continued to employ him. And in *Parsons v Fisons Ltd* the company's medical advisor noted that the employee had poor vision and only narrowly averted several possible accidents. After a full discussion with the group medical advisor and her general practitioner, she was dismissed. This too was held to be fair. There was no other suitable job for her, and it was not necessary to wait until an accident occurred before taking appropriate action.

9.56 It is important to bear in mind the health and safety of other employees as well as their general comfort and working environment. In *Kenna v Stewart Plastics Ltd* the employee had a series of epileptic fits in an open plan office. The dismissal was held to be fair. The employer had a duty to ensure that other employees could do their work in reasonable working conditions which were physically and mentally conducive to work.

9.57 Fourth, the employee may be dismissed if he refuses to observe the safety instructions or wear the appropriate safety equipment. In *Frizzell v Flanders* the employee was provided with a gas mask while working in a tank. He was seen working without the mask and was dismissed. This was held to be fair. It was essential to enforce the safety precautions rigorously both for his own sake and for the sake of others, and his dismissal would serve as a warning that flagrant breaches of the safety instructions would not be tolerated.

9.58 An over zealousness on the part of the employee to be cossetted against the risks of the employment can also result in his fair dismissal. In *Wood v Brita-Finish Ltd* the employee had been provided with acid-proof gloves, goggles, wellingtons and a protective apron, all of which had been approved by the Factory Inspectorate. He refused to work unless he was also provided with an overall and was dismissed This was held to be fair. Overalls had proved to be ineffective in the past and contributed nothing to the safety of the employee. In *Howard v Overdale Engineering Ltd* the employee refused to work in a new factory because of dust caused by engineers drilling cables into the floor. The employment tribunal found that the employers were not in breach of any statutory obligation to prevent impurities from getting into the air or to prevent employees from being subjected to harmful substances, and his dismissal was held to be fair for refusing to obey a lawful order.

9.59 Although an employer is entitled to dismiss if he genuinely and conscientiously believes that there is a health or safety hazard, such dismissals should only be carried out with a full investigation of all the relevant circumstances A procedural failure is likely to result in a wrong decision being reached and hence an unfair dismissal. In *Milk Marketing Board v Grimes*, the employee was the driver of a milk float. He was almost completely deaf, and could only communicate with his employers by means of written questions and answers. Fearing that there may be an obvious safety hazard, the employee was sent for an examination by the company's occupational health advisor, who reported that the employee was unfit to drive whilst deaf and that a hearing aid would not materially improve matters. He was thus dismissed. Before the employment tribunal, the employee produced a consultant's report who concluded that the use of a hearing aid would restore his hearing to a tolerable level, which would be adequate for safe driving. Further, he was able to show that he had been driving for 34 years without an accident. Because the employers had not given the employee an opportunity to deal with the question of his incapacity, and because the procedure leading to the dismissal was flawed, the dismissal was held to be unfair.

9.60   It is not the function of the employment tribunal to determine whether or not the employer is in breach of his common law or statutory duties, as they would not always have sufficient evidence available on which to make such a finding. In *Lindsay v Dunlop Ltd*, workers in the tyre-curing department became concerned about the possible carcinogenic nature of fumes and dust. As a temporary measure, it was agreed to resume normal working with masks being provided. The claimant, however, refused to adopt this course, maintaining that his continued exposure to fumes would endanger his health. His subsequent dismissal was held to be fair. Whether or not the employers were in breach of their obligations under s.63 of the Factories Act was a matter which could only be determined by the courts and in the circumstances the employers had not acted unreasonably.

9.61   If the employee refuses to do the work unless he is provided with the necessary safety precautions, it is up to the employers to make a full and informed investigation into the reasons for the refusal, consideration of whether or not there is justification for the refusal and a communication of the results of the investigation to the employees before the decision to dismiss is taken. If employees make a complaint about the lack of safety precautions, which is sensible, *bona fide* and not frivolous, the employer must take all necessary steps to reassure the employees, and should not just treat the refusal to work as being *per se* a ground for dismissing from employment (see *Atlas Products & Services v Jones*).

9.62   To establish that it is fair to dismiss an employee for refusing to follow the safety rules, or to wear or use the precautions provided, it must be shown (a) the employee knew of the requirement, (b) the employer was consistent in his enforcement policies, and (c) the precautions were suitable for the employee and for the work he was doing. Again, a full investigation into the circumstances is called for. In *Mayhew v Anderson (Stoke Newington) Ltd* an insurance company recommended that the employee be asked to wear protective glasses, stating that the company's insurance cover would be withdrawn if she did not do so. The employers purchased a pair of safety goggles for 78p but she refused to wear them because they were not comfortable. She was warned that if she persisted with her refusal she would be dismissed, and ultimately the threat was carried out. Her dismissal was held to be unfair. She had never refused to wear reasonable eye protectors, only this particular type, which irritated her eyes and were uncomfortable. Custom-made eye protectors were available at a cost of £33, and the employment tribunal thought that these should have been provided for her, even at the risk of creating a precedent.

9.63   Finally, other reasons prompted by a genuine concern for health and safety can justify dismissal. In *Wilson v Stephen Carter Ltd* the claimant was dismissed after refusing to go on a training course which involved staying away from home for a week and this was held to be fair.

9.64   If lesser disciplinary sanctions do not succeed, the employer may ultimately dismiss a recalcitrant employee, but some employers do not consider this to be a satisfactory solution, as they would rather have the workers working than have the problem of obtaining new staff and training them all over again. At this stage it may be possible to invoke the assistance of the HSE inspectorate, who could issue a prohibition notice on the employee, which would effectively prevent him from working in contravention of the matters contained in the notice. A failure to comply with this is punishable by a fine or even imprisonment, and this may yet prove to be an effective way of dealing with the problem. At the same time, an employee could be warned that he is acting in breach of his duty under s.7 or 8 of HSWA, which again is a criminal offence.

9.65   It will be recalled (see Chapter 5) that employees and safety representatives have protection in certain cases from suffering a detriment or being dismissed in health and safety cases.

Suspension on medical grounds

9.66   Section 64 of the Employment Rights Act 1996 provides that where an employee is suspended from work on medical grounds in consequence of:

(a) any requirement imposed by or under the provision of any enactment, or

(b) any recommendation contained in a Code of Practice issued under HSWA

which, in either case, is a provision specified in s.64(3) of the Act, then that employee shall be entitled to be paid during the suspension for up to 26 weeks. The present provisions are as follows:

(a) Control of Lead at Work Regulations 1998

(b) Ionising Radiations Regulations 1999 (regulation 24)

(c) Control of Substances Hazardous to Health Regulations 1999 (regulation 11).

9.67   It will be noted that there must be a suspension on medical grounds. This means the potential effect on the health of the employee, not the actual effect. In other words, the provisions of s.64 are not relevant if an employee is actually off work sick. Nor is the suspension on medical grounds if he is unable to work because a prohibition notice has been imposed. Medical suspension payments can only be claimed when there is a suspension from work in order to comply with a requirement in any of the above provisions, but if he is incapable of working because of any physical or mental disablement, he has no legal entitlement (s.65(3)).

9.68   If he is dismissed because of one of the above requirements, he can bring a claim for unfair dismissal as long as he has been employed for a period of four weeks, instead of the more usual period of one year. Whether such dismissal would be fair will obviously depend on the circumstances. For example, it may be shown that the employee's job became redundant, etc.

9.69   Medical suspension pay is not meant to be a top-up for, or a substitution for, statutory sick pay. It is designed to meet the situation where employees are fit for work, but are prevented from doing so because of a health hazard, in particular following a recommendation that they should cease work made by a doctor from the Employment Medical Advisory Service. In *Stallite Batteries Co Ltd v Appleton and Hopkinson*, an employee fell into a skip containing lead waste. In consequence, his lead/blood level rose dramatically to 93 µg/100 ml, which was in excess of the limits laid down under the Control of Lead at Work Regulations 1998. The level decreased over the following months, but his own doctor certified that he was still unfit for work. Eight months after the incident he was dismissed and he claimed compensation for unfair dismissal and medical suspension pay. The Employment Appeal Tribunal held that as he was not available for work because of sickness, he was not entitled to medical suspension pay by virtue of the provisions of s.65(3).

9.70   If the employer still needs someone to do the work, he may decide to take on a temporary replacement. He should inform the latter in writing that his employment will be terminated at the end of the period of suspension. If, therefore, he has to dismiss the temporary employee in order to permit the first employee to return to work, the dismissal will be for "some other substantial reason" but without prejudice to the rule that the employer will still have to show that he acted reasonably in treating that reason as a sufficient ground for dismissal (s.106 of the Employment Rights Act 1996). However, since the medical suspension period is unlikely to last long enough to enable the temporary employee to obtain a sufficient qualifying period of employment, this provision is somewhat otiose.

9.71   To qualify for medical suspension payments, the employee must have been employed for more than four weeks. Further, he will not be entitled to be paid if the employer has offered him suitable alternative work (whether or not the employee was contractually obliged to do that type of work) and he unreasonably refuses to perform that work. The employee must also comply with reasonable requirements imposed by the employer with a view to ensuring that his services are available. In other words, as the employer is paying the employee wages during the suspension, the employer may require the employee to do other work, or hold himself in readiness for work. The amount of pay to be made is calculated in accordance with ss.220–225 of the Act, which depends on the contractual arrangements for pay.

9.72   An employee may complain to an employment tribunal that the employer has failed to pay him in accordance with the above provisions. The complaint must be presented within three months of the failure, and if the complaint is upheld, the employment tribunal will order the employer to pay the amount due.

9.73 The provisions relating to suspension on maternity grounds are considered in paragraph 7.6.

CHAPTER 10

The impact of international obligations

European Union

10.1   In 1951, by the Treaty of Paris, the European Coal and Steel Community (ECSC) was established, when six countries (France, West Germany, Italy, Belgium, Holland and Luxembourg) agreed to pool their coal and steel resources and create a common commercial market for their products. Subsequently, the Mines Safety and Health Commission was created to work for the elimination of occupational risks to health and safety in coalmines.

10.2   In 1957 the European Atomic Energy Commission (EURATOM) was established in order to co-ordinate and develop the peaceful uses of nuclear energy, and strong emphasis was placed on the need to ensure the protection of the health of workers as well as the community at large from dangers arising from radiation hazards.

10.3   Also in 1957, by the Treaty of Rome, the European Economic Community (EEC) was established. This has the wider objective of establishing a common market for its economic activities by the elimination of customs duties, creating common customs tariffs, permitting the free movement of capital and workers, laying down common agricultural and transport policies, and harmonising the laws of Member States to ensure that competition is not distorted and to facilitate the anticipated economic expansion.

10.4   In 1967 these three institutions were merged into the European Communities (EC), with the fusion of their executive institutions, and the result is that although the three organisations have a separate existence, they are all now under the one umbrella. By the European Communities Act 1972, the UK signified its accession to the Treaty of Rome, including its laws, which by s.2(1) of the Act are to be given legal effect without further enactment. Ireland and Denmark joined at the same time as the UK and Greece became a member in 1981. Spain and Portugal became full members in 1992. Finland, Austria and Sweden became full members in 1995.

10.5 As indicated (see paragraph 1.44) the Maastricht Treaty created the European Union, with the possibility of other European countries joining in the near future.

The working of the European Union

10.6 The nature of European law, and the structure of EU institutions have already been considered in Chapter 1. As noted, initial proposals are made by the Commission, there is a consultative process with interested parties (including the European Parliament) and final approval is given by the Council of Ministers.

10.7 The Commission operates through twenty Directorates-General (DGs) with the addition of a number of other departments. In the main, DG V, which deals with employment and social affairs, has an overall responsibility for health and safety matters, although there is an overlap with other DGs where matters of common concern arise. Directorate E of DG V is the department most closely concerned with health and safety matters, and is based in Luxembourg. It has responsibilities for (a) toxicology, biology and health effects, (b) radioactive waste, accident prevention and safety measures in nuclear installations, (c) public health and radiation protection, (d) industrial medicine and hygiene, (e) industrial safety, and (f) Mines Safety and Health Commission.

10.8 In order to advise the Commission generally on all aspects of health and safety at work, an Advisory Committee on Safety, Hygiene and Health Protection was established in 1974. This consists of two members from governments, two from employers' associations, and two from trade unions, making a total of six from each Member State. This Committee assists the Commission in the preparation and implementation of activities in the field of safety, health and hygiene relating to work activities, with the exception of those areas which are dealt with by the Mines Health and Safety Commission and EURATOM.

10.9 The Advisory Committee's terms of reference are as follows:
  (a) conducting, on the basis of information available to it, exchanges of views and experience regarding existing or planned regulations
  (b) contributing towards the development of a common approach to problems which exist in the field of safety, hygiene and health

protection at work, and towards the choice of Community priorities, as well as the measures necessary for implementing those priorities

(c) drawing the Commission's attention to areas in which there is an apparent need for the acquisition of new knowledge and for the implementation of appropriate educational and research projects

(d) defining, within the framework of Community action programmes, and in co-operation with the Mines Safety and Health Commission, the criteria and aims of the campaign against the risks of accidents at work and health hazards within the undertaking, and methods enabling undertakings and their employees to evaluate and to improve the level of protection.

Consultative bodies

10.10   Before EU legislation is passed, a tremendous amount of consultative work takes place. There are 17 External Advisory Groups, consisting of some 278 experts from all EU countries. Their role is to be consulted on the scientific and technical content of the thematic programmes put forward. Proposals need to be supported by relevant scientific or technical data or surveys, national experts are consulted, advisory committees are asked for opinions and initial proposals will then be drawn up. These are then transmitted to the European Parliament, to the Economic and Social Committee and to the Council of Ministers. At all stages, representations can be made by national groups representing employers, trade unions and other interested parties.

10.11   When proposals reach the UK, a Government department (generally known as the "lead department") which is most closely concerned with the proposal, will take charge of the consultative process. Usually, on health and safety matters, this will be the Department of Transport, Local Government and the Regions, but it may be some other department which has a major interest in the proposals (eg Department of Trade and Industry). Discussions will continue with the TUC, CBI, trade associations, etc and an explanatory memorandum will be prepared by the lead department and submitted to Parliament for consideration by the scrutiny committee of each House. These committees may call for written or oral evidence, make recommendations for change, or request a Parliamentary debate. Once the Government has formulated its views, the matter can be transmitted back to the Council of Ministers for consideration by a working group.

Here, the respective views are collated, the text may be revised, and the final proposals formulated and ultimately adopted. Not surprisingly, it can take many years before an initial proposal is finally transformed into a binding directive.

Procedure for making Directives

10.12   In order to adopt a Directive under Article 137 of the Treaty of Rome, the "co-operation procedure" must be followed. The Commission submits proposals to the Council of Ministers. The European Parliament and the Economic and Social Committee are then consulted and give their opinion. The Commission may then amend the proposals (but is not obliged to do so) and they are resubmitted to the Labour and Social Affairs Council of the Council of Ministers. A "common position" is then adopted, if necessary by a qualified majority vote. This is then reconsidered by the European Parliament, which may then (a) approve the common position, or (b) propose further amendments, or (c) reject them, in which case the proposals must be adopted by the Council of Ministers unanimously.

10.13   Once a Directive relating to health and safety at work has been adopted, HSC draws up the necessary legislative proposals in order to implement it. Again, it will engage in a series of consultations with interested parties, but since all concerned should have been involved in the earlier discussion, the subject matter will occasion little surprise, and the only problems which are likely to arise will stem from the detailed arrangements which may be necessary in order to ensure that the final legislative proposals (usually made by regulations) will meet the European standards. Indeed, HSC takes pride in considering that it already anticipates European legislation as part of its own ongoing programme, and is thus in a favourable position to influence the European standards. Indeed, "The Commission's aim in negotiations is to influence the shape of EC proposals during their embryonic stages and where practicable to advance UK policy and practice as a model for adoption across the Community" (*Annual Report* 1989/1990, page 1).

EU Directives

10.14   As already noted (see paragraph 1.42) the Treaty of Rome was amended in 1986 by the Single European Act, which aimed to create a

Europe without economic barriers by the end of 1992. One of the amendments was the inclusion of a new Article 118A, which read as follows.

1. The Member States shall pay particular attention to encouraging improvements, especially in the working environment, as regards the health and safety of workers, and shall set as their objective the harmonisation of conditions in this area, while maintaining the improvements.

2. In order to help achieve the objective laid down in the first paragraph, the Council, acting by a qualified majority on a proposal from the Commission and after consulting with the European Parliament and the Economic and Social Committee, shall adopt, by means of Directives, minimum requirements for gradual implementation, having regard to the conditions and technical rules obtaining in each of the Member States. Such Directives shall avoid imposing administrative, financial and legal constraints in a way which would hold back the creation and development of small and medium-sized undertakings.

3. The provisions adopted pursuant to this Article shall not prevent each Member State from introducing more stringent measures for the protection of working conditions compatible with the Treaty.

10.15   The result was the adoption by the Council of a Directive on the introduction of measures to encourage improvements in the health and safety of workers at work, the so-called Framework Directive (89/391/EEC). Its provisions were given effect by the Management of Health and Safety at Work Regulations 1992 (now replaced by the 1999 regulations — see Chapter 5). In addition, a number of "daughter" Directives were adopted, ie Workplace Directive (89/654/EEC), Use of Work Equipment Directive (89/655/EEC), Personal Protective Equipment Directive (89/656/EEC), Manual Handling of Loads Directive (90/269/EEC) and Display Screen Equipment Directive (90/270/EEC). The provisions of these Directives have been implemented by the respective regulations outlined in Chapters 5–6.

10.16   Several further directives on health and safety at work have been adopted by the Council, which have either been implemented by respective regulations, or are under active consideration. These include the following.

Adopted Directives

(1) Carcinogens Directive (90/394/EEC)

10.17   This Directive was implemented by the Control of Substances Hazardous to Health Regulations 1994 (now replaced by the Control of Substances Hazardous to Health Regulations 1999), together with a revision of the supporting Approved Codes of Practice. The Directive applies to substances which may cause cancer, and to certain further substances and processes specified in Annex 1 of the Directive. Employers must make an assessment of the risk of exposure and, dependent on that assessment, replace the substance with a less harmful or less dangerous substance or use the substance in a closed system. If this is not possible, exposure must be reduced to as low a level as is possible. There must be suitable procedures for dealing with situations of abnormal exposure and emergency conditions, monitoring and health surveillance must be adopted, and the employer must provide adequate training, information and instructions concerning the risks to the health of workers, the precautions to be taken, and the results provided of any health surveillance. This Directive was amended in 1997 (95/C/317/06) and again in 1999 (99/38/EC).

(2) Asbestos Worker Protection Directive (91/382/EEC)

10.18   This was implemented by the Control of Asbestos at Work Regulations 1987, as amended in 1992, and the Asbestos (Prohibitions) Regulations 1992. The Directive amends and updates the EC Directive on the protection of workers from risks relating to exposure to asbestos at work (83/477/EEC). Generally it increases the protection afforded to workers using asbestos, and, in particular, it requires employers to draw up a plan of work before starting on the removal from buildings of asbestos-containing products. Specific essential features of the plan are to be communicated to the competent authority.

(3) Temporary Workers Directive (91/383/EEC)

10.19   This Directive was implemented by the Management of Health and Safety at Work Regulations 1992 (now replaced by the Management of Health and Safety at Work Regulations 1999). The Directive applies to all workers with fixed duration contracts, and also to those who are seconded from one employer to another. Employers must give appropriate training and information to temporary workers, and they must receive medical surveillance on the same basis as permanent employees. The transferee employer is to be responsible for the health and safety of workers who are seconded to him.

(4) Biological Agents Directive (90/219/EEC)

10.20   The Council has already adopted two Directives on genetically modified micro-organisms and the release into the environment of genetically modified organisms and these have been implemented by the Genetically Modified Organisms (Contained Use) Regulations 2000 and the Genetically Modified Organisms (Deliberate Release) Regulations 1992. The Biological Agents Directive deals with the protection of workers from the risks related to exposure to biological agents whilst at work, although it does draw a distinction between exposure which is incidental to work activity (eg health care, farming, etc) and where there is a conscious decision to work with such agents, eg a micro-biological laboratory. Employers must make a risk assessment, reduce the risks of exposure, provide training, instruction and information to workers, provide health surveillance, notify their activities to competent authorities and take special measures related to health care. The Directive has also been implemented by an amendment to the COSHH Regulations, which were consolidated in 1994 and again in 1999.

(5) Construction Sites Directive (92/57/EEC)

10.21   This Directive will apply to building and civil engineering works, and any site at which the construction, equipping, alteration, renovation, repair, upkeep, maintenance and demolition of all types of buildings or structures is taking place. A project manager will have to be appointed to ensure that health and safety is considered from the concept of the project to its completion. Work plans will be required, with particular reference to specific hazards. There will be duties on designers and developers to ensure that the work is done in a safe manner, with additional reference to the safety of the end users. This Directive has been implemented by the Construction (Design and Management) Regulations 1994.

(6) Safety Signs Directive (92/58/EEC)

10.22   This Directive replaces Directive (77/576/EEC), which was given effect to in the UK by the Safety Signs Regulations 1980. The new Directive requires employers to use a safety sign whenever there is a risk which cannot be adequately controlled by other means, taking into account the risk assessments made. In addition, the term "safety sign" includes other means of communication, such as hand signals, coding of pipework, marking of traffic routes, acoustic signals (eg fire alarms) and luminous signs. The number of conventional signs have been increased (with particular reference to identifying fire fighting equipment). The Directive has been implemented in the UK by the Health and Safety (Safety Signs and Signals) Regulations 1996.

(7) Pregnant Women Directive (92/85/EEC)

10.23   This Directive is designed to protect the health and safety of women workers who are pregnant, or who have recently given birth, or who are breast-feeding. An assessment will have to be made of the chemical, physical and biological agents and industrial processes which are considered to be hazardous for such workers. Reference will have to be made to movement and posture, mental and physical fatigue, and other types of stress connected with the work. An assessment will also have to be made of any risks to health and safety which could arise from an appended list of agents, processes or working conditions, and pregnant women are to be informed of the result of the assessment. If it is revealed that there is a risk to health or safety, or that there would be an effect on pregnancy or breast-feeding, the employer will be required to avoid the risk either by making a temporary adjustment to the working conditions, or move the worker to another job. If such methods are not possible, the worker is to be given leave for the period necessary to ensure her health and safety. Pregnant women, or those who have recently given birth, must not be obliged to do night work if they produce a medical certificate stating that this would be detrimental to their health or safety.

10.24   The Directive contains further provisions concerning the employment rights of pregnant women, including maternity pay, maternity leave of absence, and protection from dismissal because of pregnancy. The Directive was implemented in the UK by the Management of Health and Safety at Work (Amendment) Regulations 1994, now revoked and incorporated into the Management of Health and Safety at Work Regulations 1999. The employment rights aspects of the Directive have been met by various amendments to the law, now found in the Employment Rights Act, ss.66–85 (see paragraph 7.4).

(8) Working Time Directive (93/104/EEC)

10.25   In *UK v Council of European Union* (1997 IRLR 30) the European Court dismissed a challenge that the Working Time Directive (93/104/EEC) was not valid, and held that it was properly made under Article 118A of the Treaty of Rome (which enables Directives dealing with health and safety matters to be passed by the majority voting procedure). Strictly speaking, the Directive was due to have been implemented by 23 November 1996, which exposed those employers who are "emanations of the State" (see *Foster v British Gas*) to "Francovitch" type claims (which must be brought in the ordinary courts see *Gibson v East Riding of Yorkshire*). However, the European Court did hold that the requirement in the Directive that a weekly rest period shall in principle include Sunday was not valid, there being no evidence to suggest that Sunday was more closely connected with health and safety that any other day of the week.

10.26   The Directive, which provided for maximum working hours, rest breaks, rest periods, annual holidays and limits on night work, etc was implemented by the Working Time Regulations 1998 (see paragraph 5.74).

(9) Young Workers Directive (94/33/EEC)

10.27   The Protection of Young People at Work Directive (94/33/EEC) has now been adopted, and was required to be implemented by Member States by 1996. The Directive requires that the minimum working age for children is 15, although children under that age may be permitted in certain circumstances to undertake work experience/training, or certain light work for a limited number of hours each week. The Directive is not likely to pose many difficulties so far as UK law is concerned, as there is already a well-defined scheme regulating the employment of children and young persons.

10.28   The Health and Safety (Young Persons) Regulations 1997, which amended the Management of Health and Safety at Work Regulations 1992, were passed to implement this Directive. These regulations have now been revoked by and incorporated into the Management of Health and Safety at Work Regulations 1999 (see paragraph 5.68).

(10) Use of Work Equipment Directive (95/63/EC)

10.29   This Directive amends the original Directive on the provision and use of work equipment (89/655/EEC). It deals principally with the hardware requirements for mobile and lifting equipment. The new Provision and Use of Work Equipment Regulations 1998 and the Lifting Operations and Lifting Equipment Regulations 1998 implement this Directive.

(11) Seveso II Directive (96/82/EC)

10.30 This Directive repeals the original Seveso Directive (82/501/EC and 87/716/EC) following a fundamental review of the problems revealed in dealing with major accident hazards. The object is to prevent such incidents by providing a stringent Control regime, and to limit the consequences of any such incident for people and the environment. The Directive removes the distinction between "process" and "storage", improves on the generic categories of substances, to include, for example, substances which are dangerous to the environment, and extends cover to land planning. Operators are required to draw up a major accident prevention policy, and the competent authority is required to examine safety reports and set up an inspection system. Emergency plans must be implemented and tested. The Directive has been implemented by the Control of Major Accident Hazards Regulations 1999 (COMAH).

(12) Basic Safety Standards Directive (96/29/Euratom)

10.31 This Directive lays down the basic safety standards for the protection of the health of workers and the general public against the dangers arising from the use of ionising radiation. Other Directives deal with dangers to outside workers (90/641/Euratom) and the protection for individuals liable to medical exposure as a result of work with ionising radiations (97/43/Euratom). The Ionising Radiations Regulations 1999 implement these Directives.

Proposed Directives

10.32 A number of Directives with health and safety implications are currently being discussed at the various stages of procedure (see Appendix 3).

10.33 The Fifth Framework Programme for the period 1999/02 has been adopted, which will emphasise environment and health, major natural and technological hazards, organisation of production and work, and measurements, testing and standardisation.

Product Safety Directives

10.34 In addition to directives under Article 137, the EU is attempting to harmonise the laws of Member States on product safety and supporting standards. These Directives are made under Article 95 of the Treaty — sometimes referred to as "New Approach" Directives. These will depend on the availability of harmonised European standards because different laws in the various Member States could cause technical barriers to trade.

10.35 Directive (83/189/EEC) requires Member States to inform the Commission of any new technical regulation, which is then circulated to other Member States for comment. If it is thought that· the proposed regulation would create a barrier to the free movement of goods, the state may not implement it for a period, and the Commission may then decide to propose or adopt a directive on the subject of notification.

10.36 "New Approach" Directives set out essential requirements (eg on safety) which must be complied with before products may be sold anywhere in the Community. They also state how manufacturers are to meet those essential requirements. Once these are complied with, the product may carry the "CE" marking, which means that they can be sold anywhere in the EU.

10.37 There are two European bodies which prepare European Standards. One is the European Committee for Standardisation (CEN), the other is the European Committee for Electrotechnical Standardisation (CENELEC). These bodies work with the national standards organisation in the respective States. In the UK, this body is the British Standards Institution (see paragraph 2.74). The European Committees achieve an acceptable consensus, and the standard is then adopted by the weighted majority system (see paragraph 1.42).

10.38 The following "New Approach" Directives have a particular interest to those involved in health and safety matters.

10.39 (a) Personal Protective Equipment Directive (89/686/EEC) (PPE). This Directive covers any device or appliance designed to be worn or used or held by an individual for protection against one or more safety or health hazards. It also covers combined PPE and interchangeable components which are essential to its satisfactory functioning.

10.40   PPE must preserve the health and ensure the safety of users, must not harm other people, domestic animals or goods when properly maintained and used for its intended purpose. This Directive has been implemented by the Personal Protective Equipment (EC Directive) Regulations 1992 (as amended).

10.41   (b) Machinery Safety Directive (89/392/EEC and 91/368/EEC). Machinery must satisfy the essential health and safety requirements set out in the Directive, including the materials used in the construction, lighting, design, controls, stability, hazards relating to moving parts, fire, noise, vibration, radiation, emission of dust and gases, maintenance, warnings and instruction handbooks. This Directive has been implemented by the Supply of Machinery (Safety) Regulations 1992.

10.42   Other "New Approach" Directives deal with such topics as mobile machinery and lifting equipment, non-automatic weighing instruments, gas appliances, medical devices, and so on (see Appendix 3).

European legislation on health and safety

10.43   A collection of all legislative material on occupational health and safety in the fifteen Member States of the European Union is now held by HSE. There is also a Language Service Unit which provides a translation service to HSE staff, and a Translation Bulletin (available free of charge), indicating the topics translated and the cost of providing these to interested parties.

International Labour Organisation

10.44   The International Labour Organisation (ILO) was formed in 1919. It consists of representatives of national governments, employers' and workers' organisations and is now an agency of the United Nations. It has worked consistently to improve international labour standards relating to such matters as conditions of work, training, freedom of association, social security, industrial relations, and many other similar topics. It holds international conferences, provides technical advice and assistance to individual countries, and generally acts as an international forum for the promotion and improvement of standards throughout the world.

10.45   A major part of the work of the ILO consists of adopting conventions and recommendations. These are submitted to national governments for consideration, for they are not automatically binding. A convention may be ratified by a nation state, which amounts to a pledge to implement its provisions. However, any state is free to denounce a convention it has adopted, and is then free to ignore its provisions. A recommendation does not require ratification, but merely serves as a guide if national action is to be taken on a particular topic.

10.46   Since its inception, the ILO has passed over 150 Conventions, many relating to occupational health and safety matters. It has also passed over 160 recommendations covering similar topics, and has published a large number of reports and studies.

10.47   The ILO also produces research papers, suggests international classification standards, and issues Codes of Practice giving guidance on practical measures which may be taken to safeguard workers' health against occupational hazards.

APPENDIX 1
Useful Addresses

HEALTH AND SAFETY EXECUTIVE (HSE)

Information Services

HSE Information Services

General enquiries and information are available from a national telephone public service called HSE Infoline. Tel: 08701 545500. Open 8.30am to 5.00pm Monday to Friday. Queries can also be faxed on 02920 859260 or e-mailed on hseinformationservices@natbrit.com There is also an HSE website at www.hse.gov.uk

HSE Information Centres

HSE Information Centres are for personal callers who want to consult the information held there. Written general enquiries should be addressed (or faxed) to the Sheffield Information Centre.

Sheffield Information Centre (for
personal callers and written/faxed
enquiries)
Health and Safety Executive
Health and Safety Laboratory
Broad Lane
Sheffield S3 7HQ
Fax : 0114 2892333

There are also HSE Information Centres in London and Bootle for personal callers who want to consult the information held there.

London Information Centre
Health and Safety Executive
Rose Court
Ground Floor North
2 Southwick Bridge
London SE1 9HS

Bootle Information Centre
Health and Safety Executive
St Hugh's House
Trinity Road
Bootle
Merseyside L20 3QY

Both the above centres are open 9am to 5pm, Monday to Friday, to personal callers only.

HSE PUBLICATIONS

All HSE publications can be obtained from:

HSE Books
PO Box 1999
Sudbury
Suffolk CO10 6FS
Tel : 01787 881165.
Fax : 01787 313995
Website : www.hsebooks.co.uk

OFFICES OF THE HEALTH AND SAFETY EXECUTIVE

Contact details for the HSE's head and regional offices are provided below.

Head Office

Rose Court
2 Southwark Bridge Road
London SE1 9HS
Tel: 020 7717 6630/31/11/13

Regional Offices

Inspectors are based in office organised into divisions. The asterisk (*) shows an office where inspectors dealing with the manufacture, processing and storage of chemicals and onshore major hazards including gas transmission and distribution, pipelines and the road transport of dangerous substances may be contacted.

London and South East Division

Covers the counties of: Kent, Surrey, East Sussex, West Sussex and all London Boroughs

St Dunstans House
201–211 Borough High Street
London SE1 1GZ
Tel: 020 7556 2100
Fax: 020 7556 2200

3 East Grinstead House
London Road
East Grinstead RH19 1RR
Tel: 01342 334200
Fax: 01342 334222

Home Counties Division

Covers the counties of: Bedfordshire, Berkshire, Buckinghamshire, Cambridgeshire, Dorset, Essex (except London Boroughs in Essex), Hampshire, Hertfordshire, Isle of Wight, Norfolk, Suffolk and Wiltshire

14 Cardiff Road
Luton
Bedforshire LU1 1PP
Tel : 01582 444200
Fax : 01582 444320

(*)39 Baddow Road
Chelmsford CM2 OHL
Tel : 01245 706200
Fax : 01245 706222

(*)Priestley House
Priestley Road
Basingstoke RG24 9NW
Tel : 01256 404000
Fax : 01256 404100

Wales and West Division

Covers: Wales and the unitary authorities of Cornwall, Devon, Somerset, North West Somerset, Bath and North East Somerset, Bristol, South Gloucestershire, Gloucestershire, Hereford and Worcester, Shropshire and Staffordshire

(*)Brunel House
2 Fitzalan Road
Cardiff CF2 1SH
Tel : 029 2026 3000
Fax : 029 2026 3120

The Marches House
Midway
Newcastle-under-Lyme ST5 1DT
Tel : 01782 602300
Fax : 01782 602400

Inter City House
Mitchell Lane
Victoria Street
Bristol BS1 6AN
Tel : 0117 988 6000
Fax : 0117 926 2998

Midlands Division

Covers: West Midlands, Leicestershire, Oxfordshire, Warwickshire, Derbyshire, Lincolnshire and Nottinghamshire

(*)McLaren Building
2 Masshouse Circus
Queensway
Birmingham B4 7NP
Tel : 0121-607 6200
Fax : 0121-607 6349

(*)1st Floor
The Pearson Building
55 Upper Parliament Street
Nottingham NGI 6AU
Tel : 01159 712800
Fax : 01159 712802

(*)5th Floor
Belgrave House
1 Greyfriars
Northampton NN1 2BS
Tel : 01604 738300
Fax : 01604 738333

North West Division

Covers the North West: Cheshire, Cumbria, Greater Manchester, Lancashire and Merseyside

Quay House
Quay Street
Manchester M3 3JB
Tel: 0161-952 8200
Fax: 0161-952 8222

(*)Victoria House
Ormskirk Road
Preston PR1 1HH
Tel : 01772 836200
Fax : 01772 836222

(*)The Triad
Stanley Road
Bootle
Merseyside L20 3PG
Tel : 0151-479 2200
Fax : 0151-479 2201

Yorkshire and the North East Division

Covers Yorkshire and the North East: Hartlepool, Middlesbrough, Redcar and Cleveland, Stockton-on-Tees, Durham, Hull, North Lincolnshire, North East Lincolnshire, East Riding, York, North Yorkshire, Tyne & Wear, and the Metropolitan Boroughs of Barnsley, Doncaster, Rotherham and Sheffield.

8 St Paul's Street
Leeds LS1 2LE
Tel : 0113 283 4200
Fax : 0113 283 4296

(*)Sovereign House
110 Queens Street
Sheffield S1 2ES
Tel : 0114 291 2300
Fax : 0114 291 2379

(*)Arden House
Regent Centre
Regent Farm Road
Gosforth
Newcastle-upon-Tyne NE3 3JN
Tel : 0191-202 6200
Fax : 0191-202 6300

Scottish Division

Covers Scotland: all the Scottish unitary authorities and island councils

Belford House
59 Belford Road
Edinburgh EH4 3UE
Tel : 0131-247 2000
Fax : 0131-247 2121

375 West George Street
Glasgow G2 4LW
Tel : 0141-275 3000
Fax : 0141-275 3100

HSE CONTACT POINTS FOR SPECIFIC ACTIVITIES

Mining

Mines Inspectorate
Room 611
Daniel House
Trinity Road
Bootle
Merseyside L20 7HE
Tel: 0151-951 4136

Railways

Railway Inspectorate
2nd Floor SW
Rose Court
2 Southwark Bridge
London SE1 9HS
Tel: 020 7717 6533

Nuclear industry

Nuclear Safety Directorate
Information Centre
St Peter's House
Balliol Road
Bootle
Merseyside L20 3LZ
Tel: 0151-951 4103

Offshore oil and gas industry

Offshore Safety Division Information Centre, Lod Cullen House, Fraser Place Aberdeen AB23 3UB *Tel:* 01224 252652

Manufacture, tranpsort, handling and security of explosives

Explosives Inspectorate
St Anne's House
Stanley Precinct
Bootle
Merseyside L20 3RA
Tel: 0151-951 4025

Manufacture, processing and storage of chemicals and other onshore major hazards including gas transmission and distribution, pipelines and the road transport of dangerous goods

Contact the HSE offices marked (*) above. Enquires may also be sent to:

Chemicals and Hazardous Installations Division
St Anne's House
Stanley Precinct
Bootle
Merseyside L20 3RA
Tel: 0151-951 3235.

APPENDIX 2

Publications

Approved Codes of Practice and legislative guidance

The following have been approved or authorised by the Health and Safety Commission. Copies are available from HSE Books (Tel: 01787 881165), along with a free catalogue of all HSE priced and free guidance documents. British Standards may be ordered from the British Standards Institution (Tel: 020 8996 9000).

Accidents and emergencies

L73 A guide to the Reporting of Injuries, Diseases and Dangerous Occurrences Regulations 1995
L74 First aid at work
L75 Guidance for railways, tramways, trolley vehicle systems and other guided transport on RIDDOR 95

Agriculture

L116 Preventing accidents to children in agriculture
HSG89 Safeguarding agricultural machinery (revised)

Asbestos

L11 A guide to the Asbestos (Licensing) Regulations 1983 (as amended)
L27 The control of asbestos at work
L28 Work with asbestos insulation, asbestos coating and asbestos insulating board
HSG189/1 Controlled asbestos stripping techniques for work requiring a licence
HSG189/2 Working with asbestos cement

Confined spaces

L101 Safe work in confined spaces

Construction

L54 Managing construction for health and safety
L96 A guide to the Work in Compressed Air Regulations 1996
L102 Construction (Head Protection) Regulations (revised)
HSG32 Safety in falsework for in situ beams and slabs
HSG33 Health and safety in roofwork (revised)
HSG47 Avoiding danger from underground services
HSG141 Electrical safety on construction sites
HSG144 Safe use of vehicles on construction sites
HSG150 Health and safety in construction
HSG151 Protecting the public — your next move
HSG168 Fire safety in construction
HSG185 Health and safety in excavations: Be safe and shore

Dangerous substances

COP 14 Road tanker testing: Examination, testing and certification of the carrying tanks of road tankers and of tank containers used for the conveyance of dangerous substances by road
L5 General COSHH ACOP and Carcinogens ACOP and Biological Agents ACOP
L8 The prevention or control of legionellosis (including legionnaires' disease)
L9 The safe use of pesticides for non-agricultural purposes
L60 Control of substances hazardous to health in the production of pottery
L62 Safety data sheets for substances and preparations dangerous for supply. Guidance on regulation 6 of the CHIP regulations 1994
L67 Control of vinyl chloride at work
L86 Control of substances hazardous to health in fumigation operations
L88 Approved requirements and test methods for classification and packaging of dangerous goods for carriage
L90 Approved carriage list: information approved for the carriage of dangerous goods by road and rail
L100 Approved guide to the classification and labelling of substances and preparations dangerous for supply (4th edition)
L124 Approved supply list (6th edition)
HSG97 A step by step guide to COSHH assessment
HSG110 Seven steps to successful substitution of hazardous substances

HSG126 CHIP2 for everyone
HSG173 Monitoring strategies for toxic substances
HSG193 COSHH Essentials: easy steps to control chemicals

Display screen equipment

L26 Display screen equipment work
HSG90 VDUs: an easy guide to the regulations

Diving

L103 Commercial diving projects inland/offshore
L104 Commercial diving projects
L106 Media diving projects
L107 Scientific and archaelogical diving projects

Docks

COP 25 Safety in docks. (Docks Regulations 1988)
HSR27 A guide to the Dangerous Substances in Harbour Areas Regulations 1998
HSR28 A guide to the Loading and Unloading of Fishing Vessels Regulations 1998
HSG186 The bulk transfer of dangerous liquids and gases between ship and shore

Electricity and Electrical Systems

HSG85 Electricity at work: Safe working practices
HSG87 Safety in the remote diagnosis of manufacturing plant and equipment
HSG107 Maintaining portable and transportable electrical equipment
HSG118 Electrical safety in arc welding
HSG180 Application of electro-sensitive protective equipment using light curtains and light beam devices to machinery
HSR25 Memorandum of guidance on the Electricity at Work Regulations 1989

Explosives

L10 A guide to the Control of Explosive Regulations 1991
L13 Guide to the Packaging of Explosives for Carriage Regulations 1991
L66 Guide to the Placing on the Market and Supervision of Transfers of Explosives Regulations (POMSTER) 1993

First Aid

COP32 First aid on offshore installations and pipeline works
L74 First aid at work

Food/Catering

HSG31 Pie and tart machines
HSG45 Safety in meat preparation: Guidance for butchers
HSG55 Health and safety in kitchens and food preparation areas
HSG156 Slips and trips: Guidance for the food processing industry

Gas and oil-fired equipment

COP20 Standards of training in safe gas installation
L56 The Gas Safety (Installations and Use) Regulations 1998
L80 A guide to the Gas Safety (Management) Regulations 1996
L81 The design, construction and installations of gas service pipes
HSG16 Evaporating and other ovens

Healthcare

L55 Preventing asthma at work. How to control respiratory sensitisers
HSG116 Stress at work: A guide for employers
HSG137 Health risk management: A practical guide for managers in small and medium-sized enterprises
HSG174 Anthrax: Health hazards

Health services

Management of health and safety in the health services
The management of occupational health services for healthcare staff
Safe disposal of clinical waste

Violence and aggression to staff in the health services: Guidance on assessment and management
Manual handling of loads in the health service

Ionising radiation

L49 Protection of outside workers against ionising radiation
L121 Work with ionising radiations: Approved Code of Practice and Guidance
HSG94 Safety in the use of gamma and electron irradiation facilities (revised)

Lead

COP2 Control of lead at work

Leisure

Safety at outdoor activity centres
COP15 Zoos: Safety, health and welfare standards for employers and persons at work. Approved Code of Practice and guidance notes
HSG79 Health and safety in golf course management and maintenance
HSG105 Health and safety in horse riding establishments
HSG112 Health and safety at motor sport events
HSG154 Managing crowds safely
HSG175 Fairgrounds and Amusement Parks. Guidance on safe practice. Practical guidance on the management of health and safety for those involved in the fairgrounds industry
HSG179 Managing health and safety in swimming pools

Lifts

L113 Safe use of lifting equipment: Approved Code of Practice and guidance notes. Lifting Operations and Lifting Equipment Regulations 1998

Lift trucks

L117 Rider operated lift trucks: Operator training
HSG6 Safety in working with lift trucks
HSG136 Workplace transport safety: Guidance for employers

Management of Occupational Health

L21 The management of health and safety at work
L87 Safety representatives and safety committees
L95 A guide to the Health and Safety (Consultation with Employees) Regulations 1996
HSG65 Successful health and safety management
HSG96 The costs of accidents at work
HSG101 The costs to Britain of workplace accidents
HSG137 Health risk management: A practical guide for managers in small and medium-sized enterprises
HSG183 Five steps to risk assessment: case studies

Manual handling

L23 Manual handling
HSG115 Manual handling: Solutions you can handle
Manual handling of loads in the health service

Mines

COP28 Safety of exit from mines underground workings
COP34 The use of electricity in mines
L42 Shafts and winding in mines
L43 First aid at mines
L44 The management and administration of safety and health at mines
L45 Explosives at coal and other safety-lamp mines
L46 The prevention of inrushes in mines
L47 The Coal Mines (Owners' Operating Rules) Regulations 1993
L71 Escape and rescue from Mines Regulations 1995

New and expectant mothers

HSG122 New and expectant mothers at work: A guide for employers

Noise

L108 Reducing noise at work: Guidance on the Noise at Work Regulations 1989
HSG138 Sound solutions: Techniques to reduce noise at work

Offshore

L65 Prevention of fire and explosion, and emergency response on offshore installations
HSG125 A brief guide on COSHH for the offshore oil and gas industry
HSG142 Dealing with offshore emergencies

Personal protective equipment

L25 Personal protective equipment at work
HSG53 Respiratory protective equipment: A practical guide for users

Pesticides

L9 The safe use of pesticides for non-agricultural purposes

Petroleum spirit

COP6 Plastic containers with nominal capacities up to 5 litres for petroleum spirit: requirements for testing and marking or labelling

Pressure systems

L122 Safety of pressure systems: Pressure Systems Safety Regulations 2000: Approved Code of Practice

Quarries

L118 Health and safety in quarries: Quarries Regulations 1999: Approved Code of Practice

Safety representatives and committees

L87 Safety representatives and safety committees
L95 A guide to the Health and Safety (Consultation with Employees) Regulations 1996

Safety signs

L64 Safety signs and signals

Vibration

HSG88 Hand-arm vibration
HSG170 Vibration solutions: Practical ways to reduce the risk of hand-arm vibration injury

Violence

Preventing violence to retail staff
Violence and agression to staff in the health services: Guidance on assessment and management

Work equipment

L22 Work equipment
L112 Safe use of power presses
L113 Safe use of lifting equipment
L114 Safe use of woodworking machinery

Workplace

L24 Workplace health, safety and welfare
HSG37 Introduction to local exhaust ventilation
HSG38 Lighting at work
HSG54 The maintenance, examination and testing of local exhaust ventilation
HSG57 Seating at work

HSG60 Work related upper limb disorders: a guide to prevention
HSG132 How to deal with sick building syndrome
HSG155 Slips and trips: Guidance for employers on identifying hazards and controlling risks

Young persons

HSG165 Young people at work: A guide for employers

Zoos

COP15 Zoos: safety, health and welfare standards for employers and persons at work

APPENDIX 3
List of EU Directives Relating to Health and Safety

Available in the Official Journal Legislation series (OJ L) from The Stationery Office. Tel: 0870 600 5522.

* These Directives have been implemented by UK Regulations.

67/548/EEC* Directive on the approximation of laws, regulations and administration provisions relating to the classification, packaging and labelling of dangerous substances (Dangerous Substances Directive) OJ L196, 16.8.67

83/477/EEC* Directive on the protection of workers from the risks related to exposure to asbestos at work OJ L263, 24.9.83

89/391/EEC* Directive on the introduction of measures to encourage improvements in the safety and health of workers at work (Framework Directive) OJ L183, 29.6.89

89/392/EEC* (91/368/EEC) Directive on the approximation of the laws of the Member States relating to machinery, as amended (Machinery Directive) OJ L183, 29.6.89; OJ L198, 22.7.91

89/654/EEC* Directive concerning the minimum safety and health requirements for the workplace (Workplace Directive) OJ L393, 30.12.89

89/655/EEC* Directive concerning the minimum safety and health requirements for the use of work equipment by workers at work (Use of work equipment Directive) OJ L393, 30.12.89

89/656/EEC* Directive on the minimum health and safety requirements for the use by workers of personal protective equipment at the workplace (Personal Protective Equipment Directive) OJ L393, 30.12.89

89/686/EEC* Directive on the approximation of the laws of EC Member States relating to personal protective equipment (Personal Protective Equipment "PPE" Directive) OJ L399, 30.12.89

90/269/EEC* Directive on the minimum health and safety requirements for the manual handling of loads where there is a risk particularly of back injury to workers (Manual Handling of Loads Directive) OJ L156, 21.6.90

90/270/EEC* Directive on the minimum safety and health requirements for work with display screen equipment (Display Screen Equipment "VDU" Directive) OJ L156, 21 6.90

90/394/EEC* Directive on the protection of workers from the risks related to exposure to carcinogens at work (Carcinogens Directive) OJ L196, 26.7.90

90/679/EEC* Directive on the protection of workers from the risks related to exposure to biological agents at work (Biological Agents Directive) OJ L374, 31.12.90

91/382/EEC* Directive amending Council Directive of 19.9.83 (83/477/EEC: OJ L263, 24.9.83) on the protection of workers from the risks related to exposure to asbestos at work (Asbestos Worker Protection Directive) OJ L206, 29.7.91

91/383/EEC* Directive on the measures to encourage improvements in the safety and health of temporary employees (Temporary Workers Directive) OJ L206, 20.7.91

92/57/EEC* Directive on the implementation of minimum safety and health requirements at temporary or mobile construction worksites OJ L245, 26.8.92

92/58/EEC* Directive on the minimum requirements for the provision of safety and/or health signs at work (Safety Signs Directive) OJ L245, 26.8.92

92/69/EEC* (17th adaptation) Directive on the approximation of laws, regulations and administrative provisions relating to the classification, packaging and labelling of dangerous substances

93/21/EEC* (18th adaptation) (Dangerous Substances Directive) OJ L383, 29.12.92; OJ L110, 4.5.93

92/85/EEC* Directive on the introduction of measures to encourage improvements in the safety and health at work of pregnant workers and workers who have recently given birth or are breast-feeding (Pregnant Workers Directive) OJ L348, 28.11.92

93/44/EEC* Directive amending Directive (89/392/EEC) on the harmonisation of the laws of Member States relating to machinery OJ L175, 19.7.93

93/88/EEC* Directive amending Directive (90/679/EEC) on the protection of workers from the risks related to exposure to biological agents at work OJ L268, 29.10.93

93/104/EEC* Directive concerning certain aspects of the organisation of working time (Working Time Directive) OJ L307, 13.12.93

93/112/EEC* Directive amending Directive (91/155/EEC), defining and laying down detailed arrangements for the system of specific information relating to dangerous preparations in implementation of Article 10 of Council Directive (88/379/EEC) OJ L314, 16.12.93

94/9/EEC* Directive on the approximation of laws of the Member

States concerning equipment and protective systems intended for use in potentially explosive atmospheres OJ L100, 19.4.94

94/33/EC* Directive on the protection of young people at work (Young Workers Directive) OJ L216, 20.8.94

94/51/EC* Directive adapting to technical progress Council Directive (90/219/EEC) on the contained use of genetically modified micro-organisms OJ L297, 18.11.94

94/55/EC* Directive on the approximation of the laws of Member States with regard to the transport of dangerous goods by road OJ L319, 12.12.94

94/60/EC* Directive amending the Dangerous Substances Directive (76/769/EEC)for the 14th time OJ L365, 31.12.94

95/50/EC* Directive on uniform procedures for the checks on the transport of dangerous goods by road OJ L249, 17.10.95

95/63/EC* Directive 89/655/EEC on the minimum safety and health requirements for the use of equipment by workers at work OJ L335, 30.12.95

96/29/EURATOM Directive laying down the basic safety standards for the protection of the health of workers and the general public against the dangers arising from ionising radiation OJ L159, 29.6.96

96/35/EC* Directive on the appointment and vocational qualifications of safety advisors for the transport of dangerous goods by roads, rail and inland waterway OJ L145, 19.6.96

96/49/EC Directive on the approximation of the laws of the Member States with regard to the transport of dangerous goods by rail OJ L235, 17.9.96

96/82/EC* Directive on the control of major-accident hazards involving dangerous substances OJ L10, 14.1.97

97/23/EC Directive on the approximation of the laws of the Member States concerning pressure equipment OJ L181, 9.7.97

97/56/EC Directive amending for the 16th time Directive 76/769/EEC on the approximation of the laws, regulations and administrative provisions of the Member States relating to restrictions on the marketing and use of certain dangerous substances and preparations OJ L333, 4.12.97

98/8/EC Directive concerning the placing of biocidal products on the market OJ L123, 24.4.98

98/24/EC Directive on the protection of the health and safety of workers from the risks related to chemical agents at work (fourteenth individual Directive within the meaning of Article 16(1) of Directive

(89/391/EEC)OJ L131, 5.5.98

98/81/EC Directive amending Directive (90/219/EEC) on the contained use of genetically modified micro-organisms OJ L330, 5.12.98

99/36/EC Directive on transportable pressure equipment OJ L138/20, 1.6.99

99/38/EC Directive amending Directive 90/394/EEC on the protection of workers from risks related to exposure to carcinogens at work OJ L 138/66, 01.06.99

99/82/EC Directive amending Directive 67/549/EEC on dangerous substances. Amendment to include criteria for classifying preparations dangerous to the environment

99/92/EC Directive on minimum requirements for improving the safety and health protection of workers potentially at risk from explosive atmospheres OJ 1023/57, 28.01.00

Other Relevant EU Documents

90/326/EEC *Recommendation* concerning the adoption of a European schedule of occupational diseases OJ L160, 26.6.90

Regulation (EC) 2062/94 *Regulation* on establishing a European agency for safety, hygiene and health at work (Safety Agency) OJ L216, 20.8.94

Proposed EU Directives

The following Directives are still at the draft stage and may be amended or even withdrawn before being approved by the Council or adopted.

Proposal for a Directive on the minimum health and safety requirements regarding the exposure of workers to the risks arising from physical agents. This will be specifically for the protection of workers from the risks from vibration at work: OJ C77, 18.3.93; amended proposal OJ C230, 19.8.94.

Draft proposal for a Second Indicative Limit Value Directive: No published text

Proposals for amendments to the Asbestos Worker Protection Directive 83/477/EEC: No published text

Proposal to amend the Safety Data Sheets Directive (91/155/EEC) to incorporate changes required by changes made by the Dangerous Preparations Directive (99/82/EC)

Proposals to amend the Use of Work Equipment Directive

(89/655/EEC) to improve worker safety when using work equipment for temporary work at height

Proposals to amend the Machinery Directive (89/392/EEC) to include market surveillance as part of the enforcement process and introduce a new procedure for dealing with dangerous parts of machinery

New Approach Technical Directives

The following table shows the main New Approach Technical Directives and the regulations that implement those directives.

Reference	Directive	UK Implementing Regulations
73/23/EEC	Low Voltage	Electrical Equipment (Safety) Regulations (SI 1994 No. 3260)
87/404/EEC	Simple Pressure Vessels	Simple Pressure Vessels (Safety) Regulations 1991 (SI 1991 No. 2749) as amended
88/378/EEC	Toy Safety	Toys (Safety) Regulations 1989 (SI 1989 No.1275) as amended
89/106/EEC	Construction Products	Construction Products Regulations 1991 (SI 1991 No. 1620)
89/336/EEC	Electromagnetic Compatibility	Electromagnetic Compatibility Regulations 1992 (SI 1992 No. 2372) as amended
98/37/EC	Machinery	Supply of Machinery (Safety) Regulations 1992 (SI 1992 No 3073) as amended

89/686/EEC	Personal Protective Equipment	Personal Protective Equipment (EC Equipment Directive) Regulations 1992 (SI 1992 No. 3139) as amended
90/384/EEC	Non-automatic Weighing Instruments	Non-automatic Weighing Instruments (EEC Requirements) Regulations 1992 (SI 1992 No. 1579) as amended
90/385/EEC	Active Implantable Medical Devices	Active Implantable Medical Devices Regulations 1992 (SI 1992 No. 3146) as amended
90/396/EEC	Appliances Burning Gaseous Fuels	Gas Appliances (Safety) Gaseous Fuels Regulations (SI 1992 No. 711) and the Gas Appliances (Safety) Regulations 1995 (SI 1995 No. 1629)
98/13/EC**	Telecommunications Terminal Equipment and Satellite Earth Station Equipment	Telecommunications Terminal Equipment Regulations 1992 (SI 1992 No. 2423) as amended
92/42/EEC	New hot water boilers fired with liquid and gaseous fluid (efficiency requirements)	Boiler (Efficiency) Regulations 1993 (SI 1993 No. 3083)

93/15/EEC	Explosives for civil uses	Placing on the Market and Supervision of Transfers of Explosives Regulations 1993 (SI 1993 No. 2714) (except Art. 10)
93/42/EEC	Medical Devices	Medical Devices Regulations 1994 (SI 1994 No. 3017)
94/9/EC	Equipment and protective systems intended for use in potentially explosive atmospheres	The Equipment and Protective Systems Intended for Use in Potentially Explosive Atmospheres Regulations 1996 (SI 1996 No. 192)
95/16/EC	Lifts	Lifts Regulations 1997 (SI 1997 No. 831)
97/23/EC	Pressure Equipment	Pressure Equipment Regulations 1999 (SI 1999 No. 2001)

APPENDIX 4

GLOSSARY

This glossary of technical legal terms is designed for use by non-legal professionals in order to make the body of the text more accessible. It covers, in particular words, with legal meanings that may differ from their everyday meanings. The glossary is intended to meet the demands of those concerned with health and safety at work.

Absolute:	Without conditions; complete. In criminal law absolute or strict liability means that an offence may be committed even though there is no intention to commit it.
Accessory:	A person who is involved in a criminal offence to a lesser extent than the principal offender.
Acquiescence:	Consent which is expressed or implied from conduct.
Amenity:	Something which is conducive to comfort or convenience.
Appellant:	A person making an appeal.
Apportionment:	Division into proportionate parts.
Body corporate:	A company or corporation.
Breach:	The infringement of a legal right or duty.
Case stated:	A procedure whereby an appeal is made on a point of law from a magistrates' court to the Divisional Court.
Causation:	The relationship between cause and effect, subject to detailed legal rules. In criminal cases it must be proved beyond reasonable doubt that the accused caused the unlawful act.
Chattel:	Technically, anything other than freehold land.
Child:	A person who has not attained the age of 18 (formerly infant/minor).
Citation:	1. A summons ordering a person to appear before a court. 2. Reference to case law in support of an argument.
Civil (action court/law):	Civil courts are those which deal with private rights as distinct from those which deal with allegations of crime. See also "Crime, Criminal" below.

Claimant:	A person making a legal claim (formerly plaintiff).
Claim form:	The document on which the claim is made (formerly writ).
Clause:	A subdivision of a document or a Parliamentary Bill.
Common law:	The meaning used in this book is that body of law created by judicial decision rather than by Parliament.
Consolidation:	A procedure whereby all relevant statutory provisions are brought together in one statute or regulation (no changes in the law are made by this process).
Construction, rules of:	Principles established by the courts for ascertaining the meaning of words and phrases in documents and legislation.
Contract:	The law of contract is the body of rules governing agreements intended to create legal obligations.
Corporeal:	Visible; tangible.
Corpus delicti :	The facts amounting to a breach of law.
Crime, Criminal:	An act, deemed to be an offence against the State, which is punishable.
Curtilage:	A garden, yard, field or other piece of ground included within an area belonging to a dwelling-house.
De minimis (non curat lex):	The law is not concerned with trifles.
Deemed:	Supposed.
Defendant:	A person against whom a legal claim is brought.
Derogation:	The restriction of the strength of an obligation or right.
Dictum :	A statement by a judge in the course of a decision. See also " *Obiter dictum*", below.
Disclosure:	An order that relevant documents, etc in the possession of one party be disclosed to another party (formerly discovery of documents).
Egress:	Means of exit.
Enactment:	An Act of Parliament or part of an Act, including bye-laws and regulations made under an Act.

Exemption clause:	Part of an agreement excluding the liability of the parties in specific circumstances.
Express:	Clearly stated as opposed to implied.
Further information:	Requests made by one party to the other party for further information as to the nature of the claim or defence (formerly interrogatories/request for further and better particulars).
Held:	Decided.
Hereditament:	An inheritable interest in land. A mere licence to use land is not a hereditament because it is a personal right and would not pass to an heir. A corporeal hereditament is a physical object. An incorporeal hereditament is a right, for example a right of way.
In private:	A hearing before a judge in his private chambers (formerly in camera).
Indemnity:	A contract of indemnity is created when a person promises to give security against injury or loss which might be suffered by another.
Indictable, indictment:	An indictment is a written statement accusing a person of a criminal offence which is to be tried in the crown court before a judge and jury.
Ingress:	Means of entry.
Injunction:	A court order requiring a person to do or refrain from doing a particular thing.
Inspection:	An order whereby the court or a party to the proceedings may inspect documents, etc in the possession of the other party.
Instituted:	Commenced.
Inter alia :	Among other things.
Latent:	Not apparent at first sight.
Legislation:	Acts of Parliament and regulations made thereunder.
Liability:	Legal obligation or duty.
Litigant:	A person who takes legal action.
Litigation friend:	A person who brings a claim in his own name on behalf of another who cannot do so, eg a child (formerly next friend).
Mandatory:	A mandatory injunction (see above) directs a person to do a positive act.
Material:	Relevant.

Mens rea :	A guilty mind, ie a deliberate intention to do a wrongful act.
Negligence:	A technical legal concept, generally meaning careless conduct, but subject to strict and complex legal rules.
Obiter dictum :	A statement of law during the hearing of a case, not forming part of the decision in the case. See also "Precedent", below.
Onus:	Burden of proof.
Part 20 Claim:	A counter claim, or the joining of another person to the action.
Part 36 Offer:	An offer to settle the claim (generally without admission of legal liability).
Part 36 Payment:	A payment into court prior to the commencement of proceedings, generally without an admission of legal liability.
Particulars of claim:	Details of the claim.
Patent defect:	Arising at first sight, on the face of it.
Penal legislation:	Acts of Parliament creating criminal offences.
Per incuriam :	Without full legal argument.
Permission:	With the leave of the court.
Plaintiff:	A person who commences legal proceedings.
Precedent:	A judicial decision, creating a rule of law, which applies to later cases involving similar facts.
Prima facie :	On first impression; at first sight; on the face of it.
Procedure:	The normal method of conducting legal proceedings.
Res ipsa loquitor:	The facts speak for themselves.
Respondent:	A person who is defending or resisting an appeal.
Revocation:	Annulment.
Sanction:	A measure of punishment.
Sentence:	The penalty imposed upon a convicted person, normally subject to a statutory maximum.
Statement of case:	The court document which will contain details of the claim and defence.

Status quo (ante):	The same state as before.
Statute:	An Act of Parliament passed by the House of Commons and House of Lords and signed by the Sovereign.
Substantive:	Definite, complete.
Summary:	An offence which may only be dealt with in the magistrates' court.
Tort:	The branch of law dealing with liability for civil wrongs. The normal remedy for a tort is damages in compensation for the wrong done, or an injunction to prevent repetition of the wrong.
Tortfeasor:	A person alleged or proved to have committed a tort.
Vicarious liability:	Liability arising through one person's relationship with another. An employer may be liable for wrongful acts committed by an employee during the course of employment.
Volenti non fit injuria:	Consent to a risk of injury does not give rise to legal liability.
Without notice:	An application to a court made without notifying the other side, eg in an emergency (formerly ex parte).
Witness statements:	Sworn statements made by the witnesses (formerly affidavits).

Note A number of changes to civil procedures have been made recently, known generally as the Woolf reforms. Legal terminology has been simplified, and, in particular, Latin tags are no longer to be used. Some examples of Woolf terminology are included in the glossary.

Subject Index

Introduction

The index covers Chapters 1 to 10, but not the Appendices. Index entries are to paragraph numbers. Alphabetical arrangement is word-by-word, where a group of letters followed by a space is filed before the same group of letters followed by a letter, eg "Gas installations" will appear before "Gasholders". In determining alphabetical arrangement, initial articles and prepositions are ignored.

lead at work 6.190
manual handling 6.147–6.155
radiation 6.280–6.289
injuries at work compensation *see*
Injuries at work
liability insurance 1.4, 2.46, 4.1–4.9
non-employees, duties
to 3.2, 3.71–3.81
safety policies *see* Safety policies
safety rules, enforcement
of 9.42–9.65
shared workplaces, co-operation
and co-ordination 4.25, 5.42–5.44
**Employment Appeal Tribunal
(EAT)** 1.74
Employment contracts
breach, working time
regulations 5.98
**Employment Medical Advisors
(EMA)** 2.66, 2.68, 4.43
**Employment Medical Advisory
Service (EMAS)** 2.64, 3.9
functions 2.65
HSE control 2.31, 2.32
management 2.66
powers 2.68–2.71
responsibilities 2.67
**Employment National Training
Organisation** 5.190
**Employment Nursing Advisors
(ENA)** 2.66, 2.70
Employment protection 5.146–5.148,
5.164–5.182
Employment tribunals 1.73
application for review 3.164–3.165
costs 3.166
remedies to employees 1.17, 5.178
working time regulations 5.94–5.97
**ENA (Employment Nursing
Advisors)** 2.66, 2.70
Enforcement 3.115–3.203, 9.1–9.2
appointment procedures 9.3–9.7
employees
action by 9.33–9.41

dismissal on safety
grounds 9.52–9.65
suspension on medical
grounds 9.66–9.73
employer action 9.42–9.65
employment protection 5.164–5.182
enforcement notices 3.116–3.118
appeals against 3.133–3.140
fire precautions 4.28
enforcing authorities
HSE 2.36–2.50, 2.56–2.58
local authorities 2.51–2.55
self inspection 2.59
transfer of authority 2.60–2.63
factories 4.56
fire precautions 4.26–4.28
safety representatives and safety
committees 5.157–5.163
working time regulations 5.92–5.98
works rules 9.8–9.14, 9.32
drunkenness 9.19–9.21
eating and drinking 9.17
fighting 9.18
hygiene observance 9.25
ill health 9.26–9.27
neglect 9.29
safety equipment, failure to
use 9.24
safety rules, breach of 9.23
skylarking 9.22
sleeping on duty 9.30
smoking 9.15–9.16
training 9.31
vandalism 9.28
Environment Agency 2.1
pollution responsibilities 2.63, 3.89,
4.32
**Environmental Health Officers
(EHO)** 2.53, 4.38
Environmental protection 4.31–4.37
**Environmentally hazardous
substances** 3.19–3.20
Epileptics 7.146–7.149
Equal pay 1.54

National Vocational Qualifications (NVQs) 5.187
NEBOSH (National Examination Board in Occupational Safety and Health) 2.81, 5.186–5.189
Neglect, works rules on 9.29
Negligence
care, employers' duty of *see* Care, employers' duty of
common law claims 1.5, 8.18–8.52
contributory 1.5, 8.65
defences 8.53–8.54
causation 8.64
contributory negligence 8.65
denial 8.55–8.58
sole fault of employee 8.59–8.63
limitations of actions 8.66–8.68
proof of 8.50–8.52
NIGs (National Interest Groups) 2.33
Night workers, working hours 5.76
NIOSH (National Institute of Occupational Safety and Health) 7.3
Noise at work 6.298–6.310, 7.188–7.189
Non-employees 3.19
employers' duties to 3.2, 3.71–3.81
as safety representatives 5.140
Non-smokers *see* Smoking at work
Non-specific arm pain (NSAP) 7.137
Northern Ireland
application of health and safety law 3.10
legal system of 1.125
Noxious substances 3.89
NRGs (National Responsibility Groups) 2.33
NSAP (non-specific arm pain) 7.137
Nuclear installations
safety of, HSC advisory committee on 2.21
NVQs (National Vocational Qualifications) 5.187

Occupational diseases 7.71
Occupational exposure standards (OES) 6.317
Occupational health
HSC advisory committee on 2.24
services 5.197–5.199
Occupiers' liability 8.87–8.91
OES (Occupational exposure standards) 6.317
Offensive substances 3.89
Offices, shops and railway premises
agreements, power to modify 4.67
application of the Act 4.68
defences 4.66
definitions 4.60
health, safety and welfare 4.59–4.68
multi-occupancy buildings 4.62–4.63
notification of employment 4.64
offences 4.65
power to modify agreements 4.67
Offshore installations
construction work 1.127
Cullen Report 1.128
HSE responsibility 1.128, 2.31
HSWA, application of 3.11, 3.21
oil and gas installations 1.127
personal protective equipment 6.139
pipeline work 1.127, 3.11, 3.21, 6.139
protective legislation 1.127–1.128, 4.69–4.70
safety representatives and safety committees 5.163
Oil and gas installations, offshore *see* Offshore installations
Orders
nature 1.30
Regulations distinguished 1.31
Overlap of the law 1.98
Overseas working 7.25–7.27

Parental leave 7.10
Paris Treaty 10.1

personal protective
equipment 6.132–6.134
private vehicles, use at work 7.169
representatives of employee
safety 5.146–5.147
safety representatives 5.130–5.139
safety signs 6.219
work equipment 6.69–6.70
**Transparent/translucent surfaces,
workplace** 6.29–6.30
Travelling first-aid kits 6.269
Treaty of Amsterdam 1.43
Treaty of Paris 10.1
Treaty of Rome 1.19, 1.41–1.43, 1.54,
1.59, 1.72, 10.3, 10.14
**Treaty on European Union
(Maastricht Treaty)** 1.44, 10.5
Triable either way offences 1.62

Unfair dismissal 7.12
University premises 3.85
Upper limb disorders 7.125–7.137
**Use of Work Equipment
Directive** 1.12, 6.54, 10.15, 10.29

Vandalism 9.28
VDU (visual display units) *see*
Display screen equipment
Vehicles
construction (health, safety and
welfare) 6.376
fork-lift trucks 6.92
private, use at work 7.169–7.171
Ventilation 6.12–6.13
Ventilators 6.31
Vibration White Finger (VWF)
7.138–7.143
Vicarious liability 8.74–8.84
Violence against employees 6.251,
7.72–7.79

**Visiting armed forces, exemption
certificates** *see* Exemption
certificates, armed forces
Visiting workers, safety of 5.45–5.48
Visitors *see* Non-employees
Visual display units *see* Display
screen equipment
**VWF (Vibration White
Finger)** 7.138–7.143

Wales, Assembly 1.125
Walls 6.29–6.30
Warning signs 6.223
Washing facilities 6.39–6.40
Waste materials 6.18–6.19
Water for drinking 6.41
Water sealed gasholders 4.48
Weather protection
construction (health, safety and
welfare) 6.383
Weights, lifting *see* Manual handling
operations
Welfare 3.19, 3.55–3.58
see also Health and Safety at Work,
etc Act 1974
construction (health, safety and
welfare) 6.381
safety committees'
involvement 5.153
Welfare Orders 1.1
Welsh Assembly 1.125
Windows 6.29–6.32
Women
employment 7.1–7.3
hours of work 1.1–1.3, 7.1
lead at work 6.191, 6.200, 6.202, 7.1,
7.207
maternity leave 7.10
maternity rights 7.4–7.20
pregnancy *see* Pregnancy
radiation exposure 7.1
risk assessments 5.62–5.67, 7.7–7.8,
7.192